REASON & RELIGIOUS BELIEF

REASON &
RELIGIOUS BELIEF

An Introduction to
the Philosophy of Religion

Second Edition

MICHAEL PETERSON
WILLIAM HASKER
BRUCE REICHENBACH
DAVID BASINGER

New York   Oxford
OXFORD UNIVERSITY PRESS
1998

OXFORD UNIVERSITY PRESS

Oxford   New York
Athens   Auckland   Bangkok   Bogota   Bombay   Buenos Aires
Calcutta   Cape Town   Dar es Salaam   Delhi   Florence   Hong Kong
Istanbul   Karachi   Kuala Lumpur   Madras   Madrid   Melbourne
Mexico City   Nairobi   Paris   Singapore   Taipei   Tokyo   Toronto   Warsaw

and associated companies in
Berlin   Ibadan

Copyright © 1998 by Oxford University Press, Inc.

198 Madison Avenue, New York, New York 10016
Published by Oxford University Press, Inc.

Oxford is a registered trademark of Oxford University Press

Library of Congress Cataloging-in-Publication Data
Reason & religious belief : an introduction to the philosophy of
religion / Michael Peterson . . . [et al.].—2nd ed.
p.   cm.
Includes indexes.
ISBN 0-19-511347-0 (pbk.)
1. Religion—Philosophy.   2. Christianity—Philosophy.
I. Peterson, Michael L., 1950–   .
BL51.R326   1997   210—dc21

Printing (last digit): 9 8 7 6 5
Printed in the United States of America
on acid-free paper

CONTENTS

Contents

Contents

Contents

PREFACE TO THE SECOND EDITION

We have been very gratified by the reception that the first edition of *Reason and Religious Belief* received. Suggestions and criticisms from many of those who used the book have been helpful in preparing this revision. In addition, we decided to add several topics not covered in the previous edition.

We offer this edition of *Reason and Religious Belief* in the hope that it will continue to be helpful to those interested in a first course in philosophy of religion. In doing so, we remain committed to the primary task undertaken in the previous edition: to analyze important concepts and evaluate major arguments in the field, with the aim of finding the most reasonable position on the issues.

Asbury College   M. P.
Huntington College   W. H.
Augsburg College   B. R.
Roberts Wesleyan College   D. B.
January 1997

PREFACE TO THE
FIRST EDITION

Reason and Religious Belief grows out of our many years of collective experience reflecting upon the issues in philosophy of religion and teaching them to undergraduate students. So, in our writing, we have been especially conscious of the need to communicate the issues in ways that students can understand.

Perhaps more than anything else, though, the book was born out of long-standing friendship and intellectual interaction among the four of us. We dare to hope that the enjoyment and even the excitement of the type of philosophical discussion we have shared will show through these pages and become contagious. Our different interests and specializations within the philosophy of religion are welded together by our complete agreement on the nature of the philosophical task in general: to analyze important concepts and evaluate major arguments, with the overall aim of finding the most reasonable position on any issue.

No project of this magnitude can be successful without help from others. We wish to thank the Faculty Research and Development Committee of Asbury College for providing a small grant to defray the costs of producing this manuscript. And we are grateful to Robert Audi and George Mavrodes for reading and making valuable suggestions on earlier drafts of the manuscript.

Asbury College	M. P.
Huntington College	W. H.
Augsburg College	B. R.
Roberts Wesleyan College	D. B.
April 1990	

INTRODUCTION

Interest in philosophy of religion has virtually exploded in the past couple of decades. Professional philosophers are bringing new techniques to bear on traditional problems and are pioneering important new territory as well. In 1980, *Time* magazine reported this resurgence of interest in the philosophical examination of religion, stating that "God is making a comeback." It is becoming increasingly obvious to more and more people that the issues surrounding belief in God are extremely significant. This text has been written as an introduction to the basic issues and options in the exciting field of philosophy of religion. We try to provide a very accessible, comprehensive text in the philosophy of religion—one that is as current as possible, historically informed, theologically sophisticated, and philosophically challenging.

The present text does not assume background in philosophy on the part of the reader. Thus, undergraduate, graduate, and seminary students with no previous exposure to philosophy should be able to handle the book. Since no prior mastery of introductory terms and concepts is required, the text should be accessible even to thoughtful and diligent readers who study it apart from any formal course setting. While this text is designed as a basic presentation of matters in the philosophy of religion, there is a good deal of general philosophy along the way, supplying helpful background about major philosophers and their ideas as the book develops.

The essential strategy of this introductory text is to distill and discuss the main issues in the field, extracting the intellectual dialogue with which the more complex and difficult primary literature is occupied. We have also created an anthology—*Philosophy of Religion: Selected Readings* (Oxford, 1996; hereafter referred to as PRSR)—that is exactly correlated to the structure of the present text and thus enhances the student's ability to follow the dialogue emerging out of the original sources.

We invite students to participate in that great debate about religion that has occupied many historical and contemporary philosophers. Our primary emphasis is on the *structure* of the issues. We want students to understand precisely what each issue is, the shape of its logic, what is at stake, and the main options it presents. Our ultimate goal is to help students be able to form reasonable opinions about the issues and acquire the ability to continue to think about them in meaningful and helpful ways.

Knowing the pedagogical advantage of finding a point of contact with students, we begin each chapter with a concrete story, example, or quotation and gradually develop the larger issue under discussion. We try to draw students naturally into the issues and encourage thoughtful response, striving throughout for clarity and friendliness of presentation. For a number of years, we have employed this technique in our own teaching of the subject and have confidence in its effectiveness.

While there is something of a logical order in the sequence of the first several chapters, instructors using this text can assign chapters in almost any order, as the topics are somewhat independent. Obviously, supplementary readings, preferably of original works, can be coordinated with the individual chapters. Study questions are included at the end of each chapter in order to aid private review as well as classroom discussion. Suggested reading is included for each topic so that students can further pursue the issues. A general index and a names index enable students to trace efficiently the occurrence of particular concepts and viewpoints.

Since the long-standing interest among Western philosophers has been in theism, this text is devoted largely to the issues related to the view that there exists a Supreme Spiritual Being, transcendent from the world, who is omnipotent, omniscient, and perfectly good. This, of course, is the view known more precisely as *classical theism*. The major theistic religions (Judaism, Christianity, and Islam) basically share this view of God. While focusing primarily on issues pertaining to classical theism, we do consider some issues or variations of issues that pertain more specifically to *Christian* theism, primarily because interest in Christian theism is quite common among contemporary Anglo-American philosophers of religion. At appropriate points, we also indicate how the issues treated here apply to other major religions and theological conceptions, thus acquainting students to some degree with Hinduism, Buddhism, and other non-Western traditions. In fact, we believe that references to non-Western religious traditions enhance the students' perspective on the central issues at hand.

A study of this sort almost inevitably assumes some familiarity with the religious tradition or theological conceptions being examined. We try to make the most minimal assumptions along these lines. Ideally, our readers will be somewhat acquainted with Western religious faith and the sorts of beliefs that are characteristic of theistic religions generally. However, we supply enough description and exposition of these beliefs along the way so that even the neophyte should be able to grasp quickly the religious concepts and doctrines under discussion. Beyond this, we do not assume that readers are theists or religious believers of any persuasion.

We cover all of the issues that are typically treated in standard philosophy of religion texts and a few topics that are rarely treated but that many instructors would like to see included. Chapter 1 begins by surveying the pervasive religiosity of the human race and defining exactly what a philosophical examination of religion would be. Chapter 2 examines what is perhaps for many people their most familiar and concrete contact with religion—religious experience. We examine such questions as whether there is a common core or structure to all religious experiences and whether these experiences can serve to justify religious beliefs. We move beyond experience in Chapter 3 and consider whether religious commitments are subject to rational evaluation. After looking at two extreme positions—hard rationalism and fideism—we adopt a posture that we call "critical rationalism." Critical rationalism is committed to the analysis and evaluation of religious beliefs but does not maintain that these beliefs are subject to conclusive proof or disproof. Then we devote Chapter 4 to the attributes traditionally associated with the theistic deity, attributes that define more precisely the Being who is the subject of further argument and debate. We do not neglect, however, the trenchant critique of the traditional concept of deity offered by process thinkers.

In the following two chapters, we address the arguments for and against the existence of God, the main fare of natural theology and natural atheology, respectively. In Chapter 5, we examine the classic arguments for the existence of God, arguments that still fascinate and challenge those who think about whether it is possible to provide rational support for theistic belief. Then, in Chapter 6, the problem of evil—widely recognized as the most serious rational objection to belief in God—is analyzed and discussed. Although natural theology and atheology constitute a significant portion of traditional philosophy of religion, the aims and methods of these enterprises have come under severe criticism since the 1980s. Philosophers began to argue that belief in God need not rest on rational argument but can be "basic" in the framework of our beliefs. This position, considered in Chapter 7, is so new that almost no other introductory text addresses it.

In the remaining six chapters, we proceed to a variety of enduring issues. In Chapter 8 we discuss the problem of religious language, of how human words can meaningfully apply to God. Although the day has just passed when this subject was at the very forefront of philosophy of religion, many of the issues involved are fundamental to making progress in other areas of the field. In Chapter 9, we consider the problem of miracles. Since Christian theism has historically involved a belief in miracles, this chapter first probes the difficulty of definition; then it faces the problem of whether miracles are possible and, if so, whether they are identifiable. Chapter 10 focuses on the problem of life after death, allowing us to show that concepts of postmortem survival vary with views of the human self. We also scrutinize several arguments for the reality of life after death.

In Chapter 11, we look closely at the relation of religion and science, a topic covered in only a small portion of texts in philosophy of religion. When the topic is treated, it is usually developed in terms of current issues—say, the creation-evolution debate or the possibility of producing life with the DNA molecule—rather than in terms of some overall understanding of religion and science as human activities. We bring some order to the confusing discussion by making vital conceptual distinctions between the natures of these fields. In the succeeding chapter, we take up an increasingly pressing issue: the problem of religious diversity. This problem alone is inspiring numerous new courses in colleges and universities. Here, in Chapter 12, we see that through modern communication and travel, people have become acutely conscious of the great differences among the many religious and cultural traditions, making us wonder how such divergent belief-systems can all be said to be true. In Chapter 13, we explore the connection between religion and ethics. We raise such questions as whether ethical norms can originate in God and whether religion offers a distinctive vision of human moral fulfillment.

Coming near the end of our study, we recognize that one historically important way in which philosophy has intersected with religion has been the explication and analysis of its doctrines. Therefore, we devote Chapter 14 to an examination of some representative contemporary efforts in this area. Current work on key doctrines in Christian theology, such as the Incarnation and the Atonement, provides rich material for reflection and discussion. Much of the work on these topics is quite fresh and is only lately becoming widely known. Chapter 15, the final one in the book, serves as a capstone to our study of the philosophy of religion, summarizing the main lessons that can be learned and inviting readers to continue exploring the issues in that fascinating field.

In an introductory treatment of intellectually significant issues, we are convinced that the impact on readers is determined not so much by *what* particular issues are selected for treatment as it is by *how* those issues are handled. Hence, the posture or stance of the authors is of major consequence. We have sought to strike a balance between pure neutrality, on the one hand, and outright advocacy, on the other. While we attempt to be fair to various positions, we sometimes indicate which one seems most reasonable to us among alternatives. This approach is more personal than "pure neutralism" and, we believe, helps enlist readers in the activity of critical thinking about the issues.

It is certainly true that undertaking the present study in the philosophy of religion can help those who are already believers to develop a deeper understanding of their faith as well as become aware of responsible objections to it. But it is equally true that those who do not have faith can gain a better understanding of the multitude of important issues to which religious faith gives rise.

Introduction

We believe that a serious study of philosophy of religion is both intellectually stimulating and personally rewarding, and we have diligently tried to design this text to facilitate such outcomes. If we have met our philosophical and pedagogical objectives in sufficient measure, then we dare to hope that all of our readers will find this exploration of the philosophy of religion to be genuinely worthwhile.

CHAPTER 1

THINKING ABOUT GOD: THE SEARCH FOR THE ULTIMATE

Religion is a powerful force in human life. The evidence for this fact is both clear and abundant:

- Cro-Magnon societies buried persons in fetal position, surrounding them with useful objects—weapons, necklaces, and cooking utensils—as though they might experience another life.
- An aboriginal tribe prays to the great spirit of the sky to be favorable toward them and not withhold rain.
- In Japan, a Zen Buddhist meditates on the unity between the "I" and the "not-I."
- During the Islamic holy month of Ramadan, a devout Moroccan family practices fasting from dawn to sundown.
- On Easter Sunday, Christian believers all over the world celebrate the Resurrection of Jesus just as Christians have done for two thousand years.

From the birth of civilization, a multitude of religions has developed, each very complex. We know that prehistoric tribes manifested their religious impulse in animistic and totemistic practices. More advanced world religions have highly sophisticated concepts of God or Ultimate Reality: for Jews it is Yahweh, for Christians it is the Triune God, for Muslims it is Allah, for Hindus it is Shiva or Vishnu, for Theravada Buddhists it is Nirvana.[1]

Equally ample evidence shows that countless numbers of people are not religious at all. In contemporary culture, millions adhere to no religious tradition, practice no forms of worship or meditation, and thus seem to possess no religious faith. There are also individuals and organizations that actively promote some version of atheism or at least the rejection of religion. Well known in popular culture are Madalyn Murray O'Hair and the Association of American Atheists, which she founded.[2] More intellectually sophisticated is the American Humanist Association.[3] Yet even those persons and groups who deliberately reject all forms of religion witness in a peculiar way its impact on human life.

DEFINING RELIGION

What exactly is religion? Arriving at a precise definition of *religion* is notoriously difficult, since almost each one that is offered seems subject to counterexample.[4] C. P. Tiele wrote that "Religion is, in truth, that pure and reverential disposition or frame of mind which we call piety." F. H. Bradley stated that "Religion is rather the attempt to express the complete reality of goodness through every aspect of our being." And James Martineau claimed that "Religion is the belief in an ever living God, that is, in a Divine Mind and Will ruling the Universe and holding moral relations with mankind." It is apparent that each of these definitions specifies a different characteristic: Tiele accents the attitude of piety, Bradley links religion with goodness, and Martineau focuses on belief in ethical monotheism. Other attempted definitions of religion touch upon additional traits, such as ritualistic acts, prayer and communication with gods, and so on, and each definition seems to have some measure of relevance.

Wisdom counsels us, however, not to elevate any isolated feature to the status of a universal definition. Religions are more complex than that. There are primitive, shamanistic religions, for example, that seem not to involve feelings of genuine piety so much as prudential or utilitarian acts of obeisance. Thus, Tiele's definition is incomplete. Likewise, there are polytheistic religions (such as those of ancient Egypt and Greece) that do not recognize a single divine ruler of the universe. Thus, the definition given by Martineau fails to cover all religions. Counterexamples for most definitions could be found.

We can begin to see that speaking too generically about religion risks being imprecise and may even distort the rich and complicated details of actual religions. For example, religion is almost always associated with the supernatural or the divine, but not always. The notion of a supernatural realm does not occur, for example, in the nontheistic schools of Buddhism and functions in very different ways, say, in Taoism, Hinduism, and Islam. The great differences among religions make it difficult to find a least common denominator or to talk of religion in general.

On the other hand, focusing on just one specific religion often ignores or underestimates some of the very broad traits that all religions seem to share, such as those noted by Ninian Smart.[5] All religions have an experiential dimension, ranging from a quiet sense of the presence of the divine in ordinary life to the mystic consciousness of union with the divine. Each religion has a mythic dimension that conveys a large-scale understanding of God or Ultimate Reality to the faithful in terms of symbolic speech and stories. The doctrinal dimension articulates and organizes the basic beliefs of a religion. The ethical dimension of a religion concerns the sphere of moral action and practical life orientation. Ritual is a dimension of all religions that pertains to the prescribed behaviors, both public and private, related to worship of the divine. The last dimension, the social, pertains to how a religion organizes all sorts of interpersonal relationships.

In spite of the difficulties in defining and applying the term "religion," we need to arrive at a tentative, working definition. For our purposes, we assume that *religion is constituted by a set of beliefs, actions, and experiences, both personal and corporate, organized around a concept of an Ultimate Reality.* This Reality may be understood as a unity or a plurality, personal or non-personal, divine or not, differing from religion to religion. Yet it seems that every cultural phenomenon that we call a religion fits this definition. The prescribed actions vary from ritualistic patterns to ethical living; the desired emotions vary from feelings of piety and humility to a sense of optimism about life and the universe.

As the title of this text suggests, our present study of philosophy of religion is directed at *beliefs,* specifically, *religious* beliefs. But how shall we think about this? *Beliefs,* for our purposes, are statements (i.e., propositions) that are taken as true; they are truth-claims. In a certain sense, every religion rests on beliefs. These religious beliefs tend to revolve around five basic areas. First, humans find themselves in a predicament (e.g., sin for Judaism and Christianity, *samsara* for Hinduism, mortality for Taoism). Second, humans need a way to resolve the predicament (e.g., salvation, liberation). Third, there exists something transcendent that assists us or is the goal of our existence (e.g., Ultimate Reality, God, Brahman, Nirvana). Fourth, this "something" can be known or approached in some specified way (e.g., holy scriptures, shamans). Fifth, we must do something to achieve salvation or liberation (e.g., have faith, deny self, engage in meditation, follow the Five Pillars of Islam).

Such beliefs in a given religion account for the particular actions and emotions that it endorses. These beliefs may be made official and presented in the form of doctrine and teaching, or they may be somewhat implicit in the daily practice of the religion. Yet the numerous details of any religion are, in a real sense, an extension of how the fundamental beliefs about Ultimate Reality are interpreted and expressed in real life.

Accordingly, when we find some group of human beings involved in a network of beliefs, actions, and experiences that focus on some Ultimate Reality, we are justified in saying that we have an instance of religion. Obviously, some cultural phenomena embody all of the relevant features to a remarkable extent and thus provide clear and uncontroversial examples of a religion. Roman Catholicism and Orthodox Judaism are unmistakable instances of religion according to our definition. Other groups less obviously possess the set of relevant characteristics but are still arguably instances of religion, such as certain forms of Buddhism and even Unitarianism. It has even been argued that secular humanism and communism are religions or at least strongly exhibit religious characteristics.

Of course, we cannot fully understand a given religion—its preferred attitudes and emotions, its prescribed rituals, its important stories and myths, and its recommended way of life—simply by looking at it. Many subtle factors—psychological, sociological, anthropological, historical—are not obvious to the untrained eye. That is why an expert, say, in the psychology of religion or the sociology of religion can reveal fascinating insights to the novice. However, these disciplines do not ask questions about the meaning, truth, consistency, or explanatory adequacy of the belief systems in the religions they study. That is the purview of the philosophy of religion.

WHAT IS PHILOSOPHY OF RELIGION?

Since philosophy is the discipline that closely examines *beliefs*, we may rightly expect it to be interested in *religious beliefs*. Philosophers often raise critical questions about whether certain beliefs are *meaningful, true, probable,* or *plausible*. They seek to *clarify* beliefs and are concerned about whether they are *consistent* and *coherent*. They are interested in whether beliefs have *explanatory power* and about what their *implications* are. So we will find philosophers of religion asking these same kinds of questions about religious beliefs.

Philosophers of religion also bring insights and interests from other areas of philosophy (e.g., *epistemology, metaphysics,* and *ethics*) to bear on their consideration of religion. For example, philosophers of religion might think about the epistemology of religious belief, pondering questions about the sources and justification of religious knowledge. Or they might analyze various metaphysical theories of the nature of God and the structure of the divine attributes, or the metaphysics of human free will in relation to divine sovereignty. They might even trace the connection between a given religious tradition and a certain ethical way of life.

(The particular approach one takes to the philosophy of religion depends on precisely how one conceives of the philosophical task in general. The *traditional* conception of philosophy, dominant throughout the history of Western thought, was that philosophy should be used in the service of comprehensive, systematic outlooks—even those that are religious or theological in orientation. The name *natural theology* became a label for the enterprise that presumed that belief in the existence of God and other religious beliefs could, and indeed should, be established by philosophical argument.[6]

Since the early decades of the twentieth century, the *phenomenological* approach to religion has had its proponents, thinkers who promise to provide a new method for describing and understanding phenomena as they really are.[7] They do this by "bracketing" (or suspending) preconceptions as well as critical questions about truth or falsity, in order to "disclose" or "lay bare" its essence as actually experienced by its own adherents.[8]

Yet, for most of this century, the principal philosophical approach among English-speaking philosophers has been *analytic*. Narrowly conceived, this approach restricts the task of philosophy solely to the clarification and analysis of the logic of our ideas, as it denies that philosophy can address questions of truth or falsity in our beliefs.[9] More broadly conceived, the analytic approach is seriously concerned with clear analysis and logical rigor, but as a prelude to more substantive considerations of truth and reasonableness.

The present study is basically analytic in its style, seeking to clarify and analyze important concepts and arguments. Yet it is not narrowly analytic, for it seeks to point out, where possible, those positions that seem most correct and fruitful. In this way, our current venture preserves much of the spirit of the traditional approach, without adopting wholesale the old model of natural theology. No sustained attempt is made in these pages to apply phenomenological techniques, since such an approach is appropriate to an entirely different kind of inquiry.

While our explanation of the relationship of philosophy to religion is somewhat loose and approximate, it is on equal footing with philosophy of art, philosophy of science, philosophy of history, and a number of other studies in which philosophy thoroughly inspects a specific subject matter. Obviously, all such studies are doubly difficult to define because both the nature of philosophy and the discipline under study can be conceived in a variety of ways. Here we simply assume that the enterprise of philosophy is to be conducted according to our foregoing description. So, we are now in a position to propose a working definition for *philosophy of religion: the attempt to analyze and critically evaluate religious beliefs.* In order to make our study more manageable, we now need to narrow the set of religious beliefs that we will investigate in the chapters to follow.

THE GOD OF THEISM

All major religious systems merit serious philosophical investigation. Worthwhile exercises in philosophy of religion can be conducted by inquiring into the specific beliefs of any one given religion or by comparatively studying various religions. For the past twenty-five hundred years in Western culture, the chief interest of philosophers who study religion has been the theistic concept of deity. *The theistic deity is conceived as a transcendent spiritual being who is omnipotent, omniscient, and perfectly good.* We might call this view *classical theism* or *standard theism.* Theism itself, of course, is not a religion but expresses an important belief framework of three living religions. Amid their differences, Judaism, Christianity, and Islam share this basic view of God.

William Rowe calls the core beliefs of standard theism *restricted theism*. Restricted theism conjoined with other distinctive beliefs that arise from the creeds and doctrines and sacred texts of a particular living religion he calls *expanded theism*.[10] Contemporary Anglo-American philosophers of religion continue to be interested in issues surrounding restricted theism as well as those that relate to various versions of expanded theism. In this vein, the present study treats a variety of key issues related to theistic belief.

Some contend that purely intellectual interest in God (in this case, the God of theism) misses the heart of true religion. They contend that the abstract analysis of religious concepts and the logical examination of theological beliefs fail to appreciate the intimate, personal involvement of religious faith. Contending that "the God of the philosophers" is not "the God of faith," they often argue that rigorous intellectual investigation has nothing to offer to devout faith. However, while intellectual interest—or, more precisely, philosophical interest—in religion is not the same thing as passionate religious commitment, it is our belief that faith cannot be totally divorced from reason.

Although religious faith certainly involves an element of personal trust in God, that trust is normally based on a number of *beliefs* about what God is like and how a person becomes properly related to God. It is surely true that having faith in God and living in a manner that manifests that attitude amount to *more* than intellectually adopting beliefs that God exists and that God is perfect in power, knowledge, and justice. But having faith in God is *at least* a matter of accepting such beliefs. In some cases, religious believers may not have a clear and self-conscious understanding of their own beliefs or may not be particularly adept at articulating them. However, this does not alter the fact that religious faith rests on beliefs about the kind of object in which one has faith.[11]

Besides, the instant a believer makes some sort of claim of faith, some statement about her relation to the God she worships, she has automatically entered the arena of rational discussion and dialogue. Likewise, any time someone denies some particular religious belief or rejects all religious beliefs generally, that stance is also open to *rational evaluation*. Wittingly or unwittingly, the believer as well as the nonbeliever has stated some intellectual beliefs, uttered truth-claims that are subject to being criticized as well as defended. Even the belief that faith is immune from critical examination and must be either accepted or rejected on other grounds must itself be rationally evaluated.

Actually, it is not just outsiders or critics who have the right to examine the belief-component of religious faith. Believers themselves may want to seek deeper understanding of their faith by probing its beliefs further. In fact, all major religions recognize their own intellectual dimension, or belief-component, and contain self-critical activities. In addition, they recognize that they must confront criticism from outside. They realize that if religion in modern life is to have any relevance to people who are intellectually honest and morally sensitive, it must be open to continued scrutiny.

Over the centuries, the theistic view of God has produced a rich legacy of dialogue and debate, an ongoing discussion in which the reader of this text is invited to participate.

THE RELIGIOUS AMBIGUITY OF LIFE

Now that we have reached at least a working definition of religion, become acquainted with the role of philosophy of religion, and narrowed our scope to theism, how shall we proceed? Specifically, how might we characterize the initial situation in which we find ourselves as we start thinking philosophically about theistic belief? We might remind ourselves of the dual facts with which we opened this chapter: that many people embrace religion and that many people do not. Since we are going to narrow our discussion to theistic religion, we could readily say that many people accept theistic belief and many people do not. Opinion is obviously divided.

We need to make a further distinction between two general categories of people: *reflective* and *unreflective*. Obviously, people exhibit the tendency to be rationally reflective in varying degrees: some are highly reflective, some seem not to be reflective at all, and others fall somewhere in between. Believers and nonbelievers fall into such categories. Clearly, many people have not seriously pondered the important issues related to the coherence or incoherence, plausibility or implausibility, or truth or falsity of theism, and yet they have decided either to accept or to reject theistic claims. Some say that they just believe in an all-powerful and all-good God, or that prayer is valid, or that miracles happen—and that this is the end of the matter for them. Others claim that they do not believe in God, or that prayer is pointless, or that the idea of miracles seems silly—and that is the end of the matter for them. But neither the believers nor the unbelievers here have made a serious attempt to reflect on the grounds for their opinions. What we have, then, is *unreflective belief* and *unreflective nonbelief*, respectively.

The study before us cannot be concerned with unreflective belief or disbelief. Philosophy is preeminently an enterprise of *reflective reason*, seeking to get beyond superficial approaches to important issues. It seeks to look responsibly at all relevant arguments, clarify key ideas, and carefully trace out implications of beliefs. So, we are interested here in how things look "upon reflection." Interestingly, and perhaps disturbingly for some, we get mixed opinions even from reflective people about the truth of theism. It is not just that unreflective people split on the issue; reflective ones divide as well. Seemingly responsible, earnest, thoughtful people who look hard at the evidence and arguments do not agree!

Most *reflective believers* with a theistic orientation realize that the truth of God's existence is not immediately obvious. For some, God's "hiddenness" constitutes a problem and challenges us to search for him. St. Anselm (1033–1109) wrote:

Lord, if thou art not here, where shall I seek thee, being absent? . . . And, by what marks, under what form, shall I seek thee? I have never seen thee, O Lord my God; I do not know thy form. What, O most high Lord, shall this man do, an exile far from thee?[12]

Anselm stands in a long line of thoughtful believers who have sought to give a rational account for why they believe in God and hold other theistic ideas. They attempt to search out God's existence, to try to construe the facts to see if they point us to God and help us make sense of related religious beliefs—an exercise that Anselm himself called "faith seeking understanding."[13] Not all theists, of course, claim God to be hidden, and not all agree on the degree of divine hiddenness. Some claim to have strong experiential grounds for belief or to have witnessed miracles. Yet some of the most honest and sensitive theistic literature revolves around the theme of the hiddenness of God. And in our contemporary period, this theme is becoming more commonly discussed.

Reflective nonbelievers also agree that the existence of God is not plainly evident. However, in attempting to be reasonable and reflective about the matter, they have concluded that there are no good grounds for believing in God and often cite positive grounds for disbelief. In "A Free Man's Worship," Bertrand Russell stated that the universe appears to be ultimately meaningless:

That man is the product of causes which had no prevision of the end they were achieving; that his origin, his growth, his hopes and fears, his love and beliefs, are but the outcomes of accidental collocations of atoms, that no fire, no heroism, no intensity of thought and feeling, can preserve individual life beyond the grave; that all the labors of the ages, all the devotion, all the inspiration, all the noonday brightness of human genius, are destined to extinction in the vast death of the solar system, and that the whole temple of Man's achievement must inevitably be buried beneath the debris of a universe in ruins—all these things, if not quite beyond dispute, are yet so nearly certain, that no philosophy which rejects them can hope to stand. Only within the scaffolding of these truths, only on the firm foundation of unyielding despair, can the soul's habitation henceforth be safely built.[14]

For Russell, as for numerous other thoughtful nonbelievers, the prima facie nonexistence of God is "upon reflection" taken as a correct conclusion.

OUR TASK

We indicated earlier that the present study attempts to think critically about the issues related to the theistic concept of God. We acknowledge not only that these issues are very complex but that they are issues on which reasonable, responsible, reflective persons can legitimately disagree. In a universe that can be honestly and sensitively characterized by "mystery" or "divine hiddenness" or perhaps even "divine absence," we should not expect unanimity of opinion on the existence and nature of Ultimate Reality. There is a long tradition of theistic thinkers who believe that they can make good, rational sense of the existence of God, faith, prayer, miracle, and other theistic concepts. By contrast, down through the centuries, there has been a notable array of people with very fine intellects who believe that such concepts must be rejected.

Hence, as we embark upon our study, we are committed to a posture that respects serious and responsible thought, regardless of the outcome. That does not mean, however, that we will adopt a purely neutral stance as we sort through the issues, evaluating the arguments and counterarguments. We believe that respect for the rational process also demands that we indicate at points where we stand on key issues. This is not to succumb to blind bias, which lies at the opposite extreme from pure neutrality, but it is to attempt to model a kind of interested objectivity. The form of objectivity that we seek strives to be fair to various positions and to acknowledge when appropriate which one seems most reasonable among alternatives.

The present venture, then, is open to all who are seeking understanding and who are committed to subjecting all beliefs, religious or otherwise, to rigorous philosophical examination. The results of this process are hard to predict. For some, it will lead to the modification of certain views. For others, it could lead to either the acceptance or rejection of theism. For still others, it may lead to deeper commitment.

STUDY QUESTIONS

1. Formulate your own definition of "religion." Test your definition to see if it applies to various cultural phenomena normally labeled religious.

2. Try to define "philosophy." What are some of its main concerns?

3. What is the philosophy of religion? Explain how approaches to philosophy of religion are influenced by different approaches to philosophy itself.

4. Discuss the importance of considering matters of consistency, coherence, plausibility, truth, and meaning with respect to religious beliefs.

5. What is meant by the "hiddenness of God"? Evaluate the significance of this concept.

6. Is it possible to remain completely neutral in the study of religion? Is it desirable to remain neutral? What kind of objectivity should we seek in the investigation of religion (or any important subject)?

7. At the outset, what issues in religion would you identify for philosophical analysis and discussion? Prior to reading this book, have you ever read any material that subjects religious beliefs to rational scrutiny?

8. Try to state in your own words the basic position of classical theism. Discuss its relationship to some specific concrete religions.

9. Show how some major issues in philosophy of religion arise on the basis of certain events and experiences in ordinary life.

10. Explore the objection that philosophical interest in religion misses the essence of religious faith. Do you think that religion or religious faith is subject in any way to rational investigation?

NOTES

1. For an excellent study of the religions of the world, past and present, see Ninian Smart, *The Religious Experience*, 4th ed. (New York: Scribners, 1991).

2. See, for example, the *American Atheist* magazine that is published by O'Hair's group. Also see Robert G. Ingersoll, *Atheist Truth vs. Religion's Ghosts* (1900: reprint ed., Austin, Tex.: American Atheist Press, 1980).

3. See the listing for this organization in *Directory of American Philosophers 1996–97*, 18th ed., Archie Bahm, ed. (Bowling Green, Ohio: Philosophy Documentation Center, 1996), p. 186. For the general position of humanistic atheism, also see P. Kurtz, ed., *Humanist Manifestos I and II* (Buffalo, N.Y.: Prometheus Books, 1973).

4. The following definitions are cited in William P. Alston, "Religion," *Encyclopedia of Philosophy*, vol. 7 (New York: Macmillan, 1967), p. 140.

5. Ninian Smart, *Worldviews: Crosscultural Explorations of Human Beliefs* (New York: Scribners, 1995).

6. We may distinguish other disciplines that are also thought to have a supportive function for theistic belief are as follows. *Dogmatic* (or *confessional*) *theology* begins from the assumption that a certain religious tradition is authoritative. Dogmatic theologians seek to provide ways of elucidating and systematizing accepted doctrines but do not challenge their acceptance. Philosophy of religion is also distinct from *apologetics*, which is concerned to defend a given religious position from intellectual objections. Apologetic projects may be either negative or positive: *negative apologetics* seeks to show that certain criticisms of a specific religion position fail, whereas *positive apologetics* seeks to show that the position is reasonable or credible. Apologetics often has a very practical side, lending itself readily to the practical activity of persuasion. While philosophical awareness and logical skill are relevant to the enterprises of dogmatic theology and apologetics, these activities are not philosophical in the fundamental sense that they begin from a position of relative openness to alternative views and willingness to critique their own most basic commitments.

7. The father of this movement is Edmund Husserl. See his *The Idea of Phenomenology*, trans. W. Alston and G. Nakhnikian (The Hague: Nihoff, 1964).

8. Gerardus van der Leeuw's *Religion in Essence and Manifestation* (New York: Harper and Row, 1963) is a work that takes this approach.

9. One of the classic sources in the analytic tradition, which denies substantive content to philosophy, is A. J. Ayer, *Language, Truth, and Logic* (New York: Dover, 1936). A classic source that promotes philosophy as the enterprise of elucidation and not of advancing truth-claims is Ludwig Wittgenstein, *Philosophical Investigations*, trans. G. E. M. Anscombe (New York: Macmillan, 1953).

10. William Rowe, "Evil and the Theistic Hypothesis: A Response to Wykstra," *International Journal for Philosophy of Religion* 16 (1984): 95.

11. This point is expanded in H. H. Price, "Belief 'In' and Belief 'That'," *Religious Studies* 1, no. 1 (1965): 1–27.

12. St. Anselm, *Proslogium*, in *St. Anselm, Basic Writings*, pt. 1, 2nd ed., trans. S. M. Deane (LaSalle, Ill.: Open Court, 1974).

13. Ibid.

14. Bertrand Russell, *Why I Am Not a Christian and Other Essays on Religion and Related Subjects*, ed. Paul Edwards (New York: Simon and Schuster, 1957), p. 107.

SUGGESTED READING

Alston, William. "Problems of Philosophy of Religion." In *Encyclopedia of Philosophy.* Vol. 6. New York: Macmillan, 1967.

Burtt, Edwin A. *Types of Religious Philosophy.* Rev. ed. New York: Harper and Brothers, 1951.

Hick, John. *An Interpretation of Religion: Human Responses to the Transcendent.* New Haven: Yale University Press, 1989.

Lewis, H. D. "History of Philosophy of Religion." In *Encyclopedia of Philosophy.* Vol. 6. New York: Macmillan, 1967.

Livingston, James C. *Anatomy of the Sacred: An Introduction to Religion.* New York: Macmillan, 1989.

Morris, Thomas. *Making Sense of It All.* Grand Rapids, Mich.: William B. Eerdmans, 1992.

Schellenberg, J. L. *Divine Hiddenness and Human Reason.* Ithaca, N.Y.: Cornell University Press, 1993.

CHAPTER 2   RELIGIOUS
EXPERIENCE: WHAT
DOES IT MEAN TO
ENCOUNTER
THE DIVINE?

People in every religion not only claim to experience some Ultimate Reality but also feel that such experiences give significant meaning and direction to their lives. In the eighth century B.C., the Hebrew prophet Isaiah recorded his experience of God:

> In the year that King Uzziah died, I saw the Lord seated on a throne, high and exalted, and the train of his robe filled the temple. Above him were seraphs, each with six wings, . . . calling to one another: "Holy, holy, holy is the Lord Almighty; the whole earth is full of his glory." . . . "Woe to me!" I cried. "I am ruined! For I am a man of unclean lips, and I live among a people of unclean lips, and my eyes have seen the King, the Lord Almighty."[1]

One of the more famous experiences of the divine is found in the writings of the North African Christian theologian Augustine (354–430):

> I was asking myself these questions ['Why not make an end of my ugly sins at this moment?'], weeping all the while with the most bitter sorrow in my heart, when all at once I heard the sing-song voice of a child in a nearby house. Whether it was the voice of a boy or a girl I cannot say, but again and again it repeated the refrain 'Take it and read, take it and read.' At this I looked up, thinking hard whether there was any kind of game in which children used to chant words like these, but I could not remember ever hearing them before. I stemmed my flood of tears and stood up, telling myself that this could only be a divine command to open my book of Scripture and read the first passage on which my eyes should fall.[2]

Some experiences make less, or even no, appeal to sensory data but nonetheless provide focus to human life. This is illustrated by the following description of an awareness of the universal Self:

Not by sight is It grasped, not even by speech,
Not by any other sense-organs, austerity, or work.
By the peace of knowledge, one's nature purified --
In that way, however, by meditating, one does behold Him
    who is without parts.[3]

How are we to understand religious experiences? In this chapter we explore what a religious experience is, whether we can use religious experience to justify our religious beliefs, and whether described religious experiences have a common core.

TYPES OF RELIGIOUS EXPERIENCE

An *experience* is an event that one lives through (either as a participant or an observer) and of which one is conscious or aware. For example, to experience a World Series baseball game is to play in it, attend and watch the game, or (in an extended or mediated sense) see it on television or hear it on the radio. *Religious experiences* differ, in part, from ordinary experiences in that what is experienced is taken by the person to be some supernatural being or presence (God either in himself or as manifest in some action), a being related to God (a manifestation of God or personage such as the Virgin Mary), or some indescribable Ultimate Reality (such as the nondual Absolute [Brahman] or Nirvana).

It is important to distinguish religious experience from gaining a religious insight.[4] Religious experience, as we are understanding it, requires that persons have or believe that they have an encounter with God or Ultimate Reality, whereas those having a religious insight need not believe that they are encountering God or Ultimate Reality. For example, one might get an insight into the way sin proliferates and conquers us by noting, when digging in one's garden, that if the roots of a nearby tree are not continually removed from the soil, they gradually spread and choke out the vegetable plants. Although some concept of God is necessary to understand the concept of sin (which is an offense against God), the gardener need not believe that he or she has experienced God to achieve this religious insight. Some event in our ordinary experience might suffice to trigger an insight into our spiritual condition or the relation of God to the world without our ever experiencing or believing that we have experienced God in that event. Of course, a religious experience *can* be the source of religious insight. Both Isaiah and Augustine claimed that their experiences of God gave them understanding both about the nature of God and about their own sinfulness. But one can have religious insight without either experiencing God or believing that God exists, whereas to have a religious experience requires that God or Ultimate Reality be either the object of the experience or taken to be such.

We should note, however, that religious traditions often treat both insight and religious experience as important, if not necessary, to achieve the ultimate goal of liberation or salvation. For example, Buddhists hold that since our human predicament or bondage (suffering or *dukkha*) is caused by ignorance, insight into the nature of reality is necessary to liberate us. By seeing that all, including ourselves, is insubstantial, impermanent, changing, one is freed from the ignorance that takes things as objects worthy of desire. Cravings and desires (*tanha*) can be eliminated ultimately only by terminating their root causes, which according to the twelve–spoked wheel of dependent origination, include sensation, consciousness, and ultimately ignorance. Thus, religious experience can be directed properly to the cessation of sensation and conceptualization, to mindlessness, wherein no cognitive activity, including insight, remains:

> By the transcendence of all conceptualizations of form, by the disappearance of conceptualizations based upon sense-data, by paying no attention to conceptualization of manifoldness, having attained to the sphere of infinite space [the practitioner] remains therein, thinking 'space is unending'. By entirely transcending the sphere of infinite space [infinite consciousness; of nothing at all; of neither conceptualization nor non-conceptualization], having attained to the sphere of infinite consciousness [nothing at all; neither conceptualization nor non-conceptualization; the cessation of sensation and conceptualization] [the practitioner] remains therein.[5]

We claim to experience God or Ultimate Reality in a variety of ways. Richard Swinburne (1934–) suggests five types of religious experience, classified *from the perspective of the experiencer.*[6] These types he considers mutually exclusive and totally exhaustive of the possibilities.

1. *Experience of God or Ultimate Reality mediated through a common, public, sensory object.* For example, one might claim to see God in an icon, sunset, or ocean. Icons or sunsets are not God but that in and through which God or the supernatural is encountered:

> Crossing a bare common, in snow puddles, at twilight, under a clouded sky, . . . I have enjoyed a perfect exhilaration. . . . In the wood, is perpetual youth. Within these plantations of God, a decorum and sanctity reign, a perennial festival is dressed. . . . Standing on bare ground,—my head bathed by the blithe air, and uplifted into infinite space,—all mean egotism vanishes. I become a transparent eyeball; I am nothing; I see all; the currents of the Universal Being circulate through me; I am part or particle of God.[7]

2. *Experience of God or Ultimate Reality mediated through an unusual, public, sensory object.* For example, one might claim to experience the supernatural through an appearance of the Virgin at Lourdes, a figure seen in a cloud formation, or in a bush that burned but was not consumed:

> Now Moses was keeping the flock of his father-in-law, Jethro. . . . And the angel of the Lord appeared to him in a flame of fire out of the midst of a bush; and he looked, and lo, the bush was burning, yet it was not consumed. . . . God called to him out of the bush, "Moses, Moses!"[8]

The appearance is public, in that many people present could (in theory) observe what is happening and experience God through it. However, the appearance is unusual; few assert they have seen the Virgin at Lourdes, and only Moses claimed to witness a burning bush that was not consumed.

One might also claim to experience something unusual, even though someone else in the same situation might take it to be common or ordinary. Swinburne provides the example, described in the New Testament, of the encounter between two persons and a man walking to Emmaus. The two eventually understood this companion to be the risen Jesus Christ, whereas another "might have had the same visual sensations . . . and yet not had the religious experience." [9]

3. *Experience of God or Ultimate Reality mediated through private sensations that can be described in normal sensory language.* For example, a person might claim to experience God in a dream or vision, as did Peter who, in a trance, saw a cloth filled with nonkosher animals lowered from heaven.[10] Visions, dreams, locutions, and the like, despite being described in sensory language, are available only to one person:

> I was sitting in a certain chapel, and while I was taking pleasure in the delight of some prayer or meditation, I suddenly felt within me an unwonted and pleasant fire. When I had for long doubted whence it came, I learned by experience that it came from the Creator and not from creature, since I found it ever more pleasing and full of heat.[11]

4. *Experience of God or Ultimate Reality mediated through private sensations that cannot be described in normal sensory language.* Here one feels or claims to experience something, but it cannot be spoken about; it is ineffable. For example, St. Teresa of Avila (1512–1582) relates the following experience:

> I was at prayer on a festival of the glorious Saint Peter when I saw Christ at my side—or, to put it better, I was conscious of Him, for neither with the eyes of the body nor with those of the soul did I see anything. I thought He was quite close to me and I saw that it was He Who, as I thought, was speaking to me. . . . All the time Jesus Christ seemed to be beside me, but as this was not an imaginary vision, I could not discern in what form: what I felt very clearly was that all the time He was at my right hand, and a witness of everything that I was doing.[12]

5. *Experience of God or Ultimate Reality that is not mediated by any sensations.* The person claims to be intuitively and immediately aware of God or the One. A Western mystic, Nicholas of Cusa (1401–1464), writes, "I behold Thee, O Lord my God, in a kind of mental trance, for if sight be not sated with seeing, nor the ear with hearing, then much less is the intellect with understanding."[13] This type is most richly illustrated by the higher meditational states of Hinduism and Buddhism:

> Of one who has entered the first trance the voice has ceased; of one who has entered the second trance reasoning and reflection have ceased; of one who has entered the third trance joy has ceased; of one who has entered

the fourth trance the inspirations and expirations have ceased; of one who has entered the realm of the infinity of space the perception of form has ceased; of one who has entered the realm of the infinity of consciousness the perception of the realm of the infinity of space has ceased; of one who has entered the realm of nothingness the perception of the realm of the infinity of consciousness has ceased.[14]

In reality, perhaps few experiences fall neatly into one given type, for experiences contain richly diverse elements. For example, Nicholas commends beginning meditational experience with an icon, though the ultimate experience of God is nonsensory:

> But I perceive, not with my fleshly eyes, which look on this icon of Thee, but with the eyes of my mind and understanding, the invisible truth of Thy face, which therein is signified, under a shadow and limitation. Thy true face is freed from any limitation, it hath neither quantity nor quality, nor is it of time or place, for it is the Absolute Form, the Face of faces.[15]

Hence, it is less important to try to categorize each experience than to understand more generally the diversity of ways persons understand their religious experiences. Mystical experience (generally categorized as types 4 or 5) provides one kind of religious experience but does not exhaust all possibilities.

Given this typology of how people *understand* their religious experiences, the question remains concerning what people *really* experience. Do they *really* experience God, or do they only interpret certain experiences or feelings religiously? Philosophers have suggested three different perspectives on the *reality of religious experience*.

RELIGIOUS EXPERIENCE AS FEELING

In his influential nineteenth-century writings, Friedrich Schleiermacher (1768–1834) contended that religious experience is not an intellectual or cognitive experience but "a feeling of absolute or total dependence upon a source or power that is distinct from the world."[16] It is self-authenticating, intuitive, and unmediated by concepts, ideas, beliefs, or practices. Since it is a feeling, preceding conceptual distinctions, we cannot describe it. It is an affective rather than a cognitive experience.

This view influenced many, including Rudolf Otto (1869–1937). He admits that some aspects of God can be grasped by reason. By analogy we can ascribe to God attributes such as spirit, purpose, good will, omnipotence, and selfhood. "All these attributes constitute clear and definite *concepts*: they can be grasped by the intellect; they can be analyzed by thought; they even admit of definition."[17] Yet in respect to God's deeper nature—his holiness—God cannot be rationally known; God is ineffable. We must apprehend God's holiness by something that goes beyond the rational, namely, by feeling.

Otto understands religious experience as a feeling, or better, a complex of feelings. This feeling comes in many forms:

> The feeling of [the *mysterium tremendum*] may at times come sweeping like a gentle tide, pervading the mind with a tranquil mood of deepest worship. It may pass over into a more set and lasting attitude of the soul, continuing, as it were, thrillingly vibrant and resonant. . . . It may burst in sudden eruption up from the depths of the soul with spasms and convulsions, or lead to the strangest excitements, to intoxicated frenzy, to transport, and to ecstasy.[18]

Otto finds the numinous manifested in three specific types of feeling. We experience the feeling of dependence, that we are mere creatures, "submerged and overwhelmed by [our] own nothingness in contrast to that which is supreme above all creatures."[19] We can also experience the feeling of religious dread (awe) and of being overpowered before the *mysterium tremendum*. We shudder and quake at the "sight" of God. And finally, we have a feeling of longing for the transcendent being that fascinates us. Built into us is a restlessness, a longing for God.[20]

William James (1842–1910) contends that since "feeling is the deeper source of religion,"[21] philosophical and theological reflection are secondary products, outgrowths of religious experience. Were there no religious experience, there would be no theologies or religious philosophies. "The attempt to demonstrate by purely intellectual processes the truth of the deliverances of direct religious experience is absolutely hopeless."[22]

James is correct in his contention that there would be no philosophy of religion if people had no religious experience. At the same time, for religious experience to generate the myths, dogmas, and theologies that are the stuff of philosophy of religion, religious experience cannot be "private and dumb, and unable to give an account of itself."[23] That is, it is hard to see how one can generate cognitive religious truth-claims, as found in theology and religious philosophy, out of noncognitive feelings. If both the experienced and the experience are ineffable, and if the latter is so fundamental that it precedes cognitive distinctions, what religious truths can follow upon it? Even attempts to describe the experience by analogy presuppose that the event can be cognitively understood, so that one can appreciate which analogies are appropriate to the experience and which are not.

A second objection is that defenders of this view have misunderstood the nature of feelings and emotions. Emotions are not more fundamental than beliefs or behavior. Indeed, emotions, like beliefs and acts, depend on concepts. Emotions

> are in part constituted by concepts and judgments. To say that a concept is constitutive of an emotion is to say that the emotion cannot be specified without reference to that concept. . . . In order to specify an emotion it is necessary to specify the quality of the feeling, the object of the emotion and the rational grounds by which the subject justifies the emotion. We

can now see that among those grounds are the subject's beliefs about the causes of his state.[24]

But if concepts in part constitute emotions, religious experience cannot be completely divorced from the cognitive.

At the same time, however, one might contend that both objections place too much emphasis on the cognitive aspect of religious experience. In some religious traditions, religious experience involves a gradual weaning of the individual from cognitive consciousness to a state that, at best, can be described as pure consciousness or pure emptiness (*shunya*). In Buddhism, for example, the goal is to transcend all conceptualization in order to attain to the sphere of pure consciousness and from there to the state of emptiness. The experiencer seeks not knowledge but to free himself from the cravings and desires of being a self. Once he realizes that there is no self, he can remove the cravings and desires that flow from desire for self and consequently remove the suffering that pervades our existence. Religious experience, at this stage, is fundamentally directed toward liberation, not cognitive understanding. Indeed, by overcoming the subject-object distinction, cognitive understanding is rendered impossible. Religious experience in this tradition is not feeling, but it is ultimately noncognitive.

RELIGIOUS EXPERIENCE AS PERCEPTUAL EXPERIENCE

A second view is that some religious experiences are a type of perception. William Alston (1921–), for example, holds that religious experience often has the same structure as perception.[25] We can discern three elements in our ordinary, sensory perception (for example, seeing a cat): the perceiver (the person who sees the cat), the perceived object (the cat that is seen), and the phenomenon (the appearance of the cat). Similarly, it is held, there are three elements in religious experience: the religious experiencer; God (Reality), who is experienced, and the appearance or presentation of God to the perceiver. Philosophers debate precisely how perception is to be analyzed. In particular, they raise questions concerning the status of the phenomenon. But philosophers generally agree that in perception objects present themselves to us in ways that enable us to know them. Similarly, in religious experience God presents himself in ways that enable us to know God and his actions.

Some might think it strange to understand religious experience as a kind of perception. It appears that ordinary perceptual or sense experience differs in important ways from religious experience. Sense perception is a common experience, whereas religious experience is unusual, perhaps even rare; sense perception yields a great deal of information about the world, whereas religious experience yields apparently little information about God; all humans have the capacity for sense perception, but many seem not to have the capacity for religious experience. These differences, however, do not show that religious experience has a structure that is unlike perception. For one thing, neither the frequency of an experience nor the amount of information it yields tells us anything about its structure. Further, some people have limited sensory and hence perceptual capacities because they cannot see or hear, but this fact casts no doubt on the claim that seeing and hearing are forms of perception. Similarly, that many do not have religious experiences is irrelevant to the claim that religious experience is structured like perceptual experience.

Some philosophers, however, point to one significant difference that allegedly shows that religious experience is not a type of perception. It concerns the nature of the perceptual appearance or presentation (the phenomenon). Ordinary perception is sensory; the perceived object presents itself as bearing certain sensory qualities. For example, the desk in front of me appears brown, hard, rectangular, and wooden. But those who have religious experiences sometimes report that what they perceive, namely, God, bears perceptual qualities that are *not* sensory. The qualities they experience in God are divine goodness, power, love, sovereignty, and giving strength. As we noted earlier, sometimes religious experience does have sensory content, but when it does, often that content comes from what mediates the experience (for example, sunsets and icons), rather than from the object of the experience (God).[26] But the characteristics of the sunset are not the characteristics of God. The problem, then, is this: If the characteristics of what is allegedly perceived (the phenomenon) in religious experience differ so much from ordinary perceptual experience, is not the structure of religious experience so different that it is a mistake to understand religious experience as a form of perception?

Alston admits that the perceived qualities of religious experiences of God—properties such as power, beauty, and goodness—are not sensory. Some of these, for example, concern God's dispositions or the attitudes behind his actions. However, for Alston that does not mean that they cannot be the content of a perception. He distinguishes between phenomenal qualities (the way something looks to me at the moment) and objective qualities (the disposition of an object to look in a certain way in certain circumstances). When we describe an experienced object, he claims, frequently our description refers to its objective and not its phenomenal qualities. We do not describe the object by saying how the thing *appears* at the moment. That is, if you asked me to describe my house, I would not list the particular sense data that I am now receiving—that my house appears to me dark brown and beige, darker in the shadows, trapezoidal beneath the roof, and so on. If we always gave descriptions of objects in terms of how they look to us at the moment, the description would be both indefinitely large (in order to reflect the large quantity of received sensory data) and so unique (since, for example, I perceive objects under indefinitely many lighting conditions and from indefinitely many angles) that we could not construct usable concepts from such diverse patterns. Rather, we often speak about the thing's objective or dispositional qualities by using assumed or unstated *comparative* concepts.[27] That is, when I describe an object, I state how it would look under *normal* conditions. For example, to the question "What is the color of your house?" I would respond that it is beige, though at night it does not appear beige.

To put this point more simply, just ask yourself what the door of your classroom looks like from where you are sitting. More than likely you will say that it is rectangular. Yet rectangularity is not its phenomenal property at the moment; rather, from where you are sitting it probably appears trapezoidal. But you usually give its objective property (rectangularity) when asked what the door you see is like.

In a similar fashion, God's qualities of power, goodness, and love are reported using not phenomenal or sensory language, but comparative concepts. They characterize how God could be expected to appear under certain "normal" conditions (his objective rather than phenomenal properties). If we describe our experience of God using comparative concepts, the way we report objects of sense perception distinctly parallels how we report our perception of God. Just as we frequently report our perception of things not by talking about how the things appear at the moment but rather by using comparative concepts referring to how they would look in normal circumstances (their objective properties), so our reports of our experience of God appeal to comparative rather than phenomenal concepts.

An objection might be raised to the effect that we know how houses, cars, and trees appear in normal circumstances because we could, if pressed, provide the relevant phenomenal description. Ultimately, the objective properties are also phenomenal. How do religious experiencers know how God would appear in normal circumstances, since they cannot provide a phenomenal description of God?

Alston suggests that our experience with humans who are more or less good gives us some idea of what it is like to experience God showing his goodness. But does knowing how good people act give us an expectation of how we should experience God's goodness? Here again we are moving from a point of comparison that contains sensory information (how good people act) to a point that lacks it (how God acts). Further, don't we have to have some idea of the phenomenal conditions under which we could experience God in order to anticipate how God would manifest his goodness under normal circumstances?

Alston replies that the religious experiencer need not determine this, for it is not uncommon for persons to have perceptual experiences of things without being able to specify what they would look like under normal circumstances. But having some notion of how God would be perceived under normal circumstances is essential for suggesting that religious experience parallels ordinary perceptual experience, since in many cases we do know what objects normally look like. In short, the absence of phenomenal concepts in experiences of God raises questions about whether religious experience is a kind of perceptual experience.

The question concerning how God would appear gives rise to a second problem. Whereas human sensory perception is generally consistent, allowing us to check the accuracy of any particular perception by appealing to other perceptual experiences, religious experiences are extremely diverse. Thus, the accuracy of any particular experience cannot be so easily confirmed. Religious experiences are conditioned by distinctive cultural and religious perspectives, so what people in various religions experience differs widely. The Ultimate Reality that a Hindu experiences is very different from the personal God a Christian experiences. But we cannot easily confirm which experience is correct independent of the distinctive religious systems. This, of course, does not show necessarily that religious experience is not perceptual; it may only mean that religious experiences are more open to individual interpretation. We return to this problem later in this chapter.

RELIGIOUS EXPERIENCE AS INTERPRETATION IN SUPERNATURAL TERMS

Defenders of a third view reject the thesis that religious experiences need be actual perceptual experiences. According to Wayne Proudfoot (1939–), to call an experience a perception entails a claim not only about the person's awareness of the event (something must have been presented to or appeared to the perceiver) but also about the cause of the experience. For our experiences really to be perceptions, the perceived object must be there and make a causal contribution (of the right sort) to our experience of it. For example, to say that a person sees a cat is to grant both that a cat exists and that the cat causally contributes to the person's seeing it. If the cat does not exist and does not in some way cause the perception, then we say, not that the person perceives or sees the cat, but rather that the person hallucinates a cat or mistakes something else for a cat.

If religious experience is a kind of perceptual experience, the same conditions must hold true for it. That is, if religious experience is *truly* a perceptual experience, what is perceived must exist and make a causal contribution of the right sort to our experience of it. Now, if we restrict our consideration to how persons *interpret* their experience (what might be called a *phenomenological description*), Proudfoot holds that we can use the model of perception to understand religious experience. Embedded in the experiencers' understanding of their experience is a claim about its cause. Such persons believe that they actually have perceived God, God's activity, or some being related to God. Their religious experience cannot be understood apart from their belief that they encountered God or Ultimate Reality.

However, to describe a religious experience as an actual perceptual experience would be too restrictive. We want to be liberal in allowing that people of diverse faiths have religious experiences. But this formulation would commit us to the belief that the objects of or the alleged causes of those religious experiences really exist. That is, we could not admit that someone had a religious experience without admitting that what he or she perceived existed. To avoid this unsatisfactory result, Proudfoot holds that our characterization of religious experience must be broad enough to permit another person to admit that people have religious experiences that they describe in terms of experiencing something supernatural, without having to grant that they actually experienced any such supernatural object.

A religious experience, then, is an experience that the person who has it *takes* or interprets as religious. To take an experience as religious means that the *experiencer believes* that a naturalistic explanation of the experience is insufficient; it is inappropriate to locate the cause of the experience in the experiencer's digestive processes, emotions, wish fulfillment, or subconscious. Rather, she can explain the experience only by appeal to some Reality beyond herself who is speaking to or encountering her.[28]

According to this view, then, it is important to distinguish the *description* of the experience from the *explanation* of the experience. In *describing* the experience, the perspective of the subject dominates. A religious experience cannot be described apart from the experiencer's belief system, including the belief that the experienced object exists. This means that a description of a religious experience will invoke the existence of the supernatural that caused the experience. For example, one cannot describe Augustine's religious experience without reference to his belief that God exists and can communicate through spoken and written words. So described, religious experience cannot be reduced to any other kind of experience; to do so is to misidentify the experience. As such, scientific accounts that dispense with the supernatural element are irrelevant to describing the experience, for whereas science attempts to explain the experience in terms of its natural causes, those who have the religious experience require the supernatural explanation as part of its description. So far this is consistent with Alston's perceptual account of religious experience.

However, for Proudfoot, the fact that experiencers understand the experience in terms of the supernatural does *not* mean that they really experienced the supernatural or that there is no adequate natural *explanation* for their experience. Here is where Proudfoot departs from Alston's perceptual account. In the case of Augustine, it might just have happened that, apart from any divine activity or intention, a child nearby was playing a game, of which the sing-song—"take it and read"—was a part. However, were this true, it would not make Augustine's experience any less religious. It simply means that what he took as its ultimate cause—God himself—might not be its cause. In other words, an experience can be a genuine religious experience for a person because of its locus in his or her belief system even though no supernatural object actually is perceived. All that is required is that experiencers *interpret* their experiences in terms of categories and beliefs about the supernatural.

All experience is mediated by concepts and beliefs and shaped by language. When people have an experience, they identify that experience under some set of concepts and rules. There is no uninterpreted datum that is experienced and then later interpreted. The experience itself is embedded both in some interpretation of the world and in some commitment to a certain set of religious beliefs and practices. Thus, for example, some mystics are committed to the belief that their religious experience of God is ineffable and yet communicates knowledge about God; should some experience not satisfy these criteria, it simply is not a mystical experience. This means that there will be no single description of religious experiences; there will be numerous accounts, each reflecting the belief structure of the perceiver.

But how can we evaluate whether a person really has experienced God? If each person's concepts and beliefs shape his religious experience, how can we determine which account—the natural or the supernatural— provides the best explanation? Proudfoot is correct when he argues that, though the outside party (Jane) must describe the experience Joe has in terms of Joe's beliefs about the cause of the experience, Jane need not endorse those beliefs. Proudfoot goes on to assign to the analyst the task of trying to ferret out why people who have had religious experiences understand them as they do, and he contends that "what we want is a historical or cultural explanation."[29] But this assignment begs the question concerning which belief-system provides the appropriate framework for explaining the events, for why should one assume that a historical or cultural explanation is more to the point than a supernatural or theistic one?

One response is that we can evaluate the veracity of religious experience-claims only within particular belief systems. That is, the explanation of the experience must be internally consistent with the set of beliefs and concepts that the experiencer uses. But then persons with a belief-system different from that of the religious experiencer cannot evaluate the religious-experience claim, for they lack the particular set of beliefs and concepts the experiencer uses to explain the experience.

CAN RELIGIOUS EXPERIENCE JUSTIFY RELIGIOUS BELIEF?

We cannot doubt that people have religious experiences. But what interests the philosopher of religion most is whether these experiences can provide the basis or grounds for making knowledge claims about reality. Some theists contend that religious experience plays a valuable role in justifying religious beliefs. As one bumper sticker puts it, "God is not dead—I talked with him this morning!" But whether the alleged experience of God can be used to ground our beliefs depends, in part, upon how one characterizes religious experience.

First, suppose that religious experiences are *merely* feelings. Schleiermacher thought that not only could he generate the structure of religious belief by an appeal to these feelings, he also could justify that structure by the same feelings. But can feelings justify cognitive belief? The difficulty arises from the claim that both God (as transcendent) and our experience of God (as feeling, unstructured by concepts and beliefs) are ineffable. But for the experience to have cognitive significance, it must be mediated by rational beliefs and concepts.

Otto faces a similar problem. He grants that the conceptual descriptions of the numinous are not "genuine intellectual 'concepts,' but only a sort of illustrative substitute for a concept."[30] He calls the concepts used to describe the experience "ideograms," imperfect analogies drawn from our ordinary experience. Yet he designates certain concepts as appropriate for marking the numinous. To distinguish what appropriately designates it from what does not implies that there is some conceptual system by which the numinous can be grasped. The experience of the numinous, therefore, must have some intellectual content.

In short, those who describe religious experience as mere feeling encounter a dilemma. If the religious experience is ineffable, then it cannot be used to ground religious beliefs, for it provides no content for the grounding. If, however, the experience has conceptual content, then it cannot be independent of conceptual expression and immune from criticism. Those who make religious experience into *mere* feeling cannot have it both ineffable and the foundation for religious conceptual systems.

Now suppose that one characterizes religious experience as Proudfoot does, namely, as experience that is interpreted by the experiencer as caused by something supernatural. Then the very designation of an experience as religious requires that experiencers have certain beliefs about what they take to be its cause. The identification of the cause is part of the description of the experience. But then, it might be argued, religious experience cannot be used to justify belief in the existence of that cause. To do so would be to argue in a circle: the experience is religious because someone took it as being caused by God, and that person has good reason to believe that God exists because of this religious experience.

The consequence of this view is that religious experience is meaningful insofar as it finds its place within a particular religious worldview. The experience makes sense because a person already has a set of beliefs that includes the supernatural. The existence of the supernatural is not properly inferred from the experience but is part of its very description and, hence, a presupposition of the experience.

This argument, however, might be mistaken. If the fact that our experiences are interpreted in terms of our belief structure means that our experiences cannot be used to justify our beliefs, then none of our experiences can justify our beliefs, for all experiences invoke our belief structures. The result would be that the experience I describe as my seeing a cat in the tree would not justify my belief that there is a cat in the tree, for it would presuppose that there are such things as cats, trees, and cats in trees. But what then would justify this belief? Such a view would leave all experiential beliefs unjustifiable.

It appears that justification in terms of our experience needs to be understood in terms of what best explains that and similar experiences. If the best explanation for a perceptual experience of a cat is in terms of a cat, then that experience might provide evidence for the existence of a cat. Similarly, if the best explanation for a religious experience is in terms of a supernatural cause, then that experience might provide evidence for God's existence. Others may offer a completely naturalistic explanation of the experience. However, the more experiences that can be explained cogently by appeal to the supernatural, and the more these experiences fit in with a coherent belief structure, the more one is justified in believing that this explanation of the experience is correct. This reply suggests that religious experiences can be reasonably considered authentic perceptual experiences, and this brings one closer to Alston's position.

Those who hold that religious experience is a perceptual experience argue that religious experience can be used to justify religious beliefs in the same way that we commonly use our perceptions to justify our beliefs about the world. For example, we are justified in believing that there is a robin on the lawn when we see a robin on the lawn and have no reason to think that the perceptual conditions are unusual or that our perceptual apparatus is not working properly. Similarly, religious persons are justified in believing that God exists, loves them, or answers their prayers on the basis of their religious experiences.

THE PRINCIPLE OF CREDULITY

But cannot we be mistaken about our religious experiences, and, if so, how can they provide evidence to justify religious belief? Of course we can be mistaken, but this is neither contrary to our normal perceptual experience nor sufficient to deny that religious experience justifies religious belief. When people say they see a robin outside, we ordinarily grant that there is a robin that they see. Swinburne calls this the *Principle of Credulity: when it seems to someone that something is the case, it probably is so, unless there are special considerations to mitigate the claim.*[31] That is, the way things appear to be provides good grounds for believing that this is the way things are. We are justified in holding the belief until someone introduces contrary considerations that cast doubt upon either this particular perception or the accurate functioning of our perceptual apparatus. This does not mean we could not be mistaken about the experience, but it places the burden of proof on those who would claim that the experience was not genuine.

If religious experience is also a kind of perceptual experience, we can apply the Principle of Credulity to religious experience as well. In the absence of special considerations, religious experience should be taken by experiencers as providing good grounds for the belief that God or Ultimate Reality exists or has certain properties. This does not mean that experiencers could not be mistaken in their experience or belief. But like perceivers in ordinary sensory experience, persons are entitled to their belief about their religious experience until they are given good reason to think that the belief conflicts with other justified beliefs (for example, about God's nonexistence) or that there is some shortcoming in their perceptual apparatus. The religious experience provides a prima facie justification for beliefs about God.

But can we accept the Principle of Credulity? And can we apply the Principle of Credulity to religious experience? Are there not special considerations that cast doubt on its applicability to religious experience? One criticism is raised by Michael Martin (1932–). He notes that many people have tried to have religious experience but have failed. Hence he posits a negative principle of credulity: if it seems to someone that something is absent, then probably it is absent. For him, the perceptual experience of the absence of God is as telling as the perceptual experience of God is for others.[32]

A second criticism is developed by C. B. Martin (1924–), who argues that in order to be justified in making knowledge claims based on perceptual experience, the experience must be checkable or verifiable. When someone claims to see a robin on the lawn, that person is justified in holding the belief that a robin actually is on the lawn only if that person or others can check out the perception by other perceptions. But the special consideration involved in religious experience is that it lacks verifiability. "If the believer says, 'I had a direct experience of God at 6:37 p.m., May 6, 1939,' this is not an empirical statement in the way other [perceptual experience] statements are."[33] Martin sees this as a product of the religious believer's attributing religious experience either to a kind of sixth sense that differs from the other five but borrows language from them in a way that can only be metaphorical or to a unique way of knowing that only those who have it can understand (just as only those who are sighted can understand what it is for something to be blue). In both cases, Martin claims, the experience is uncheckable, so the believer is not justified in making knowledge claims on the basis of that experience.

Martin notes that those who have religious experiences often claim indubitability for their experience. But claims of perceptual indubitability are more like claims about appearances (what seems to the perceiver to be the case) than about something perceived (which is dubitable). That someone has an appearance of a blue ball is indubitable. But from the fact that a person has an appearance of a blue ball he cannot conclude that there really is a blue ball that he sees. Hence, believers are caught in a dilemma. Either claims based on religious experience are indubitable and hence are only about what appears (appearance claims) and not about any object of the experience (like God), or they are about God but unverifiable. In neither case can knowledge claims about God's existence and character follow from religious experiences.

William Wainwright (1935–) replies that it is true that there are some disanalogies between religious experience and other perceptual experiences. For one, religious believers generally disregard differing claims. If others disagree with their claims, then perhaps those critics did not use the proper meditative techniques. Believers may change their mind about their experience when faced with opposing claims, but they need not do so. For another, the religious experiencer does not make verifiable predictive claims (at least verifiable in this life). Wainwright argues, however, that these disanalogies occur because of the nature of the object perceived. Since God differs from the sense objects we normally perceive, one cannot require that everyone perceive God in the same way or that the experience of God yield verifiable predictions. Religious experience is more analogous to perceiving a person than to perceiving inanimate sensory objects; one person might perceive another person as dispassionate and distant, whereas a second might perceive that same person as warm and friendly.

Beyond this, Wainwright contends that there are tests for checking religious experience claims. One kind of test involves evidence to show that God exists, such as provided by the arguments for God's existence. Of course, someone like Martin might not accept this evidence, but the critical rationalist does not require that an argument be convincing to everyone to hold that it provides justificatory evidence. The point here is that tests are part of a larger framework of beliefs that one takes to be justified.

Wainwright's other tests relate indirectly to the religious experience: whether it produces for the believer a life marked by virtues, the effect the believer has on others, the profundity of what the believer says, the coherence of the experience with orthodox religious claims, its coherence with the experiences of others, and the pronouncements of an authority.[34]

It might be objected that these tests are indirect, whereas we test ordinary perceptual experience more directly. I check to see if my visual sensation of a computer in front of me is true by reaching out and touching it. But Wainwright notes that if direct, sensory tests provide the only type of verification available to us, we are committed to an infinite regress that precludes any verification. If one perception is confirmed by a second, and the second is suspect, then the second must be confirmed by a third, and so on. Hence, indirect tests of experience must be appropriate.

DIVERSITY OF RELIGIOUS EXPERIENCES

One of Wainwright's tests is the coherence of the beliefs that arise from believers' religious experiences. Some would object here that the beliefs of those who have religious experiences do not cohere with each other. Whereas the way we report both ordinary perceptual experiences and the objects of those experiences is fundamentally uniform, reports about religious experiences and what is allegedly experienced are very diverse and not always mutually coherent. As we noted earlier, persons give incompatible descriptions of the Reality experienced. For example, Christians describe the God they encounter as triune and really distinct from themselves, whereas Hindus characterize Brahman as the whole of reality and describe the relation of the self (*atman*) to Brahman nondualistically. Can incompatible descriptions of what is experienced be reconciled?

Perhaps these differing descriptions cannot be reconciled. However, this is not necessarily fatal to the Principle of Credulity. The principle does not require that all perceptions be veridical. Where perceptions yield conflicting testimony, we must turn to other experiences and rational arguments to determine the truth of the various claims. That is, where there are incompatible accounts, additional considerations must be introduced to help decide which, if any, of the religious experiences are veridical. Although the reports provide a prima facie ground for their acceptance, not all beliefs based on such experiences are true. Just as we at times doubt perceptual claims for good reasons (seeing the mirage of a water puddle in the road on a hot day), we might do the same for claims based on religious experience. Consonance with other justified beliefs about God and religious practices might be one way to winnow out less reliable claims.

At the same time, however, the presence of conflicting claims does raise questions about whether one can use such experiences to justify religious beliefs. It suggests that religious experiences lack a general reliability. Indeed, these experiences seem to rely rather heavily upon the personal religious backgrounds of the respective reporters of the experiences. In such cases, naturalistic accounts in terms of culture, rather than supernaturalistic accounts in terms of some divine being or reality, might better explain the religious experiences.

The objection from conflicting claims must be carefully crafted if it is to be telling. It is very important to note that it is not mere diversity of religious experiences that poses a problem but incompatibility of the religious claims based on them. For one thing, there is no reason that people might not have different experiences. Ordinary perceptual experience is very diverse; different people experience different things or the same thing from different perspectives. For another, different descriptions of what is experienced do not by themselves pose a problem for justification. For example, although two people may describe a painting in front of which they are standing in different ways, the existence of the painting will not be in doubt. Similarly, that religious experiencers give different names to what is experienced or that different people experience different beings (Mary, Krishna, angels) or receive different revelations regarding their personal lives does not establish that their respective experiences are incompatible or incapable of justifying any claim to the existence of what they perceived. All that follows is that they are different. Rather, the problem arises from the incompatibility of some of the claims made about Reality on the basis of religious experience. That is, for the objection to hold, it must be shown that the Ultimate Realty allegedly experienced by one person is *incompatible* with that allegedly experienced by another, not merely different from it.

IS THERE A COMMON CORE TO RELIGIOUS EXPERIENCE?

The discussion of the objection to religious experience from allegedly conflicting claims about reality based on religious experience raises a fundamental issue—namely, whether there is a common core to religious experience. On the one hand, there are those who argue that the diversity objection fails because all religious experiences of Ultimate Reality have something in common. Differences are to be explained by the fact that experiencers proceed to give detailed interpretative accounts that, by invoking concepts, models, and metaphors from their respective religious traditions, introduce incompatibility into the descriptions of the experience. The differences are imported from the religious doctrines they hold and are not necessarily to be found in the experiences or stimuli themselves.[35] Once the interpretations are removed, a common core remains.

This is particularly evident, according to some thinkers, in mystical experiences, which involve an immediate and noninferential consciousness of some Reality, prior to any subject-object differentiation. The mystic achieves union with Reality either epistemologically (when there is no *experienced* subject-object distinction) or ontologically (when there is no *real* distinction between experiencer and object). Mystics later interpret this experience through the use of rational concepts and categories, but to do so is already to depart from the ineffability of the original experience.

One can find the view that there is a common core to religious experiences—a core that transcends the boundaries of different religions, denominations, and cultures—in writers such as William James, Walter T. Stace (1886–1967), and, more recently, Caroline Franks Davis (1957–). Stace is concerned particularly about mystic experiences. His goal is to give a phenomenologically objective description of the mystic experience. He notes that one must be careful to distinguish between the experience and the interpretation of the experience. The interpretation is introduced in order to enable the person to understand and communicate the experience. Stace wants to ascertain the pure description of the experience itself. He lists seven distinctive core features of the mystic experience:

1. the Unitary Consciousness; the One, the Void; pure consciousness
2. nonspatial, nontemporal
3. sense of objectivity or reality
4. blessedness, peace, and so forth
5. feeling of the holy, sacred, or divine

6. paradoxicality
7. alleged by mystics to be ineffable.[36]

Yet one might ask: Does not this very classification invoke interpretation, especially when Stace speaks about the One or the Void (with a capital letter) as fundamental to this experience? Stace replies that one must distinguish levels of interpretation:

> If a mystic speaks of the experience of "an undifferentiated distinctionless unity," this mere report or description using only classificatory words may be regarded as a low-level interpretation. But this is being more fussily precise than is usually necessary, since for all intents and purposes it is just a description. If a mystic says he experiences a "mystical union with the Creator of the universe," this is a high-level interpretation since it includes far more intellectual addition than a mere descriptive report.[37]

His point is that the seven characteristics are solely descriptive. Interpretation enters later in attempts to identify the One with, for example, the God of Christianity or Brahman of Hinduism.

However, admitting that interpretation occurs in a basic description, even if only at a low level, appears to be fatal to the contention that one can discern a cross-cultural, universal core. This becomes clear when, in making the distinction between extrovertive and introvertive mystical experiences, Stace suggests that the introvertive kind is a more complete version of the extrovertive, since "consciousness or mind is a higher category than life."[38] To speak of categories and to evaluate them is to introduce interpretation into the most important of the alleged core elements.

Taking the opposite position, Steven Katz (1944–) argues that no experience is unmediated by concepts and beliefs. We process all experience through our beliefs, learned categories, and conceptual framework. Even self-consciousness—the paradigm of intuitive experience—is conceptually conditioned. Consequently, religious and cultural beliefs condition religious experience, to the extent that persons in different religious traditions actually experience differently. There is not *one* religious experience but a plurality of diverse experiences. Katz appeals to his own Jewish tradition to support his thesis:

> All these [Jewish] cultural-social beliefs and their attendant practices . . . clearly affect the way in which the Jewish mystic views the world, the God who created it, the way to approach this God, and what to expect when one does finally come to approach this God. That is to say, the entire life of the Jewish mystic is permeated from childhood up by images, concepts, symbols, ideological values, and ritual behavior which there is no reason to believe he leaves behind in his experience. Rather, these images, beliefs, symbols, and rituals define, *in advance*, what the experience *he wants to have*, and which he then does have, will be like.[39]

That is, our prior beliefs, formed by interaction with our religious tradition, shape our religious experience by preforming the schema by which we perceive and understand.

As confirmation of this position, note the role of gurus and teachers of the mystical tradition. Small groups of devotees, led by a master or teacher who instructs them in a specific method for achieving the desired goal, closely hold the relevant wisdom. Hence, the methods and beliefs instilled by the teacher condition the mystic experience. The master sanctions, if not determines, the attainment of genuine mystic insight. For example, it was Hung-jen, the fifth Zen Buddhist Patriarch, who recognized that the poem of Hui-neng, the uneducated rice-pounder,

> The Bodhi is not like a tree,
> The Clear mirror is nowhere standing
> Fundamentally not one thing exists;
> When, then is a grain of dust to cling?

showed superior insight to that of the learned Shen-hsiu, who wrote this verse:

> This body is the Bodhi-tree
> The soul is like a mirror bright;
> Take heed to keep it always clean
> And let not dust collect on it.[40]

How, then, does one account for the apparently similar descriptions of religious experience given by Stace? First, Katz holds that the similarity is only apparent. Although the descriptions of the experiences use the same terminology, there is no reason to think that the terms have the same meaning in all reports. That two persons from different traditions, for example, describe their experience as paradoxical does not mean that it is paradoxical in the same way or that the same content stands in the relationship of paradox. Indeed, the terms *paradox* and *ineffable* serve to "cloak the experience from investigation and to hold mysterious whatever ontological commitments one has," rather than to "provide *data* for comparability."[41] Second, the terms used to characterize the experience are general and vague and fail to carefully delineate the mystical experiences. James's suggestion that every mystical experience is ineffable and noetic leaves open whether the ineffability is the same and whether the noetic quality has the same content in every case. The truth-claims of Madhyamika Buddhism, with its emphasis on the emptiness of Reality, differ markedly from the truth-claims of Christianity about God and God's relation to his created world. The Realities in the two cases cannot be identified:

> Henry Suso's "intoxication with the immeasurable abundance of the Divine House . . . . entirely lost in God [of Christianity]", the *Upanishads* "sat [what is] . . . . is expressed in the word *satyam*, the Real. It comprises this whole universe: Thou art this whole universe", as well as the Buddhist's "dimension of nothingness" all can be included under these broad phenomenological descriptions of "Reality", yet . . . it is clear that Suso's Christian God is not equivalent to the Buddhist's "nothingness", and that

the experience of entering into the Divine House is not equivalent to losing oneself in Buddhist "nothingness". It becomes apparent on reflection that *different* metaphysical entities can be "described" by the same phrases if these phrases are *indefinite* enough.[42]

Katz's analysis has not gone unchallenged. One criticism is that his view cannot account for some fundamental features of mystical experience. Mystics claim to be able to achieve a state in which self-awareness and awareness of objects cease. Yogis, for example, meditate on various things, such as physical objects, invisible things, the self, and, finally, consciousness. Gradually they attain to *samadhi,* a form of inward concentration in which progressively all conscious content—consciousness of all distinctions among perceptual objects, of inner states such as joy, of oneself as a distinct being, of objects of meditation as distinct from oneself, and, ultimately, of consciousness itself—is removed. In the final intuitive state, pure consciousness unifies all—past, present, and future.

The very attaining of pure consciousness defies Katz's analysis. To reach enlightenment, mystics often specify a path or a set of techniques by which they intentionally "forget" or bracket their previous experiences and categories of understanding. The Hindu school of Yoga, for example, specifies eight methods or types of practices directed toward the realization of pure consciousness. The first five, sometimes referred to as external aids, include a lifestyle of self-restraint and abstention (practicing celibacy, never stealing, and commiting no injury), moral observances (practicing contentment, doing penance, and studying), practice of bodily postures, and breath control. The last three involve concentration on objects (*dharana*), meditation (*dhyana*), and contemplation (*samadhi*). Adherents claim that following such disciplines ends their automatic perceptual and conceptual responses to what they experience. Ultimately, the yogi achieves pure consciousness, in which all categories, ideas, and external input are forgotten. In the final stages the subject-object, knower-known dualism that characterized our treatment of religious experience earlier in this chapter is replaced by a more unitary experience, devoid of distinctions.

The methods used, such as concentration for extended periods on a particular object—or, in the case of some Zen Buddhists, wall meditation— have been duplicated in the laboratory. Experimentees whose eyes were exposed only to a patternless field (by taping halves of ping-pong balls over them or by mounting a tiny projector on a contact lens so that the same object always appears) did not report seeing nothing (which still involves making conceptual distinctions) but described an end of seeing, "a complete disappearance of the sense of vision for short periods."[43]

In short, if forgetting and the like are possible, and if the mystic can attain a state of pure consciousness in which there is neither object nor content of consciousness, then Katz's thesis must be reconsidered. Since all categories and experiences are transcended, there is nothing in the higher-stage mystical states to be conditioned by prior conceptual categories or experiences.

In conclusion, the issue of a common core to religious experience is significant to addressing whether religious experience can be used to justify religious belief. If Stace is correct, then the differences among religions need not affect the more basic contention that religious experience can justify a basic core of beliefs. There is no ultimate incompatibility. What religious experience does not do, however, is by itself provide grounds for more developed or detailed (ramified) religious beliefs. A more comprehensive case would have to be structured to move beyond the common core. If Katz is correct that the diversity of religious experience is not only great but conditioned by the prior beliefs of the experiencer, religious experience is so conditioned by prior concepts that it cannot provide a sound basis for religious beliefs. Indeed, even if the mystic is correct that pure consciousness provides an exception to this thesis, there is still no sound basis for religious beliefs as long as the very exceptions are countentless states. In short, whether we should look to religious experience to justify religious beliefs remains to be further carefully explored.

STUDY QUESTIONS

1. What are the five types of religious experience suggested by Richard Swinburne? Find an example of two of them from some religious, philosophical, or devotional literature.

2. Compare and contrast the view of religious experience as perception (Alston) with the view that religious experience is what the experiencer takes as not capable of being explained by natural causes (Proudfoot). In what ways would their explanations of a particular account of religious experience be similar and in what ways different?

3. If you know people who have had a religious experience, ask them how they describe the experience. Which of the three explanations of the nature of religious experience does their account best illustrate, and why?

4. Give an argument (either from this chapter or your own) either for or against the thesis that religious experience can be used to justify religious beliefs. What view of religious experience have you presupposed? What objection might be raised against your argument?

5. If you are religious and do not use religious experience to justify your religious beliefs, to what do you appeal? Why do you think this provides better grounds for your beliefs than religious experience?

6. Compare and contrast arguments that might be given for and against the thesis that there is a common core to religious experience. Which perspective do you think is correct, and why? Might there be a common core to higher-state mystical experiences but not to other types of religious experience?

7. In what ways are the religious experiences of Asian religions like Buddhism and Hinduism different from those of Western religions like Christianity, Islam, and Judaism? Why are they different (here you might consider the fundamental perspectives on reality these religions hold)?

NOTES

1. Isa. 6:1–3, 5 (NIV).

2. Augustine, *Confessions*, vol. 8, trans. R. S. Pine-Coffin (New York: Penguin Books, 1961), p. 12.

3. *Mundaka Upanishad*, III, i, 8, in Sarvepalli Radhakrishnan and Charles A. Moore, eds., *Indian Philosophy* (Princeton: Princeton University Press, 1957), p. 54.

4. Some who treat religious experience do not make such a distinction and consequently arrive at a different typology of religious experience. See Carolyn Franks Davis, *The Evidential Force of Religious Experience* (Oxford: Clarendon Press), chap. 2, who categorizes religious experience into interpretive, quasi-sensory, revelatory regenerative, numinous, and mystical experience.

5. *Digha-Nikaya* 2.71.2–17, quoted in Paul J. Griffiths, *On Being Mindless* (LaSalle, Ill.: Open Court, 1986), p. 17.

6. Richard Swinburne, *The Existence of God* (Oxford: Oxford University Press, 1979), pp. 249–52. [See also Peterson, *et al.*, *Philosophy of Religion: Selected Readings* Part 1, pp. 42–43. Hereafter we cite this book as *PRSR*.]

7. Ralph Waldo Emerson, "Nature," "Essays and Addresses," in *Selected Writings of Ralph Waldo Emerson*, ed. W. Gilman (New York: New American Library, 1965), p. 189.

8. Exodus 3:1–4.

9. Swinburne, *Existence of God*, p. 250.

10. Acts 10:10–16.

11. Richard Rolle, *I Sleep and My Heart Wakes*, in Elmer O'Brien, ed., *Varieties of Mystic Experience* (New York: Holt, Rinehart and Winston, 1964), p. 161.

12. E. Allison Peers, ed., *The Life of Teresa of Jesus* (Garden City, N.Y.: Image Books, 1960), p. 249. [See *PRSR*, Part 1, p. 7.]

13. Nicholas of Cusa, *The Vision of God* (New York: Frederick Ungar, 1960), p. 78.

14. *Samyutta-Nikaya* XXXVI, 11$_5$, in Henry Clarke Warren, ed., *Buddhism in Translations*, (New York: Atheneum, 1973), p. 384.

15. Nicholas of Cusa, *Vision*, p. 23.

16. Friedrich Schleiermacher, *The Christian Faith* (Edinburgh: T. & T. Clark, 1928), p. 17.

17. Rudolf Otto, *The Idea of the Holy* (London: Oxford University Press, 1958), p. 1.

18. Ibid., p. 12.

19. Ibid., p. 10.

20. Augustine, *Confessions*, I, 1; C. S. Lewis, *Pilgrim's Regress* (Grand Rapids: William. B. Eerdmans, 1958).

21. William James, *The Varieties of Religious Experience* (New York: New American Library, 1958), p. 329. [See *PRSR*, Part 1, p. 19.]

22. Ibid., p. 346.

23. Ibid., p. 331 [see *PRSR*, Part 1, p. 19].

24. Wayne Proudfoot, *Religious Experience* (Berkeley: University of California Press, 1985), pp. 87, 108.

25. William Alston, *Perceiving God* (Ithaca, N.Y.: Cornell University Press, 1991), chap. 1. [See *PRSR*, Part 1, p. 25.]

26. If the religious experience is of an embodied personage such as Jesus, the Virgin Mary, or Krishna, the problems developed here do not arise, for presumably their appearances would have sensory content.

27. William P. Alston, " Experience of God: A Perceptual Model," paper read at Wheaton College, Wheaton, Ill. [Reprinted as "Religious Experience as Perception of God" in PRSR. See Part 1, p. 26.]

28. Proudfoot, Religious Experience, pp. 176–88. [See PRSR, Part 1, pp. 33–34.]

29. Ibid., p. 223.

30. Otto, Idea of the Holy, p. 19.

31. Swinburne, Existence of God, p. 254.

32. Michael Martin, Atheism: A Philosophical Justification (Philadelphia: Temple University Press, 1990), p. 166. [See PRSR, Part 1, p. 52.]

33. C. B. Martin, Religious Belief (Ithaca, N.Y.: Cornell University Press, 1959), p. 67.

34. William Wainwright, Mysticism: A Study of Its Nature (Madison: University of Wisconsin Press, 1981), pp. 86–87.

35. Davis, Evidential Force, chap. 7.

36. W. T. Stace, Mysticism and Philosophy (New York: Macmillan, 1960), pp. 131–32. I have given the characteristics of his introvertive type. The extrovertive type differs slightly in items 1 and 2, but he considers this type to be a lower level, an "incomplete kind of experience."

37. Ibid., p. 37.

38. Ibid., p. 133.

39. Steven T. Katz, "Language, Epistemology, and Mysticism," in Steven T. Katz, ed., Mysticism and Philosophical Analysis (Oxford: Oxford University Press, 1978), p. 33.

40. D. T. Suzuki, Essays in Zen Buddhism (New York: Grove Press, 1949), pp. 205–7.

41. Katz, "Language, Epistemology, and Mysticism," p. 54.

42. Ibid., p. 51 (brackets in original text).

43. Robert K. C. Forman, "A Construction of Mystical Experience," Faith and Philosophy 5, no. 3 (1988): 259–65.

SUGGESTED READING

Alston, William. Perceiving God. Ithaca, N.Y.: Cornell University Press, 1991.

Brakenhielm, Carl. Problems of Religious Experience. Uppsala: University of Uppsala, 1985.

Clark, Ralph W. "The Evidential Value of Religious Experiences." International Journal for the Philosophy of Religion 16 (1984): 189–202.

Davis, Caroline Franks. The Evidential Force of Religious Experience. Oxford: Clarendon Press, 1989.

Hardy, Alister. The Spiritual Nature of Man: A Study of Contemporary Religious Experience. Oxford: Clarendon Press, 1979.

James, William. The Varieties of Religious Experience. New York: New American Library, 1958.

Katz, Steven T., ed. Mysticism and Philosophical Analysis. Oxford: Oxford University Press, 1978.

Lewis, H.D. Our Experience of God. London: Allen and Unwin, 1959.

Otto, Rudolf. The Idea of the Holy. London: Oxford University Press, 1958.

Proudfoot, Wayne. *Religious Experience.* Berkeley: University of California Press, 1985.

Rowe, William L. "Religious Experience and the Principle of Credulity." *International Journal for the Philosophy of Religion* 13 (1982): 85–92.

Smart, Ninian. *The Religious Experience.* London: Macmillan, 1991.

Stace, W. T. *Mysticism and Philosophy.* New York: Macmillan, 1960.

Swinburne, Richard. *The Existence of God.* London: Oxford University Press, 1979.

Underhill, Evelyn. *Mysticism.* Cleveland: Meridian Books, 1955.

Wainwright, William. *Mysticism: A Study of Its Nature, Cognitive Value, and Moral Implications.* Madison: University of Wisconsin Press, 1981.

Yandell, Keith. *The Epistemology of Religious Experience.* Cambridge: Cambridge University Press, 1993.

CHAPTER 3   FAITH AND REASON: HOW ARE THEY RELATED?

November 18, 1978, marked one of the most horrifying religious tragedies of modern times. Virtually the entire population—men, women, and children—of the community of Jonestown, Guyana, perished overnight. This was not the result of natural disaster, disease, or violence inflicted by enemies. Rather, some 914 human beings died as a result of drinking Kool-Aid laced with cyanide in a collective religious ritual of "revolutionary suicide."[1]

The founder of Jonestown, the Reverend Jim Jones, was a Midwestern Protestant preacher whose church, the Peoples Temple, had moved to Redwood Valley in California, and a social activist who had pushed hard for racial integration. Jones's teachings increasingly deviated from those of mainstream Christianity until he claimed to be a living god and to have raised some forty-three people from the dead. Under increasing pressure and criticism, he and many of his congregation migrated to Guyana in 1977, carving the Jonestown community out of the jungle. But criticism and pressure continued, especially from disaffected former members, until the Jonestown leadership despaired of any hopeful future and the mass suicide was chosen as the way out of a desperate situation as well as the prelude to a happy reunion on "the other side."

Why did it happen? How could people do such a thing? It is impossible not to ask such questions, and yet the answers, at one level, are not hard to come by. The people of Jonestown believed in Jim Jones as the living god among them, and in his words as a divine message. And that message told them that the right thing to do, the only act that would maintain integrity in a hostile and threatening world, was to take their own lives and those of their children. The deed followed logically upon their beliefs and the commands of their divine leader.

But this pushes the question a step further back: How could people believe such insane things? Why didn't common sense and ordinary reasonableness show them that Jones could not possibly be what he said and that his message was not credible? But once again, the answer is not far to seek. These were people of faith, and for them, as for many believers, what faith requires is first of all that faith itself be strengthened and nurtured; doubt and questioning are the antithesis of faith and the bitter enemies of the religious life. So in asking Jones's followers to use human reason to discern that Jones's message was not to be trusted, we would be asking them to negate the very faith by which they lived—and died.

CAN REASON BE TRUSTED?

The case of Jonestown is an extreme example, but the relationship between faith and reason has seldom been tranquil or peaceful; rather, conflict and controversy appear at every turn. In fact, quite a few people, many of them serious religious thinkers, have said things that suggest that faith[2] and reason are not compatible *at all*—that their relationship is, and must be, one of mutual rejection and hostility. The apostle Paul wrote, "See that no one makes a prey of you by philosophy and empty deceit" (Col. 2:8). The early Christian writer Tertullian (160–220) asked, "What has Athens to do with Jerusalem?" (By "Athens" he meant Greek philosophy; by "Jerusalem," the Christian church.) The implied answer is, "Nothing—faith and philosophy have nothing in common; they are totally opposed." Pascal (1623–1662) wrote, "The heart has its reasons which reason does not know," and he implied that some persons might have to take steps to dull their reasoning faculties in order to be able to believe![3]

Still, it is much harder to bring about a clear-cut separation of faith from reason than these statements might indicate. Those who stress faith and attack reason often place a great deal of emphasis on *religious experience:* as the bumper sticker says, "God is not dead—I talked with him this morning!" However, as we saw in the previous chapter, religious experience is by no means a purely emotional "happening"; rather, it involves *concepts* and *beliefs* about the Being that is experienced. If we tried to separate religious experiences from such concepts and beliefs—from the *religious belief-system*, as we shall call it—then there would be no way of saying *who or what it is that is experienced* or of explaining what sort of difference the experience ought to make to the person who has it. Yet such a religious belief-system needs to be *understood*, at least to some degree—and it is hard to see how understanding it is not going to involve the use of reason.

In fact, none of the religious thinkers mentioned totally repudiates reason. It has been argued persuasively that the apostle Paul's warnings are directed at a *certain kind* of reasoning, namely, "worldly wisdom," which is the product of "human conceit that shuts itself up against the truth," not against the use of reason as such.[4] Even a cursory reading of his letters shows that he frequently makes use of reasoning, analysis, and arguments in the course of his religious teaching.[5] Tertullian, in spite of his diatribe against philosophy, was himself trained in philosophy and can be shown to have made use of it in his explanations of Christian doctrines. And while Pascal, like Paul, was severely critical of *a certain kind* of reasoning, one of the major projects of his life was the construction of an "apologetic" (a rational defense) for Christianity.

The real question, then, is not whether reason has any place in religion—the answer to that question is obviously yes—but what kind of place reason does and should have.[6] But here also, at least part of the answer is relatively uncontroversial. All religious communities *in fact* make use of reason, and in effect sanction its use, in the process of *teaching* the religion's belief-system to children and new converts and in enabling the faithful to *understand,* so far as possible, what their faith is about. Such uses of reason really do not need to be debated. The really controversial question is this: What role (if any) should reason play in the *validation* (or invalidation) of religious belief-systems? Granted that we may have to make use of reason in understanding the faith, is it also true, in any sense, that having faith at all depends (or should depend) on *having good reasons to believe* that one's faith is *true?* That is the real core of the "problem of faith and reason," and that is the question to which the rest of this chapter is devoted.

STRONG RATIONALISM

The first answer to our question[7] that we will consider is that of *strong rationalism,* the position that holds that *in order for a religious belief-system to be properly and rationally accepted, it must be possible to prove that the belief-system is true. Rationalism,* as used here, contrasts with *irrationalism* or *fideism;* in general, rationalism in this sense implies a reliance on reason, or intelligence, in deciding our beliefs and actions.[8] The word "prove," to be sure, is somewhat ambiguous; for our present purposes, we understand it to mean *show that a belief is true in a way that should be convincing to any reasonable person.* This means that the *premises,* or assumed truths, on which a proof is based must be such that any reasonable person who takes the trouble to investigate them should be able to determine that they are true (or, at least, that they probably are true). And the *methods of reasoning* that are employed in a proof must also be such that any reasonable person who investigates them should be able to see that they are correct—that, assuming the premises are indeed true, the conclusions arrived at by those methods of reasoning are either guaranteed true or at least very likely to be true as well.

The central idea of strong rationalism was stated forcefully by the English mathematician W. K. Clifford (1845–1879), as follows:

> It is wrong always, everywhere, and for anyone, to believe anything upon insufficient evidence.

> If a man, holding a belief which he was taught in childhood or persuaded of afterwards, keeps down and pushes away any doubts which arise about it in his mind . . . and regards as impious those questions which cannot easily be asked without disturbing it—the life of that man is one long sin against mankind. . . .
>
> Inquiry into the evidence of a doctrine is not to be made once for all and then taken as finally settled. It is never lawful to stifle a doubt; for either it can be honestly answered by means of the inquiry already made, or else it proves that the inquiry was not complete.[9]

Why does Clifford set such high standards for our beliefs? In answering this, he emphasizes the serious consequences, for oneself and especially for others, that may result from accepting a belief without adequate evidence:

> A shipowner was about to send to sea an emigrant ship. . . . Doubts had been suggested to him that possibly she was not seaworthy. These doubts preyed upon his mind, and made him unhappy. . . . Before the ship sailed, however, he succeeded in overcoming these melancholy reflections. . . . He watched her departure with a light heart, and benevolent wishes . . . and he got his insurance money when she went down in mid-ocean and told no tales.
>
> What shall we say of him? Surely this, that he was verily guilty of the death of those men. It is admitted that he did sincerely believe in the soundness of his ship; but the sincerity of his conviction can in no wise help him, because *he had no right to believe on such evidence as was before him.*[10]

We all sympathize with Clifford in his condemnation of the ship-owner; he goes on to argue, as we have seen, that *any* belief held upon insufficient evidence is reprehensible.

One objection often raised against Clifford's kind of view is that there are many people, especially those who must work hard for a living and have little education, who simply do not have the time or, perhaps, the ability to do the kind of serious thinking he requires before one is entitled to have faith. Clifford takes note of this objection and rejects it: " 'But,' says one, 'I am a busy man; I have no time for the long course of study which would be necessary to make me in any degree a competent judge of certain questions, or even able to understand the nature of the arguments.' Then he should have no time to believe."[11]

Clifford's opinion, very thinly concealed, is that *no* religious belief-system is capable of meeting the high standards of proof that should govern all of our believing, and so a reasonable (and moral) person must do without religious beliefs. But not all strong rationalists, by any means, have been hostile to religion. John Locke (1632–1704) was a Christian whose standards for proper belief were essentially the same as those later stated by Clifford; he thought that Christianity, when properly understood and defended, could meet those standards.[12]

Thomas Aquinas (c. 1224–1274) differed in some of his views from

Locke and Clifford, but he agreed with Locke in holding that by careful rational investigation it was possible to make a convincing case for the truth of Christianity.[13] A contemporary philosopher of religion whose position is very close to strong rationalism as here defined is Richard Swinburne (1934–).[14]

The appeal of this perspective on faith and reason is undeniable. Which of us has not felt frustrated, even angry, at the many things people (perhaps especially religious people) claim to "know" but are unable to give any good reasons for? In view of this frustration, the desire to have "real proof" for the things we believe is very understandable. The strong rationalist doesn't make any sloppy appeals to "faith"; she offers to *prove* that her view is correct—and challenges you to do the same for your view, if you disagree with her.

All the same, there are reasons to question whether strong rationalism is the right view to take. For one thing, it can be questioned whether the kind of rational guarantee the strong rationalist insists on is even *desirable* from the standpoint of religious faith. There is a very common and widespread view among religious people that in faith one "steps out beyond" what can be proved or rationally guaranteed and that this "stepping out," with its attendant risk and uncertainty, is an important, even essential element in faith. (Kierkegaard, discussed in the next section of the chapter, expresses this very powerfully.) Of course, this idea that faith must involve risk and uncertainty could be wrong, but it is common enough among religious people that it needs to be taken seriously. And if the idea is correct, then strong rationalism cannot be the right way to approach religious faith.

Another question about strong rationalism is this: Can it be made to work? That is, is it actually possible to do what the strong rationalist demands and show that a particular religious belief-system is true in a way that should be convincing to any reasonable person? The strong rationalist (if she is religious) thinks that it is and is prepared to show you how it can be done. Against this, though, there is the undeniable fact that, in spite of centuries of argument by strong rationalists and others, no one religious belief-system shows any signs of being proved in a way that "satisfies all reasonable people." What is the problem here?

The mere fact that not everyone is convinced by her arguments is not immediately devastating to the strong rationalist. What she will say is that her arguments are sound and *ought* to be convincing to anyone, but something has gone wrong in this particular case. Perhaps the other person simply has not studied the arguments carefully enough or has not understood them correctly. Alternatively, someone may lack the training or even the intellectual capacity to understand some arguments that in themselves are perfectly good. (This would be true of most of us in the case of some of the advanced arguments in mathematics, for instance.) Finally, the other person may be "blinded by prejudice" so that, even if he seems a reasonable person in most everyday situations, his prejudices simply do not allow him to see the truth in religious matters.

All the same, the way the discussions of religious arguments have actually gone is not very encouraging to the strong rationalist. If her perspective is correct, one would expect that in the case of at least some religious arguments the misunderstandings and resistances would gradually be overcome, and over a period of time more and more thinkers would recognize these arguments as sound and rationally compelling. What seems actually to happen is almost the reverse: even philosophers who accept a particular argument as correct are likely, as they continue to study it, to find that it contains loopholes such that an intelligent person *could* refuse to accept the argument without being obviously unreasonable. Rather than a movement in the direction of consensus, the trend seems to be toward a recognition that *no* such arguments are convincing for all reasonable persons. It is noteworthy that the great diversity of beliefs that is so prominent a feature of contemporary society is by no means limited to uninformed or unreflective persons. On the contrary, it is found also among thoughtful, sincere, and knowledgeable individuals.

It is important to realize that this lack of universally convincing arguments applies not only to religious belief-systems but to *all* arguments supporting *worldviews*—general, overall accounts of what reality is like. Sometimes the impression is given that if one wants to be religious one has to rely on "pure faith" but that if one's worldview is based on science one can have solid proof. This is a very serious mistake. It is true that many results in various branches of science are so firmly established that no reasonable person is likely to dissent from them. (A "flat-earther" is, after all, our favorite example of someone who sticks to his views in defiance of the evidence.) But science as a total worldview—the idea that science can tell us everything there is to know about what reality consists of—enjoys no such overwhelming support. This worldview (often termed *scientific naturalism*) is just one theory among others and is no more capable of being "proved to all reasonable people" than are religious belief-systems. To claim that the strong support enjoyed by, say, the periodic table of the elements transfers over to scientific naturalism as a worldview is highly confused if not deliberately misleading.

Yet another problem with strong rationalism is this: Strong rationalism assumes that "reason" exists in human beings as a faculty that is "neutral" as between conflicting worldviews, and thus can be used to prove things to everyone (prejudice aside), regardless of what worldviews people are initially inclined to accept. But *is* reason really neutral in this way? It seems clear in everyday life that people's belief-systems—their worldviews—*do* have a considerable impact on which sorts of arguments they find convincing and believable. Philosophers, aware of this fact, have invested immense effort in trying to establish a totally "pure" and "presuppositionless" approach to philosophy. The attempt of Descartes (1596–1650) to begin his philosophizing from a stance of "universal doubt" is a well-known example.[15] Perhaps not quite all the returns are in on this effort, but a preponderance of contemporary philosophers seem to be convinced that the thing cannot be done—that there *is* *no* pure, assumption-free standpoint on which our knowledge can be based in a way that is independent of "where we are coming from." [16] But if this is correct—if the goal of totally eliminating from our belief-systems prior convictions and "prejudices" is unattainable—then the approach of strong rationalism cannot be made to work.

FIDEISM

The second kind of view we are going to examine is commonly called *fideism* [17]—"faith-ism." Fideism is defined in a number of ways by different writers, but for our purposes we define it as the view that *religious belief-systems are not subject to rational evaluation.* To say, for instance, that we have *faith* that God exists and that he loves us is to say that we accept this in a way that does *not* depend on any evidence or reasoning and that we refuse to have anything to do with trying to prove or disprove God's love for us.

Is this just a stubborn rejection of reason on the fideist's part? Not necessarily. The fideist reminds us that an argument (*any* argument) must rest on premises or assumptions of some kind. If someone will not grant any assumptions to begin with, then it is impossible to argue with such a person. (This, in effect, is what the philosophical skeptic does—which is what makes it so frustrating to argue with a skeptic!) Now, what is assumed as a premise in one argument may be established as a conclusion in another argument, but this process cannot go on forever; somewhere along the line we must come to our *fundamental assumptions,* those things we accept without proof just because they are so absolutely basic that there is nothing more basic by which they could be proved.

The important point that needs to be seen, according to the fideist, is this: *For a sincere religious believer, the most fundamental assumptions are found in the religious belief-system itself.* Religious faith *itself* is the foundation of one's life—it is, in the phrase of Paul Tillich (1886–1965), one's "ultimate concern." But if this is so, then the idea of testing or evaluating one's faith by some external, rational standard is a terrible mistake, which very likely reflects a lack of true faith. Thus, it is sometimes said that if we test God's Word by logic or science, we are really worshiping science or logic rather than God!

For some people the idea that religious faith must be accepted without any proof or evidence might seem uncomfortable, even frightening. But a true fideist sees no problem in lack of proof; rather, he revels in it. Sören Kierkegaard (1813–1855), a Danish thinker, heaps scorn on those who would seek the truth of religion in an objective, detached way through evidence and argument. They forget that what is at stake here is their own existence as human beings. (It is almost comparable to selecting one's spouse on the basis of points scored in a beauty or body-building contest!) Furthermore, he points out, objective, rational inquiry is an "approximation-process" in which one comes closer and closer to the ultimate answer but never quite reaches it; there is always one more bit of evidence to consider, one more book or article to read and evaluate. And this, of course, means that the decision for or against God is put off indefinitely. But the person truly concerned about his soul realizes that "every moment is wasted in which he does not have God."[18] In fact, if we could *prove* God's existence and his love for us, it would then be impossible to have *faith* in God—so even if our inquiry were successful, it would frustrate rather than facilitate the goal of coming to know God! As Kierkegaard says,

> Without risk there is no faith. Faith is precisely the contradiction between the infinite passion of the individual's inwardness and the objective uncertainty. If I am capable of grasping God objectively, I do not believe, but precisely because I cannot do this I must believe. If I wish to preserve myself in faith I must constantly be intent upon holding fast the objective uncertainty, so as to remain out upon the deep, over seventy thousand fathoms of water, still preserving my faith.[19]

But if assembling arguments and evidence in favor of belief in God is useless, how *does* one come to have faith? The answer is simple: you must *commit* yourself, you must take the "leap of faith," believing without having (or wanting) any reasons or evidence to show that your belief is true. The idea of a leap of faith can be illustrated by the following story. You are attending an outdoor party with a group of friends. After a while the party gets a bit slow, and just to keep things moving one of your friends offers you a bet: he bets you fifty dollars that you will not dive into your host's swimming pool in total darkness. (The pool is down the hill, well away from the lighted patio where the party is going on.) You are a good diver, so you accept the bet, strip down to your cut-offs, and proceed to the pool. Naturally, the whole group trails along behind; the fact that people cannot see where they are going makes it all the more fun. Finally, you reach the bottom of the diving board and begin climbing the ladder, surrounded by cries of "Do you think he'll really do it?" "Wait and see—he'll chicken out!" But as you reach the top of the ladder, a horrible thought occurs to you. It is quite early in the spring, and the last time you saw the pool by daylight it had been drained for the winter. It is *very* dark, and strain as you will, you cannot see whether the pool has any water in it or not. Furthermore, your host has something of a reputation as a practical joker; it just might appeal to him to let you jump into an empty pool. If you descend the ladder to check, everyone will say you copped out and you will lose the bet, and you really cannot afford to lose fifty dollars. So, you jump. . . .

When religious people are introduced to Kierkegaard's idea of faith, many of them find it very attractive. It seems to be closer to their own idea, and perhaps experience, of faith than the "hard-nosed" logical approach recommended by strong rationalism. The idea that faith involves *commitment* and *risk taking* seems to make a great deal of sense to many religious people. The extent of Kierkegaard's influence is seen in the fact that he is the primary inspiration of the philosophical movement known as existentialism, as well as of the "neo-orthodox" theology of such men as Karl Barth (1886–1968) and Rudolph Bultmann (1884–1976).[20]

Still, there are some real problems with fideism. One problem is this: Given that faith is a leap, how does one decide *which* faith to leap for? For a person who already is committed, that may not seem to be a problem— but what about the person who is searching for a faith and sees several alternative possibilities that seem about equally plausible—say, Roman Catholicism, charismatic Protestantism, and Bahai? It would seem that a reasonable approach would be to carefully examine the alternatives and see which of them is most likely to be true—but that, of course, is precisely what the fideist says cannot be done. But surely it is essential to have *some* reasonable way in which the claims of competing belief-systems can be assessed. When people "buy into" religious belief-systems without giving careful consideration to whether the beliefs are reasonable and have a chance of being true, they sometimes accept ideas that are bizarre and even dangerous. (Jim Jones's Peoples Temple, mentioned earlier, and the Branch Davidians, led by David Koresh, are two example of this.)

The notion that religious belief-systems represent the believer's "most fundamental" assumptions and thus cannot be tested by anything else may involve an ambiguity in the word *fundamental.* For the sincere believer, her beliefs are "fundamental" in the sense that they provide the basic, overarching guidance for the way she lives her life; they establish her direction, her goals, and her reason for living. But it does not follow from this that these beliefs are "fundamental" in the sense of being *more evident,* and *more obviously true,* than anything else she knows or believes. In fact, we all find that there are obvious facts in everyday life—things we perceive through sight and touch and hearing—that more or less force themselves upon us in a way that has very little to do with what religious belief-systems we accept or reject. Simple truths of arithmetic, too, seem to have a self-evidence about them that is apparent to people regardless of the worldviews they embrace. Such truths as these are, in a way, "fundamental" *in our knowledge* ("epistemologically fundamental," as philosophers would say), though they by no means provide the sort of "fundamental guidance" for our living that is offered by religious beliefs. But if so, then it may be feasible to *use* such epistemologically fundamental beliefs in order to *test* religious belief-systems.

Nor does it seem to be true that one cannot test one's faith by rational standards without losing the faith itself. On the contrary, there are many cases in which this has actually been done. Martin Luther (1483–1546) thought that Copernican astronomy, with its view of the earth as moving through the heavens, was incompatible with faith: When the Hebrew leader Joshua wanted to prolong the daylight so that his troops could complete their victory in a battle (Josh. 10:12–14), he commanded the *sun*, not the earth, to stand still—so, it must have been the sun, *not* the earth, that was moving in the first place! More recently, Christians (including Kierkegaard and other modern fideists) have found that the damage to one's faith from accepting modern astronomy is entirely negligible. And many believers have had the experience of coming to believe that some of their views concerning God involve logical contradictions. (For instance, one might conclude that one's belief in absolute divine control of everything that happens is inconsistent with one's belief in human free will.) In consequence of this, these believers have sometimes modified their religious understanding of things, but few experience this as a "loss of faith." To the charge that testing one's faith by logic is placing logic above God, the retort might be that a really strong and sound faith involves the confidence that one's beliefs can *pass* any properly conducted test on the basis of logic and evidence.

Can we not, in fact, go even further than this and say that in order to be taken seriously by a reasonable person, a religious belief-system *must* be subjected to the tests of logical consistency and factual correctness? What would we make of a religious person who, calmly and deliberately, tells us that she is well aware that some of her beliefs are logically contradictory or conflict with well-known facts but that this is no obstacle to her holding these beliefs? Wouldn't we conclude that either (1) she is badly confused and doesn't know what she is saying, or (2) she is not seriously interested in the *truth* of her beliefs but is determined to maintain them (perhaps for the comfort they give her) *whether they are true or not?*[21] In fact, even fideists usually avoid admitting straight out that their beliefs are logically contradictory or in conflict with established facts. Usually they say that their beliefs contain *apparent* contradictions, thus holding out the hope that, from a more ultimate perspective, it will be seen that there is not a real contradiction after all.[22] If challenged with conflicting facts, they question the reliability of the "secular" sources of the "alleged facts" that conflict with their beliefs—thus, "young-earth creationists" challenge the scientific credentials of "mainstream" astronomy and geology, which support the conclusion that the universe is many billions of years old. But in refusing to admit *real* conflicts between their own views and logic or well-established facts, aren't these believers admitting, in effect, that it *is* valid to use logic and evidence to test the soundness of religious beliefs?

In fact, it is surprisingly difficult to avoid engaging in the rational evaluation of belief-systems. In conversations with religiously oriented persons, it often seems they are quite happy to use arguments as long as they think they have good arguments available; it is when they are stuck, or when the argument seems to be going against them, that appeals to "pure faith" begin to surface. But even sophisticated fideists are likely to be inconsistent here. They may not make any attempt to "prove" that their own faith is correct, but they are quite likely to begin pointing out flaws, inadequacies, and inconsistencies in other, competing religious belief-systems. In all fairness, though, it must be admitted that if such flaws pointed out in another's belief-system tend to cast doubt on that system, then similar flaws in one's *own* belief-system, as pointed out by others, must tend to cast doubt on whether one's own beliefs are correct. Simply ignoring such challenges leaves one open to the suspicion that one is really interested not in what is *true* but only in holding on to one's present beliefs regardless. What seems to be called for, then, is to *answer* the criticisms of one's convictions—to show that the objections to one's faith are mistaken or not serious or can be met by a minor reformulation of one's beliefs that leaves the substance of the faith unchanged. But to do this, of course, is precisely to *engage in the rational evaluation of religious belief-systems*, which is what the fideist says cannot be done!

CRITICAL RATIONALISM

Suppose we conclude, then, that both fideism and strong rationalism are mistaken. Unlike fideists, we will say that it *is* possible to rationally criticize and evaluate religious belief-systems; in contrast with strong rationalists, we will say that this evaluation cannot be expected to result in a conclusive, universally convincing *proof* that some particular system is correct.

If we accept this, then we are in effect affirming *critical rationalism*,[23] here defined as the view that *religious belief-systems can and must be rationally criticized and evaluated although conclusive proof of such a system is impossible.* Like strong rationalism, critical rationalism tells us to *use* our rational capabilities, to the greatest extent possible, in assessing religious beliefs. This involves developing the best arguments we can—the best "case," so to speak—for a belief-system and then comparing this with the case made for alternative systems. (Such a case for theism is developed in Chapter 5.) It also involves considering the main *objections* to the belief-system in question. (A major objection to theism is discussed in Chapter 6.) And it may involve the consideration of rational foundations for belief that do *not* take the form of arguments (for this see Chapter 7). Critical rationalism tells us to do all these things, but it warns us not to be overconfident or overly optimistic about the conclusiveness of such an investigation. This view is "critical" in two ways: it emphasizes the role of reason in criticizing, or critically evaluating, religious beliefs, as opposed to conclusively establishing such beliefs as true. And the view is also "critical" with regard to the view of reason itself; it takes a more modest and limited view of reason's capabilities, in contrast with the excessively optimistic estimate of reason incorporated in strong rationalism.

Critical rationalism, as we have seen, emerges almost automatically if we reject both strong rationalism and fideism.[24] All the same, it will be helpful to say a bit more about it, in order to get more of an idea about how it works out in practice. Just how should we proceed if we want to evaluate religious beliefs in the way critical rationalism recommends?

There are two somewhat different answers to this question, depending on whether we are concerned with some specific, relatively limited item of belief (such as the belief in life after death) or with the religious belief-system or worldview taken as a whole.

Suppose, then, that we have selected some particular belief for investigation. This belief may be one we are ourselves inclined to accept or one whose truth or falsity seems especially important to us—or it could even be determined by a course assignment!

Having selected a belief for study, the next step is to make sure that we *understand* the belief as accurately as possible. This involves deciding on definitions of key terms and exploring the implications of the belief—determining what other beliefs are required if this one is accepted and what other beliefs are excluded by it. If the belief in question is one we are not personally inclined to accept, we should pay careful attention to those who *do* accept it, so as to avoid misunderstandings resulting from our own lack of familiarity and possible prejudice. If, on the contrary, the belief is one we do accept, then we need to listen to the questions and criticisms of opponents so as to become aware of problems and ambiguities in the belief we may have overlooked through familiarity.

Once we are fairly sure we understand the belief to be studied, the next step is to look at *reasons* for and against accepting the belief. At best, such reasons will fall short of conclusive, universally convincing proof, but that does not mean they have no value at all. It has been pointed out by George Mavrodes (1926–) that in many cases the success of reasons and arguments for a belief is "person-relative"—that is to say, there are arguments that are convincing for one person and that actually enable her to come to know the truth about some subject, and yet these same arguments may fail completely for another, equally intelligent person.[25]

But why should this be so? Sometimes it may be simply that the premises of the argument are known to be true by one person but not by another. All of us know some things others are ignorant of, and vice versa—and a person cannot be expected to find an argument convincing if she does not know that its premises are true. In general, of course, knowledge and information can readily be communicated from one person to another—but not always. Sometimes the force of an argument can be appreciated only by persons who have special training that is time-consuming and laborious to acquire. At other times one may have knowledge of some occurrence but be unable to convince others about this. (You may be very confident of your own recollection of a conversation at which you were present, and yet others may tell the story differently.) Sometimes the basis for one's belief may be in part a personal experience that cannot be adequately described or communicated to someone who has never had a similar experience. And last, but by no means least important, we all have preconceptions and prejudices that bias us towards seeing things in one way rather than in another.

None of this means that there is no such thing as the truth or that we should despair of ever being able to discover the truth. It is important to realize that while conclusive *proof* of a religious belief is difficult to achieve, conclusive *disproof* may sometimes be possible. If a belief can be shown to involve a logical contradiction or to be in conflict with well-established facts, then a rational person will have no choice but to modify or abandon that belief. And if certain views can be eliminated in this way, that narrows the range of remaining options. It may even be that, given unlimited time, patience, and good will, all of us could eventually overcome the differences caused by our diverse starting points and arrive at a consensus about the truth of things. But, in practice, such a goal is likely to prove elusive. And in the absence of universal consensus, there is really only one way to proceed: each of us must seek the truth on the basis of the other things he or she knows or reasonably believes to be true, using methods of reasoning that, upon careful reflection, commend themselves to us as likely to lead to the truth. We do not *create* the truth for ourselves; that way lies madness or the quagmire of relativism. But we must, each one of us, *seek* the truth for ourselves, and that is what philosophy is all about.

These considerations apply even more strongly when what is in question is not a particular item of belief but rather a religious worldview taken as a whole. Such worldviews are typically quite complex, involving claims about the nature of reality (metaphysics), the nature of knowledge and the methods of attaining it (epistemology), and the nature of goodness and of a good life (ethics). The complexity of worldviews means that the task of assessing them is also complex. We will want to consider whether the worldview is *logically consistent* or whether, on the contrary, contradictions are lurking among its essential beliefs. We will also want to know whether the worldview is *consistent with known facts*—and in assessing this we will, of course, be depending on various sources for these "facts" that we have come to regard as reliable. We need to ask about the *explanatory power* of the worldview: Does it fit things into a comprehensive pattern in an illuminating way, or does it leave us with a view of things possessing no coherent unity? A final question—difficult to formulate precisely, but immensely powerful in its influence—is this: To what extent does this worldview enable us to make sense of the actual living of our lives? Does it enable us to understand both our successes and our failures, and does it energize us to move in the direction of that which, upon reflection, we recognize as best and most worthwhile? Or does it fail, in the end, to cast any real light upon our actual living? (This was the central point of Kierkegaard's insistence that we must pay attention to *our own existence*. What is the point, he asked, of a worldview that gives us no help here, however dazzling it may be in other respects?)

Reflecting upon the rationality of religious worldviews along the lines sketched out is no short or easy task, but we believe it can be a rewarding one. Sometimes the process may result in a firmer grasp and a deeper commitment to the faith-perspective one has already accepted. At other times, more or less serious modifications may seem to be called for. And it does happen that, as a result (at least in part) of such reflection, a person may undergo a "conversion" to some entirely different way of seeing the world. Whatever the specific result may be, it is to be hoped that the process will leave one with a deeper understanding of the religious worldview(s) that are investigated and a better appreciation of what is at stake either in accepting such a worldview or rejecting it.[26]

We believe that critical rationalism, as outlined here, has significant merits as an answer to the question of faith and reason. It cannot be denied, however, that the study of religious beliefs according to the principles of critical rationalism sometimes proves to be rather frustrating. In a sense, the critical rationalist is in a more exposed, more vulnerable position than either the fideist or the strong rationalist. The critical rationalist is committed to the task of rational evaluation of religious beliefs, unlike the fideist who makes his "leap of faith" and is then able to ignore issues of rational justification. But the critical rationalist, unlike the strong rationalist, has no assurance that by proceeding properly she will be able to prove conclusively that one particular position is correct and that others are mistaken. So, unlike the adherents of either of the other two views, the critical rationalist is *never* in the position of being able to decide, finally and for good, that the discussion concerning the truth and validity of her religious beliefs has reached its ultimate conclusion.

Broadly speaking, the approach taken throughout this text is that of critical rationalism. If we were fideists, then many of the arguments we put forward and discuss concerning the truth or falsity of religious beliefs would lose their point. If we were strong rationalists, the arguments might remain, but they would be used in a different way, and we would be making stronger claims for their conclusiveness than we in fact find ourselves able to make. Critical rationalism fits together well, furthermore, with the emphasis on the consideration of alternative religious views that is present throughout the text. In a sense, the critical rationalist *needs* alternative views, and the proponents of these views, more than either the fideist or the strong rationalist. The strong rationalist *proves*, and *knows with certainty*, that her own view is right, so her concern with other views can be limited to studying them to determine their errors, as well as looking for the best way by which their proponents can be persuaded to embrace "the truth." And the fideist, once he has performed the "leap of faith," has very little need for alternative views—at most, they may be of use, by way of contrast, in displaying the excellence of the "chosen" view—which, judged by its own internal standards, will always emerge as superior in any comparison.[27] The critical rationalist, in contrast, has *no* absolute rational assurance that her own view is correct, so she needs the competing views both in order to assess their merits in comparison with her own and for the sake of the penetrating criticism of her own view that is most likely to come from those who do not share it.

We have laid a good deal of stress on the continuing, open-ended nature of critical reflection as advocated by critical rationalism. But it may seem that this serves to show that Kierkegaard was right after all in saying that those who try to judge faith by objective, critical reflection will go on forever that way and will never reach the point of *having* faith and of *being* religious. Does not this emphasis on an open-ended, never-final process simply confirm what he said?

Not necessarily. A person may recognize that she cannot support her belief with evidence that will be convincing to all rational persons, and yet she herself may find the evidence for those beliefs rationally conclusive. Or, she may recognize that, even from her own point of view, the evidence is less than conclusive, and yet she may be deeply committed to carrying out those beliefs in her life. Kierkegaard, then, was right about at least one thing: religious faith often, perhaps always, involves a *commitment,* a "*stepping out*" and *entrusting ourselves* to something that goes beyond what we have conclusive proof of. (And on the other hand, those who reject religion may have to come to terms with the fact that their own reasons for disbelief are less conclusive than they might wish.) Those who live the life of faith tell us that their commitment is *not* a tentative, partial, "fingerscrossed" sort of thing, carefully proportioned to the exact degree of rational evidence they may have for a particular conclusion. Some of the ancient Israelites were inclined to reason like this: "It seems pretty likely that our God, Yahweh, really is the one who is running the show, so by all means let's worship him, 'pay our dues,' make the appropriate sacrifices, and so on. Still, it is also true that Baal, the God of the Canaanites, has some pretty impressive credentials of his own. So, the smart thing to do is to hedge our bets a little—we will sacrifice to Yahweh, all right, but we will also do what we can to keep on the right side of Baal—just in case." According to the biblical text, Yahweh was not very happy about this approach to the matter—in fact, those who proceeded in this way were in deep trouble. A believer's commitment to God is supposed to be *total* commitment, even when one does not have total proof that one's belief in God is correct! And critical rationalism in no way *speaks against* such total commitment. Rather, it tells us that we should not pretend to greater rational certainty than is in fact available, but neither should we fail to exercise our powers of reflection and rational thought while we are making the most important decision of our lives.

It is true enough that this combination of religious commitment to "total devotion" with a mental attitude that is rational, reflective, and open to alternatives is likely to create some inner tension. But this tension is not necessarily of the destructive, ultimately harmful kind—rather, it is one that is actually lived out, in a rewarding and productive way, in the lives of many reflective religious persons.[28]

STUDY QUESTIONS

1. Do you think there is a danger in today's society of persons acting in irrational and harmful ways because of religious beliefs they hold? If so, give examples. What do you think is the best solution for this problem?

2. Which of the viewpoints on faith and reason sketched in this chapter most closely matches the approach taken by most religious persons you know? Discuss.

3. Explain strong rationalism, and discuss the reasons making this plausible as a view of faith and reason.

4. Which of the objections against strong rationalism strikes you as most convincing? Discuss.

5. Explain fideism, and explain the fideist's reasons for saying that religious beliefs cannot be rationally evaluated.

6. What are some of the factors that make fideism attractive to many religious persons?

7. Have there been situations in which you, personally, have taken something like a "leap of faith"? If so, describe one of these situations.

8. Are the objections to fideism given in the text convincing or not? Discuss.

9. Is it possible to test religious beliefs by logic and evidence without ceasing to have *faith* in these beliefs? Discuss.

10. Explain critical rationalism, showing how it differs from strong rationalism and from fideism.

11. What do you see as the strong points of critical rationalism? What are its weaknesses?

12. Is it possible to be a critical rationalist, admitting that one's beliefs cannot be conclusively proved, without becoming "wishy-washy" in one's faith?

NOTES

1. For an account of the episode, with an interpretation of the religious worldview that lay behind the tragedy, see David Chidester, *Salvation and Suicide: An Interpretation of Jim Jones, the Peoples Temple, and Jonestown* (Indianapolis: Indiana University Press, 1988).

2. The term "faith," as used in religious contexts, is rather complex in its meaning. Faith usually involves a *cognitive* aspect; it involves *believing* that the doctrines of the religion are true. But it also is often thought of as involving, or implying, a *volitional* aspect, expressed in *commitment* to the object of faith and *obedience* to what is commanded; there may also be an *affective* aspect of *trust* or *love*. In this chapter we have in mind primarily the "belief" aspect of faith, but we in no way wish to minimize the importance of the other aspects.

3. See Blaise Pascal, *Pensées*, tr. W. F. Trotter, and *The Provincial Letters*, tr. Thomas M'Crie (New York: Random House, 1941), p. 83. [A selection is found in *PRSR*, Part 2.]

4. See Paul W. Gooch, *Partial Knowledge: Philosophical Studies in Paul* (Notre Dame, Ind.: University of Notre Dame Press, 1987), p. 42.

5. See, for example, I Corinthians 15.

6. Note the difference between "does" and "should"—while it is clear that reason does in fact have *some* place in religion, we cannot automatically assume that the place it actually has in people's thinking about religion is the place it *should* have.

7. The three main positions discussed in this chapter result from a present-day analysis of the issues; they were not applied as self-descriptions by the historical philosophers mentioned. Some thinkers, indeed, may not be too easy to classify: many of Pascal's statements, for example, sound like fideism, yet his position as a whole seems rather to be that of "critical rationalism." Somewhat similar analyses of the alternatives on the faith-reason issue have been put forward by William J. Abraham (*An Introduction to the Philosophy of Religion* [Englewood Cliffs, N.J.: Prentice-Hall, 1985], chaps. 7, 8, 9, and 10) [see the selection in *PRSR*, Part 2], and by C. Stephen Evans (*Philosophy of Religion: Thinking about Faith* [Downers Grove, Ill.: InterVarsity Press, 1985]), chap. 1.

8. There is another use of "rationalism" in epistemology, in which it contrasts with *empiricism*. Rationalism in this sense is the view that the most important truths are known by "pure reason" without reliance on sense perception. That is *not* the way "rationalism" is used in this chapter.

9. William K. Clifford, "The Ethics of Belief," in George I. Mavrodes, ed., *The Rationality of Belief in God* (Englewood Cliffs, N.J.: Prentice-Hall, 1970), pp. 159–60. [Also in *PRSR*, Part 2.]

10. Ibid., pp. 152–53.

11. Ibid., p. 160.

12. For an excellent discussion of Locke's views, see Nicholas Wolterstorff, "The Migration of the Theistic Arguments: From Natural Theology to Evidentialist Apologetics," in *Rationality, Religious Belief, and Moral Commitment*, ed. Robert Audi and William J. Wainwright (Ithaca, N.Y.: Cornell University Press, 1986), pp. 38–81.

13. An important difference is that Thomas, unlike Clifford and Locke, did not lay on *each individual believer* (or even on each *adult* believer) the responsibility for providing rational justification for his or her beliefs. For Thomas's views, see the article by Wolterstorff cited in note 12 and also Ralph McInerny, "Analogy and Foundationalism in Thomas Aquinas," in the same volume, pp. 271–88.

14. See Richard Swinburne, *The Existence of God* (Oxford: Oxford University Press, 1979), and *Faith and Reason* (Oxford: Oxford University Press, 1981).

15. More recent philosophers who have pursued this ideal include Edmund Husserl (1859–1938) and Bertrand Russell (1872–1970).

16. Among the important philosophers who argue against the ideal of "pure, presuppositionless reason" are Ludwig Wittgenstein (1889–1951) and Hans-Georg Gadamer (1900–).

17. FEE-day-ism; the word is derived from the Latin word *fides*, meaning "faith."

18. Söven Kierkegaard, *Concluding Unscientific Postscript*, trans. David F. Swenson and Walter Lowrie (Princeton: Princeton University Press, 1941), pp. 178–79. [A selection is found in *PRSR*, Part 2.]

19. Ibid., p. 182.

20. Several scholars have argued that Kierkegaard's overall position allows a larger place for the rational evaluation of faith perspectives than is suggested by the excerpts given earlier. (See Marilyn Gaye Piety, "Kierkegaard on Rationality," *Faith and Philosophy* 10, no. 3 (July 1993); C. Stephen Evans, "The Epistemological Significance of Transformative Religious Experiences: A Kierkegaardian Exploration," *Faith and Philosophy* 8, no. 2 (April 1991); and Merold Westphal, *Kierkegaard's Critique of Religion and Society* (Macon, Ga.: Mercer University Press, 1987).) To the

extent that this is correct, Kierkegaard may be less a "pure fideist" than is implied in the text; this would serve as a confirmation of the observation that it is difficult for a reflective person to completely avoid engaging in the rational evaluation of his beliefs.

21. It should we noted that many of us sometimes find ourselves in a position somewhat similar to this. We may be aware that a set of beliefs contains or implies a contradiction, but we may have no idea *which* of the beliefs needs to be given up or modified; each of the beliefs, taken separately, seems to have strong evidence in its favor. In this case we may well decide, for the time being, to continue to accept all of the beliefs in question, since under the circumstances giving up any one of them might well leave us worse off than we were originally. This situation, however, is quite different from that of the fideist described in the text. In the situation described, we are well aware that there *is* falsehood somewhere in our beliefs; we just don't know how to identify and correct it. The fideist in the text, on the other hand, is simply unconcerned about the presence of contradictions in her belief-system.

22. For an incisive criticism of this strategy, see David Basinger, "Biblical Paradox: Does Revelation Challenge Logic?" *Journal of the Evangelical Theological Society* 30 (1987): 205–213.

23. The term "critical rationalism" is found in the writings of Karl Popper, and the meaning given to this term here is broadly consistent with Popper's use of it. See his *The Open Society and Its Enemies*, vol. 2 (Princeton: Princeton University Press, 1971), p. 231,

24. Although our discussion here is limited to three main options, the reader should be aware that these could be further subdivided; there are actually a large number of different positions in the faith-reason controversy. The issue of *evidentialism* vs. *anti-evidentialism*, introduced in Chapter 7, to some extent cuts across the threefold division in this chapter. Another interesting distinction concerns the distinction between *positive apologetics* and *negative apologetics* that we made in Chapter 1. Negative apologetics concerns itself with rebutting objections to a religious belief-system, without attempting to make a positive case in support of the system. Positive apologetics, on the other hand, develops a constructive argument for the favored belief-system.

25. See George I. Mavrodes, *Belief in God* (New York: Random House, 1970), pp. 17–48.

26. A good description of the process of worldview evaluation is given in William Abraham, *An Introduction to the Philosophy of Religion*, pp. 104–109. [And see the selection in PRSR, Part 2.] Abraham sketches out a scenario in which, as a result of such reflection, a person adopts a particular religious perspective. Real-life examples may be found in two books recounting the "spiritual autobiographies" of contemporary philosophers: Kelly James Clark, ed., *Philosophers Who Believe: The Spiritual Journeys of Eleven Leading Thinkers* (Downers Grove, Ill.: InterVarsity, 1993), and Thomas V. Morris, ed., *God and the Philosophers: The Reconciliation of Faith and Reason* (New York: Oxford, 1994).

27. It must be said in fairness that fideists, and strong rationalists, sometimes exhibit in practice a more generous appreciation of conflicting views than these descriptions might suggest. Still, it is probably true in general that fideists and strong rationalists have *less* interest in the consideration of alternative views than do critical rationalists.

28. For an excellent depiction of this tension from the standpoint of evangelical Protestantism, see Daniel Taylor, *The Myth of Certainty* (Waco, Tex.: Word Books, 1986). The tension is also discussed and/or illustrated in several of the essays in Morris, ed., *God and the Philosophers.*

SUGGESTED READING

Abraham, William J. *An Introduction to the Philosophy of Religion.* Englewood Cliffs, N.J.: Prentice-Hall, 1985.

Evans, C. Stephen. *Philosophy of Religion: Thinking About Faith.* Downers Grove, Ill.: InterVarsity Press, 1985.

Hick, John. *Faith and Knowledge.* Ithaca, N.Y.: Cornell University Press, 1957.

Mavrodes, George I. *Belief in God.* New York: Random House, 1970.

————, ed. *The Rationality of Belief in God.* Englewood Cliffs, N.J.: Prentice-Hall, 1970.

Mitchell, Basil. *The Justification of Religious Belief.* Oxford: Oxford University Press, 1981.

Pascal, Blaise. *Pensées.* Tr. W. F. Trotter. *The Provincial Letters.* Tr. Thomas M'Crie. New York: Random House, 1941.

Penelhum, Terence. *God and Skepticism.* Dordrecht: D. Riedel, 1983.

Placher, William. *Unapologetic Theology: A Christian Voice in a Pluralistic Conversation.* Louisville, Ky: Westminster/John Knox Press, 1989.

Swinburne, Richard. *The Existence of God.* Oxford: Oxford University Press, 1979.

————. *Faith and Reason.* Oxford: Oxford University Press, 1981.

(See also Suggested Readings for Chapter 7.)

CHAPTER 4   THE DIVINE ATTRIBUTES: WHAT IS GOD LIKE?

"Put this piece of salt in the water and come to me tomorrow morning."

Shvetaketu did as he was told. Then his father said to him: "Do you remember that piece of salt you put in the water yesterday evening? Would you be good enough to bring it here?"

He groped for it but could not find it. It had completely dissolved.

"Would you please sip it at this end? What is it like?" he said.

"Salt."

"Sip it in the middle. What is it like?"

"Salt."

"Sip it at the far end. What is it like?"

"Salt."

"Throw it away, and then come to me."

He did as he was told but that did not stop the salt from remaining ever the same.

His father said to him: "My dear child, it is true that you cannot perceive Being here, but it is equally true that it *is* here.

"This finest essence,—the whole universe has it as its Self: That is the Real: That is the Self: That *you* are, Shvetaketu!"

—CHANDOYA UPANISHAD[1]

In this text from the sacred writings of India, Shvetaketu and his father are probing a topic of intense interest to religious people—they are considering the *nature of God.* The answer they arrive at, to state it all too simply, is that God is the Being that is the inner reality of everything whatever. The salt is imperceptible to touch or vision; nevertheless, it pervades every drop of the water. Similarly, God—or Being or Brahman—is imperceptible to human senses, yet nevertheless completely pervades all of reality, including the inquirer who raises the question concerning the nature of God: "That *you* are, Shvetaketu!"

This question concerning the nature of God occupies us throughout the present chapter. We do not, however, concern ourselves primarily with the specific answers found by Shvetaketu and his father and by others in the Hindu religious tradition. Rather, we focus most of our attention on a view of God known as *classical theism;*[2] this is the conception of God that has been held, with some variations, by the vast majority of thinkers in the great "theistic" religions of Judaism, Christianity, and Islam. But the view of God seen in the selection from the Upanishads, often termed *pantheism,* is not neglected entirely; instead, it is introduced from time to time as a contrast and an alternative to classical theism. We also, from time to time, explain and comment on another sort of conception of God that has recently become popular in some Christian and Jewish circles, a view known as *process theism.*[3]

At this point, however, a question may be occurring to the reader. What is the point, it may be asked, of inquiring about the *nature* of God when, as yet, we have not even established whether there *is* any such being as God? Would it not make more sense first to show that there *is* a God and then to discuss his (or her, or its) attributes or characteristics?

There is certainly some point to this, but consider a counterquestion: If we have no idea *what* God is, then what sense is there in asking whether God *exists* or not? Lewis Carroll wrote a marvelous poem entitled "The Hunting of the Snark," but it would make little sense to ask whether there really are snarks, because Carroll never tells us clearly what sort of creature a snark is supposed to be. If we are similarly "in the dark" as to God's nature, what meaning can we attach to the question whether God exists or not?

Probably the reason that the question of God's existence seems to most of us to make reasonably clear sense is that we *do* have an idea of what God is like, and when we ask whether God exists it is *that kind* of being whose existence is being asked about. Many readers of this book, furthermore, will have a background of familiarity with the theistic religious traditions, and the conception of God's nature these readers will be presupposing is one that is at least fairly close to the classical theism we study in this chapter. So it seems important to become as clear as possible about that conception of God before we proceed with other matters.

The right way to understand what is going on in this chapter, then, is this: we are not meaning to assert at this point that there *really is* a being, called God, with the various characteristics discussed throughout the chapter. Rather, we are *presenting a hypothesis* concerning the nature of a being whose existence will be investigated later on. The questions we ask are of two kinds: First, what *is* the conception of God's nature held by classical theism (and, from time to time, the conceptions held by pantheism and by process theism)? And second, is this conception one that is *coherent* and *logically consistent?* If it should develop that a certain idea of God suffers from unreconcilable internal contradictions, then with regard to *that* conception we need proceed no further: a "God" whose nature can be stated only in contradictions cannot possibly exist, and to suppose that there is such a God as that is nonsense.[4]

How will we arrive at the characteristics we attribute to God? In part, the question is one of history and tradition: the attributes considered here are some of those that *in fact* have been ascribed to God by theistic thinkers. Many such thinkers, however, would assert that there is more to it than this; they would claim that the theistic concept of God possesses an *internal unity and coherence* that go far beyond any list of characteristics that merely happen to be ascribed to God in a certain tradition. And an important source of this unity and coherence lies in the attributes considered in the next section.

PERFECT AND WORTHY OF WORSHIP

In developing our conception of God, it would be foolish to overlook the fact that, above all, *God is a being who is the object of worship.* God's "worshipability"—or, to use a word that is no longer very familiar, his "worshipfulness"—is of primary religious importance, so a conception of God that is lacking at this point is unacceptable regardless of other merits it may possess. Whatever else may be true of God, it must at least be said that *God is worthy of worship.*

But what sort of God is required, if God is to be worthy of our worship? The attitude or activity of worship is no doubt complex and difficult to describe completely and accurately. But there can be little doubt that worship, in the full sense of the term, is supposed to involve *total devotion* of the worshiper to the one worshiped. In worship we totally dedicate ourselves to God; we place ourselves at God's disposal completely and without reservation. Any hint of "bargaining" with God, any mental reservation by which, however subtly, we "keep our options open" with respect to a possible shift of allegiance, detracts severely from the complete commitment that worship properly requires of us.

But if this is the case, we can ask, What must be true of God in order to make such unreserved devotion appropriate—in order, that is, for God to be "worthy of worship"? It is fairly clear, to begin with, that *God must be the greatest of all beings.* How could it be reasonable, or even plausible, to offer to God such total devotion if there exist other beings equally or even more worthy of our adulation, obedience, and so on? Under such circumstances as these, the response of a reasonable person would seem to be that God might, indeed, be entitled to a measure of honor and obedience because of his superiority to all others in the immediate vicinity—but not unreserved trust and honor and obedience, not *total devotion*. One would give to God his due, while keeping in mind the possibility that someone else might appear to whom even more was due. God would merit respect, honor, and a degree of obedience—but not worship.

God, then, must be the greatest of all beings. But we can go farther than this. Suppose it is plain to us that, though God is *in fact* the greatest of all beings, it is entirely possible that there should have been a being *superior* to God in one or several ways. Would this not inevitably detract from the unreserved devotion that is required for worship? As a matter of fact, we are supposing, God is the greatest of all beings, and there is nothing else in existence that could supplant him in our esteem. But things perfectly well could have been different; there might very well have been some other being able to rival or even excel the God whom we worship. If so, then even in the midst of our worship, would we not occasionally find ourselves with a touch of regret for the greater things that might have been?[5]

With this line of thought in mind, we are ready to appreciate the point of a definition of God offered by the great medieval Christian thinker Anselm (1033–1109). Addressing God, he said, "We believe that thou art a being than which nothing greater can be conceived."[6] He was saying, in effect, that God is so great that *no being is conceivable that would surpass God in any way*. God, in other words, is the *absolutely perfect being*. Not only is there in fact no other being equal or superior to God, but there could not be any such being, for God contains in himself all possible perfection and excellence.

This conception of God, as the *absolutely perfect being*, is one that, upon reflection, many religious persons have found to be deeply satisfying. It is, as we have seen, plausibly thought to be implied by the very idea of worship,[7] and it lays the foundation for a conception of God that it is very hard to challenge as inadequate.

Perfect being theology (or "Anselmian" theology, as it is also called[8]) becomes, then, the "binding thread" that ties together and unifies the discussion of the various attributes ascribed to God by classical theism.[9] Can we, indeed, go further and say that the notion of God as the perfect being gives us all the guidance we need in setting forth the divine attributes, so that our whole conception of God can be, as it were, woven in its entirety from this single thread?

Probably not, for several reasons. For one thing, although the idea of God as the perfect being has strong intuitive appeal, it is by no means the case that different theologians, even from the same religious tradition, will always agree on which conception of God's attributes has the effect of portraying God as "more perfect" than another. For example, it seemed clear to Anselm, as to Augustine (354–430) and to most other ancient and medieval theologians, that in order to be perfect God must be *impassible*—that is, God must be incapable of emotion, and in particular incapable of feeling any sorrow or suffering as a result of the afflictions of his creatures. Since suffering is negative, a harm to the being that undergoes it, a perfect being must be *incapable* of suffering. More recently, however, many theologians have rebelled against the notion of an "impassible" God, insisting that God's perfection, and in particular his attributes of love and sympathy, positively *require* that he be capable of suffering along with his creatures. Clearly, we have here a major disagreement, one that will not readily be settled by further discussions about the meaning of "perfect" as applied to God.

It should also be realized that, in setting forth God's attributes, we cannot possibly ignore the religious and theological tradition within which any given theology operates. If, for instance, one were to offer to the Jewish religious community a conception of God radically at variance with that found in the Hebrew Bible and in Jewish tradition, that conception would not be warmly received, no matter how plausible a case one could make for the "perfection" of God so conceived. An interesting historical example of this is the philosopher Baruch de Spinoza (1632–1677). Born a Jew, he was excommunicated from the synagogue for his "heretical" conception of God, which was in fact closer to pantheism than to traditional Jewish theism. As we have noted, intuitions about perfection may vary, and a philosopher of *religion* who is seeking to apply that notion would do well to pay attention to the conception of God that actual religious communities have found to best represent perfection and worshipfulness.

A further consideration that must guide our application of the notion of divine perfection is that of *logical consistency and coherence.* As was already noted, any conception of God that is supposed to represent an actual being must at least meet the requirement of logical consistency. To be sure, a set of divine attributes that is logically inconsistent could not possibly be part of the description of a perfect being, so this criterion may already be included in the very idea of "perfect being" theology. But while this reasoning may be valid, it is also true that humans can be quite ingenious in imagining and ascribing to God seemingly marvelous characteristics that in fact are logically inconsistent. It is important, then, to carefully investigate the logical consistency of the various attributes we wish to ascribe to God.

NECESSARY AND SELF-EXISTENT

We begin with a pair of attributes that at first may seem abstract and difficult to grasp, yet are important for pointing out the fundamental difference, according to classical theism, between God and everything else whatsoever. First, consider *self-existence.* It is a familiar thought to us that for many things—especially living creatures of all kinds—it may take energy and often effort simply for the thing to remain in existence. We live our lives "from within," and when the inner vitality needed to do this becomes weak, we feel our own existence as imperiled and insecure. But we also depend on external beings and circumstances in various ways for our existence. Other beings brought us into existence, and we depend on food, water, air, and so on to sustain us in existence. Furthermore, we are all too aware of various things that might damage or destroy our existence; in a sense, then, we are dependent on the *non*occurrence of these sorts of things for our continued life and well-being.

Now, consider the idea of a being that is dependent on other things in none of these ways. It owes nothing to any other being for its origin or sustenance, and it is entirely incapable of being threatened, harmed, or destroyed by anything else whatsoever. Such an entity would exist wholly "from within," entirely "on its own steam." It would be, in a word, *self-existent*.

Now we introduce two additional terms: *necessary* and *contingent*. To say something is contingent is to say that it depends on things or circumstances other than itself; contingency plans are plans for what may or may not be done, depending on other things that may or may not happen. If, on the other hand, a being is *not* contingent in any way and will exist regardless of anything that may happen to other things or circumstances, then its existence is inevitable, inescapable. It is, in other words, a *necessary being*, a being that *depends on nothing but itself, and, given that it exists, its nonexistence, either in the past or in the future, is absolutely impossible*.

It is very clear that God, as conceived by classical theism, is a necessary and self-existent being in the senses I have just explained. God is eternal; no other being is relevant to his coming into existence, since he never in fact came into existence, and nothing whatever can in any way threaten or endanger God's existence. It is, then, simply impossible that God should not exist. We further note that God's necessity and self-existence are essential elements in his perfection; it seems clear that God is greater if he depends on nothing outside himself than if he were so dependent.

These characteristics of necessity and self-existence fundamentally distinguish God from all other things in existence. In particular, there is nothing in the natural world, the world revealed to us by the sciences, about which it is at all plausible to say that it is necessary and self-existent. All the familiar things of everyday life—people and animals, cars and houses, trees and mountains, stars and galaxies—come into being and pass away and are clearly contingent beings. Even the fundamental constituents of matter—the so-called "elementary particles"—are not immutable but form, disappear, and are changed into others, as attested by high-energy physics. According to the Big Bang theory (now a consensus view among cosmologists), it seems that the very matter-energy of the universe itself had an origin. So if there is anything at all other than God that is necessary and self-existent, we have no idea what it might be and no reason to suppose that anything of the sort exists at all.

There is, however, another, even stronger sense in which something may be said to be "necessary." Some propositions are said to be *logically necessary,* meaning that it is logically impossible that they be false; the falsehood of such a proposition would in some way involve a contradiction. (For example, it would involve a contradiction to deny that "Every triangle has three angles"; this is a *logically necessary proposition.*) Picking up on this, we can say that a *logically necessary being* is a being whose *existence* is logically necessary, whose *nonexistence* would be contradictory and logically impossible. It should be noted that if God's existence is logically necessary, it will also be necessary in the sense previously explained, but the converse does not hold; God might be self-existent, and in *that* sense necessary, without being logically necessary.

Should God be understood as a logically necessary being? This question is deeply controversial. A good many theistic philosophers and theologians—perhaps the majority—have asserted that God's existence *is* logically necessary, but many others have disagreed. On the face of it, "God exists" does not *seem* to be a logically necessary truth, and the proposition "There is no God" does not seem, at first glance, to be logically contradictory. This proposition has even been accepted as *true* by quite a few persons who are in general quite expert in the detection of contradictions. And Immanuel Kant (1724–1804) has persuaded many philosophers with his argument that *no* proposition asserting the *existence* of something can be logically necessary. (Thus, "Every triangle has three angles" is necessary, but "A triangle exists" is not necessary.) [10]

Still, it may be that none of these considerations is decisive. Kant's arguments, while impressive, have been strongly disputed, especially in recent years. [11] And we should not be misled by simple examples into thinking that it is always easy to determine whether a given proposition is either logically necessary or self-contradictory. Mathematics, for example, contains a great many necessary propositions whose necessity (and truth) are far from obvious, and some mathematical statements have resisted even the most intensive efforts of mathematicians to determine whether or not they are necessarily true.

The question of the logical necessity of God's existence is pursued further in Chapter 5 as part of the discussion of the ontological argument for God's existence. In closing, we note the following: If, on the one hand, God's existence *is* logically necessary, then this surely counts as a "perfection" of God, one of the many excellences that set God apart from all lesser beings. If, on the other hand, God's existence is *not* logically necessary, it is also the case that it is *impossible* that God existence should be necessary. And in that case, "necessary existence" does *not* count as a perfection; rather, it is just another of the many logically incoherent attributes that we humans, in our confusion, have invented and ascribed to God. [12]

PERSONAL AND FREE CREATOR

We now turn to some attributes that are more familiar to ordinary religious people. To say that God is *personal* is to say at least the following things: God has *knowledge and awareness*; God *performs actions*; God is *free* in the actions he performs; and God can *enter into relationships* with persons other than himself. These requirements seem minimal, in that a God lacking in any of them would seem *not* to be fully personal; on the other hand, if God does meet these requirements, then it would seem appropriate to describe God as "personal" even though there may be many respects in which God is very different from the human persons we know.[13]

From the standpoint of theism, it seems evident that personality, or personhood, should be considered as a perfection of God. Many of the finest things we know—love, intelligence, creativity, and moral goodness, for example—are attributes exclusively of persons, and if God were not personal he would be debarred from possessing any of these excellences. There is also the extremely important point that for many theists, worship and the religious life generally are conceived in terms of a *personal relationship* with God; thus, if God were *not* personal, their entire idea of the religious life would collapse.

God, according to classical theism, is also the *creator* of all things other than himself. The idea of creation is important in all the theistic faiths, and it seems essential to the idea of an absolutely perfect being that, if there are beings other than God in existence, God should be their creator. God's status as creator ensures his superiority, mastery, and ownership over all the things he has created in a way that could hardly be done otherwise. God is said, furthermore, to have created "out of nothing" (Latin, *ex nihilo*). This is not to be understood as if "nothing" were the name of some sort of mysterious "stuff" out of which God created the universe. Instead, to say that creation is out of nothing means that there *was no* material out of which God created; rather, all things other than God exist solely because he wills them to exist and have no other basis at all for their existence. Creation out of nothing contrasts with, and is superior to, two other modes in which the production of things might be imagined. It is superior to production from preexisting materials because in the latter case God's act of creating would be dependent upon, and probably to some extent limited by, the materials he had to work with. (There would also be the question of how to account for the existence of the materials.) And it is superior to creation *ex deo*, "out of God's own being," because this would tend to compromise the absolute distinction between creator and creature that is the hallmark of theistic metaphysics.

The God of classical theism is not only the creator but also the *sustainer* of finite things. This is to say, created things are *totally dependent on God for their existence from moment to moment.* A dramatic but not inaccurate way of putting this is to say that, were God for a single instant to completely forget about his creation, in that instant the entire creation would collapse into nothingness.

God, furthermore, enjoys *freedom* in creating, sustaining, and governing the world. To say that God is free means that God cannot be forced, constrained, or controlled by anything outside himself. Unlike creatures, God has no need to adjust himself to an environment; rather, all environments exist only in virtue of his creating and sustaining activity. Moreover, God has the freedom to *choose* what sort of world to create and how to dispose of that world. To be sure, given God's essential goodness, it is impossible that God should choose anything that conflicts with that goodness. But this leaves God still with a very wide range of possibilities, among which he chooses the ones he will bring about. Indeed, it has generally been held that God was perfectly *free either to create a world or to refrain from creating*; prior to creation, there were no creatures to whom the "right to exist" was owed, nor would the goodness of creation "add to" the greatness and goodness of God in such a way that creating was for him necessary and inevitable. So the decision to create was itself a free and generous choice on God's part.

These attributes fundamentally distinguish the theistic God from God as conceived in pantheism. To see this, we consider briefly an especially interesting form of pantheism, the *advaita vedanta* of the Hindu thinker Shankara (788–820).[14] The sole ultimate reality, according to Shankara, is Brahman, which is wholly nonempirical, entirely beyond ordinary human experience, though its existence and nature can be grasped intuitively through yogic meditation. Our ordinary experience, to be sure, indicates that both the world of nature and individual human personalities exist as independent realities. Such experience, however, is to be viewed as we view dream experiences: within the dream, we cannot help but consider the objects of the dream experiences as real, but once we awaken, this is seen to have been an illusion. Similarly, in our ordinary state of ignorance we cannot help regarding the objects and persons of everyday life as real, but from the higher, enlightened standpoint, all of this—including one's own personal existence!—is seen to be illusory. Indeed, this "ignorance" is the principal obstacle that needs to be overcome in order to reach true spiritual illumination.

Brahman, then, is *not* personal; rather, it is the ultimate, impersonal "true being" that is the reality behind all the illusory appearances of the world. Other versions of pantheism describe the situation somewhat differently, but for none of them is God the creator, for creation implies a distinction between God and the universe that is alien to pantheism. Furthermore, an impersonal "being" cannot *act* and therefore cannot be *free* in its actions; rather, it simply and changelessly *is*.

The God of process theism is like the God of classical theism in being personal. But the relationship between God and the universe is considerably different. Process theism rejects both the idea of creation ex nihilo and the radical distinction between God and the world posited by classical theism. Process theism's conception of God's relation to the world is best expressed by saying that the world is *God's body*, through which he lives his life as we live our lives through our bodies. This means that God and the universe are not wholly distinct from each other, as for classical theism; rather, all finite things, including human beings, are in a sense included in God's own being. Perhaps the best way of conceiving this is to imagine that each individual cell in a human body is possessed of its own consciousness and awareness, however limited, of what is happening to it and is going on around it. Then imagine that these individual "cell-consciousnesses" are, as it were, caught up and included in the *unified* consciousness that is the "mind" of the entire body, a consciousness that both transcends and includes each one of them. In some such way as this, each of us is a "cell" in the body of God, and because of this, God is able literally to *share*, in a most intimate way, in all of our experiences, our joys and our sorrows. In the words of A. N. Whitehead (1861–1947), the philosopher whose works inspired process theism, "God is the great companion—the fellow-sufferer who understands."[15]

All of this means that the relationship between God and the universe is conceived very differently in process theism than in classical theism. In classical theism, there is a *one-sided dependence* of the universe upon God, whereas in process theism the relationship is better described as one of *interdependence and mutuality* between God and the universe. Whitehead went so far as to say, "It is as true to say that God transcends the World, as that the World transcends God. It is as true to say that God creates the World, as that the World creates God."[16] Since God needs his body through which to live, even as we need our bodies, it must be concluded that *God can never be without a body*—that is, without a universe. That does not necessarily mean that the present universe is, like God, without beginning and without end, though this is a possibility. But if, as scientific evidence seems to suggest, our present physical universe had a beginning in time, we may be assured that before it there was another universe, or perhaps an endless series of universes, so that God has never been without a body—without a world.

ALL-POWERFUL, ALL-KNOWING, AND PERFECTLY GOOD

God is *all-powerful*, or *omnipotent*, he is *all-knowing*, or *omniscient*, and he is *perfectly morally good*. All of these attributes are fundamental to the theistic view of God, and each of them involves difficulties in understanding and formulation.

Apparently the natural way to understand God's omnipotence is simply to say that God can do anything whatever. But this quickly runs into difficulties. Can God create a square circle, or cause it to be true that $1 + 2 = 17$? At least since the time of Thomas Aquinas (c. 1224–1274), it has been recognized that the exercise of God's power must be limited to what is *logically possible.*[17] The expression *square circle* is one that could not possibly apply (correctly) to anything, and so the fact that God cannot make one implies no defect in God's power. Other limitations on what God can do stem from God's own nature; God cannot do things that require embodiment (such as climbing Mount Everest) or that imply limitations (such as, for instance, forgetting something). Perhaps more significant, it is generally held that God cannot do things that imply a moral fault, such as breaking one of his promises. In view of such considerations as these, we may say that God's omnipotence means that *God can perform any action the performance of which is logically consistent, and consistent with God's own nature.*[18]

Philosophers have devised a great many puzzles with which to test definitions of omnipotence; one of the most intriguing is the "paradox of the stone." Consider the following question: Can God create a stone that he cannot lift? If he cannot, there is something he cannot do, and he is not omnipotent. (It is obvious that making something one is unable to lift is a logically possible thing to do—home builders, for example, do this all the time.) Suppose, on the other hand, that God *can* create a stone he cannot lift. So far, so good, but now there is *another* task that God cannot perform—namely, to lift the stone in question! So either way, God is not omnipotent. (So as not to cut short the reader's attempt to wrestle with this puzzle, the solution is relegated to an endnote.[19])

The most immediately obvious way of expressing God's *omniscience* is to say that God knows everything—or better (since only *true* propositions can be *known*), that God knows all true propositions. A difficulty arises, however, in that it seems there are propositions that are true at some times but not at others. Consider the proposition "Martha was married last Sunday." Assuming that Martha does indeed marry on a Sunday, this proposition is true for exactly one week, from midnight on the Sunday of the wedding to Sunday midnight one week later. God, presumably, *knows* this proposition for exactly as long as the proposition itself is true—though to be sure, he would know *after* the time period in question that this proposition *had been true* during that period.[20] In view of this, we can modify our definition to say that at any time, God knows all the propositions that are true at that time.

But do we also need a clause, similar to the one in the definition of omnipotence, that excludes true propositions that are such that it is *logically impossible* that God should know them? *Are* there any true propositions of this sort? One possible candidate consists of propositions about decisions God himself is going to make. It seems likely that it is not possible for anyone, including God, to be in the process of making a decision and also, while making it, already to know what the decision will be. So if God *does* make decisions (as theism says he does), there may be truths God logically cannot know while he is making those decisions. To be sure, it might be held that God does not decide things in time, but rather, in some peculiar way, before time or outside of time. But even if this is true, it does not entirely blunt the force of the point made: there would still be an "aspect" of God's life, even if not a period of time, in which he must operate without knowledge of certain true propositions. (Other candidates for true propositions that God logically cannot know are discussed in the next section of this chapter.)

There is one further point to be made before we present our full definition of omniscience. We humans not only *know* things; we also *believe* things, some of which are true and others of which are false. It may be that God has *no* beliefs over and above his knowledge, and certainly he holds no false beliefs. But then our definition of omniscience needs to be crafted so as to explicitly exclude God's holding false beliefs.

With these considerations in mind, we can define God's omniscience as follows: *At any time, God knows all propositions that are true at that time and are such that God's knowing them at that time is logically possible, and God never believes anything that is false.* The most controversial element in this definition is the clause stating that God knows only what it is logically possible for him to know. But this really should not cause any difficulty: If there are no truths it is logically impossible for God to know, then the clause in question excludes nothing from God's knowledge, but that does not mean that the definition is incorrect or inadequate.

It is a matter of consensus among theists that God is *perfectly morally good.* Whatever character traits, principles of action, and so on it may take to qualify a being as morally perfect must definitely be held to characterize God. What needs to be clarified here mainly involves two things: What is the *content* of perfect moral goodness? And, what is the *relation* between moral goodness and God?

The specific content of moral goodness—whether, for instance, love is more important as a divine attribute than holiness and justice, or the reverse, or whether they are all equally important—is something theists find it hard to agree about. One's answers to these kinds of questions are likely to depend in important ways on particular theological views about the ways in which God acts and deals with people, and so these matters are perhaps best left to be dealt with within the various theological traditions. In what follows we speak generally of God's "goodness," "love," "justice," and the like, without claiming to specify exactly what each of these means or how they are related to each other.[21]

With regard to the *relation* between goodness and God, an initial question is whether God is capable of acting contrary to moral goodness. A few philosophers have thought that, in order for God to be morally praiseworthy, he must be capable of doing evil, even though he never in fact does so.[22] The vast majority of theistic thinkers, however, have held that God is *essentially* morally perfect—that his very nature is such that it is impossible for him to act in a way that is morally wrong. This view was, in fact, anticipated in our discussion of omnipotence, when we assumed that God is *incapable* of breaking one of his promises.

Another question about the relation between goodness and God concerns the source of the standard of moral goodness. Does there exist, independent of God, a standard of goodness to which God, like all other persons, is morally obligated to conform? Or, on the other hand, do moral good and evil owe their existence entirely to the will and command of God? Or is there some further possibility for the relation between God and the standard of moral goodness? For the time being, we defer engaging this question until Chapter 13.

None of the attributes discussed in this section can properly apply to God as conceived in pantheism. The pantheistic God can, to be sure, be said to possess "all power" and "all knowledge," since whatever power and knowledge there may be are, by definition, *its* power and knowledge; it is the ultimate substance, the "inner soul," of everything that exists. But the pantheistic God possesses no *individual mind* that would enable it either to *know* or to *act* as we understand these notions. According to Spinoza, "Neither intellect nor will pertain to God's nature," and if we were to attribute intellect and will to God, they "would have nothing in common with [human intellect and will] but the name; there would be about as much correspondence between the two as there is between the Dog, the heavenly constellation, and a dog, an animal that barks."[23] Perhaps the most striking point to be made, however, is that *the God of pantheism cannot distinguish between good and evil. All* actions performed in the universe are *equally* manifestations of the power of God; the notion that some of these actions are in an ultimate sense "good" and others "evil" must in the end be dismissed as an illusion. Pantheists may be, and often are, extremely upright and scrupulous in their personal ethics, but in the ultimate perspective good and evil—or, what *we call* good and evil—are transcended. And this contrasts the pantheistic God very sharply with the God of theism, who is a fighting God, a God who is unambiguously *for* good and *against* evil.

There is no reason why the God of process theism need be greatly different from the God of classical theism with respect to knowledge and goodness. The process theist's attitude toward divine power, on the other hand, is markedly different, as shown in the title of a book by Charles Hartshorne: *Omnipotence and Other Theological Mistakes.*[24] Why is omnipotence a mistake? Because classical theism depicts God as having the power to impose his will unilaterally on things and persons in his creation, as exercising coercive power over them. Process theism, on the other hand, maintains that God's power can never be coercive, but must always be persuasive. God does not have the power to unilaterally impose his will on nature—thus, the process God performs no miracles. Furthermore, he is not able to compel human beings to do his will—rather, he "lures" them, as Whitehead said, by holding before their minds the highest and best possibilities to which they can attain by voluntarily complying with his intentions.[25]

Classical theists typically see this as greatly diminishing the power and greatness of God—as making God distinctly less "worthy of worship" than if he were omnipotent. The reply to this is that, because of the inherent moral superiority of persuasive over coercive power, God's greatness is enhanced, not diminished, by his inability to use coercive power. However that may be, it is clear that this stance places process theism sharply in conflict with the theological traditions of all the theistic faiths, all of which clearly portray God as capable of exercising *both* persuasive and coercive power.[26]

GOD, PROVIDENCE, AND HUMAN FREEDOM

One of the religiously most crucial attributes of God is that God is *provident*. This means that God in some way directs and controls the course of the world and of human events so as to bring about an outcome that is in line with God's purposes and with the ultimate welfare of God's people. How exactly this goes varies considerably according to the different theologies that come into play here. But it is clear that for the religious person it is supremely important to understand, so far as may be possible, how God is working in the world and what must be done in order to align one's own purposes and efforts with God's.

God's providence involves all of the attributes discussed in the previous section—God's power, knowledge, and goodness. It also depends in important ways on the account that is given of human freedom. There are two very different ways in which free will has been understood. According to the *compatibilist* conception, a human action is "free" if the following requirements are met: (1) the immediate cause of the action is a desire, wish, or intention internal to the agent; (2) there is no external event or circumstance that compels the action to be performed; and (3) the agent could have acted differently, if she had chosen to. If these criteria are satisfied, the action comes, as we might say, "from within"; it cannot rightly be said that the agent is *forced* to perform it. This is "compatibilist" free will, because it holds that free will is compatible with deterministic causation so long as the three conditions given are satisfied.

A good many philosophers and theologians are not satisfied with this way of understanding free will, because they do not think this sort of freedom is sufficient to make humans morally responsible for their actions. These philosophers and theologians insist, on the contrary, that in order for an action to be truly free, it must have been *really possible,* with *all the antecedent conditions remaining exactly the same,* for the agent to have chosen differently. One philosopher has expressed this *libertarian* view of free will by saying that, when a person is free with respect to performing an action, she "has it in her power to choose to perform A or choose not to perform A. *Both A and not A could actually occur*; which *will* actually occur has *not yet been determined.*"[27]

With these distinctions in mind, we are in a position to consider some different views of divine providence. On one extreme is *process theism,* where God's control of worldly events is really quite minimal. As has been noted already, God's action is limited to persuading humans and other agents to follow the course he knows to be best for them; beyond this, it is impossible for God to intervene directly to secure the outcome he desires. This means that the outcome of many situations is quite uncertain and uncontrollable, even for God; on the other hand, according to process theism God bears very little responsibility for the evils that occur in the world.

At the other extreme is *theological determinism*, sometimes termed "Calvinism" because of the prominence of this view in the theology of John Calvin (1509–1564). Theological determinism accepts a compatibilist view of free will, which means that human actions can be "free" even though they are entirely predetermined and controlled by God. (God knows exactly the physical and psychological makeup and predispositions of each person and can place a person in precisely the right situation so that she will freely decide exactly what God intends for her to decide. Alternatively, God can simply *decree* what the person will *freely* choose to do.) This view allows God total, unconditional control over all events—something that many believers find immensely comforting and reassuring.[28] On the other hand, theological determinism encounters serious difficulties in accounting for the evil in the world; it seems compelled, in fact, to assert that everything that happens, including all the terrible evils of human history, is exactly as God wanted it to be. (See Chapter 6 for more on this topic.)

In between these extremes, there is a type of view that is held by probably a majority of Jews and Christians and a minority of Muslims. Humans are said to have libertarian free will, so God does not have direct control of everything that occurs. Humans may, and in fact often do, act in ways contrary to God's will, and when they do this they, and not God, are responsible for the evil that results. But God is not absolutely limited to persuasion, as in process theism. Rather, God is able to act directly in the natural world (see Chapter 9 on miracles); God is also able to influence human actions and may even, in specific instances, overrule the free will of creatures in order to secure his objectives. Thus, God is able to retain ultimate control over the direction and goal of the world's history, while allowing genuine freedom to human beings.

Most people who have held this view have held that God has, in advance, complete and detailed knowledge of everything that will ever actually happen, including the free choices to be made by his creatures. Some also believe God knows exactly what *would happen* given each of the options open to a person; this, of course, involves knowing what various persons *would freely choose to do* under various conditions that are never actually realized. Given this knowledge, God is able to guide persons to perform precisely those actions that will have the best results. This latter type of knowledge (knowledge of the free choices that would be made in various hypothetical circumstances) is termed *middle knowledge*; it has become the topic of controversies that are too complex to be explored here.[29]

It has been questioned whether complete and certain knowledge of the future on God's part is compatible with genuine free will. This question has received especially intensive scrutiny in recent decades.[30] In order that the reader may understand what is at issue here, we include the following sample of an argument for the *incompatibility* of foreknowledge and free will. The example concerns a certain Clarence, known to be addicted to cheese omelets. Will Clarence have a cheese omelet for breakfast tomorrow morning, or won't he? The argument proceeds as follows:

1. It is now true that Clarence will have a cheese omelet for breakfast tomorrow. (Premise)
2. It is impossible that God should at any time believe what is false or fail to believe anything that is true. (Premise: divine omniscience)
3. God has always believed that Clarence will have a cheese omelet tomorrow. (From 1,2)
4. If God has always believed a certain thing, it is not in anyone's power to bring it about that God has not always believed that thing. (Premise: the unalterability of the past)
5. Therefore, it is not in Clarence's power to bring it about that God has not always believed that he would have a cheese omelet for breakfast. (From 3,4)
6. It is not possible for it to be true both that God has always believed that Clarence would have a cheese omelet for breakfast and that he does not in fact have one. (From 2)
7. Therefore, it is not in Clarence's power to refrain from having a cheese omelet for breakfast tomorrow. (From 5,6) So Clarence's eating the omelet tomorrow is not an act of free choice.[31]

It will be noted that step (2) consists of a definition of divine omniscience *without* the stipulation about what it is logically possible for God to know; thus, the conclusion is that Clarence does *not* have free choice about what to eat for breakfast. If we find the conclusion unacceptable (that is, if we believe that human beings do possess libertarian free will), then a reasonable response would be to adopt a definition of omniscience that includes the requirement of logical possibility as given in the previous section; we could then conclude that the truth about Clarence's breakfast is one of the things it is logically impossible for God to know. Note, furthermore, that there is nothing in any way special about Clarence's decision with regard to the omelet. On the contrary, what is established here about this decision can be generalized to any decision made by anyone at any time. The conclusion will be, then, either that no created beings ever make any free choices at all or that God is unable—*logically* unable—to know these decisions with certainty before they are made.

Is the argument given correct? The matter is very much in dispute, and the arguments about it have become so complex that to pursue them here is impossible. By far the most common reply to arguments of this kind is to insist that, for instance, God's knowledge of Clarence's choice does not in any way *cause or compel* Clarence to make the choice he does. But while this may be true, it is hard to see how it constitutes an answer to the argument. The argument, after all, never claims that God's knowledge causes Clarence's action. The argument merely observes that it is impossible for it to be the case *both* that God believes that Clarence will eat the omelet and that Clarence does not in fact eat one. And this is assuredly true. But as we have already observed, the discussions of this topic are far too complex to be pursued in detail here; the interested reader is urged to consult the appropriate literature.[32]

It should be clear, in any case, that the conclusion that comprehensive divine foreknowledge is inconsistent with human freedom does *not* require the abandonment of divine omniscience. Rather, this would simply be a striking instance of a group of truths that it is logically impossible for God to know. If it does not demean God's omnipotence that he cannot draw an "undrawable" figure such as a square circle, then neither does it detract from his omniscience that he cannot know unknowable truths about future free actions. As soon as these truths are available, God will be the first to know!

Nevertheless, this doctrine of *limited foreknowledge* (as we may call it) does imply that God's knowledge concerning the future is a good deal less complete than many theists have supposed it to be. Whether this constitutes a serious problem for theistic philosophy and theology, is simply another aspect of the continuing dispute over freedom and foreknowledge.[33]

GOD ETERNAL—TIMELESS OR EVERLASTING

That God is eternal is a common conviction among theists. But how is this to be understood? The most straightforward and readily understandable way to interpret God's eternity is simply to say that God *always has existed and always will exist*. God, then, exists *through time* like other persons and things, but, unlike the others, his existence has neither beginning nor end. In a word, God is *everlasting*.

Some philosophers and theologians, however, have found this to be an inadequate interpretation of God's eternity. They have said, rather, that God is *timeless, outside of time altogether*. God, on this view, does *not* experience the world moment by moment as we finite persons do; rather, he experiences the world's history all at once, in a total simultaneous present. For God, they say, there is no past, nor present, nor future; God simply *is*. And all of time is present to God, all at once and changelessly, in his eternal present. Augustine put it like this:

> Nor dost Thou by time, precede time: else shouldest Thou not precede all times. But Thou precedest all things past, by the sublimity of an ever-present eternity; and surpassest all future because they are future, and

when they come, they shall be past; but Thou art the Same, and Thy years fail not. Thy years neither come nor go; whereas ours both come and go, that they all may come. Thy years stand together, because they do stand; nor are departing thrust out by coming years, for they pass not away; but ours shall all be, when they shall no more be. Thy years are one day; and Thy day is not daily, but To-day, seeing Thy To-day gives not place unto to-morrow, for neither doth it replace yesterday. Thy To-day, is Eternity. . . .[34]

One benefit often found in this view is that it seems to resolve the problem of freedom and foreknowledge, discussed in the previous section. The argument for the incompatibility of freedom and foreknowledge, it will be recalled, relied heavily on the fact that God, in the past, already has known what each of us will do in the future. But if God is timelessly eternal, this is not true. It is not that God knew, in the past, what we would do; rather, God timelessly *knows* this, and he knows it as a present reality, for all times are present to him. As Thomas Aquinas said: "He who goes along the road does not see those who come after him; whereas he who sees the whole road from a height sees at once all those traveling on it."[35] The "height," of course, is God's eternity, from which he sees at once the whole "road" of time, which we temporal travelers come to know only bit by bit as we make our way along it.

Now the fact that some action is known in the present, as it occurs, has no tendency to show that the action is not done freely; no more, then, should the fact that God in *his* present knows eternally what we do detract from the freedom of the action.

Whether this solution succeeds or not is itself, as one might expect, a disputed question. In any case, this is not the only reason, and perhaps not the most important reason, that the theory of divine timelessness has been accepted. The more fundamental reason seems to be the conviction, which has its roots in Greek philosophy and especially Neoplatonism, that the *changeability* that must characterize God if he exists through time is unacceptable as an attribute of the "most real being." A recent defense of divine timelessness puts it this way: "Such radically evanescent existence [as that of temporal beings] cannot be the foundation of existence. Being, the persistent, permanent, utterly immutable actuality that seems required as the bedrock underlying the evanescence of becoming, must be characterized by genuine [i.e., timeless] duration, of which temporal duration is only the flickering image."[36]

The doctrine of divine timelessness continues to be a topic of controversy among philosophers of religion. Probably the trend in recent years has been away from this view and towards accepting the view that God is everlasting, which is both easier to understand and apparently more in agreement with the scriptures, which depict God as acting in time and history.[37] Yet timelessness continues to find able defenders and advocates. The discussion of the various divine attributes earlier in this chapter has been carried on in terms of the idea of God as everlasting, since this is the more familiar and easily understood concept. But the same attributes can, with appropriate modifications, be restated as attributes of a timeless God. The issue between these rival conceptions, then, remains very much in doubt.[38]

Here, then, we bring to a conclusion our exposition of the theistic concept of God. The concept seems to be logically consistent, though in view of its complexity it is difficult to be absolutely certain about that. And it is one that has fascinated and intrigued generation after generation of philosophers and theologians. But is it more than this? Is the concept one that applies to a *real being,* one who in very truth is the creator and sustainer of all things other than himself and who enters powerfully and intimately into the world-process and especially into the lives of his worshipers? It is this question that must be addressed in subsequent chapters.

STUDY QUESTIONS

1. Describe briefly the conception of God implied in the story of Shvetaketu and his father. How does this differ from the understanding of God you are familiar with?

2. How is the concept of God defined in the religious tradition with which you are most familiar? How (if at all) does this idea of God differ from that of classical theism, as explained in the text?

3. Does it seem correct to you to say that only a God who is absolutely perfect could be fully worthy of worship? Discuss.

4. Explain what is meant by saying that God is a "necessary being." Does it seem to you that an adequate conception of God should include this idea? Discuss.

5. Explain what it means to say that God is the creator. Why is the idea of creation an important part of the concept of God?

6. Do we have a more adequate idea of God if we think of God as wholly distinct from the universe (classical theism) or if we think of God as including the universe within himself (process theism)?

7. Does it lessen one's appreciation of divine power to say that God cannot do things that are logically impossible, such as changing the laws of arithmetic? Is it better to say that God is able to act in ways that are cruel and deceitful or that God is unable to do these things?

8. Is God greater and more perfect if he exercises both persuasive and coercive power (as in classical theism) or if he exercises only persuasive power (as in process theism)?

9. In defining God's power and God's control over the world, is it important to preserve the possibility of free will for human beings? If so, how should free will be defined?

10. If it should turn out that it is logically impossible for there to be both comprehensive divine knowledge of the future and genuine free will for human beings, which is more important? Discuss.

NOTES

1. Quoted in Ninian Smart, *The Religious Experience of Mankind,* 2d ed. (New York: Scribner's, 1976), p. 106.

2. A note on terminology: we use *classical theism* to denote a group of views that are in the broad mainstream of the theistic traditions, in contrast with pantheism and process theism. Views within this mainstream differ from each other in a number of ways, some of them explored in the chapter. In some other writings, "classical theism" is used in a more restrictive way, to designate views that hold that God is timelessly eternal, simple, impassible, and absolutely immutable. These views form a subset of classical theism as it is defined here. Throughout this chapter, *theism* and *theistic,* when used without qualification, refer primarily to classical theism; some but not all of what is said about "theism" applies also to process theism.

3. For process theism, see John B. Cobb and David Ray Griffin, *Process Theology: An Introductory Exposition* (Philadelphia: Westminster Press, 1976). [See the selection in *PRSR,* Part 3.] A good exposition of the conceptions of ultimate reality held by the various schools of Vedanta is found in John M. Koller, *Oriental Philosophies,* 2d ed. (New York: Scribner's, 1985), pp. 82–99.

4. Some religious traditions do seem to insist on characterizing God in contradictory terms. In many cases, the best way to understand this is that the contradictory description is attempting to convey a "deeper truth" about the divine that is not expressable in literal language. Still, unless we are somehow able to grasp this deeper truth, the contradictory description is of little help. If the contradictory description is interpreted literally—for instance, if it is said to be literally true both that God is unembodied and that he has a body—then there is no way of understanding what is thereby said about God.

5. This point is not uncontroversial. One philosopher suggested that we might feel no such regret were we to learn that God did not know some unimportant theorem of mathematics, especially if God *could* know the theorem if he wanted to. (Presumably, he just has not taken the time to work it out.)

   This may or may not be correct. But if it is correct, it seems likely that we would feel no regret because we do not, in the case described, really feel that God is significantly inferior, or lacking in excellence, as a result of not knowing that particular theorem. Suppose, on the other hand, that God is *unable* to know the theorem: "God is great at algebra, but he just can't seem to get the hang of solid geometry." Most likely this would indeed be disturbing to us, because in this case it would seem clear that God is less great than he might conceivably be.

6. *St. Anselm: Basic Writings,* trans. S. N. Deane (La Salle, Ill.: Open Court, 1962), p. 7. [See the selection in *PRSR,* Part 4.]

7. It could be pointed out, to be sure, that people have often worshiped gods that were very much inferior to this "perfect being" conception. But this is not a decisive objection, for two reasons: First, the religious attitudes in question may very well fall short of *worship,* in the strong sense that has been given to this word in our discussion. But second, insofar as it becomes generally recognized that a particular kind of god falls short of maximal excellence and perfection, gods of that kind

tend to be *eliminated* as serious objects of worship—thus, for example, the decline in polytheistic worship that tends to occur in many advanced cultures.

8. A recent volume exploring this theme is Thomas V. Morris, *Anselmian Explorations: Essays in Philosophical Theology* (Notre Dame, Ind.: University of Notre Dame Press, 1987).

9. Process theists also think of God as the "absolutely perfect being," but their conclusions about what is implied by perfection are, as we shall see, somewhat different. Pantheists would probably say that God is *perfect* but not *a perfect being,* since according to pantheism God is not *a being* at all.

10. For Kant's arguments, see "The Ideal of Pure Reason," in Kant, *Critique of Pure Reason,* trans. N. K. Smith (New York: St. Martin's, 1965), pp. 487–507.

11. See Robert Merrihew Adams, "Has It Been Proved that All Real Existence Is Contingent?" and "Divine Necessity," both in Adams, *The Virtue of Faith* (New York: Oxford, 1987); also Alvin Plantinga, *The Nature of Necessity* (Oxford: Clarendon Press, 1974).

12. For additional reading on God's existence as logically necessary, see J. N. Findlay, "An Ontological Disproof of God's Existence," in *New Essays in Philosophical Theology,* ed., Antony Flew and Alasdair McIntyre (London: Macmillan, 1955), pp. 47–56 [reprinted as "God's Necessary Existence Is Impossible" in *PRSR,* Part 3]; and Thomas V. Morris, *Our Idea of God* (Downers Grove, Ill.: InterVarsity Press, 1991) [see selection in *PRSR,* Part 3].

13. Note that we say God is *personal,* not that God is *a person.* The latter assertion would be a controversial one, accepted by some theists but not by all. According to the Christian doctrine of the Trinity, there are *three* persons in God, designated as Father, Son, and Holy Spirit; these persons are capable of personal relationships *among themselves* as well as with created persons. Jews and Muslims, on the other hand, emphatically reject the doctrine of the Trinity.

14. *Vedanta* refers to the Hindu holy books on which this system claims to be based; *advaita* means "nondual," referring to the lack of duality between Brahman and the empirical world. It should be noted that this is only one of many ways of understanding God in Hinduism, which taken as a whole permits an almost unlimited variety of conceptions of the divine. Many Hindus worship personal deities such as Vishnu and Shiva, which are sometimes said to be "aspects" of Brahman.

15. Alfred North Whitehead, *Process and Reality,* corrected ed., ed. David Ray Griffin and Donald W. Sherburne (New York: Free Press, 1978), p. 351.

16. Whitehead, *Process and Reality,* p. 348.

17. See Thomas Aquinas, *Summa Theologica* I, 25, 3. [Reprinted as "God is Omnipotent" in *PRSR,* Section 3.]

18. It should be noted that our conception of omnipotence and other divine attributes will make an important difference to our understanding of the "problem of evil"; see Chapter 6 for more on this.

19. What seems the best solution is due to George Mavrodes ("Some Puzzles Concerning Omnipotence," *Philosophical Review* 72 (1963): 221–23) [reprinted in *PRSR,* Part 3]. The solution may be stated as follows. The question asks whether God "can create a stone that he cannot lift." Can God accomplish this task, or not? Now, in order to have before us a definite task, it is necessary to specify *who* it is that is to be incapable of lifting the stone. (A stone that the average philosophy professor cannot lift may present no challenge for Arnold Schwarzenegger!) In the present case, the person who is to be unable to lift the stone is God himself. But God is, by definition, capable of lifting a stone of any size whatever. So the task set for God is that of creating a stone so big it cannot be lifted by a being who is capable of

lifting a stone of any size at all—and this, clearly, is self-contradictory, just like the task of creating a round square. But as we've already seen, omnipotence does not include the ability to do what is self-contradictory, so God's inability to create a stone that God cannot lift creates no difficulty for the claim that God is omnipotent.

20. Some philosophers have maintained that, while the *sentence* "Martha was married last Sunday" is tensed, the *proposition* expressed by that sentence is *not* tensed and does not change in truth-value over time. There seems at present, however, to be a majority view that this solution will not work and that we must accept the existence of tensed propositions.

21. It should be noted, however, that the philosopher of religion cannot well remain completely neutral concerning the nature of divine goodness; among other things, the view taken on this point has an important effect on one's approach to the problem of evil.

22. On this point see Bruce Reichenbach, *Evil and a Good God* (New York: Fordham University Press, 1982), chap. 7.

23. *Chief Works of Benedictus de Spinoza,* vol. II, trans. R. H. M. Elwes (New York: Dover, 1955), pp. 60–61.

24. (Albany, N.Y.: SUNY Press, 1984).

25. In Chapter 6 we discuss the employment of these process ideas to respond to the problem of evil.

26. For a thorough critique of the process view of God's power, see David Basinger, *Divine Power in Process Theism: A Philosophical Critique* (Albany, N.Y.: SUNY Press, 1988).

27. David Basinger, "Middle Knowledge and Classical Christian Thought," *Religious Studies* 22 (1986): 416.

28. Mainstream or Sunni Muslims are strongly committed to theological determinism; Shiites, on the other hand, acknowledge the reality of libertarian free will.

29. The best exposition and defense of the theory of divine middle knowledge is found in Luis de Molina, *On Divine Foreknowledge (Part IV of the Concordia),* trans. with introduction by Alfred J. Freddoso (Ithaca, N.Y.: Cornell University Press, 1988). For a critique of middle knowledge, see William Hasker, *God, Time, and Knowledge* (Ithaca, N.Y.: Cornell University Press, 1989), chap. 2.

30. A classic statement of this argument is given by Nelson Pike, "Divine Omniscience and Voluntary Action" *Philosophical Review* 74 (1965): 57–73 [reprinted in *PRSR*, Part 3].

31. Hasker, *God, Time, and Knowledge,* p. 69.

32. Recent books on the topic include Jonathan L. Kvanvig, *The Possibility of an All-Knowing God* (New York: St. Martin's, 1986); Hasker, *God, Time, and Knowledge*; and Linda Zagzebski, *The Dilemma of Freedom and Foreknowledge* (New York: Oxford University Press, 1991).

33. For further discussion of many of the issues considered in this section, see Clark Pinnock et al., *The Openness of God: A Biblical Challenge to the Traditional Understanding of God* (Downers Grove, Ill.: InterVarsity Press, 1994), pp. 134–54.

34. *The Confessions of St. Augustine,* trans. Edward B. Pusey (New York: Random House, 1949), Bk. 11, pp. 252–53.

35. Thomas Aquinas, *Summa Theologica,* trans. Fathers of the English Dominican Province, 2d ed. (London: Burnes, Oates & Washbourne, 1920), I, 14, 13, reply obj. 3.

36. Eleonore Stump and Norman Kretzmann, "Eternity," *Journal of Philosophy* 79 (1981): 444–45.

37. For argument in support of this view, see Nicholas Wolterstorff, "God Everlasting," in C. Orlebeke and L. Smedes, eds., *God and the Good* (Grand Rapids, Mich.: Eerdmans, 1975), pp. 181–203 [reprinted in *PRSR*, Part 3].

38. The best recent presentations are found in Stump and Kretzmann, "Eternity," and in Brian Leftow, *Time and Eternity* (Ithaca, N.Y.: Cornell University Press, 1991). For additional discussion, see Kvanvig, *Possibility of an All-Knowing God*, pp. 150–71, and Hasker, *God, Time, and Knowledge*, pp. 144–85.

SUGGESTED READING

Basinger, David. *Divine Power in Process Theism: A Philosophical Critique*. Albany, N.Y.: SUNY Press, 1988.

Basinger, David, and Randall Basinger, eds. *Predestination and Free Will: Four Views of Divine Sovereignty and Human Freedom*. Downers Grove, Ill.: InterVarsity Press, 1986.

Cobb, John B., and David Ray Griffin. *Process Theology: An Introductory Exposition*. Philadelphia: Westminster Press, 1976.

Gale, Richard M. *On the Nature and Existence of God*. New York: Cambridge University Press, 1991.

Hartshorne, Charles. *Omnipotence and Other Theological Mistakes*. Albany, N.Y.: SUNY Press, 1984.

Hasker, William. *God, Time, and Knowledge*. Ithaca, N.Y.: Cornell University Press, 1989.

Kenny, Anthony. *The God of the Philosophers*. Oxford: Oxford University Press, 1979.

Koller, John M. *Oriental Philosophies*. 2d ed. New York: Scribner's, 1985.

Morris, Thomas V. *Our Idea of God: An Introduction to Philosophical Theology*. Downers Grove, Ill.: InterVarsity Press, 1991.

Pinnock, Clark, Richard Rice, John Sanders, William Hasker, and David Basinger. *The Openness of God: A Biblical Alternative to the Traditional Conception of God*. Downers Grove, Ill.: InterVarsity Press, 1994.

Stump, Eleonore, and Norman Kretzmann. "Eternity," *Journal of Philosophy* 79 (1981): 429–58.

Swinburne, Richard. *The Coherence of Theism*. Rev. ed. Oxford: Oxford University Press, 1993.

Wierenga, Edward R. *The Nature of God: An Inquiry into Divine Attributes*. Ithaca, N.Y.: Cornell University Press, 1989.

Zagzebski, Linda. *The Dilemma of Freedom and Foreknowledge*. New York: Oxford University Press, 1991.

CHAPTER 5   # THEISTIC ARGUMENTS: IS THERE EVIDENCE FOR GOD'S EXISTENCE?

In 1961 Yuri Gagarin circled the earth in a Soviet spaceship and pronounced that God did not exist because he did not see God out his tiny window. Although most people would have been surprised had Gagarin glimpsed God, they continue to wonder whether there is any good evidence to support the claim that God exists. Some believe that evidence such as unjustified pain and suffering counts strongly against God's existence. Others claim that evidence is not necessary for a rational belief in God. (We pursue these two perspectives in Chapters 6 and 7, respectively.) Some believe there is no evidence and so conclude that there is no reason to believe in God, while others argue that the available evidence for God's existence can be used to ground belief.

The arguments produced by the latter group are frequently referred to as *theistic arguments* or *theistic proofs*. Over the centuries theistic philosophers have sharpened and refined these arguments, while nontheists have developed serious critiques of them. In this chapter we first examine the nature and function of proof, then present four different types of theistic arguments and their respective critiques, and finally look at the role of cumulative case arguments for theism and atheism.

THEISTIC ARGUMENTS AS PROOFS

Before we consider particular theistic arguments, something must be said about what they purport to show or establish. Traditionally these arguments were termed *proofs*. This language raises three questions: What is a proof? Is the theist required to produce proofs of God's existence? Should we adopt the terminology of proof in speaking about providing evidence for or against God's existence?

In Chapter 3 we suggested a *person-relative view of proof*. A proof in this sense possesses three characteristics.[1] First, the argument must be *sound*; that is, the premises must be true, and the conclusion must follow validly (without breaking certain formal rules of reasoning) from the premises. Second, proofs are events having to do with knowledge. But knowledge is always had *by* someone. Therefore, a proof is a sound argument that someone *knows* to be sound. The person for whom it is a proof must know that the premises are true and that the conclusion follows validly. Since, on this view, not every rational person must be capable of recognizing that the argument is sound for it to be a proof, an argument functions as a proof *only* to the person who knows the argument to be sound. Third, the function of proofs is to *extend our knowledge*. This suggests two things: (1) The premises must be more readily knowable than the conclusion. This is important because in a proof one wants to move from the more to the less readily knowable. (2) The person for whom it is a proof must know the truth of the premises without inferring them from the conclusion. This is important to avoid begging the question. In short, a proof is a sound argument that the person for whom it is a proof knows to be sound and whose premises that person knows as true without inferring them from the conclusion.

However, if proofs are person-relative, why all the fuss over theistic proofs? In particular, is it necessary that theists have proofs of God's existence? First, we cannot require proofs for everything we know; otherwise either the conclusion we are supporting is a reason for one of the premises for that conclusion, or we have an infinite series of arguments, each supporting the premises in the logically subsequent argument. The former is unacceptable, for by inferring from the conclusion the premise that supports the conclusion we argue in a circle. The latter is unacceptable because no finite person could ever construct the requisite infinite series of arguments.

Second, despite the fact that we frequently use the term "proof"—note the colloquial response "Prove it!"—proofs play a minor role in our intellectual life. There is very little that we can prove, and what we can prove is generally quite uninteresting. Hence, though theists are within proper bounds when they put forth and evaluate arguments that purport to prove God's existence, one cannot *require* that theists prove that God exists or, correlatively, that nontheists prove that God does not exist.

Some might reply that, at the very least, persons should have proofs for those claims that are both not obviously true and really important or significant. But how are we to know what is really important or significant? We might attempt to prove what is trivial while missing what is really significant. Moreover, we have no reason to think that the class of really important things belongs to the class of provable rather than nonprovable things. The fact that something is important (to us or to anyone else) fails to inform us whether it can be derived from premises less controversial than it. It might at best be inductively defensible or belong to a class of basic truths for which there is no proof.

So it seems that theists do not need to prove God's existence (or non-theists God's nonexistence). At the same time, however, it seems proper to ask theists to present grounds or evidence of some sort for their contention that God exists, since for many people such a claim is not obviously true. Though that evidence *might* consist of proofs, it need not. Inductive reasoning or immediate experience might provide a basis for rational belief.

This leads to our third question: Should we speak of *arguments* rather than *proofs?* Many contemporary theists, following the example set by Richard Swinburne (1934–) have abandoned the deductive model of arguing for God's existence, in which proofs must be formally valid, for the inductive model.[2] Whereas Swinburne doubts that deductive forms of the theistic arguments are successful, he has confidence that inductive forms do establish the probability that God exists.

Whether one can stretch the notion of "proof" to include evidence that *tends* to establish the truth of a position gets us into a debate that we will not pursue, though some dictionaries[3] allow this extension. Clearly, if we are to do justice to both the classical arguments and contemporary developments, both deductive and inductive arguments must be considered. Consequently, in what follows we adopt "argument" in place of "proof"; this accommodates theists who offer both deductive and inductive evidence for God's existence, while maintaining our emphasis on the person-relative nature of the argument.

THE ONTOLOGICAL ARGUMENT

Without doubt the most intriguing and puzzling of the theistic arguments is the ontological argument. According to the Christian theologian Anselm (1033–1109), we can form the concept or idea of a being than which none greater can be conceived. That is, a being than which none greater can be conceived exists as an idea in some mind. But that than which none greater can be conceived cannot exist only in the mind or understanding. Suppose it were to exist only in the mind. Then it would not be the being than which none greater can be conceived, for existence in reality is greater than existence only in the mind. But we assumed at the outset the concept of a being than which none greater can be conceived. Hence, this being, which we name God, must exist in reality as well as in the mind.[4]

We might formalize the argument as follows:

1. Persons have the idea of a greatest possible being.
2. Suppose the object of this idea exists only as an idea in the mind.
3. Existence in reality is greater than existence only in the mind.
4. Therefore, we can conceive of a being greater than the greatest possible being, that is, a being that also exists in reality.

5. But there can be no being greater than the greatest possible being.

6. Therefore, the greatest possible being exists in reality.

Anselm does not deny that some persons can fail to see that God (the greatest possible being) exists. However, for him this happens because they have not properly understood the concept of God. Once one sees that God really is the greatest possible being, God's existence is undeniable.

There seems to be something seriously wrong with an argument that, like Anselm's, moves from a premise about *ideas* in our minds to establishing that something exists in *reality*. Yet, despite these suspicions, philosophers have found it difficult to discern precisely where the argument is vulnerable and to make a strong case that this point of suspicion is a vice rather than a virtue.

One who tried to expose the vulnerability of the argument was the monk Gaunilo, a contemporary of Anselm. Gaunilo suggested that the first premise of Anselm's argument is false; one cannot conceive of the greatest possible being.[5] This being is unlike any other reality. When I conceive of "humans," I know what the term means because I have had experience with humans. But when I hear the words "being than which none greater can be conceived," I can understand the meaning of the individual words, but I cannot understand the being they signify. I can form concepts of things that are finite and familiar but not of a transcendent God.

But Anselm's point is not that we can completely comprehend God's nature, that we can know God as God knows himself. Rather, he holds that we can know enough about God to know that, at the very least, God must be the greatest possible being. And should the one who denies God's existence reflect on what it is to be God, that person must understand that God exists.

Gaunilo also wondered whether one could use Anselm's argument structure to prove the existence of all sorts of unreal things. He argued in the following manner. Suppose I conceive of an island more excellent than any other, an island that has inestimable wealth and delights. But what exists in reality is more excellent than what exists solely in the mind. Therefore, this island exists. By this argument we could (absurdly) prove the existence of all manner of imaginary and nonexistent things. The reductio ad absurdum argument Anselm used on the fool Gaunilo uses on Anselm.

Anselm never fully and adequately replied to this argument,[6] but others have. One reply is that Anselm's ontological argument applies only to things capable of having perfections. It does not apply to things like islands because they are finite and hence incapable of perfection. The properties that would make an island perfect might include mineral wealth, smoothness of sand, a vast number of palm trees, and abundance of fruits. But for any island that one conceives that possesses these properties, one can think of an island with more of them. These properties have no intrinsic maximum. Without characteristics that have a maximal limit, one cannot have a perfect island. However, the properties that apply to the greatest possible being include properties for which there are maximums: knowledge, power, and moral perfection. God can be omniscient, omnipotent, and morally perfect. Hence, the form of Anselm's argument cannot be used, as Gaunilo suggested it could, to establish the existence of all sorts of nonexistent, finite things.[7]

Yet might there not be some nonexistent things that possess properties with maximums that could be plugged into Anselm's argument form? Consider the idea of the greatest possible thousand-dollar bill. Would an argument similar to Anselm's show that this bill necessarily exists? Of course, there could be a bill greater in value—say a one-million-dollar bill—but that is not the point. The point is that there could not be a greater thousand-dollar bill, for any bill with this property is worth its maximum. One might question whether its other properties have intrinsic maximums—for example, being unwrinkled or of uniform color—but these are irrelevant to its being a bill worth one thousand dollars, that is, a bill of a certain denomination. In this essential aspect there is a maximum, and, hence, using Anselm's argument form, such a bill would have to exist.[8] Perhaps Gaunilo was correct in his thesis but chose the wrong example in the island.

A different criticism of Anselm's argument focuses on premise 3. For Anselm, existence is a perfection. A perfection is something that makes whatever has it better or greater. For example, to say that health is a perfection is to say that being healthy is better, all else being equal, than being not-healthy. Similarly, to say that existence is a perfection is to say that something is better or greater because it exists, all else being equal. Or, put another way, it is better for a thing to exist than to not exist. One has to be careful here. Anselm is not saying that it is better for *us* that things exist rather than not-exist. This is obviously false, since there are many things—dust on my furniture, typing errors, mosquitoes, cancer—that I would be better off without. Rather, Anselm's point is that it is better *for the thing itself* to exist in reality than merely as a concept in a mind.

Is existence a really perfection? Norman Malcolm (1911–), for one, is doubtful:

> The doctrine that existence is a perfection is remarkably queer. . . . A king might desire that his next chancellor should have knowledge, wit, and resolution; but it is ludicrous to add that the king's desire is to have a chancellor who exists. Suppose that two royal counselors, A and B, were asked to draw up separately descriptions of the most perfect chancellor they could conceive, and that the descriptions they produced were identical except that A included existence in his list of attributes of a perfect chancellor and B did not. One and the same person could satisfy both descriptions. More to the point, any person who satisfied A's description would *necessarily* satisfy B's description and vice versa![9]

Contrary to Malcolm, one could argue that A and B do not produce the same description of the perfect chancellor, for a nonexistent chancellor could satisfy description B but not description A.[10] We could assume that all descriptions presuppose the existence of what is being described, but that begs the issue in question.

To inquire whether existence is a perfection is to ask whether existence is a property, for every perfection is a property. When we say, "God is good," good is a perfection and property of God. The problem is that the word "exist" functions differently from other property words. For example, it makes sense to say, "Some libraries do not have good organization," but not to say, "Some libraries do not exist." Yet from an example like this it does not follow that existence is not a property, only that, if it is a property, it is an unusual one. But whether this unusualness is enough to vitiate Anselm's argument is unclear. Perhaps the problem has less to do with whether existence is a property than with the fact that there are different kinds of existences—in the understanding, in reality, in mythology—and that it is not clear how or on what grounds these are comparable.

CONTEMPORARY VERSIONS OF THE ONTOLOGICAL ARGUMENT

Recently, some philosophers claim to have found a second, more persuasive argument in Anselm.[11] For example, Charles Hartshorne (1897–) notes that while great attention has been paid to the Anselmian argument presented here, a second, more persuasive argument in Anselm's *Proslogium* has been largely ignored. A major difference between the two arguments is how existence is to be treated. Hartshorne agrees with critics of Anselm that one cannot always treat existence as a property. However, it does not follow that existence is never a property. Although existence per se is not a property, *necessary existence* is. Consequently, for any two objects, if one exists necessarily and the other not (that is, exists contingently, such that it could either exist or not exist), the first is greater than the second.

It follows, then, that if God's existence were contingent, God would exist by sheer chance or luck or due to some cause. Hence, God would not be the greatest conceivable being. But God, as the greatest possible being, possesses necessary existence.[12] Therefore, God's existence is either logically necessary or logically impossible. God's existence is not logically impossible. Hence, it is logically necessary.[13]

To make their argument succeed, Hartshorne and others interpret the necessity of God's existence as logically necessary existence (existence the denial of which is or entails a self-contradiction). But why should one think that God (or anything, for that matter) possesses logically necessary existence? Some have thought that Anselm, in his alleged second argument, held this view of God, but there is textual evidence to the contrary. John Hick (1922–), for example, argues that Anselm meant not the modern notion of logical necessity but *ontological or factual necessity.* Such a necessary being is not dependent on any other being for its existence; it has its existence from itself.[14] It can neither come into nor pass out of existence. If it exists, it always has existed and always will exist. If it does not now exist, it never has and never will exist.

Modern Anselmians reply that logical necessity is necessary for an adequate conception of God. God must be conceived as maximally perfect, as exemplifying "necessarily a maximally perfect set of compossible [mutually compatible] great-making properties."[15] And since necessary existence is a great-making property, God cannot not-exist. If a maximally perfect being (God) is impossible, then such a being cannot exist. But if a maximally perfect being is possible, then by virtue of possessing the great-making property of necessary existence, a maximally perfect being (God) exists. The debated issue concerns not only the status of necessary existence as an alleged great-making property but the very conception of God.

Michael Tooley (1941–) has questioned the coherence of the concept of maximal greatness that lies behind this revised ontological argument.[16] After the fashion of Gaunilo, he contends that we can construct arguments that parallel those used in the ontological argument for other maximal properties but that turn out to yield a contradiction. For example, one might argue that it is reasonable to believe that the property of being a maximal universal solvent existing in every possible world and capable of dissolving anything in that world is exemplified in a possible world. But a similar argument might be made for the property of being maximally insoluble, that is, existing and being insoluble in every possible world. But if the form of the argument can establish the reasonableness of believing that both of these properties are exemplified and thus generate a contradictory conclusion, there must be something wrong with the argument form, an objection that applies to establishing maximal greatness as much as to maximal solubility.

It is not hard to see that for many, the jury is still out on this argument. Some believe that the ontological argument is obviously fallacious, for one cannot argue from concepts to reality. Others believe it is sound but not necessarily convincing, since it requires, among other things, belief that God's existence is possible.

THE COSMOLOGICAL ARGUMENT

A second argument frequently given by theists is the cosmological argument. The cosmological argument is less a specific argument than an argument form. It begins by invoking an empirical fact about the world (contingent beings exist; there is something in motion; the universe began to exist). Then it seeks the cause or explanation of this fact. It argues that an infinite series of causal conditions cannot provide an adequate explanation. Finally, it concludes with the existence of some necessary being, first cause, or personal agent. Two importantly different versions of this argument can be discerned. One, advanced by Thomas Aquinas (c. 1224–1274), Samuel Clarke (1675–1729), Frederick Copleston (1907–1994) and Richard Taylor (1919–),[17] considers the explanatory causal conditions in terms of their logical rather than their temporal relation to the effect, so that the first cause to which the argument concludes is not necessarily a first cause in time but a cause on which all else depends for its continued existence. The other, advanced by Arabic philosophers such as al-Kindi (c. 870) and al-Ghazali (1058–1111) and more recently defended by William Craig (1945–), argues for a first cause in time. Let us begin with the second version of the argument, referred to as the *kalam* argument.

THE KALAM COSMOLOGICAL ARGUMENT

We can formulate the *kalam* argument as follows:

1. Everything that begins to exist has a cause of its existence.
2. The universe began to exist.
3. Therefore, the universe has a cause of its existence.[18]

Premise 1 states a version of the causal principle that lies at the root of all cosmological arguments. Craig holds that this premise is intuitively obvious; no one, he claims, seriously denies it.

However, some do deny it, arguing that the claim that something should suddenly spring out of nothing is intelligible.[19] Some philosophers go beyond an intuitive appeal to base their case against the causal principle on recent work in quantum physics.[20] It appears that electrons can pass out of existence at one point and then come back into existence elsewhere. There is no way of tracing their intermediate existence or determining what causes them to come into existence at one point rather than another. One cannot precisely determine or predict where they will reappear; the location is only statistically probable.[21]

Craig responds that appeals to quantum phenomena do not affect the *kalam* argument. He notes that in modern physics a vacuum is not nothing, but rather a state of minimal energy, so that electrons do not simply appear out of nothing. The electron phenomenon results from vacuum fluctuations.[22]

It is difficult to know what to say about this argument from quantum physics, given our present knowledge. Some argue that the indeterminacy phenomena of quantum physics result from the limits of our investigative equipment. We simply are unable at this time to discern the intermediate states of the electron's existence. Others argue that the very introduction of the observer into the arena so affects what is observed that it gives the appearance that there are effects without causes. But there is no way of knowing what is happening without introducing observers and the changes they bring. Still others maintain that though the causal principle operates at the supra-atomic level, the principle is inapplicable at the sub-atomic level and hence is not universally true. The implications of indeterminacy phenomena are unclear at this point. What can be said is that any demonstration that indeterminacy is a real feature of the world would have significant negative implications for the more general causal principle that underlies the cosmological argument.

Returning to the original *kalam* argument, what can be said about premise 2? Why should we think that the universe had a beginning in time? Craig provides four arguments, two a priori and two a posteriori, to support this premise. We have space only to look briefly at one of each. One a priori argument proceeds as follows:

4. An actual infinite cannot exist.

5. A beginningless temporal series of events is an actual infinite.

6. Therefore, a beginningless temporal series of events cannot exist.

In defense of premise 4, Craig notes that an actual infinite, which is a timeless totality that neither increases nor decreases in the number of members it contains, cannot exist, for it leads to absurd consequences. For example, imagine a library with an actually infinite number of books. Suppose that the library contains an infinite number of red books and an infinite number of black books. It follows that there are as many red books in the library as there are books in the library, that there are as many red books as there are red and black books combined, and that there are as many books in the library as black books minus the red books, for no infinite has more members than another. But this is absurd. Hence, though an actual infinite exists in the ideal world of mathematics, it cannot exist in reality.

Craig's point is that, with respect to actual infinites, either there is a correspondence between members of sets, so that where they correspond one-to-one they are equivalent, or else there is no correspondence between the members of the sets and the whole is greater than the sum of its parts. The former leads to the absurdity that subsets are equivalent to the whole set. The latter leads to the absurdity that two sets, one a subset of the other, though both infinite, have different numbers of members.[23] In effect, since both options lead to absurdity, there cannot be an actual infinite.

But why should one think that a beginningless series is an actual rather than a potential infinite (premise 5)? Craig contends that, since the beginningless series of past events can be numbered and conceptually collected together, the series is an actual infinite. The fact that the events do not occur at the same time is irrelevant. If there were a starting point, so that events were added to or subtracted from this point, we would have a potential infinite that increased through time by adding new members. But since in the beginningless past there is no such starting point, the infinite is an actual, not a potential, infinite.

Part of the problem here concerns Craig's definition of actual and potential infinite. For Aristotle, the actual finite was an infinite that existed at a particular time, whereas a potential infinite was realized over time by addition or division. Hence, the temporal series of events, as formed by successively adding new events, was a potential, not an actual, infinite.[24] For Craig, however, an actual infinite is a timeless totality that cannot be added to or reduced. Hence, there remains a disagreement over whether a time factor is involved in determining whether something is an actual infinite and, hence, whether the beginningless series of events is an actual or a potential infinite. If it is an actual infinite, Craig's argument has substantial import.

The a posteriori argument in defense of premise 2 relies upon recent developments in astrophysics. In 1965 two scientists at Bell Laboratories discovered background radiation in the universe. This radiation appears to be the remnant of some gigantic early explosion, called the Big Bang. Two widely held but competing models of the origin of the universe are compatible with this datum.

According to the *Oscillating Universe model*, the universe goes through repetitive cycles of expansion and contraction. Following the big explosion, it expands to a certain point, where the gravitational force of matter takes over to slow and eventually end its expansion. This force pulls the universe back together, until it reaches a point of compact density (the Big Crunch), explodes, and begins to expand outward again. This process repeats indefinitely, though not necessarily in the same way. For this still to be possible, our universe must not have passed the critical threshold beyond which the gravitational force can no longer reverse its expansion.

The other model is the *Infinitely Expanding Universe model.* According to it, the Big Bang occurred but once, and since then the universe has been expanding outward, until sometime in the future it will die a cold death (the Big Freeze).

Determining which model is correct depends, in part, upon calculations of the total amount of matter in the universe. Some hold that the density of the matter is now insufficient to halt the expansion of the universe. Having passed the critical gravitational threshold, the universe will continue to expand forever. Others maintain that there is a great quantity of currently undetected invisible or dark matter in the universe, scattered in dust clouds within or between the galaxies, so that we have not yet passed the critical threshold beyond which contraction of the universe is possible. Clearly, evaluation of the argument depends upon our knowledge of the universe at any given time.

Though in an argument it is generally inappropriate to attack the conclusion, if there is reason to think that the conclusion is false and the argument valid, this indicates that one of the premises is false. This is, in part, the criticism that has been raised recently against a Big Bang theistic argument. Contrary to the conclusion of the *kalam* argument, on what is termed the "inflationary" theory of the origin of the universe, the universe did come into existence without a cause. The universe, it is contended, was originally a vacuum, with no space-time dimensions. But this universe "found itself in an excited vacuum state," a "ferment of quantum activity, teeming with virtual particles and full of complex interactions,"[25] which, subject to a cosmic repulsive force, resulted in an immense increase in energy. Due to this repulsive force, the universe rapidly expanded in size. But what is the origin of this increase in energy, which eventually made possible the Big Bang? The response is that the law of conservation of energy, which now applies to our universe and holds that the total quantity of energy in the universe remains fixed despite transfer from one form to another, does not apply to the initial expansion. The cosmic repulsion caused the energy to increase from zero in the vacuum to a huge amount. This great explosion released energy, from which all matter emerged. In effect, contrary to the ancient Parmenidean principle, out of nothing—a primeval vacuum—everything came. Consequently, since the conclusion of the *kalam* argument is false, one of the premises of the argument—in all likelihood the first—is false.

The issues in this version of the *kalam* argument begin to get technical and speculative. This is a mark neither for nor against the argument; it merely suggests that what initially appears to be a simple argument is exceedingly complex. The final verdict on this a posteriori version of the *kalam* argument must await further developments in theoretical astrophysics.

AN ATHEISTIC ARGUMENT FROM THE BIG BANG

In a turnabout on the Big Bang argument, Quentin Smith (1952–) argues that Big Bang cosmology is actually incompatible with a belief in God. He argues as follows:

1. If God exists and there is an earliest state of the universe, then God created that earliest state.

2. God is omniscient, omnipotent, and perfectly benevolent.

3. A universe with life is better than an inanimate universe.

4. Therefore, if God created that earliest state, then it must either contain life or eventually lead to a universe containing life. (from 1 and 3)

5. There is an earliest state of the universe, and it is the unique event of the Big Bang.

6. The earliest state of the universe involves the life-hostile conditions of infinite temperature, infinite curvature, and infinite density.

7. Since the Big Bang event is inherently unpredictable and lawless, there is no guarantee that it will lead to a universe with life.

8. Therefore, there is no guarantee that the earliest state of the universe will lead to life. (5 and 7)

9. Therefore, God could not have created that earliest state. (4 and 8)

10. Therefore, God does not exist. (1 and 9)[26]

The problematic (and key) statement is 4. Two objections can be raised. First, why is it necessary that God create a universe with life? The reason, given in 3, is that a universe with life is better than one without, and God is under obligation to create the best possible world. But many theists have doubted that God is under such an obligation, since such a notion is incoherent.[27] Of course, God could have a reason for creating a world with life, for example, a reason dealing with the good God wants to bring about. But God's having a reason to create such a world does not impose a necessity on God.

Second, and more important, God could ensure a universe with life through God's subsequent intervention. There is no logical necessity that this life-engendering capacity be present at the outset. Smith responds that were God to intervene, it would be "a sign of incompetent planning. . . . The rational thing to do is to create some state that *by its own lawful nature leads* to a life-producing universe."[28] But God's intervention after the initial Big Bang is not illogical. Further, why must God create the universe in the most efficient way, one that excludes subsequent intervention? As Thomas Morris (1952–) points out,

> Efficiency is always relative to a goal or set of intentions. Before you know whether a person is efficient in what she is doing, you must know what it is she intends to be doing, what goals and values are governing the activity she is engaged in. . . . In order to be able to derive the conclusion that if there is a God in charge of the world, he is grossly inefficient, one would have to know of all the relevant divine goals and values which would be operative in the creation and governance of a world such as ours. [29]

Indeed, Morris goes on to wonder why we need to ascribe efficiency to God at all. It is not a property required by God's perfection, such that he is deficient without it. It might be a good property to have if one has limited time or power, but presumably God lacks neither. In short, one might question whether Smith's counterargument from the Big Bang succeeds.

THE ATEMPORAL COSMOLOGICAL ARGUMENT

The atemporal type of cosmological argument does not attempt to prove the existence of a first cause in time. The universe might well have been eternal. Yet the universe is contingent and, hence, dependent on something else for its continued existence. Thus, the cause to which the argument concludes might best be termed a sustaining cause, rather than a first creative cause. It is required for anything to exist at any time.

Although the argument appears in various writers with different first premises, the fundamental structure and resulting issues are basically the same:

1. A contingent being exists.
2. This contingent being has a cause or explanation of its existence.
3. The cause or explanation of its existence is something other than the contingent being itself.
4. What causes or explains the existence of this contingent being must be either other contingent beings or include a noncontingent (necessary) being.
5. Contingent beings alone cannot cause or explain the existence of a contingent being.
6. Therefore, what causes or explains the existence of this contingent being must include a noncontingent (necessary) being.
7. Therefore, a necessary being exists.

We introduced the terms *contingent being* and *necessary being* in Chapter 4. We noted that a *contingent being* is one that, though it exists, might not have existed. Not being self-sufficient, it depends on something else for its existence. For example, you are a contingent being. Although you exist now, your nonexistence at this moment was at least possible (for example, you could have died last night). So understood, premise 1 is true.

Premise 2 invokes a version of the *principle of causation.* According to this version, every contingent being has a cause of its existence.[30] Perhaps the most common defense of this principle is that reason must hold such a principle to make reality intelligible.

One might object that though the causal principle applies to descriptions of how we *know* the world, this does not mean that it describes what actually goes on in the real world. Principles of thought need not mirror the principles of reality.

Two replies are possible. First, defenders of the causal principle argue that the success with which we have applied this principle refutes the thesis that reality does not operate according to the causal principle. If we consistently used this principle but it did not apply to reality, we should have bumped up against numerous contradictions by now. Second, if we begin at this fundamental point to drive a wedge between thought and reality, the outcome can only be skepticism about what the world is really like.

One might also object to the principle of causation on grounds arising from quantum physics. The reader might want to review the discussion of this objection presented earlier in this chapter when we considered the *kalam* argument.

Premise 3 makes the obvious claim that something cannot be a causal condition for its own existence; to do so it would have to exist already. The point here is not primarily about time but rather a logical point: something that is contingent cannot account for its own existence.

Some, like Immanuel Kant (1724–1804), object to conclusion (7), that a necessary being exists. When the cosmological argument concludes with the existence of a necessary being, Kant contends, it argues for the existence of a being whose existence is absolutely necessary, whose nonexistence is absolutely inconceivable. But the only being that meets this condition is the most real being, the concept of which lies at the heart of the ontological argument. Accordingly, he claims, the cosmological argument presupposes the cogency of the ontological argument. But since the ontological argument is suspect, the cosmological argument that depends on it likewise must be suspect.[31]

However, the contention that the cosmological argument depends on the ontological argument is based on a confusion. As we noted when we discussed the ontological argument, the term *necessary being* can be understood in different ways. Kant, like some modern defenders of the ontological argument, understands "necessary being" as having to do with logically necessary existence, that is, with existence that is logically undeniable. But this is not the sense in which "necessary being" is understood in the cosmological argument. Necessity is understood in the sense of ontological or factual necessity described in Chapter 4. A necessary being is one that, *if* it exists, cannot not exist: it is self-sufficient and self-sustaining. That something is a necessary being still leaves open the question whether it actually exists.

The critical premise of this version of the cosmological argument is 5. In its defense, some argue that if all the causal conditions were contingent, then each of them would require a cause of its existence. The result would be that the conditions responsible for the effect would be infinite. But an infinite set of causal conditions cannot explain the existence of the contingent being. Two types of arguments are given in defense of this.

The first argument is that there cannot be an actually infinite set of anything in reality. Although in mathematics we can speak about actual infinites, mathematical actual infinites concern only the ideal world of mathematics. If actual infinites were to exist in the real world, absurdities would result. Earlier in this chapter we provided an example of this in terms of the absurdities that would result if there existed an infinite number of books in a library. If the actual infinite cannot exist, then one cannot appeal to an actual infinite of present causal conditions to explain the existence of any given contingent being. Hence, the causal conditions must contain at least one noncontingent causal condition or being.

According to the second argument in defense of 5, even if an actually infinite set is possible, such a set of causal conditions cannot explain something's existence. Where each causal condition is contingent, each one itself needs an explanation for its existence. Since each being in an infinite series of contingent beings needs a reason for its existence, an infinite series of contingent beings cannot explain the existence of any contingent being. It is as if one had a chain holding up a lamp; though each link holds up the next link in the chain, the infinity of the chain does not explain why the lamp is suspended.

Why, it might be asked, do we need to explain the existence of every contingent causal condition in order to explain another thing's existence? Richard Swinburne terms this requirement the *completist fallacy*.[32] Cannot we circumvent both arguments simply by providing those causal conditions that are necessary and sufficient for the thing in question to exist? An explanation is provided once we derive the existence of the contingent thing from some relevant theory plus the existence of what is necessary for its existence.[33]

The contemporary defender of the cosmological argument probably should concede that each contingent thing exists because of the causal activity of other contingent things in the universe. However, even with this concession, the question still remains as to why there are contingent beings at all when conceivably there could have been none. In particular, why is there a universe (as a collection of contingent things) rather than not?[34] "When the existence of each member of a collection is explained by reference to some other member *of that very same collection* then it does not follow that the collection itself has an explanation. For it is one thing for there to be an explanation of the existence of each dependent being and quite another thing for there to be an explanation of why there are dependent beings at all."[35] To say that there always have been dependent things fails to provide a sufficient reason for why there are any such things rather than not.

Bertrand Russell (1872–1970) argues that we cannot ask about the cause of the universe, that it is "just there, and that's all."[36] But perhaps there is good reason to think that the universe is contingent and hence requires an explanation for its existence. The argument is that since everything in the universe is contingent, the universe itself must be contingent.

Russell is correct in noting that general arguments of this type can commit the fallacy of composition. For example, the argument that since all the bricks in the wall are small, the wall is small, is fallacious. Yet sometimes the totality has the same character as the parts on account of the parts—we built the wall out of bricks; therefore, it is a brick wall. The universe's contingency, it is argued, is like the second case. If all the contingent parts of the universe, including matter and energy, ceased to exist simultaneously, then the universe itself, as the totality of these parts, would cease to exist. But if it can cease to exist, it is contingent and requires an explanation for its existence.

Some reply that this reasoning to the contingency of the universe is still fallacious, for even if every contingent being fails to exist in some possible world or other, it remains possible that there is no possible world in which every contingent being fails to exist. That is, though there is no being that would exist in every possible world, some contingent being would exist in every world. Hence, one cannot proceed from the contingency of the parts to that of the whole.

If all the parts are contingent, it is possible that they all could not exist simultaneously, and this possibility makes the universe contingent. Some have argued that the simultaneous nonexistence of all contingent things might not be possible, for the existence of one contingent being may be necessary for the nonexistence of some other contingent being.[37] But the reasoning here can be questioned. That something's nonexistence is necessary for the existence of something else holds for certain properties: the nonexistence of any siblings is necessary for someone to be an only child. But it is not clear that something's existence is necessary for something else's nonexistence per se, which is the claim with regard to the argument for the contingency of the universe.

William Rowe (1931–) develops a different argument to support the thesis that the universe must be contingent. He argues that it is necessary that if God exists, then it is possible that there are no dependent beings. Since it is possible that God exists, it is possible that there are no dependent beings, and hence the universe is contingent.[38]

As one can readily see, the issues surrounding the cosmological argument, in whatever form it takes, are complex. But one further question remains: Even if the argument succeeded, would it show, as Aquinas held, that God (understood religiously) exists? Whether the argument establishes the existence of God understood religiously depends on whether the necessary being or first cause to which the argument concludes is the God of religion. Some suggest that the universe is the necessary being, but we have seen that there is reason to doubt this. Without any other reasonable candidate, it is likely that the necessary being is God. But much more would have to be said concerning its properties to establish that the necessary being is to be identified with a being who is personal, loving, good, all-knowing, and omnipotent and who acts purposively.

THE ANALOGICAL TELEOLOGICAL ARGUMENT

Undoubtedly, the most popular argument for the existence of God is the teleological argument. Like the cosmological argument, it is a causal argument. But it emphasizes the order or *telos* that is found in the universe. Also like the ontological and cosmological arguments, it has a long history and reflects the prevailing scientific worldview of the time. In our discussion we leave aside the Thomistic argument constructed on an appeal to final causes and instead focus on modern conceptions of the argument— the analogical version and the anthropic version.

Still found widely in popular religious literature, the analogical teleological argument has shown amazing resilience. It can be traced back at least to the Enlightenment and is best exemplified by William Paley's (1743–1805) argument that nature is analogous to a watch. On analyzing a watch, we are impressed with its intricate means-ends adaptation. All the wheels, gears, and springs are made and adjusted so that by their motion the watch keeps perfect time. Seeing this, we cannot help but conclude that the watch had an intelligent maker who fashioned it according to a design for a purpose. When we look at nature, we quickly discover the same intricate means-ends adaptation. "Every indication of contrivance, every manifestation of design, which existed in the watch, exists in the world of nature; with the difference, on the side of nature, of being greater and more, and that in degree which exceeds all computation."[39] Just consider, for example, the astounding means-ends ordering between all the parts of the eye and the end of seeing; each part is well suited to contribute to the whole, so that if just one part functions poorly, sight is affected. Since the effects—nature and the watch—are analogous, it is reasonable to conclude that nature, like the watch, has an intelligent, purposeful maker.

Yet, we may ask: Will the analogy work? David Hume (1711–1776), anticipating Paley's argument, advanced three criticisms of an analogical teleological argument. First, the strength of the argument depends upon the similarity between the things held to be analogous (the analogs). The greater the similarity, the stronger the argument; the weaker the similarity, the weaker the argument. Hume argued that the two analogs are greatly disparate.[40] Our world is not like watches and other humanly contrived things. Indeed, containing vegetation and animals, it is as much organic as mechanical.

Second, it is unreasonable to think that the principle governing our creation of machines—that reason is required for means-ends adaptation— governs all of nature. There are many natural principles besides reason: reproduction, photosynthesis, gravity. Indeed, the number of principles might be indefinitely large. Why choose reason or mind as the ultimate governing or forming principle of the universe? Reason might be operative only here on earth and only in human endeavors. Why not choose, for example, photosynthesis as the dominant principle? Further, each principle rules over its own natural domain: photosynthesis in plants, generation in animals. We cannot project a governing principle from one limited area to another part of nature, to the whole of the universe, or to its formation.

Third, suppose we grant that there is a mind that accounts for the order in the universe. Does not the principle of causation hold for mind and its ideas just as much as for the material world?[41] If so, this mind must have a cause for its order. Hence, we have an infinite regress of causes for any event, since we cannot invoke either the mental or the material to be the ultimate cause or explanation. But an infinite regress of causes yields no satisfactory explanation for the resulting order. Hence, either we deny the principle of causation (and do not require a cause for the means-ends adaptation in the material world) or we affirm the principle of causation and allow evidence showing that each area, material as well as mental, can organize itself.

Philosophers prior to this period generally doubted that matter could organize itself. To provide such an account, however, is one of the significant contributions of Charles Darwin (1809–1882). He argued that the order in the universe is not the product of conscious activity but the result of natural selection. Individual examples of apparent purpose result when modifications produced by random mutations either are preserved when they benefit (or at least do not harm) the individual or are discarded when they prove detrimental to survival or reproduction. But genetic mutation and natural selection are strictly natural processes; they do not require a divine mind for their operation. Evolutionary naturalism, it is held, provides a reasonable alternative for explaining particular instances of means-end order in nature, confirming Hume's suspicion that matter can organize itself.

THE PROBABILISTIC TELEOLOGICAL ARGUMENT

Contemporary proponents of the teleological argument grant that individual examples of *means-ends* ordering in the organic realm can be explained in terms of *evolutionary principles*. Evolution, with its auxiliary hypothesis of natural selection, functions as a broad paradigm that enables us to account for natural biological processes. However, the universe manifests certain other features that are best explained by appeal to an intelligent, purposive designer. Abandoning the argument from analogy, contemporary proponents construct a different kind of inductive argument, a cumulative argument based on *probability*. They bring several important considerations to bear on the matter.

First, *natural selection* does not so easily explain certain aspects of the universe. Since natural selection is a biological principle and not a principle of chemistry, we must appeal to other principles to explain why living things came from the nonliving. An analysis of the elemental chemical-physical components of the universe reveals that life is possible. But natural selection and random mutation can neither explain *how* these components gave rise naturally to life nor *why* these components should give rise to *living* rather than to nonliving things. Many possibilities have been suggested, the most prevalent having to do with amino acids arising in primeval, prebiotic soups made up of water, ammonia, and methane. In more recent scenarios, chemists suggest that the repetitive crystalline structure of certain clays served as a medium for the reproductive processes necessary for life to begin; planetary scientists suggest that asteroids brought the necessary organic molecules to earth. Yet experimental replications of these current origin accounts have failed to produce unqualified, corroborative results. Indeed, as some have argued, this is to be expected, since it is extraordinarily unlikely that life should emerge from a methane soup, ocean bubbles, or electrical field of pyrite. "The trouble is that there are about two thousand enzymes, and the chance of obtaining them all in a random trial is only one part in $(10^{20})^{2000} = 10^{40,000}$, an outrageously small probability that could not be faced even if the whole universe consisted of organic soup."[42] That life arose because of the design and act of some intelligent being is much more likely.

Second, the entire process of organic development invokes information processing. Especially here, the theist holds, there are hints that something more than natural selection is required to explain the ordered phenomena. In particular, how does one get the information-chains found in RNA out of the basic physical elements of protons, neutrons, electrons, and so on? Once there are RNA sequences, we can understand how they combine and recombine. Indeed, RNAs can act as both blueprints and catalysts to stimulate reactions between themselves and other molecules. But prior to there being sequences, what could order the *information-neutral* physical-chemical elements into *information-bearing* paired nucleotides, reproducing themselves, eventually to be linked as DNA on a double helix spiral?

Further, information is meaningless unless it is read, but prior to there being living organisms nothing existed to read the information. Both the information and the reading of it must arise simultaneously in order for either aspect to be beneficial and hence worthy of being preserved. The problem is a version of the old chicken-and-egg dilemma, except that here the question is not which arose first but what led to their arising together. It appears more likely or probable that a kind of directedness moved the basic physical elements toward simultaneously being information carriers and readers.

A third teleological consideration is that natural selection, as a scientific theory concerning the processes of change in organic life, is directionless; it says only that the fit survive, but it places no requirements or direction on the fit. This means that, although natural selection can account for individual cases of organic adaptation, it cannot account for the fact that species do not merely sustain their existence but show evidence of development toward complex organisms. Indeed, that there is direction and progression to complexity in the evolutionary process is one of the more striking features of nature. Many organisms have become increasingly more complex, even to the point of having psychical components. Yet survival is not necessarily related to complexity; among the fit survivors are both extremely complex and simple organisms.

The teleologist holds that the best explanation is that some creative mind lies behind this process, anticipating the process from the very beginning, creating the elements that make possible progress to more complex life forms and directing the process (perhaps through quantum events) toward the end of living, sentient creatures. The teleological argument here appeals no longer to individual cases of adaptedness but to the apparent direction and, hence, the directedness of the entire evolutionary sequence.

A fourth argument is sometimes referred to as the *Anthropic Argument.* Its defenders note that the inorganic world contains a vast complex of seemingly unrelated conditions. Many of these conditions have a very low antecedent probability, given what we know about the prior natural causes. That is, the occurrence of each of these conditions, by themselves, seems highly improbable. If any of the initial conditions at the universe's origin had been different from what they were, there would be no life as we know it. And, most important, we as conscious beings would not be here to witness the process. For example, had "the Big Bang expanded at a different rate, life would not have evolved. *A reduction by one part in a million million* at an initial stage would have led to recollapse before temperatures could fall below ten thousand degrees. An early *increase* by one part in a million would have prevented the growth of galaxies, stars and planets."[43] Or if the gravitational force had been slightly greater, all the stars would be blue giants whose life span is too short to allow the evolution of intelligent life. But if it had been slightly less, the universe would be devoid of many elements essential to life. Further, "if the electric charge of the electron had been only slightly different, stars either would have been unable to burn hydrogen and helium, or else they would not have exploded,"[44] giving us the heavier chemical elements. Or again, "if the 'strong force,' which binds the nuclei of atoms together, were stronger, helium nuclei would dominate the universe, and no hydrogen would be left over; without hydrogen there would be no water" and hence no life.[45] Finally, the universe must be so big to be so old, and it must be so old to create the chemicals necessary for the evolution of life. In particular, the basic element of life—carbon—could be formed only after the universe had cooled down from the Big Bang. But the time required for the evolution of the only possible basis for spontaneous generation of life requires a universe so big.

What this shows is that we could not be what we are—living, knowing, valuing, aesthetic beings, who in part comprehend the process—unless the universe had these specific conditions. The inorganic improbably fits into the extraordinarily narrow window of conscious life-making possibilities. What is antecedently unlikely is necessary for the very possibility of conscious beings knowing it.

Then how does one best explain why these conditions have precisely the conscious life-engendering or life-fostering value that they have? On a nonteleological schema, the antecedent probability of the occurrence of the particular scenario that resulted in carbonous life is extremely remote. Someone has calculated the odds against our universe's formation as one in $10,000,000,000^{124}$. However, on a teleological schema, viewed from our present perspective, the features of the scenario are necessary for the present state of affairs (specifically, for there being human observers). Thus, though we can describe the development of the physical events naturally, that they occurred at all and in the pattern and narrow range necessary for observing life that they did points to the likely existence of a conscious designer. Hence, it is reasonable to claim that the best explanation for there being a universe that produces conscious life requires more than mere natural causes and laws.

Stephen Gould (1941–) argues that this reasoning is flawed, for though it is antecedently unlikely that any given historical event will occur, something has to happen. Think, for example, how improbable it is that you and everyone else in the world are precisely in the position you and they are in *right now*. Even if what occurred was surprising, it is not surprising that something did occur, and hence no special explanation must be given for that fact.[46] Natural explanations suffice.

Yet the fact that *something* must happen does not remove the necessity for giving an explanation for the extraordinariness of what happens. The argument depends not merely upon the claim that the formation of a universe resulting in conscious life was extraordinarily improbable. This improbable scenario also resulted in conscious beings capable of comprehending the unique events.

Richard Swinburne gives the example of a madman who imprisons a victim with a card-shuffling machine. He tells the victim that unless that machine draws ten aces of hearts sequentially from ten decks, the machine will set off an explosion that will kill him. The madman then starts the machine to make the required draws, and to the amazement of the perspiring victim it draws ten successive aces. The grateful victim claims that the machine was rigged, but the madman replies that these fortunate draws needed no explanation, since the machine had to select some card and this was the only sequence of draws the victim could have observed. But "the fact that this peculiar order [of ten aces] is a necessary condition for the draw being perceived at all makes what is perceived no less extraordinary and in need of explanation."[47]

It is true that the improbability of an event does not mean that one cannot provide a natural explanation. Natural explanations are compatible with mere possibility. However, the possibility that these facts about the universe result from natural events does not affect the argument, for the point of the argument is that what is sought is the best possible explanation not only of the conditions themselves but also of the fact that among all the possibilities only those that make intelligent life possible exist. What requires explanation, the theist notes, is not so much that those conditions exist as that they are what they must be for conscious life to be possible at all. The appeal to a conscious, purposive designer better explains the life-anticipating conjunction of these extremely narrowly ranged physical conditions and natural laws.

Fifth, the teleologist draws attention to the structure of the entire developmental process. What is striking is the way in which the various parts of nature and the individual scientific laws result in an all-pervasive order that conforms to mathematical formulas that we can both understand and use to predict future events. The Darwinian schema employs natural laws to explain how life in its particular and diverse forms developed from complex molecules. But what it cannot explain is those very laws themselves. "Science thus explains particular phenomena and low-level laws in terms partly of high-level laws. But from the very nature of science it cannot explain the highest-level laws of all; for they are that by which it explains all other phenomena." Not a scientific but a personal explanation of "the vast uniformity in the powers and liabilities possessed by material objects,"[48] in terms of a conscious, purposive being, is indicated.

In sum, the post-Darwinian, inductive teleological argument asks not who made the ameba or the elephant but how one accounts for the entire system that, developing from the simple to the complex, from the nonliving to the living, portends conscious life. The more one reflects on the narrow window that makes sentient life possible, the more this question becomes significant. Law-governed, life-anticipating order appears in a number of areas not directly linked; yet at the same time it is antecedently unlikely. If teleology made sense only in one area, there would not be much of a case. But the fact that appealing to purposive ordering best explains a number of antecedently improbable conditions lends credence to the contention that a more probable explanation of the universe appeals to the activity of a purposeful being. In other words, the argument is both cumulative and probabilistic.

Furthermore, theists hold, this explanation gains additional credence when the teleological argument is viewed not as an independent argument but as one that follows upon or adds to the cosmological argument. If the cosmological argument is sound in concluding to the existence of a necessary being, that is, if a necessary being exists, it then becomes reasonable to suggest that the teleological argument supplies a further important characteristic of this being, namely, that the necessary being has conscious intelligence. That is, if the necessary being is the sustaining cause of things, and if what is sustained manifests purposive design, it is reasonable to infer that this sustaining cause is a conscious being that acts purposefully in the world.

THE MORAL ARGUMENT

The final argument at which we look is the moral argument. This argument was espoused by Thomas Aquinas in his fourth way, in the context of a postulational metaphysic (where we can postulate something must be the case only in order to explain something else) by Immanuel Kant,[49] and more recently in the popular writings of C. S. Lewis (1898–1963). Although a version of Kant's argument has found some recent qualified support,[50] we focus on Lewis's treatment.

For Lewis, our moral discussions and moral behavior presuppose that there is an *objective moral law*. We can rationally determine moral acts to be truly right or truly wrong. He rejects moral relativism, according to which what a group or person thinks is right is right for them. For one thing, unless there is an objective moral law, we have no standpoint from which we can critique the moral behavior or ideologies of others. If what a person thinks is right is right for that person only, the only possible grounds for criticism are a person's failure to act on what the person thinks or believes is right. But then the moral beliefs of Adolph Hitler and Joseph Stalin would be morally equivalent to those of Jesus and the Buddha. Second, if moral relativism is true, there could not be moral progress. To progress in one's moral beliefs, one must be able to be mistaken about one's moral beliefs, and one set of moral beliefs must be better than another. But this is impossible when whatever persons or a group thinks is right, is right for them. Further, those who advocate ethical relativism often do so on the grounds that moral relativism promotes tolerance, advances the good of the community, or preserves the species. But this only reintroduces objective moral values, for unless some values are better than others—tolerance better than intolerance, preservation of the species better than its demise—there is no ground for praising these values, other than that we approve them. Finally, Lewis argues that those who argue from belief relativism, which is the view that different persons or societies have different moral beliefs, to ethical relativism have failed to notice that various cultures substantially agree about what is morally acceptable and what is forbidden. The differences between cultures are less matters of value than of fact. For example, what constituted murder in Aztec society, which practiced ritual killing, differs from what constitutes murder in our society, which does not practice ritual killing.

This objective moral law, if it is to be justified and not mere opinion, must be grounded in or based on something. Lewis suggests two possible grounds: the factual reality of human experience (what he calls "matter") and mind. It cannot be grounded on the factual reality observed by science, for the laws of nature tell us only what things actually do, while the moral law deals with what *ought* to occur. Put another way, we ultimately cannot help but obey the laws of nature, but we have a choice about obeying the moral law. Even though we are commanded to obey it, we can refuse. The moral law must be grounded in mind, for only mind can give instructions regarding doing the right. This mind cannot be a human mind, for the moral law continues to hold despite the births and deaths of individual human persons. Hence, there must be a power or mind behind the universe, "urging me to do the right and making me feel responsible and uncomfortable when I do wrong. I think we have to assume it is more like a mind than it is like anything else we know—because after all the only other thing we know is matter and you can hardly imagine a bit of matter giving instructions."[51]

Is Lewis correct that a naturalistic account of ethics cannot suffice? There are traditions of naturalistic ethics that give a rational though material basis for moral obligations. For example, Aristotle (384–322 B.C.) argued that we can ground moral judgments in the final causes of the universe. By seeing how things necessarily are, we can discern how we ought to act. The *ought* is grounded not in the *is* but in what *necessarily is* the case, in the ideal structure that must be realized in order to maximize the self-fulfillment of the organism.

It might be replied that contemporary philosophers can no longer appeal to Aristotelian ethics because they have long abandoned the notion of final causation. This is true, but the point of the objection is simply to affirm that the moral argument cannot conclude directly that the ground of the moral law *must* be mind. Of course, this means that it is incumbent on contemporary ethical naturalists to show that it can be adequately grounded in something else. At this point, the discussion must turn to evaluate recent attempts to develop sophisticated naturalistic or intuitionist ethics, a subject beyond our present scope.[52]

What, then, can be said about the moral argument? Some doubt whether it can function soundly as an independent theistic argument. All of Lewis's premises have been challenged. Some theists might respond, however, that these challenges can be answered, so that it might function as part of a cumulative case that includes the cosmological and teleological arguments.

CUMULATIVE CASE ARGUMENTS AND GOD

We have advocated a person-relative notion of argument, in which each person must evaluate the soundness or strength of the argument and what he or she knows about the truth of the premises. One must be careful here. The fact that arguments are person-relative does not mean that "anything goes." Since we think and work in a community, an argument that does not meet with at least some measure of acceptance by persons in the community, that only one individual or a few think to be sound or reasonable, should raise some serious questions in the advocate's mind. Though acceptance by the community does not make any claim true, the community functions as a check against mere rationalization of any position.

It might be replied, correctly, that the term "community" is still vague. We function in many communities, not merely one. To which community should the theist present grounds or evidence? To the theistic community? To the nontheistic community? And what kind of criteria for evaluation are to be invoked? At the bare minimum, logical criteria should be accepted by all sides. But beyond this, the appropriate criteria for communal judgments are matters for ongoing discussion. [53]

One more set of objections to the arguments must be considered. Michael Martin (1932–), in his extensive, detailed defense of atheism, takes on each theistic argument individually, raising questions about both the argument and what it would show were it thought to be sound. For each argument he concludes, first, that the argument does not warrant theistic belief and, second, should it do so, it would not support a belief in the God of Christian, Jewish, or Muslim theism.[54]

Regarding the first objection, the theist could respond that generally it is a mistake to base a thesis on one argument. Just as the prosecution in a trial brings a variety of evidence to bear on the case so that if one piece of evidence is questioned, the case does not topple, so the theist should not ground his belief on any single argument or treat the arguments independently. Theistic arguments are best seen as part of a *cumulative case for theism* in which the pieces support each other in a way that enables us to make sense of the entire picture.[55] Together they indicate that there is good reason to believe in the existence of some sort of ultimate reality or God. The cosmological argument concludes that a necessary being exists, a being that if it exists is not dependent upon other beings for its existence. The teleological argument proposes that such a being, as responsible for the conscious-life-anticipating dimension of the universe, acts purposively and so has conscious intelligence and will. The moral argument suggests that this being has some relation to the moral law and that it is reasonable to conceive of the moral law as somehow grounded in it and manifested in the order of its creation.

Although Martin takes the arguments ad seriatim and claims that he could rest his case on an a priori argument that the concept of God is incoherent, he does proceed to consider other reasons as well. In doing so, one could suggest that he is constructing an elaborate *cumulative case for atheism*. In defense of *negative* atheism, he attempts to show both that religious language is cognitively meaningless and that the theistic arguments fail to provide any reason for thinking that God exists. "Although a conclusive case cannot be made for negative atheism, if a good case can be made for supposing that belief in God should be based on reason and that all the available reasons for believing in an all-good, all-powerful, and all knowing being are inadequate, negative atheism in the narrow sense will be justified as much as it can be in relation to our present knowledge."[56] In defense of *positive* atheism he advances the case that God is the sort of entity that could and should have provided evidence for his existence. Not only is such evidence lacking; the presence of evil presents a strong argument in favor of atheism.

Our point is that when considering arguments for or against theism, the case should not rest on one piece of evidence. As prosecutors would be foolish to rest their case on one piece of evidence, so those who would argue for theism or for atheism would be ill advised to justify their view by one piece of evidence or one criticism.

THE GOD OF RELIGION AND THE GOD OF PHILOSOPHY

Martin's second objection raises the important question whether the necessary, purposive being to which the arguments point is to be identified with the God of religion. His point, with which the theist might agree, is that if we are looking for the God of the Bible or the Koran to emerge from the arguments, we will be disappointed. The arguments at best yield the concept of a being that has distinctively philosophical rather than specifically religious properties. The necessary being of the arguments has not been shown to be personal, loving, worthy of worship, or concerned for our salvation. Can, then, the necessary being of the philosophers be identified with the God of religious believers?

One way theists can explore this is by what might be termed the *method of correlation*. This involves correlating the properties of the philosophical necessary being with those of the God of a particular religious tradition. Three steps are required. First, the characteristics of this necessary being must be determined. For example, it might be held to be an eternal, conscious intelligence, creatively and purposively involved in the world. Some hold that other properties, like omnipotence, omniscience, and goodness, follow from these properties. The second step is to choose a particular religious tradition and see how its Reality is described. What properties are appropriate to it? Is it held to be a conscious, purposive being, causally related to a contingent world separate from itself? Third, what properties in the two lists are consistent, inconsistent, or not duplicated? Where the lists are consistent, there is good reason to believe that they describe the same being. Where the lists are inconsistent (for example, the cosmological argument supports a dualist tradition, in which God is separate from the world, rather than a monistic or pantheistic tradition), further thinking on the part of both scholar and believer is required. Where the lists have unrelated properties (for example, the theistic arguments do not speak of a personal, loving, trinitarian being who cares about the creation), one might explore whether these properties might be derivable from the theistic arguments or at least consistent with the properties that do follow.

Whatever one concludes about the relation between the ultimate of the theistic arguments and the God of religion, it is important to note that what is at stake is a conflict or correlation not between two beings but between two conceptions of God. When seen from this perspective, the work of philosophers and that of theologians can complement each other. It is safe to say that most philosophers remains skeptical about the success of the theistic arguments, while some think that a good, cumulative for atheism can be constructed. However, for some the cumulative case of natural theology provides grounds for thinking that belief in God is reasonable. In the latter case, it is the task of theologians to put this belief in a larger, salvational, revelational context.

STUDY QUESTIONS

1. How would you argue for or against the view that one needs evidence to believe in God? If evidence is needed, who has the burden of proof, and why?

2. If you believe in God, to what evidence do you appeal to support your belief? If you do not believe in God, what argument would you give against God's existence? Carefully evaluate the strength of the arguments you give, noting the possibly problematic premises.

3. Present Anselm's ontological argument? What argument would you give to critique its central thesis that existence is a perfection, and how might a defender of the argument reply?

4. How is the contemporary version of the ontological argument similar to and different from Anselm's version? What is one of its strengths and one of its weaknesses?

5. What are the similarities and differences between the *kalam* and atemporal versions of the cosmological argument? Take one of the versions and note its critical premises, giving arguments either in support or in criticism of those premises.

6. What are the similarities and differences between the analogical and the modern inductive versions of the teleological argument? Does the teleological argument beg the question in assuming that there is order in the universe?

7. What is Gould's argument against the inductive form of the teleological argument? What is Swinburne's reply? Which do you find more convincing, and why?

8. Attempt to lay out formally the moral argument for God's existence (as we did for the ontological and cosmological arguments). Then proceed to evaluate each of the premises for its truth.

NOTES

1. George Mavrodes, *Belief in God* (New York: Random House, 1970), chap. 2.

2. Richard Swinburne, *The Existence of God* (Oxford: Clarendon Press, 1979).

3. *Webster's New World Dictionary of the American Language* (Cleveland: World Publishing Company, 1955).

4. Anselm, *Proslogium*, in *St. Anselm: Basic Writings*, ed. Sidney N. Deane (LaSalle, Ill.: Open Court, 1903), chaps. 2–4. [See *PRSR*, Part 4, pp. 145–47.]

5. Gaunilo, "On Behalf of the Fool," in Anselm, *Proslogium*, pp. 148–49. [See *PRSR*, Part 4, pp. 147–50.]

6. Anselm, pp. 158–59.

7. Alvin Plantinga, *God, Freedom and Evil* (New York: Harper & Row, 1974), p. 91 [*PRSR*, Part 4, pp. 152–53.] See also Charles Hartshorne, "What Did Anselm Discover?" in *The Many Faced Argument*, ed. John Hick and Arthur C. McGill (New York: Macmillan, 1967), pp. 330–31.

8. William J. Abraham, *An Introduction to the Philosophy of Religion* (Englewood Cliffs, N.J.: Prentice-Hall, 1985), p. 27.

9. Norman Malcolm, "Anselm's Ontological Arguments," in Hick and McGill, *The Many Faced Argument*, pp. 304–305.

10. Jerome Shaffer, "Existence, Predication and the Ontological Argument," *Mind* 71, no. 283 (1962); reprinted in Hick and McGill, *The Many Faced Argument*, p. 230.

11. Malcolm, "Ontological Arguments," pp. 301–20; Hartshorne, "What Did Anselm Discover?" pp. 321–33; Plantinga, "God, Freedom, and Evil," pp. 85–112 [see *PRSR*, Part 4, pp. 158–63].

12. Plantinga notes that one can dispense with the supposition that necessary existence is a perfection by arguing for the possibility that there exists a being with maximal greatness. A being has maximal greatness in any given world only if it has maximal excellence—which entails omniscience, omnipotence, and moral perfection—in every world. Hence, if God's existence is possible (or if maximal greatness can be instantiated), then God exists necessarily. Plantinga, "God, Freedom, and Evil," pp. 108–112 [see *PRSR*, Part 4, pp. 161–63].

13. Hartshorne is careful to insist that, though this argument establishes God's necessary existence, it does not establish his *actuality* or concreteness. For Hartshorne, God in his actuality has contingent properties; he is not necessarily unsurpassable, immutable, and independent. The ontological argument, then, establishes that God exists, but it does not tell us *how*; it does not give us his content.

14. John Hick, "A Critique of the 'Second Argument,' " in Hick and McGill, *The Many Faced Argument*, pp. 345–46.

15. Thomas V. Morris, *Anselmian Reflections: Essays in Philosophical Theology* (Notre Dame, Ind.: Notre Dame University Press, 1987), p. 12.

16. Michael Tooley, "Plantinga's Defense of the Ontological Argument," *Mind* 90 (1981): 422–27.

17. Thomas Aquinas, *Summa Theologica* I, Q.2, A. 3; *On the Truth of the Catholic Faith* I (Notre Dame, Ind.: University of Notre Dame, 1975), chap. 13. [See *PRSR*, Part 4, pp. 164–66.]; Duns Scotus, *Opus oxoniense*, I, Dist. II, Q. 1, in Allan Wolter, trans., *Duns Scotus: Philosophical Writings* (Indianapolis: Bobbs-Merrill, 1962), pp. 43–51; Bertrand Russell and F. C. Copleston, "A Debate on the Existence of God," in *The Existence of God*, ed. John Hick (New York: Macmillan, 1964), pp. 167–91; Richard Taylor, *Metaphysics* (Englewood Cliffs, N.J.: Prentice-Hall, 1983), pp. 91–99 [See *PRSR*, Part 4, pp. 167–76.]

18. William Craig, *The Kalam Cosmological Argument* (New York: Barnes and Noble, 1979), p. 63. [See *PRSR*, Part 4, pp. 176–78.]

19. J. L. Mackie, *The Miracle of Theism* (New York: Oxford University Press, 1982), p. 94. [See *PRSR*, Part 4, 196–97.]

20. Paul Davies, *Superforce* (New York: Simon and Schuster, 1984), p. 200. [See *PRSR*, Part 4, p. 220.]

21. William Lane Craig and Quentin Smith, *Theism, Atheism, and Big Bang Cosmology* (New York: Oxford University Press, 1993), pp. 182, 121–23.

22. Ibid., pp. 143–44.

23. Ibid., pp. 98–99; Craig, *Kalam Cosmological Argument*, pp. 66–95. [See *PRSR*, Part 4, pp. 178–80.]

24. Aristotle, *Physics* III, 6.

25. Davies, *Superforce*, pp. 192, 191. [See *PRSR*, Part 4, pp. 215, 214.]

26. Craig and Smith, *Theism*, pp. 200–201. We changed Smith's numbering; 9 and 10 are added to finish Smith's argument. See p. 219.

27. Bruce Reichenbach, *Evil and a Good God* (New York: Fordham University Press, 1982), chap. 6.

28. Craig and Smith, *Theism*, pp. 202–203.

29. Thomas V. Morris, *The Logic of God Incarnate* (Ithaca, N.Y.: Cornell University Press, 1986), pp. 77–78.

30. It is important to be clear about this principle. Some have mistakenly interpreted the causal principle to mean that *everything* has a cause of its existence. But then

even the first cause (necessary being or God) must have a cause of its existence, and an infinite regress of causes is inevitable. But, by definition, necessary beings are self-sufficient and self-sustaining; hence, it makes no sense to ask whether they have a cause of their existence. Accordingly, the causal principle invoked is more restricted; it claims only that *contingent* beings must have a cause of their existence.

31. Immanuel Kant, *Critique of Pure Reason*, trans. Norman Kemp Smith (New York: St. Martin's Press, 1929), A606.

32. Swinburne, *Existence of God*, p. 73.

33. Keith Yandell, *Christianity and Philosophy* (Grand Rapids, Mich.: William B. Eerdmans, 1984), pp. 59–60.

34. This argument still differs from the *kalam* argument, for whereas the *kalam* argument asks for an explanation of the universe's *coming into existence*, this argument asks for an explanation of the contingent universe's *existence* and thus is compatible with its eternal existence.

35. William Rowe, *The Cosmological Argument* (Princeton: Princeton University Press, 1975), p. 264.

36. Russell and Copleston, "Debate on the Existence," p. 175.

37. This reply was suggested to us by James Sadowsky. It is also raised by Rowe, *Cosmological Argument*, p. 164.

38. Rowe, *Cosmological Argument*, p. 164.

39. William Paley, *Natural Theology* (Charlottesville, Va.: Ibis Pub., 1986), chaps. 1, 3.

40. David Hume, *Dialogues Concerning Natural Religion* (Indianapolis, Ind.: Hackett, 1980), p. 16.

41. Ibid., Book IV.

42. Sir Fred Hoyle and N. C. Wickramasinghe, *Evolution from Space: A Theory of Cosmic Creationism* (New York: Simon and Schuster, 1981), p. 24. [See *PRSR*, Part 4, p. 206.]

43. John Leslie, "The Anthropic Principle, World Ensemble, Design," *American Philosophical Quarterly* 19, no. 2 (April 1982): 141. For a nontheistic version, see John D. Barrow and Frank J. Tipler, *The Anthropic Cosmological Principle* (Oxford: Clarendon Press, 1986).

44. Stephen W. Hawking, *A Brief History of Time* (New York: Bantam, 1988), p. 125. Though Hawking accepts one version of the anthropic principle, he does not accept the one invoked by the teleological argument.

45. L. Stafford Betty with Bruce Cordell, "God and Modern Science: New Life for the Teleological Argument," *International Philosophical Quarterly* 27, no. 4 (Dec. 1987): 415. [See *PRSR*, Part 4, p. 201.]

46. Stephen Jay Gould, *The Flamingo's Smile: Reflections in Natural History* (New York: Penguin Books, 1985), p. 183.

47. Swinburne, *Existence of God*, p. 138.

48. Ibid., pp. 139, 144.

49. Immanuel Kant, *Critique of Practical Reason* (Indianapolis, Ind.: Bobbs-Merrill Co., 1956), pp. 128–36.

50. Robert M. Adams, *The Virtue of Faith* (New York: Oxford University Press, 1987), chap. 10.

51. C. S. Lewis, *Mere Christianity* (New York: Macmillan, 1943), p. 34. [See *PRSR*, Part 4, pp. 226–27.]

52. For Lewis's argument that no naturalistic account can provide a justification of a moral belief, see C. S. Lewis, *Miracles* (New York: Macmillan, 1960), chaps. 3 and 5. For a naturalistic ethic, see Peter Railton, "Moral Realism," *Philosophical Review* 95 (1986): 163–207.

53. See Alvin Plantinga, "Advice to Christian Philosophers," *Faith and Philosophy* 1, no. 2 (July 1984): pp. 253–71 for one perspective.

54. Michael Martin, *Atheism: A Philosophical Justification* (Philadelphia: Temple University Press, 1990), pp. 97, 100, 152.

55. Basil Mitchell, *The Justification of Religious Belief* (New York: Oxford University Press, 1981), chaps. 3–5.

56. Martin, *Atheism*, p. 39.

SUGGESTED READING

Barrow, John D., and Frank J. Tipler. *The Anthropic Cosmological Principle.* Oxford: Clarendon Press, 1986.

Bertoli, F., and U. Curi. *The Conditions for the Existence of Mankind in the Universe.* Cambridge: Cambridge University Press, 1991.

Craig, William L. *The Cosmological Argument from Plato to Leibniz.* New York: Barnes and Noble, 1980.

———. *The Kalam Cosmological Argument.* London: Macmillan, 1979.

Craig, William Lane, and Quentin Smith. *Theism, Atheism, and Big Bang Cosmology.* New York: Oxford University Press, 1993.

Dore, Clement. *Theism.* Dordrecht: D. Reidel, 1984.

Flew, Antony. *God and Philosophy.* London: Hutchinson, 1966.

Gale, Richard M. *On the Nature and Existence of God.* Cambridge: Cambridge University Press, 1991.

Hallberg, Fred W. "Barrow and Tipler's Anthropic Cosmological Principle." *Zygon* 23 (June 1988): 139–57.

Hartshorne, Charles. *A Natural Theology for Our Time.* LaSalle, Ill.: Open Court, 1967.

Hick, John, and Arthur C. McGill, eds. *The Many Faced Argument.* New York: Macmillan, 1967.

Hume, David. *Dialogues Concerning Natural Religion.* Indianapolis, Ind.: Hackett, 1980.

Kelly, Charles. "Some Arguments Concerning the Principle of Sufficient Reason and Cosmological Proofs," *Thomist* 40 (April 1976): 258–93.

Kenny, Anthony. *The Five Ways.* New York: Schocken Books, 1969.

Leslie, John. "The Anthropic Principle, World Ensemble, Design." *American Philosophical Quarterly* 19, no. 2 (April 1982): 141–51.

———, ed. *Physical Cosmology and Philosophy.* New York: Macmillan, 1990.

Lewis, C. S. *Mere Christianity.* New York: Macmillan, 1943.

Mackie, J. L. *The Miracle of Theism.* Oxford: Clarendon Press, 1982.

Martin, Michael. *Atheism: A Philosophical Justification.* Philadelphia: Temple University Press, 1990.

———. *The Case Against Christianity.* Temple University Press, 1991.

Meynell, Hugo. *The Intelligible Universe: A Cosmological Argument.* Totawa, N.Y.: Barnes and Noble, 1982.

Miethe, Terry L. "The Cosmological Argument: A Research Bibliography." *New Scholasticism* 52 (Spring 1978): 285–305.

Miller, Barry. *From Existence to God: A Contemporary Philosophical Argument.* London: Routledge, 1992.

Owen, H. P. *The Moral Argument for Christian Theism.* London: Allen and Unwin, 1965.

Plantinga, Alvin. *God, Freedom and Evil.* New York: Harper and Row, 1974.

———. *The Nature of Necessity.* Oxford: Clarendon Press, 1974.

———. *The Ontological Argument.* New York: Doubleday, 1965.

Polkinghorne, John. *Science and Creation.* London: SPCK, 1988.

Prevost, Robert. *Probability and Theistic Explanation.* Oxford: Clarendon Press, 1990.

Reichenbach, Bruce R. *The Cosmological Argument: A Reassessment.* Springfield, Ill.: Charles Thomas, 1972.

Robson, John M., ed. *Origin and Evolution of the Universe: Evidence for Design?* Kingston: McGill-Queen's University Press, 1987.

Rowe, William L. *The Cosmological Argument.* Princeton: Princeton University Press, 1975.

Swinburne, Richard. *The Existence of God.* Oxford: Clarendon Press, 1979.

Taylor, Richard. *Metaphysics.* Englewood Cliffs, N.J.: Prentice-Hall, 1983.

CHAPTER 6

THE PROBLEM OF EVIL: THE CASE AGAINST GOD'S EXISTENCE

Fyodor Dostoevsky's (1821–1881) classic novel *The Brothers Karamazov* portrays the reunion of Ivan and Alyosha Karamazov, two brothers long separated by the odysseys of their different lives. Ivan, a university-educated and worldly-wise man turned atheist, seeks to elicit an answer to one of life's most profound problems from Alyosha, who has become a faithful monk:

> By the way, a Bulgarian I met lately in Moscow . . . told me about the crimes committed by the Turks and Circassians in all parts of Bulgaria through fear of a general rising of the Slavs. They burn villages, murder, rape women and children, they nail their prisoners to the fences by the ears, leave them till morning, and in the morning they hang them—all sorts of things you can't imagine. People talk sometimes of bestial cruelty, but that's a great injustice and insult to the beast; a beast can never be so cruel as a man, so artistically cruel. The tiger only tears and gnaws, that's all he can do.[1]

Ivan reveals that he collects stories of such evils, particularly those of the suffering of innocent children. His point is that God—Alyosha's God—is supposed to be mighty and just, but that the world is full of absurdity and injustice, pain and suffering. Ivan insists that he cannot embrace a system of religious beliefs that fails so utterly to make sense of life.

Examples abound of thoughtful people who reject religious belief because of the world's evil. The theologian Eugene Borowitz (1924–) writes of the Holocaust:

> Any God who could permit the Holocaust, who could remain silent during it, who could "hide His face" while it dragged on, was not worth believing in. There might well be a limit to how much we could understand about Him, but Auschwitz demanded an unreasonable suspension

of understanding. In the face of such great evil, God, the good and the powerful, was too inexplicable, so men said "God is dead."[2]

Whether encountered in the indescribable horror of the Holocaust, unrelenting hunger in underdeveloped countries, violent crime in large cities, political corruption, or the desperate suffering of terminal cancer patients—the presence of evil in our world cannot be ignored. Evil in one form or another touches all of us. Some think that theists have no intellectual right to believe in God unless they can somehow square that belief with the existence of evil.

While every major worldview, whether religious or secular, addresses the phenomenon of evil, the problem of evil for Christian theism is very acute. Naturalism, Hinduism, and other philosophies have their own distinctive explanations of what we commonly call evil. But Christian theism involves such strong claims about the moral character and lofty purposes of God that evil becomes a particularly perplexing issue. For centuries, philosophers and theologians have recognized that evil constitutes a serious difficulty for religious faith. In fact, many thinkers hold that the problem of evil is the most potent rational objection to theistic belief, what the German theologian Hans Küng (1923–) has called "the rock of atheism."[3] Just as the preceding chapter explored the major arguments for the existence of God, this chapter considers the problem of evil as constituting a significant case against the existence of God.

It might seem desirable to start with a precise *definition of evil*. Some conceive of *evil* under the theological category of "sin"; others define evil as "finitude"; and so on. However, these definitions already assume a certain theory of evil to be correct and thus bias the discussion from the outset. Therefore, let us leave open the question of definition and proceed with a broad, common-sense notion of evil.[4] After all, people may differ on their definitions of evil but widely agree on what sorts of situations really count as being evil. In philosophical parlance, they more or less agree on the set of instances to which the term "evil" *applies* but may disagree vigorously on what it *implies*. The class of situations to which the term *evil* applies includes, at the very least, extreme pain, the suffering of innocents, physical deformities, psychological abnormalities, character defects, injustice, and natural catastrophes. We may legitimately characterize such phenomena as "negative" or "destructive," since such characterizations are minimal and do not bias the further examination of the problem.

Although we must be wary of importing a more theory-laden definition into the discussion, we may readily classify evils into two broad categories, *moral evil* and *natural evil*.[5] The category of *moral evil* contains the wrongful and hurtful acts as well as the bad character traits of free human beings: actions such as murdering, lying, stealing, and traits such as dishonesty, greed, cowardice. Persons can be held morally accountable for all of these things. The category of *natural evil* covers the physical pain and suffering that result from either impersonal forces or human actions. Included here are the terrible pain and death caused by events like floods, fires, and famines as well as suffering and loss caused by diseases like cancer, tetanus, and A.I.D.S.; defects, deformities, and disabilities like blindness, deafness, and insanity must also be listed among natural evils.

THE LOGICAL PROBLEM OF EVIL

Thoughtful nontheists have made evil the basis of a strong objection to theistic belief. Actually, they have formulated the objection in two distinct ways, the *logical problem* and the *evidential problem*. Critics who advance the *logical version* of the problem allege that there is an inconsistency between certain theistic claims about God and evil. John Mackie (1917–1981) writes that "here it can be shown, not that religious beliefs lack rational support, but that they are positively irrational, that the several parts of the essential theological doctrine are inconsistent with one another."[6] On the one hand, the theist affirms that an omnipotent, omniscient, perfectly good God exists; on the other hand, he affirms that evil exists in the world. The critic, such as Mackie, who advances this version of the problem of evil, claims that these two statements are *logically inconsistent* with each other, that they both cannot be true. Since no person is rationally entitled to believe an inconsistent set of statements, the critic charges that it is not rational to believe both. If the critic is correct, then the theist has made a serious logical mistake and must relinquish at least one of the statements in the inconsistent pair.

Of course, it is not immediately obvious that a statement asserting the existence of God is inconsistent with a statement asserting the existence of evil. If there is a contradiction between them, it must be *implicit* rather than *explicit,* putting the burden on the critic to show exactly how the contradiction arises. Most critics say that some additional statements—or "quasi-logical rules," as Mackie calls them—are needed to make the contradiction explicit. Some additional statements that have been suggested include the following: that an omniscient being knows how to eliminate evil; that an omnipotent being has the power to eliminate evil; that a perfectly good being will want to or have an obligation to eliminate evil; that evil is not logically necessary; and so forth. These statements specify more fully the meaning of key terms. The critic reasons that if God has the knowledge, power, and desire to eliminate evil, and if evil is not necessary, then evil should not exist. Yet the theist claims that evil does exist. This brings to the surface the alleged inconsistency.

The exact statement about evil that critics select gives shape to their particular rendition of the logical problem. The most popular form of the problem concerns the existence of evil per se. However, some critics have been willing to admit that perhaps the *sheer existence* of evil is perhaps not inconsistent with the existence of the theistic deity but have insisted that the *amount* of evil in the world might well be. This variation on the problem, though rare in the literature, depends on conceiving of God as allowing the existence of *some* evil, but not a *great amount*. Other critics have thought that specifically *natural evil* is most clearly inconsistent with the existence of God. This variation depends on conceiving of God as allowing *moral evil* (due to human free will) but not seemingly blind, natural evil. In fact, the philosophical literature contains many formulations of the logical problem, each one employing slightly different statements about evil. What all such formulations have in common is the accusation that theism involves an inconsistent set of statements regarding God and evil and that the theist is thereby irrational in believing them. All formulations of the logical problem focus exclusively on the logical relations holding among the statements that are essential to theism and does not depend on whether these statements are true or false. Clearly, then, each formulation reflects a certain way of construing theistic claims about God and evil.

No contemporary theistic philosopher has been more energetic than Alvin Plantinga (1932–) in trying to rebut the charge of inconsistency. His rebuttal, known as the *Free Will Defense,* offers a way of showing the consistency of the relevant theistic claims. Since the critic alleges that it is *logically impossible* that both God and evil exist, the theistic defender must show that it is *logically possible*. In other words, the defender must show that both claims can be true, though he need not show that they are in fact true. As Plantinga indicates, the general strategy for proving consistency between any two statements whatsoever involves finding a third statement that is possibly true, consistent with the first statement, and in conjunction with the first implies the second statement. The third statement, of course, need not be *true* or known to be true; it need not even be plausible. The statement only needs to be *possible* because the matter of determining consistency between or among propositions has to do with whether they can all be true together, not with whether any one or all of them are in fact true. What the Free Will Defender must do therefore is to find a statement that meets these conditions.[7]

Plantinga thinks that the ideas of contemporary logicians about *possible worlds* provide a method for discovering the needed statement. A possible world is simply a total possible state of affairs, a total possible way things could have been. Plantinga's search for the third key statement begins with a description of a possible world, a brief scenario of human freedom in relation to divine omnipotence:

> A world containing creatures who are sometimes significantly free (and freely perform more good than evil actions) is more valuable, all else being equal, than a world containing no free creatures at all. Now God can create free creatures, but he cannot *cause* or *determine* them to do only what is right. For if he does so, then they are not significantly free after all; they do not do what is right *freely*. To create creatures capable of *moral good,* therefore, he must create creatures capable of moral evil; and he cannot leave these creatures *free* to perform evil and at the same time prevent

them from doing so. God did in fact create significantly free creatures; but some of them went wrong in the exercise of their freedom: this is the source of moral evil. The fact that these free creatures sometimes go wrong, however, counts neither against God's omnipotence nor against his goodness; for he could have forestalled the occurrence of moral evil only by excising the possibility of moral good.[8]

Plantinga extracts the requisite third statement from the heart of this story: God is omnipotent and it was not within his power to create a world containing moral good but no moral evil. The claim here is that it is *possible* (or possibly true) that God would create a world of free creatures who choose to do evil. In other words, for any world God might create, populated by whatever free creatures, it is not within God's power to bring it about that those significantly free creatures never go wrong.[9] And this new statement, together with one asserting the existence of God, implies that evil exists. It can now be seen to be *possible* for both God to exist and for evil to exist. Thus, the critic's charge—that it is *not possible* for both God and evil to exist—is refuted.

J. L. Mackie, Antony Flew (1923–), and other critics raise a formidable objection to Plantinga's ploy. Arguing that it is *logically possible* that there could be a world containing significantly free creatures who always do what is right and that God's omnipotence is the power to bring about any logically possible state of affairs, they conclude that God could have created a world containing free creatures who always do what is right. There is surely no contradiction in the description of such a situation. But if the critics are right about this, then the Free Will Defense is mistaken. As Mackie queries, "Why could [God] not have made men such that they always freely choose the good?"[10] After all, God is all-powerful.

Plantinga's reply to Mackie's objection involves sophisticated reasoning about the logic of omnipotence and freedom that is reminiscent of certain points discussed in Chapter 4 in this book. Plantinga's reasoning about such matters exhibits more clearly the force of the Free Will Defense. Many thinkers, both theists and their critics, accept the standard definition of *omnipotence* as *the power to bring about any state of affairs the description of which is not logically self-contradictory*. In other words, there are no *nonlogical* limits to what an omnipotent being can do. The theologians and philosophers who accept this definition of omnipotence hold that God has the ability to bring about any *intrinsically possible* state of affairs. God could bring about, for example, white polar bears and pieces of paper that are triangular because they are intrinsically possible, but he could not bring about married bachelors and pieces of paper that are both square and circular, because such things are intrinsically impossible.[11]

However, Plantinga revises the concept of omnipotence to allow for the fact that there are states of affairs that are possible *in themselves* (i.e., intrinsically) but that are not possible *for God* to bring about. This point depends on a proper understanding of the logic of free will. If a person is free with respect to an action, then whether she performs or refrains from performing that action is up to her, *not* God. Although a world in which all persons always freely do what is right is certainly possible, it is not a state of affairs that is within God's power to create; all of the free creatures in that world have to help bring it about by their own choices. The Free Will Defender insists that God cannot *determine* the actions of *free* persons.

However, Mackie and Flew counter that such insistence is based on an *incompatibilist view* of freedom (the position that free will and determinism are logically incompatible), whereas they adopt a *compatibilist view* (the position that free will and determinism, either physical or divine, are logically compatible).[12] The compatibilist typically holds that a person is free in that, if she had chosen to do otherwise than she did, she would have done otherwise; but the compatibilist holds nonetheless that the person was determined to choose in precisely the way she did. According to compatibilists Mackie and Flew, then, God could indeed have created a world containing moral good but no moral evil. In such a world, persons could have chosen, say, to perform only right actions, although all of their choices were determined.

Plantinga responds that free will is not compatible with any form of determinism and thus that God could not create just any world he pleased. He explains that God thought it good to create a world that contains significantly free creatures, beings who, like himself, are centers of creative activity. Plantinga defines very precisely the concept of *significant freedom* that functions in the Free Will Defense: "A person is free with respect to an action *A* at a time *t* only if no causal laws and antecedent conditions determine either that he performs *A* at *t* or that he refrains from so doing."[13] If this is an acceptable definition of freedom, then the Free Will Defense stands. Morally significant freedom is not compatible with any form of determinism. So, while it is possible that there could be a world containing only moral good and no moral evil, whether such a world exists is actually up to the free creatures who inhabit that world and not up to God. Further exchanges between compatibilists and incompatibilists are certainly possible, but many contemporary philosophers believe that the Free Will Defense, with its implicit incompatibilism, is a strong and effective response to the logical problem of evil.

THE EVIDENTIAL PROBLEM OF EVIL

Although the logical problem of evil marks an important phase in the literature on evil, discussion of it markedly diminished during the 1980s. It is fairly widely agreed by theists and nontheists alike that Alvin Plantinga, Keith Yandell (1938–), and other theistic philosophers have cast serious doubt on the viability of all formulations of the logical problem. Critics who still think that evil presents a problem for theistic belief have shifted focus away from the logical version of the problem and have sought to construct a viable evidential version. They have developed what is now commonly known as the *evidential problem of evil,* a challenge to theists to square their theistic commitments with the facts of evil in the world. The allegation here is not that theism is *inconsistent* but that it is *implausible*; the argument rests not on a matter of logic but on the issue of whether theistic beliefs provide a reasonable explanation of what appear to be the facts of evil. In their own ways, a number of nontheistic philosophers—such as Edward Madden (1925–), Peter Hare (1935–), Michael Martin (1932–), William Rowe (1931–), and Wesley Salmon (1925–)—have issued this kind of challenge to the theist.[14] Studying the various renditions of the evidential problem is enlightening, as they differ a great deal in quality and import.

One form of the evidential argument may be drawn from the writings of Wesley Salmon, a form we shall call the *probabilistic problem of evil.* Salmon analyzes the design argument for the existence of a supremely intelligent, powerful, and benevolent deity from the point of view of a frequency (or statistical) theory of probability. A frequency theory defines probability as the relative frequency with which a specified outcome occurs in whole set of trials. Put another way, it determines the probability of a given event as the proportion of events of one kind among events of another kind. The insurance actuary, for example, might want to know the relative frequency with which males of age 40 survive until their sixty-fifth birthday. Out of a large reference class—say, of 100,000 males—the actuary might find that 90,000 survive, or 90 percent.

Salmon interprets the design argument (as expressed by Cleanthes in David Hume's *Dialogues Concerning Natural Religion*) to claim that the universe, an object with a high degree of order, was produced by intelligent design. Salmon states that one comes to this conclusion on the basis of at least rough estimates of prior probabilities—and that these estimates are drawn from our experience. We find a disproportionately large number of orderly things in our ordinary experience, according to Salmon, that arise through mechanical production and exhibit order. He concludes that the probability of the universe's being caused by mechanical production is high, whereas the probability of its being caused by intelligent design is very low. Salmon then states that when the moral attributes of deity (e.g., goodness, love, and justice) are included in the hypothesis being evaluated, the probability drops drastically. Attempting to speak in the vein and spirit of David Hume, Salmon states that the existence of apparently gratuitous evil prevents this universe from being what we would antecedently expect of a being who is benevolent as well as omnipotent and omniscient. What we have here is a way in which a *frequentist interpretation of probability* construes evil to count against claims about the divine creation and design of the world.[15]

Both Nancy Cartwright (1944–) and Alvin Plantinga replied to the probabilistic argument from evil that Salmon included in his treatment of the design argument. Cartwright accuses Salmon of begging the question by comparing our universe as a whole with particular things within the universe that all arose by mechanical production. And she argues that a statistical or frequentist approach is completely inappropriate to treating metaphysical issues, such as that of God's existence.[16]

Plantinga's response was meant to show that no sort of probabilistic argument from evil is promising. He argued that there is no extant theory of probability—*personalistic*, *logical*, or *frequentist*—that can be used to formulate a formidable argument from evil.[17] Among the obstacles facing critics are the inherent troubles and inadequacies in modern probability studies in general (e.g, the lack of any clear criterion for assigning probability to one statement on the basis of another), as well as the temptation for critics to appeal to their own presuppositions in assessing the probability of the existence of God (e.g., the belief that the universe is a completely natural product without a divine creator). While Plantinga exposes numerous weaknesses in attempts to construct an argument from evil in probabilistic terms, he still leaves unsettled the question of whether there might be a more cogent argument from evil that is broadly inductive or evidential in character.

Edward Madden, Peter Hare, and Michael Martin insist that a formidable *evidential argument* is indeed possible, one that reflects more closely the traditional formulation of the argument from evil than does the probabilistic rendition of the argument. They speak of evil as being *evidence* against the existence of God insofar as they believe evil cannot be explained on a theistic account of the world. In their estimation, the evil with which we are all acquainted is not what one would expect if an omnipotent, omniscient, perfectly good God created and superintends the world. For most of these critics, it is not the sheer existence of evil that puts pressure on theistic belief, since *some* evil seems subject to reasonable theistic explanation. Instead, instances of evil for which there seems to be no good theistic explanation are taken to constitute prima facie evidence against the existence of God. Of course, it is generally assumed that an acceptable theistic explanation shows why the evils in question are necessary to some greater good. If no such necessary connection can be identified, then it is typically assumed that the evils in question are pointless or gratuitous. We will have more to say about this later.

In this form of the evidential argument, theism is treated as a large-scale hypothesis or explanatory theory that implies specific consequences for the way the world should be. If theism is true, then we would legitimately expect the world to turn out a certain way. Of course, complex global hypotheses seldom directly imply definite consequences on which to base our expectations, unless they are augmented by additional assumptions. In the case of the theistic hypothesis (i.e., that a certain kind of deity exists), no clear consequences follow regarding the state of evil in the world unless we supplement the hypothesis with some other statements. Such statements, at the very least, would have to specify God's disposition toward evil.

A fundamental assumption that many critics introduce here, and that theists often accept as well, is that *God would prevent or eliminate the existence of any pointless or meaningless evil.* There are different ways of expressing the assumption, but this formulation will do for present purposes. William Rowe, for example, states that such a claim "seems to express a belief that accords with our basic moral principles, principles shared by both theists and nontheists."[18] Terence Penelhum (1929–) writes: "It is logically inconsistent for a theist to admit the existence of a pointless evil."[19] On this basis, critics reason that, if God exists, we should expect no pointless or meaningless evil in the universe. Yet critics believe that pointless or meaningless evil does appear to exist; the reasons are very compelling for believing that it does. They conclude that the theistic position does not adequately explain the way things are by virtue of linking evils with offsetting or justifying goods. Thus, the evidence seems to disconfirm theism.

Both theists and their critics have traditionally thought that the key to the success or failure of the evidential argument from evil is its factual premise—the claim that pointless evil exists. Keith Yandell, a theist, writes that "the crucial question is whether it is certain, or at least more probable than not, that there is unjustified evil, whether natural or moral."[20] William Rowe, a critic, agrees that whether the theist can overturn the evidential argument depends on finding "some fault with its [factual] premise."[21] On one side, theists have typically argued that all evils are somehow justified or meaningful and thus that the factual premise must be rejected. They have developed sophisticated theories explaining how certain sorts of greater goods are connected to evils that might at first appear gratuitous (e.g., suffering builds character). Some theists who address this matter remind critics that their judgment about some evil's being gratuitous is entirely fallible and that they cannot prove conclusively that there is gratuitous evil, and so on. On the other side, critics have supported the factual premise by pointing out that there are cases of evil in which all available theistic explanations seem to break down and that the prospects are dim that any adequate explanation will be found.

Perceptive critics have even pressed the point that some cases of evil are so extreme that we cannot even sensibly imagine what sorts of justification they could ever have. Thus, as Rowe asserts, "There exist instances of intense suffering which an omnipotent, omniscient being could have prevented without thereby losing some greater good or permitting some evil equally bad or worse."[22] To establish this claim, Rowe develops a story about a fawn being trapped in a distant forest that has caught on fire during a lightning storm. The fawn is horribly burned, suffers for days, and finally dies. Rowe then says, "There does not appear to be any greater good such that the prevention of the fawn's suffering would require either the loss of that good or the occurrence of an evil equally bad or worse."[23] For Rowe, the fawn's tragic situation is apparently pointless; it is unreasonable to believe that it serves any approvable purpose.

Rowe's position prompted Stephen Wykstra (1949–) to enter the fray over the factual premise—i.e., whether it is reasonable to believe that all evils are connected to some greater goods or whether it is reasonable to believe that some evils are pointless. Wykstra challenges Rowe's claim that it "does not appear" that there are goods that justify the evil in question. Wykstra contends that accepting an *appearance-claim* in a given situation is warranted only when it is reasonable to believe that, given our cognitive faculties and our use of them, the truth of the claim would be discernible by us.[24] He proceeds to explain that he understands traditional theism to maintain that God's knowledge is above human knowledge. Wykstra concludes that it is not reasonable to think that, if there is some justifying good for a given evil, we would know it or that it would be apparent to us—i.e., that we would have "reasonable epistemic access." Using what many take to be a clear implication of theism, Wykstra concludes that Rowe is not justified in thinking that evils have no point simply on the basis that they do not "appear" to us to have a point. On Wykstra's interpretation of a theistic universe, there is no guarantee that we would know of the goods connected to the evils we witness.

Rowe replied that Wykstra's "principle of reasonable epistemic access" is not deducible from restricted theism (the claim that an omnipotent, omniscience, omnibenevolent deity exists and created the world) but is deducible only from some version of expanded theism (restricted theism plus other claims from a particular religious tradition).[25] He suggests that Wykstra has smuggled in additional claims beyond those warranted by restricted theism, claims regarding the inscrutibility of divine purposes, the limitations of human cognition, and so on. Thus, Wykstra's case fails as a defense of restricted standard theism, which was the position originally being debated. Rowe grants that Wykstra might succeed if he were defending a particular version of expanded standard theism that explicitly contained such additional claims. However, not all theistic religious traditions (forms of expanded standard theism) insist on such a great gulf between divine and human knowledge. Indeed, many of these traditions place more emphasis on the fact that humans have divinely created capacities to comprehend something of the personal and moral meanings in the universe, including those connected to evil and suffering.

It seems clear that the debate between theists and nontheists on the status of the factual premise in the argument from gratuitous evil will continue for quite some time. It may seem that theists and critics have reached a deadlock on the truth of the factual premise, a rational stalemate, with each side being able to think of a countermove to the other. However, many thinkers believe that a stalemate—if that is the net result—works to the advantage of the critic. After all, it is the theist who advances certain claims about the existence and nature of God, which he typically believes to entail still other claims about the ways God deals with the world. Then, the critic points out that the theist encounters serious difficulties in showing how such claims make sense of some very serious evils. The critic is thereby warranted in urging that the evidential problem of evil certainly reduces the credibility of the theist's position. Of course, in seeking to make a total rational assessment of theism, one would have to take into account other criticisms besides the problem of evil, as well as any positive support, such as the traditional theistic arguments. Since most critics think that the problem of evil is effective and that the traditional arguments are bankrupt or at least unconvincing, they claim to be justified in rejecting theism. A total assessment here would also have to consider the position of Reformed epistemology (thoroughly discussed in Chapter 7), a position that can be interpreted as eliminating the presumption that the theist is rationally obligated to give a theodicy.

Seeking a different way to rebut the evidential argument from evil, some theists have advocated the acceptance rather than the rejection of its factual premise.[26] They defend the factual premise on both *philosophical* and *theological* grounds. Along philosophical lines, they endorse the legitimacy of presuming the general reliability of our ordinary moral judgments, and they point out that we judge much evil in the world to be utterly pointless. Shifting to theological grounds, these theists also support the factual premise by indicating that a standard tenet of traditional Christian theism is that God created humankind with basically trustworthy rational and moral faculties. From this they conclude that it may be unwittingly inconsistent for theists to claim that the human experience of gratuitous evil is regularly and systematically mistaken. They do not intend to suggest that every judgment about an evil is correct but to admit that the weight of human experience has a bearing on the question of gratuity.

If the factual premise is not rejected, then theists must find something wrong with the generally unquestioned theological assumption that God would not allow gratuitous or pointless evil. Obviously, theists cannot remain theists and surrender the standard divine attributes. But some theists are beginning to think that the assumption that God allows no gratuity is very questionable. If theists can convincingly argue that there is a place for pointless evils within a theistic conception of the world, then they stop the evidential argument from going through.

One line of argument for gratuitous evil within a theistic universe traces out the ramifications of significant free will. Plantinga has argued that evil is possible in a theistic universe that contains morally free creatures. We can extend this point, saying that if the range of free choices available to free creatures is to be really significant rather than trivial, then creatures must be capable of the highest goods as well as the most terrible evils. For God to limit the possibility of very serious evils is to limit the range of free choice. It would seem that significant freedom involves the ability to bring about utterly meaningless evils, a risk inherent in God's program for humanity. To preserve the value of human freedom and its potential goods, God must allow the possibility of horrible evils. The *actuality* of many evils is not necessary to any greater goods; such goods could have existed without such evils being actual. But the *possibility* of these evils is necessary to the preservation of significant free will. If God narrows the scope of free choice in order to eliminate the possibility of such evils, the moral enterprise is robbed of much of its importance.[27]

If this way of drawing out the implications of Christian theism is essentially correct, then the critics' assumption—that God would not allow gratuitous evil—can be rejected. What appears to be gratuitous or pointless evil is evidence against theism only if it is assumed that the theistic deity would not allow it. Thus, it looks as if there is a way, deserving of much more discussion, of accepting the factual premise of the evidential argument from evil and still rejecting its conclusion.[28]

DEFENSE AND THEODICY

We have learned a lot from discussions of the *logical* and *evidential* problems of evil. Among other things, we have been able to sharpen the distinction between the two different versions of the problem and, likewise, to sharpen the distinction between two types of response. In response to the *logical problem, defense* was developed to establish that a given formulation of the argument fails, that it does not show theism to be inconsistent. Some theistic philosophers even extended the notion of defense to all probabilistic formulations of the evidential argument, showing that they fail to establish that theism is improbable. A defense is not concerned to offer an account or explanation for God's permission of evil that is credible, probable, or true. Technically, a defense is concerned only with neutralizing the charge that theism is inconsistent or that it is improbable. For quite some time, defense was a major preoccupation among theists. Antitheistic critics would formulate new variations of their objection from evil, which would in turn call forth innovative permutations of theistic defense. We have already seen the effectiveness of defense against the logical argument of Mackie and the evidential argument of Salmon. Yet defense never demands from theists any plausible explanation of evil.

As the success of Plantinga's Free Will Defense became widely acknowledged, discussion of the logical problem of evil gradually diminished, and discussion of the *evidential problem* increased. This trend was accompanied by a renewed interest in the prospects of *theodicy,* as opposed to defense. The evidential problem of evil came to be understood as a challenge for the theist to give a reasonable, credible account of theistic belief vis-à-vis evil in the world. In the eyes of many philosophers, defense was not sufficient for this purpose. Interest was renewed in the traditional project of *theodicy* as the attempt to give a reasonable explanation of why God allows evil in the world.

Some early disputes over the viability of theodicy raised questions about whether it was possible, or at least about the exact expectations it would be able to meet. For purposes of following the evolution of contemporary discussions of theodicy, let us consider two interesting and important objections. The first objection is that theodicy is a priori impossible.

Assuming that theodicy depends on knowing God's reasons for evil, some philosophers emphasized the disparity between the divine mind and finite human minds. Then they conclude either that we could not definitively know God's reason for a particular evil (e.g., the death of a close friend or some major catastrophe) or that we could not sketch, even in a broad and general way, a theistic understanding of the world in which evil makes sense.[29] We might grant the former point, but it is not obvious that the second, stronger claim is correct.

There are many Christian theists, by contrast, who do not construe the teachings of their faith (its Scriptures, doctrines, creeds, and all that they imply) to preclude theodicy. These theists argue that the Bible and historic church teachings affirm that it is God's good pleasure to give believers, and perhaps humanity in general, glimpses of divine purposes for the world. The basic materials for theodicy, then, can be extracted from these glimpses of God's purposes that come through the basic teachings of the faith, as well as through reflection on the human condition. Of course, it is not simply the issue of theodicy into which Christian theists claim to have some insight; they routinely declare that the teachings of their faith provide adequate, though not exhaustive, information on such important subjects as God's general purposes, the divine attributes, the significance of human life, the meaning of the incarnation and atonement, and so forth. Hence, it would be odd indeed for theistic believers to think that their central religious beliefs generate no implications whatsoever for the issue of evil. Thus, on this rendering of theism, the possibility of theodicy cannot be ruled out in principle.

The second contention—that theodicy is in principle unnecessary—is implicit in Plantinga's "Reformed objection to natural theology"[30] as well as in his "Reformed epistemology."[31] Since traditional *theodicy* is closely associated with the same impulse that motivates *natural theology*, Plantinga's criticism of natural theology (as a means of justifying religious belief) and his endorsement of Reformed epistemology (as a positive alternative to natural theology) may be applied to the enterprise of theodicy. Traditional natural theology and theodicy endeavor to show that belief in the existence of the theistic deity is entirely rational according to a certain conception of rationality. In order to accomplish this task, traditional theists consider the alleged evidence for and against the existence of God, seeking to show that the positive evidence outweighs the negative.

We discuss Reformed epistemology and related matters more completely in Chapter 7. Let us say here, however, that the Reformed objection to natural theology and, by extension, to theodicy is that these activities rest on a mistaken model of what it means to be *rationally entitled* to hold a belief. The model stipulates that we be able to give *arguments* or *evidence* for our belief. Many theists engage in natural theology and theodicy, then, in an effort to supply *arguments* and *evidence* for their religious beliefs. Plantinga tries to show that rational persuasion depends upon the theist and the nontheist sharing enough beliefs in common such that these beliefs could function as premises in a viable theistic argument. Since the nontheist does not accept many of the premises that the theist uses, she need not accept the conclusion of the theist's argument. In providing an alternative to the whole enterprise of argumentation in order to be rationally warranted in holding theistic belief, Plantinga tries to show that the theist can be rationally justified in accepting religious beliefs as *basic* (i.e., without argument). Reformed thinkers have argued that, like perceptual beliefs and memory beliefs, religious beliefs (under the right conditions) may be *properly basic.*[32] According to Plantinga, the nontheistic critic—also working from the same mistaken model of rational belief—has no grounds for demanding that the theist produce arguments and evidence to support belief in God, and the theist has no automatic obligation to supply such support. We can see how this line of reasoning renders the twin enterprises of natural theology and theodicy unnecessary.[33]

Reformed epistemologists deserve credit for showing that there are some contexts in which it is appropriate for a person to adopt certain beliefs without giving discursive arguments for them. For example, it would not be fitting to demand anything resembling a comprehensive natural theology or a systematic theodicy from an intellectually unsophisticated believer or from a believer actively engaged in religious worship. Yet there seem to be other contexts in which arguments are either very appropriate or even required. In such contexts, believers might try to produce theistic arguments for the existence of God and perhaps a theodicy to account for why evil does not militate against the existence of God. Although Plantinga admits that there might be circumstances in which arguments are not inappropriate (e.g., to meet an objection to his theistic belief), he maintains that such argumentation is secondary to the more immediate and basic way of believing in God.

Not all theistic thinkers agree with what we have posed as the Reformed objection to theodicy. For example, developing or advancing a theodicy seems completely justified to theists who construe the dialectical context of rational debate and discussion in a certain fashion. The theist might see himself not as asserting an isolated claim—such as "God exists"—but rather as advancing a whole set of logically interrelated claims regarding God's nature and purposes. He might even look at the single claim "God exists" as being invested with this larger interpretive scheme, as entailing all sorts of detailed claims about the divine nature. He maintains that the whole system of beliefs that constitute his understanding of theism offers a correct interpretation of the important features of human life and the world at large. The dialectic develops, then, when the critic alleges that this theological interpretation has difficulty accounting for evil. The theist responds by trying to elucidate and explain how his theological beliefs make sense of evil. Here the critic is not being eccentric or unfair to request that the theist make sense of his own belief in God, particularly by tracing out its ramifications for the issue of evil.

While restricted standard theism may offer some minimal directions in which theodicies might be developed, versions of expanded standard theism contain numerous additional themes that supply raw materials from which theists can draw strategies for theodicy. Different versions of Christian theism augment standard theism with specific doctrinal statements and the like, making for a richer pool of ideas. We could say the same, for example, about the way Judaism might augment restricted standard theism. Staying with our example of Christian theism, some might even argue that it already contains at least an implicit theodicy from which a more deliberate and self-conscious theodicy might be constructed. Of course, there is no guarantee that all Christian theists will work out the implications of their position in exactly the same way or that they will find sufficient common ground to persuade all critics. But it is now clear that the argument that theodicy is inappropriate or unnecessary is not sound.

Another context in which theodicy certainly seems appropriate is that of the search by theists for better understanding of their own theological beliefs. Even if we grant that they may be entitled to accept belief in God as basic under certain conditions, it is naive to think that life's experiences will never invite deeper reflection upon that belief, reflections that include questioning as well as reaffirmation. By engaging in this kind of reflection, thoughtful theists explore the implications of their unique theological perspective for a large number of important issues—moral crises, the worth of certain humanitarian projects, the hope of life after death, and the presence of evil. Thus, it is quite legitimate for theists to try to formulate some reasonable understanding of evil for themselves, and whatever understanding they obtain provides a measure of theodicy.

Over time, discussions about the viability of theodicy—whether it is impossible or unnecessary—have generally been seen as settled in favor of theodicy. Subsequent discussions on the level of metatheodicy have focused more on questions about exactly how we should conceive of the project of theodicy. For example, how much conceptual work can or ought theodicy to accomplish? How aggressive or ambitious does theodicy need to be? Is theodicy meant to suggest merely possible reasons for God's permission of evil, or is it committed to coming up with good, rationally plausible explanations for evil? Does the theodicist have to be able to provide God's reasons for individual cases or to sketch a relevant theistic explanation for large classes of evils? And where are the appropriate building blocks for theodicy to be found—in restricted theism or in some version of expanded theism? What role does our particular moral theory and even our general sense of life play in the creation of theodicy? While these questions in metatheodicy continue to be debated, the past couple of decades have witnessed a notable increase in actual theodicies that are proposed. Some theodicies seem to be rather narrowly focused, playing on a particular theme. Other theodicies are more comprehensive, usually weaving together various themes to provide a broad and systematic explanation for evil. In the next few pages, we rehearse and evaluate samples of each type of response.

THEMES IN THEODICY

Even a cursory review of the literature in theodicy over the centuries reveals a number of themes or insights that keep turning up again and again. These themes, which are taken to emerge from traditional theistic commitments, often arise in discussions among nonphilosophers as well, showing that they have broad appeal. We devote attention to several of these themes here, some because they involve worthwhile insights and others because they they make instructive mistakes.

One popular approach contends that evil is a *necessary contrast* to the good. The argument typically runs as follows: just as we learn what the color yellow is by experiencing the contrast between it and other colors, experiencing evil allows us to understand and properly appreciate the nature of goodness. While this theistic response has a certain point, it encounters enormous difficulties as a comprehensive explanation for evil. It seems that a much smaller amount of evil than we actually have would suffice to help us understand the good. Surely, we humans could get the point without all of the terrible suffering and catastrophe that occurs in our world.

Another approach that has had some uptake among religious believers is that evil is *punishment* for wrongdoing. For example, in the Old Testament book of Job, the "comforters" insisted that Job was suffering because he had sinned. They held the principle that God rewards the righteous with health, wealth, and progeny but punishes those who sin with sickness, misfortune, and loss. Yet the patriarch Job objected that he had not done anything to merit his suffering. In perceiving that the world is much more complex than the comforters' simplistic theory envisioned, Job realized that a person must have purer motivation for serving God than merely to earn reward or avoid punishment.[34] Besides, the punishment theory, when presented as a comprehensive theodicy, flirts with sheer absurdity in cases such as the death of innocent infants or the tragic destruction of the population of an entire village. This is not to deny that some people might employ the punishment theme as a partial theodicy to explain some evils.

A very interesting, but more complicated, theme aimed at explaining evil is embodied in the claim that this is the *best of all possible worlds*. In the eighteenth century, Gottfried Wilhelm von Leibniz (1646–1716) reasoned this way: a perfect God has the power to create any possible world; being perfect, God would create the very best possible world; no creaturely reality can be totally perfect but must contain some evil; so, God created a world possessing the optimum balance of good and evil.[35] Obviously, some goods are made possible only by the presence of evil (e.g., compassion is made possible by witnessing suffering; fortitude is made possible by hardship). This means that God had to weigh the total value of all possible worlds and create the one in which the evils contributed to that world's being the very best one.

Although best-of-all-possible-worlds theodicy invites long and sustained discussion, several problems immediately surface. First, the concept of a best possible world may well be logically incoherent, just as the concept of the highest possible integer is logically incoherent. There simply is no end to the system of integers. Similarly, why would we think that there is some best possible world? Second, the Leibnizian approach seems to imply that our world is not capable of improvement, an implication that runs counter to our ordinary moral judgments. The third, and perhaps most serious, problem regards the question of why a good God chose to create a world at all, given that it had to have this much suffering. Put another way, why did God create this world, if he could not create a better one? Remember Ivan Karamazov's poignant question to Alyosha: "If you were God, would you have consented to create the present world if its creation depended upon the unexpiated tears of one tortured child crying in its stinking outhouse to 'dear, kind God'?"[36] The anticipated reply to this rhetorical question is that a morally good being would not create this world at all.

Another type of theme in theodicy may be dubbed the *ultimate harmony* solution. Actually, this view is ambiguous and can be split into two distinct positions: that *all is well with the world from God's perspective* or that *all will be well in the long run*. The first approach, the *all's-well-from-God's perspective position,* can be supported by either of two characteristics attributed to deity. One divine attribute supporting the all's-well view is *omniscience,* God's perfect knowledge. Since God's knowledge of the world is complete, whereas human knowledge is partial and fragmented, only divine judgment about the state of things is ultimately valid. After all, a chord heard in isolation may sound dissonant, but when heard in context it sounds harmonious. The analogy, then, is that only God sees how the totality of events constitutes a favorable arrangement, while we puny humans cannot. Unfortunately, this approach seriously frustrates all human moral judgments, since they are always made from a limited perspective. While historic Christian theism certainly acknowledges the vast superiority of God's knowledge over that of humans, various expanded versions of it draw out the implications of this in different ways. Some versions affirm that finite persons are creatures who bear God's image and can thus make reasonably reliable moral judgments.

A second characteristic of God on which an all's-well view is based is *God's moral perfection.* This line of thought emphasizes the notion that *God's morality is higher than human morality.* So, even if we humans could see the events of the world in total context, we would not apply the same perfect moral standard as God would in appraising them. Thus, objections to belief in God based on what appear to be pointless, unjustified evils are defused. In its strongest form, this position implies that God's ways are so much "higher than our ways"[37] that everything in the world is morally acceptable to God, even though it is not acceptable to many morally sensitive human beings. Obviously, this position once again undercuts human moral judgment, since it implies that our moral judgments must be systematically mistaken. Actually, upon analysis, the concept of a higher divine morality becomes meaningless, since we would not know what such a morality would be, let alone how it could legitimately be used to the advantage of the theist trying to grapple with the problem of evil.

Ultimately, the very disturbing result of the higher-divine-morality approach is that it projects a picture of God as a moral monster, as one whose moral standards are incommensurate with our deepest moral convictions. J. S. Mill (1806–1873) renounced such a notion of God:

> In everyday life I know what to call right or wrong, because I can plainly see its rightness or wrongness. Now if a god requires that what I ordinarily call wrong in human behavior I must call right because he does it; or that what I ordinarily call wrong I must call right because he so calls it, even though I do not see the point of it; and if by refusing to do so, he can sentence me to hell, to hell I will gladly go.[38]

Theists who perceive the force of such criticisms and who understand their own religious tradition as affirming a connection between human and divine morality do not employ the higher morality theme to explain evil. They may acknowledge the perfection of God's morality and the imperfection of human morality, but they do not insist on complete discontinuity between divine and human moral standards. If there is a reasonable presumption in favor of our ordinary moral judgments, then the problem of evil cannot be answered by claiming that all is well according to the divine perspective.

The second distinct approach—the *all's-well-that-ends-well strategy*—does not claim that every evil is presently connected with a context of greater goods. Instead, this approach recognizes that many evils may not presently be linked to greater goods but insists that all evils will eventually result in higher goods in the future, either in temporal life or in eternity. While many of the considerations relevant to an assessment of renditions of the all's-well-in-God's-sight position are also relevant to an appraisal of the all's-well-that-ends-well position, a few additional points must be made. First, while there may be (or may not be) greater future goods to which present evils are connected, it is far from clear how such future goods *justify* the present occurrence of those evils. How, for example, does the fact that an orphaned child develops strong humanitarian motives and becomes a great missionary surgeon in an underdeveloped part of the globe justify, morally speaking, the brutal death of her parents at the hands of murderers? Or, how could the promised bliss and beatitude of heaven justify the excruciating suffering of a cancer victim during earthly life? It is quite a conceptual jump from the notion of a good *outweighing* an evil to the notion of *compensating* for an evil—and a very large jump to the notion of a good *justifying* the existence of an evil. In light of such difficulties, many all-will-be-well advocates simply say that we humans, with our limited powers, do not know how future goods make up for present evils but that God's inscrutable wisdom does. At the very least, there needs to be more serious discussion of the kind of moral theory that bears upon this issue before we can make full sense of what it means for a good to compensate for an evil or for a good to justify an evil.

The preceding solutions have been used to address the problem of evil generally. Nevertheless, it is helpful at this point to consider one theme that addresses specifically the *problem of natural evil*. Perhaps the most important solution to the problem of natural evil is known as the *natural law explanation*. This explanation relies on the notion that it is reasonable to think that, as part of his creative program, God would bring about a natural order. A natural order is a world constituted by objects that operate according to physical laws. The operation of physical laws of all sorts, then, makes possible a host of natural benefits, such as physiological feelings of pleasure or even helpful warnings of pain. Furthermore, a generally stable and predictable natural order supports a moral order in which rational deliberation and choice can take place and in which free choices can be carried out in action. But the possibility of natural evil is inherent in a natural system. The same water that quenches our thirst can also drown us; the same neurons that transmit pleasure can also transmit intense and unbearable pain.

Critics of *natural law theodicy*, such as H. J. McCloskey (1925–), have argued that God could greatly reduce or eliminate natural evils, either by miraculously intervening in the present natural system or by creating an entirely different natural system altogether.[39] Some theists, such as Richard Swinburne (1934–), have countered that to expect frequent divine intervention contradicts both the omni-attributes of God and the concept of a natural system.[40] After all, if God is omnipotent and omniscient, he would create a natural system in which he does not have to intervene frequently; if he is perfectly good, he would create a natural system that is good on the whole. Moreover, the very concept of a natural system implies that it is not frequently adjusted from outside the system, that it runs more or less of its own accord and would be abrogated by frequent divine intervention.

It is also helpful to consider a theme in theodicy tailored specifically for the problem of moral evil. The theme of *free will* is very familar and has been expressed on the scholarly as well as the popular levels. The appeal to free will as a basis for theodicy must be distinguished from the appeal for the purposes of defense. As we have already seen, Plantinga's Free Will Defense merely claims that it is possible that God created creatures with free will. Free Will Theodicy, by contrast, is more aggressive, affirming that it is indeed true that God created significantly free beings. This truth-claim about the creation of free creatures, along with other relevant theistic claims, is used to explain evil in an allegedly theistic universe.

A generic rendition of Free Will Theodicy runs as follows. According to the divine wisdom and goodness, God decided to create morally free beings; God knew that they would sometimes willfully choose to do wrong, but God granted free will anyway because a world of free creatures is more valuable than a world of automatons; God cannot extensively interfere with creaturely free choice because doing so would jeopardize genuine free will.[41] This scenario certainly captures a very important element in the theistic vision of the grandeur and the peril of being human.

Critics have suggested a number of ways in which the free will maneuver needs further justification. For one thing, they ask for reasons that they should accept the *incompatibilist assumption* that supports the free will explanation of evil.[42] After all, there are several compatibilist views of the nature of free will. Even among critics who are willing to concede the incompatibilist assumption, some simply argue that God could have created free human beings with stronger dispositions toward right conduct than they actually have. Doing this would surely have reduced much of the evil brought about by the misuse of free will. Theists typically respond that God has created humans with an inclination toward the good that is as strong as it can possibly be and still remain consistent with freedom of choice. And so the debate goes on.

There are many other responses to the problem of evil, but most of them have either marginal or no importance to the classic theistic tradition in general or to historic Christian theism in particular: evil as an illusion, evil as an absurd element inherent in created reality, evil as caused by demonic spirits, and so on. Many of the responses explored here are sometimes used by theists either as independent theodicies or as elements of larger, more complete theodicies.

SOME IMPORTANT GLOBAL THEODICIES

In addition to identifying specific themes that address the problem of evil, we can also identify broader explanations that weave together various selected themes. These explanations are generally more comprehensive, systematic visions of the God's ways with the universe. Let us call these large-scale visions *global theodicies*. Three of them have become very important in the literature on evil and deserve closer examination: *Augustinian theodicy, Irenaean theodicy,* and *process theodicy*.

The first view we want to treat is *Augustinian theodicy,* which traces back to the early Christian philosopher and theologian St. Augustine (354–430 A.D.). Augustine offered a large-scale vision of reality that brings together several strands of thought. One of Augustine's ideas was that the universe—that is, the whole of God's creation—is good. God creates only good things, and thus every created thing is good in its essence. Evil, then, is not a thing, not an entity. Evil does not, at least metaphysically speaking, represent the positive existence of anything; rather, it is the lack of good, the *privation* of goodness.[43] Unlike God, who is absolute and unchangeable, the universe was created out of nothing (ex nihilo) and is thus mutable or changeable. For Augustine, this explains how its original goodness is corruptible and thus can manifest evil.[44] It is particularly the misuse of free will that allows the entry of sin or evil into human experience. Augustine understood the Christian doctrine of the Fall to specify that an originally perfect creation rebelled against God through Adam's transgression. Augustine goes on to explore how this original sin brought guilt and punishment upon the whole race, how believers will be redeemed by divine grace, and how history itself will climax in the establishment of God's kingdom.[45]

Clearly, the Augustinian-type theodicy has dominated the collective imagination of Western Christendom from the fifth century A.D. onward and provides background for many of the popular Christian answers for the problem of evil even in contemporary times. It has been subject to a great deal of scrutiny. Critics have charged, for example, that Augustine failed to solve the paradox that evil poses in light of his own strong view of the majestic power and unquestionable sovereignty of God. Perhaps one of the most vexing questions is how, on Augustine's account, an originally good and free creature can engage in sin. If human beings once enjoyed an ideal state or "golden age" in which there was no evil, how is it that they would ever choose to do evil? It is well known that, in the end, Augustine recedes into the "mystery of finite freedom."[46]

A second, alternative approach to theodicy can be traced to Bishop Irenaeus (c. 130–c. 202), whose work reflects certain Greek influences and is distinct from that adopted by Augustine and the Latin fathers. John Hick (1922–), a modern-day proponent of *Irenaean theodicy*, points out that it involves a scenario quite different from the one pictured by Augustine. According to Irenaean theodicy, Adam and the original creation were innocent and immature, possessing the privilege of becoming good by loving God and fellow creatures. But it would be an error to think that original innocence can be equated with original perfection. Indeed, it is not clear that God can instantaneously create morally mature persons, since moral maturity almost certainly requires the experience of temptation over time and, according to some, the actual participation in evil. Hence, evil as we know it is to be explained not as a decline from a state of pristine purity and goodness but, rather, as an inevitable stage in the gradual growth and struggle of the human race.

Hick's rendition of Irenaean theodicy is often called *soul-making theodicy* because it paints a picture of God's grand scheme of helping human beings become morally and spiritually mature. On this view, a special kind of environment is required for the whole soul-making process. An environment conducive to personal growth must be one in which there are real challenges, real opportunities for the display of moral virtue, and real possibilities of expressing faith in God. A major component of this environment is a community of moral agents who interact in special ways and even a natural order of impersonal objects that operates independent of our wills. Obviously, in such conditions there is the genuine risk of evil—of failure and ruin, suffering and injustice. Interestingly, Hick even deems it important that the world appear as if there is no God, and evil certainly plays an important role in forming this appearance. For Hick, the potentially atheistic appearance of the world creates "epistemic distance" between creature and Creator, thus making room for genuine faith and trust in God. This point harkens back to the issues of the silence of God and the religious ambiguity of life that we discussed in Chapter 1.

For Irenaean theodicy, God's ultimate plan is the universal salvation of all persons, a process that extends beyond earthly existence and into the life after death. For those people who, for whatever reasons, depart mortal life without having achieved the proper degree of moral maturity (or soulhood, we might say), God pursues his same objective for them in the life to come. God continues his efforts in the afterlife, providing occasions for exercising love and trust, until all persons are brought into the heavenly kingdom. This affirmation of divine persistence completes the progressive, developmental, and eschatological orientation of Irenaean theodicy.[47]

Hick's very famous version of Irenaean theodicy contains elements reminiscent of *free will, natural law, character-building* explanations, as well as some distinctive concepts of his own. Various criticism have been leveled against the different aspects of his view. G. Stanley Kane, for instance, has argued that the "epistemic distance" Hick wants to postulate between humanity and God in order to make room for faith can be maintained at much less cost.[48] Severe moral and physical evils do not seem necessary to give the appearance that God does not exist, since there surely are other ways in which God can conceal his presence.

Hick's view has also been criticized as lacking in empirical support for its central claim: that the world is engaged in a program of soul making. There are enough failures in temporal life alone to cast grave doubt on whether a program of soul making is under way. Surely, there are so many people whose character is ruined rather than developed that severe critics rightly question the effectiveness or even the existence of the soul making process. Moreover, many critics wonder whether the goal of soul making, even if it did succeed in an ample number of cases, could ever justify the means used to achieve it (e.g., great hardship, suffering, catastrophe). After all, we have all heard of persons who became shining examples of humanitarian activity or of moral courage, but many of them had to fight through senseless losses of family members or had to endure severe, prolonged, and involuntary pain. Hick has shown himself keenly aware of this second point and has responded that each person must ultimately decide whether he thinks the soul-making process is worth it.

A third major theodicy emerges from the *process theodicy* of Alfred North Whitehead and Charles Hartshorne. Process philosophy modifies the classical attributes of the theistic God, giving rise to a distinctively different type of theodicy that has gained much attention in the contemporary period. Process thought in general is based on a view of reality as *becoming* rather than *being*, which is a direct reversal of the traditional approach. It is not surprising, then, that the central theme in process theodicy is the concept of change, development, evolution—both in God and in finite creatures. Creatures are conscious, ever-changing centers of activity and experience. God, for process thought, has two natures: God's Primordial Nature and God's Consequent Nature. God's Primordial Nature contains all eternal possibilities for how the creaturely world can advance; God's Consequent Nature contains the experiences and responses of creatures as they choose to actualize some of these possibilities in their lives. As God's Consequent Nature changes in response to events in the creaturely world, God may be also said to change or to be in process.

One key point in process theodicy is the rejection of the classical concept of divine omnipotence, which process thinkers take to be inadequate and laden with fallacies. Process philosophers and theologians deny that God has a monopoly on power or is "infinite in power" as traditional theology affirms. Finite creatures are also centers of power and thus can bring about new states of affairs as well. Process thinkers typically speak of this creaturely power in terms of "freedom," and thus their terminology is, at points, somewhat reminiscent of other, more traditional discussions. The process version of freedom is rooted in the very structure of reality, with each creature having the inherent power of self-determination. Thus, we may say that God has all of the power that it is possible for a being to have but not all of the power that there is. Creatures have some power of their own, power that allows them to choose good or evil possibilities for their lives. God's power, then, can meet real resistance by creatures. According to process thinkers, divine power must be viewed as *persuasive* rather than *coercive*: God can try to lure creatures toward the good and away from evil, but he cannot force them to choose the good. The process exponent David Ray Griffin (1939–) states that God cannot eliminate evil because "God cannot unilaterally effect any state of affairs."[49] Instead, God offers persons possibilities for the realization of good, adjusting his plans appropriately when finite creatures fail to live up to the divine plan and trying to lure them into fulfilling the next set of ideal possibilities, with the ultimate aim of enhancing and enriching their experience.

One intriguing theme in process theodicy is that all positive and negative experiences are ultimately conserved and reconciled in God's own conscious life. Thus, all things can be said to work out all right insofar as God "include[s] in himself a synthesis of the total universe."[50] In the Kingdom of Heaven, God brings about a kind of synthesis of all earthly experiences but does not unilaterally rectify all evils. Typically, process thinkers have not conceived "personal immortality" or "life after death" as central to the defense of God's goodness against the problem of evil, as traditional Christian thinkers sometimes do.[51] Neither is there any final, definitive, eschatological culmination of all things. Thus, for process thinkers, the continual, ongoing synthesis of all experiences in God's own conscious life is the basic hope for the triumph of good and the redemption of the world.

Process theodicy has certainly forced classical theists to rethink and refine their fundamental concepts.[52] But classical theists, as well as some nontheists, have raised a number of serious objections to process concepts as well. For example, the process concept of divine power has come under severe criticism. The process attack on the classical concept of *divine power* has been said to be pure caricature, using such loaded terms as "totalitarian" and "monopolistic." This caricature sets up the an oversimplified "either/or" distinction between *coercive* and *persuasive* power. Critics of process theodicy have suggested that there may even be a range of modes of divine power, such as "productive power" or "sustaining power or "enabling power," many of which are compatible with moral persuasion.[53] Also, there may be within the process model of power a confusion over the "possession of power" and the "ownership of power." With respect to property or things, ownership is exclusive (e.g., if one person has all of the marbles, then others have none). But with respect to power or agency, ownership is not exclusive. One person may have the power to lift the pencil from the desk, but other persons and God may also have that same power. Many classical theists have intended not a monopolistic view of divine power but only one compatible with the possession of some power on the part of finite creatures.

Another general criticism of process theodicy focuses on the concept of divine goodness, declaring that its orientation is essentially *aesthetic* rather than *moral*. If the aims of the process deity are to make creaturely experience richer and more complex, even at the cost of pain and discord, then there is the risk of violating many ordinary moral principles in the process. Classical theology seems to entail that God would not be morally perfect if he caused or allowed suffering in order to attain merely aesthetic aims. Process theists have replied that aesthetic value is a larger, more inclusive category than moral value, a maneuver that appears to make God's goodness unlike anything we are capable of recognizing and approving. Of course, hanging on the issue of whether God is not morally good is the related question of whether he is worthy of worship.

THEODICY AND THE ASSESSMENT OF THEISM

The complete list of specific themes and comprehensive theodicies into which those themes have been incorporated is much longer than we can treat in this chapter. However, the sampling of approaches here begins to acquaint us with the wide scope of moves available to theists and a number of countermoves open to critics.

We can detect one common thread running through virtually all theistic solutions, whether very specific themes or global theodicies: *God (who is omnipotent, omniscient, and wholly good) would design the universe such that evil is necessary to a greater good.* Theists have typically taken a *greater-good approach* as integral to their search for a morally sufficient reason for why God allows evil. For many who think about the problem, it seems to be a deeply held intuition that for an evil to be justified—and for God to be justified in permitting it—the evil must be necessary to a greater good. If it were not strictly "necessary," then a God who is all-powerful, all-knowing, and all-good could achieve the specified good through other means. With this strategy in the background, theistic thinkers have proposed a variety of types of goods and a range of possibilities for how they are connected with evils. The various responses to evil in the immediately preceding pages only hint at the wide spectrum of possibilities. It has been said that the greater-good strategy is the "parent" and that particular theodicies are its "children."[54]

The greater-good schema is the common root of many responses to the problem of evil, whether defensive or offensive in nature. Using a greater-good approach defensively, many theists have long endorsed the Greater Good Defense to undermine all versions of the logical and probabilistic problems of evil. However, greater-good maneuvers have also been employed to articulate full-blown theodicies that are meant to be reasonable and true explanations of why God allows evil. The free will theme, for example, is one that theists have used for both defensive and offensive purposes. For defense, it supplies a *possible* reason that God allows evil; for theodicy, it supplies a purportedly *true* reason. We focus here on the greater-good approach in theodicy.

Many theists and their critics have thought that a morally sufficient reason that God allows evil must relate evil to a good that outweighs it. These theists usually take for granted that no explanation of evil can be acceptable unless it plausibly argues that the evil in question is necessarily connected to a greater good. A wide range of theodicies, then, simply offers different ways of construing what that good is. In effect, they conclude that no existing evils are pointless or gratuitous and, thus, that they do not count as evidence against the existence of God. Here *gratuitous evil* is understood as an evil that is not necessary to the existence of a greater good. Of course, the common insight expressed in some of the most potent antitheistic rebuttals is that at least some evil or some kinds of evil do not seem necessary for a greater good. It seems either that they serve no good purpose whatsoever or that the purpose they supposedly serve is not worth the price.

In the history of debate over theodicy, several important points have been made by both sides. In future debates, perhaps critics could probe more deeply into the question of whether a greater-good justificatory scheme is viable. After all, attempting to justify evil by reference to some good essentially makes the moral weight of the evil depend on an extrinsic factor. It may well be, however, that a more promising line for the critic is to say that some actual evils are intrinsically so negative and destructive that no external good could outweigh them. This certainly is the tone of Ivan Karamozov's remarks to Alyosha with which we opened this chapter. And the writings of Madden and Hare make such a forceful case.

Theists, on the other hand, could more fully explore a distinction between two sorts of greater-good theodicy: one type claims that the *actuality* of evil is necessary to a greater good, and another type claims that the *possibility* of evil is necessary to a greater good. Clearly, many of the unacceptable greater-good theodicies are of the first type. Following this first type of approach, theists have to defend each actual evil or kind of evil by linking it to some actual good or class of goods—an effort that is extremely difficult and probably doomed. Some theists avoid many severe difficulties by denying that God is morally obligated to make each specific instance of evil turn out for the best and arguing instead that God is morally obligated to create or pursue a certain kind of world in which we have the potential for certain goods. A good kind of world would be structured according to certain general policies. Such policies would include the granting of significant freedom to human beings, the establishment of a stable natural order, and so forth. These structural features of God's created order would then make many particular evils possible, evils that may or may not always be connected to particular goods within the world system, either now or in the future. According to this approach, the greater good would be the overall structure of the world order and the values that are generally able to emerge from it. Thus, as long as the theist describes a very valuable kind of world (structured so that free creatures can make significant choices, have the opportunity to develop moral character, and so on), then the existence of such a world might well be seen as worth it.[55]

Ultimately, the dispute over evil is one of several considerations relevant to the rational acceptance or rejection of theistic belief. A reasoned judgment, therefore, must be made in light of all of the relevant arguments for and against the existence of the God of theism. What is more, a final judgment must consider how well the overall theistic position fares in comparison to other worldviews, either religious or secular.

STUDY QUESTIONS

1. Why is the problem of evil so acute for Christian theism? Explore how other worldviews might encounter their own distinctive problems of evil.

2. Carefully distinguish between the two main versions of the problem of evil. What must be the strategy of the critic of theism in pressing each problem? What must be the strategy of the theist in answering?

3. Explain the difference between defense and theodicy. Rehearse some of the arguments that can be given for why theodicy is not viable and some of the arguments for why it is. What do you think?

4. Looking for a way to construe how evil counts as evidence against the existence of God, some philosophers formulated the argument from evil in probabilistic terms. Is this a promising attack on theism? Why or why not? Is there a more promising way to formulate an evidential problem of evil?

5. Explore some of the standard answers for evil as well as full-scale theodicies that have been offered by theists. Which ones do you think are most effective? Least effective? Investigate some of the standard rebuttals to these theodicies which critics have offered.

6. Do you think that any feasible theistic answer to the problem of evil must rely somehow on a greater-good line of reasoning? Why or why not?

7. Explore the subtle distinction, as some theists have, between being committed to the *actuality* of gratuitous evil and being committed to the *possibility* of gratuitous evil.

8. Explore the complexities involved in believing that a proposition *p* is false on grounds that it "does not appear to be the case." What do these complexities teach us about "appearance claims" in general? Apply these lessons to discussions regarding what appears or does not appear to be the case in terms of whether evils in the world are connected to greater goods.

NOTES

1. Fyodor Dostoevsky, *The Brothers Karamazov,* trans. Constance Garnett (New York: Norton, 1976), p. 219. This encounter between Ivan and Alyosha constitutes one of the high points of world literature and deserves careful reading (Book Five, "Pro and Contra," chaps. 3–5).

2. Eugene Borowitz, *The Mask Jews Wear* (New York: Simon and Schuster, 1973), p. 99.

3. Hans Küng, *On Being a Christian,* trans. E. Quinn (Garden City, N.Y.: Doubleday, 1976), p. 432.

4. See this suggestion in Edward Madden and Peter Hare, *Evil and the Concept of God* (Springfield, Ill.: Charles C. Thomas, 1968), p. 5.

5. See John Hick, *Evil and the God of Love,* rev. ed. (San Francisco: Harper and Row, 1978), p. 12; also, Alvin Plantinga, *God, Freedom, and Evil* (1974; repr. ed., Grand Rapids, Mich.: Eerdmans, 1977), p. 30.

6. John Mackie, "Evil and Omnipotence," *Mind* 64 (1955): 200.

7. Alvin Plantinga, *The Nature of Necessity* (Oxford: Clarendon Press, 1974), p. 165.

8. Plantinga, *Necessity,* pp. 166–67.

9. Plantinga's own very detailed argument delves into such concepts as "Leibniz's Lapse" and "transworld depravity." It can be read in more detail in his *God, Freedom, and Evil* or in very analytical detail in his *Necessity,* Part 9.

10. J. L. Mackie, "Evil and Omnipotence," p. 209.

11. More technically, we would say: states of affairs consisting in polar bears' being white, states of affairs consisting in bachelors' being married, and so on.

12. John Mackie, "Theism and Utopia," *Philosophy* 38 (1962): 153–59; Antony Flew, "Compatibilism, Free Will and God," *Philosophy* 48 (1973): 231–44.

13. Plantinga, *Necessity,* pp. 170–71.

14. Madden and Hare, *Evil*; Michael Martin, *Atheism: A Philosophical Justification* (Philadelphia: Temple University Press, 1990), chap. 14; William Rowe, *Philosophy of Religion: An Introduction* (Belmont, Calif.: Dickenson, 1978), pp. 86–89; Wesley Salmon, "Religion and Science: A New Look at Hume's *Dialogues,*" *Philosophical Studies* 33 (1978): 143–76.

15. In order to bolster his frequentist or statistical argument, Salmon contends that a statement such as "An omnipotent, omniscient, perfectly good God exists" has a "very low" numerical probability (a value much lower than .5) in relation to some statement like "Evil exists." Conversely, he seeks to show that, given the existence

of evil, the probability of the statement "An omnipotent, omniscient, perfectly good God does not exist" is high (definitely above .5). See Salmon, "Hume's *Dialogues*," pp. 143–76.

16. Cartwright points out that the probabilistic argument from evil immediately faces the difficulty of specifying the appropriate reference class. Obviously, no person is directly acquainted with a whole class of universes such that we can arrive at a statistical measure of how many of them contain evil relative to how many were divinely created. Therefore, Salmon resorted to comparing the universe with other entities whose origins can actually be observed. But Cartwright contends that this move begs the question in advance by deciding to include entities into the reference class that are all brought about by mechanical production. Furthermore, Cartwright argues that frequentist techniques are wholly inappropriate for treating metaphysical issues, such as that of God's existence. If any type of inductive approach is appropriate, she holds that it would be the employment of experimental methods. She suggests, for example, that we imagine an experimental situation in which a bunch of random parts are thrown into a box and shaken together until they come out as a set of gears finally tuned to some end. Surely the probability of the initial random collection coming out in a highly ordered configuration is as near zero as can be, a conclusion completely opposite the one generated by Salmon's approach.

It would be interesting to explore Richard Swinburne's claim that frequentist techniques are appropriate to issues such as the existence of God. See Swinburne, *The Existence of God* (Oxford: Clarendon Press, 1979), pp. 5–21.

17. Alvin Plantinga, "The Probabilistic Argument from Evil," *Philosophical Studies* 35 (1979): 1–53.

18. Rowe, *Philosophy*, p. 88.

19. Terence Penelhum, "Divine Goodness and the Problem of Evil," in *Readings in the Philosophy of Religion: An Analytic Approach*, ed. Baruch Brody (Englewood Cliffs, N.J.: Prentice-Hall, 1974), p. 226.

20. Keith Yandell, *Basic Issues in the Philosophy of Religion* (Boston: Allyn and Bacon, 1971), pp. 62–63.

21. Rowe, *Philosophy*, p. 88.

22. William Rowe, "The Problem of Evil and Some Varieties of Atheism," *American Philosophical Quarterly* 16 (October 1979): 336.

23. Ibid., p. 337.

24. Stephen Wykstra, "The Humean Obstacle to Evidential Arguments from Suffering: On Avoiding the Evils of 'Appearance,' " *International Journal for Philosophy of Religion* 16 (1984): 85.

25. William Rowe, "Evil and the Theistic Hypothesis: A Response to Wykstra," *International Journal for the Philosophy of Religion* 16 (1984): 95–100.

26. See Michael Peterson, *Evil and the Christian God* (Grand Rapids: Baker, 1982), chap. 4. See also William Hasker, "The Necessity of Gratuitous Evil," *Faith and Philosophy* 9, no. 1 (Jan. 1992): 23–44. This article resulted from a paper read originally at the American Philosophical Association meeting, Cincinnati, Ohio, April 1988.

27. See Peterson, *Evil*, pp. 104–107. Also see Hasker, "The Necessity of Gratuitous Evil," p. 30.

28. The theist who accepts the existence of gratuitous evil on the basis of a sophisticated and highly nuanced version of theism might try a creative and venturesome counterattack. He might argue that the existence of gratuitous evil is evidence *for* the existence of God, maintaining that theism explains the exact nature of

gratuitous evil in our world (e.g., its moral depth, tragic dimensions) is explained better by a theistic, rather than any nontheistic, worldview.

29. For example, Alvin Plantinga makes the former point and at least alludes to something like the second point: "Perhaps God has a good reason [for evil], but that reason is too complicated for us to understand." Plantinga, *God*, p. 10.

30. Alvin Plantinga, "The Reformed Objection to Natural Theology," *Christian Scholar's Review* 11, no. 3 (1982): 187–98 [reprinted in *PRSR*, Part 6, pp. 309–21].

31. Alvin Plantinga, "Reason and Belief in God," in Alvin Plantinga and Nicholas Wolterstorff, eds., *Faith and Rationality: Reason and Belief in God* (Notre Dame, Ind.: University of Notre Dame Press, 1983), pp. 16–93.

32. For an excellent treatment by a Reformed epistemologist that parallels perceptual beliefs with religous beliefs, see William P. Alston, *Perceiving God* (Ithaca, N.Y.: Cornell University Press, 1991). An early paper of Alston's is also reprinted in *PRSR*, Part 1, pp. 20–29.

33. One can readily see why a theist who accepts Reformed epistemology would think that *defense* against the problem of evil is all that is rationally required. The critic advances an argument from evil against belief in God, and the theist defends against it. But the theist need not feel that he needs to have an argument for belief in God. Instead, he can simply take belief in God as basic.

34. Several major passages in the Book of Job indicate his growing awareness that the benefits and burdens of life are not equitably distributed according to merit. For example, chapters 7 and 12 of that biblical book argue that sometimes the righteous suffer and the wicked prosper.

35. Leibniz, *Theodicy*.

36. Dostoevsky, *The Brothers Karamazov*, p. 226.

37. Isaiah 55:8–9 (KJV) reads: "For my thoughts are not your thoughts, neither are your ways my ways, saith the Lord. For as the heavens are higher than the earth, so are my ways higher than your ways, and my thoughts than your thoughts." However, in light of the overall teachings of ecumenical orthodox Christianity, this passage is not best interpreted as meaning that God's purposes are radically alien to anything we could understand, that divine moral standards are completely discontinuous with human standards.

38. John Stuart Mill, selection from *An Examination of Sir William Hamilton's Philosophy* included as an appendix in *Theism*, ed. Richard Taylor (New York: Liberal Arts Press, 1957), pp. 89–96.

39. H. J. McCloskey, "God and Evil," *Philosophical Quarterly* 10, no. 39 (1960): 97–114.

40. See Richard Swinburne, "Natural Evil," *American Philosophical Quarterly* 15, no. 4 (Oct. 1978): 295–301. Also see Bruce Reichenbach, *Evil and a Good God* (New York: Fordham University Press, 1982), chap. 5.

41. See Reichenbach, *Evil*, chap. 4.

42. See, for example, Antony Flew, "Divine Omnipotence and Human Freedom," in A. Flew and A. MacIntyre, eds., *New Essays in Philosophical Theology* (New York: Macmillan, 1955), pp. 144–69. Also see Flew, "Compatibilism, Free Will and God," *Philosophy* 48 (July 1973): 231–44.

43. Augustine, *Enchiridion*, i. 8, 7.

44. Augustine, *City of God*, xii. 1, 6.

45. Augustine, *Confessions, City of God, Enchiridion*.

46. Augustine, *On Free Will*, III. xvii. 49.

47. For the specific way in which John Hick works out this type of Irenaean theodicy, see his *Evil*, Parts 3 and 4.

48. G. Stanley Kane, "The Failure of Soul-Making Theodicy," *International Journal for Philosophy of Religion* 6 (1975): 1–22.

49. David Ray Griffin, *God, Power, and Evil* (Philadelphia: Westminster, 1976), p. 280.

50. Alfred North Whitehead, *Religion in the Making* (New York: Macmillan, 1926), p. 98; also see his *Process and Reality* (New York: Macmillan, 1929), pp. 524–25.

51. We should note that there have been attempts by some process philosophers to provide a process account of personal immortality, life after death. See the discussion of this in David Ray Griffin, *Evil Revisited* (Albany, N.Y.: SUNY Press, 1991), pp. 34–40.

52. See the full-scale discussion of process theodicy in Michael Peterson, "God and Evil in Process Theodicy," *Process Theology*, ed. Ronald Nash (Grand Rapids, Mich.: Baker Book House, 1987), pp. 121–39.

53. Nancy Frankenberry, "Some Problems in Process Theodicy," *Religious Studies* 17 (1981): 181–84.

54. Melville Stewart, *The Greater-Good Defense* (New York: St. Martin's, 1993), p. ix.

55. The four coauthors of this book take this approach. See William Hasker, "The Necessity of Gratuitous Evil"; Bruce Reichenbach, *Evil and a Good God* (New York: Fordham University Press, 1982); David Basinger, *The Case for Free Will Theism* (Downers Grove, Ill.: InterVarsity Press, 1996), chap. 4; Michael Peterson, *Evil and the Christian God* (Grand Rapids, Mich.: Baker Book House, 1982).

SUGGESTED READING

Basinger, David. *The Case for Free Will Theism*. Downers Grove, Ill.: InterVarsity Press, 1996.

Griffin, David Ray. *Evil Revisited: Responses and Reconsiderations*. Albany: SUNY Press, 1991.

————. *God, Power, and Evil: A Process Theodicy*. Philadelphia: Westminster, 1976.

Hasker, William. "The Necessity of Gratuitous Evil." *Faith and Philosophy* 9, no. 1 (1992): 23–44.

Hick, John. *Evil and the God of Love*. Rev. ed. San Francisco: Harper and Row, 1978.

Howard-Snyder, Daniel, ed., *The Evidential Argument from Evil*. Bloomington, Indiana University Press, 1996.

Mackie, J. L. *The Miracle of Theism*. Oxford: Clarendon Press, 1982.

Madden, Edward, and Peter Hare. *Evil and the Concept of God*. Springfield, Ill.: Charles C. Thomas, 1968.

Martin, Michael. *Atheism: A Philosophical Justification*. Philadelphia: Temple University Press, 1990.

Peterson, Michael. *Evil and the Christian God*. Grand Rapids, Mich.: Baker Book House, 1982.

————, ed. *The Problem of Evil: Selected Readings*. Notre Dame: University of Notre Dame Press, 1992.

Plantinga, Alvin. *God, Freedom, and Evil*. Grand Rapids, Mich.: William B. Eerdmans, 1974; reprint ed., 1977.

Reichenbach, Bruce. *Evil and A Good God*. New York: Fordham University Press, 1982.

Stewart, Mel. *The Greater-Good Defense*. New York: St. Martin's, 1993.

CHAPTER 7   KNOWING GOD
WITHOUT
ARGUMENTS: DOES
THEISM NEED
A BASIS?

The French mystic Simone Weil (1909–1943) describes her first experience of God:

> In a moment of intense physical suffering, when I was forcing myself to feel love, but without desiring to give a name to that love, I felt, without being in any way prepared for it (for I had never read the mystical writers) a presence more personal, more certain, more real than that of a human being, though inaccessible to the senses and the imagination.[1]

Simone Weil's experience is all the more striking because there was so little in her background to prepare her for it. She was raised as an agnostic in a secularized Jewish home and (as she says) had read none of the mystical authors who might have led her to anticipate such an experience. Weil, who was trained in philosophy, had studied the arguments for and against the existence of God and found the question undecidable. After her experience, however, she wrote:

> When we are eating bread, and even when we have eaten it, we know that it is real. We can nevertheless raise doubts about the reality of the bread. Philosophers raise doubts about the reality of the world of the senses. Such doubts are however purely verbal, they leave the certainty intact and actually serve only to make it more obvious to a well-balanced mind. In the same way he to whom God has revealed his reality can raise doubts about this reality without any harm. They are purely verbal doubts, a form of exercise to keep his intelligence in good health.[2]

Simone Weil's claim here is both clear and striking. On the one hand, she points out, philosophers raise questions about the "reality of the external world"; we may deal with these doubts intellectually—examine them, seek to refute them, and so on—yet all this leaves completely unshaken our certainty of the reality of the bread we have eaten. On the other hand, philosophers doubt the existence of God and engage in debate using theistic and antitheistic arguments. This is all well and good—fine exercise for the mind, in fact—but for the person "to whom God has revealed his reality" these doubts no more disturb her certainty of his existence than do the philosopher's doubts about the reality of bread and trees and stones.

It is safe to say that most philosophers who have considered the question of God's existence would not agree with Weil about this. Such a certainty, based on experience, as she attests to would often be dismissed as "purely subjective"; such experiences, before we rely on them, need to be confirmed by *rational,* as opposed to purely emotional, considerations. We need, in other words, to look at the question of God's existence in the light of *evidence and arguments*—just such arguments, in fact, as have occupied us in the past two chapters.One very natural way of looking at the matter seems to be this: we estimate, on the one hand, the combined strength of the various arguments for God's existence and, on the other hand, the strength of the argument from evil, as well as other arguments against theism. Then, taking these two bodies of evidence together, we weigh them against each other, and the resulting balance determines whether it is reasonable to believe in God. Thus, if the problem of evil seems to be a strong argument against theism while none of the favorable arguments has much force, then it is rational to reject belief in God, while if the theistic arguments are powerful and the antitheistic arguments can be refuted, belief in God is reasonable and appropriate. Or, it might turn out that the evidence for and against God's existence is quite evenly balanced; in this case, it is appropriate to suspend judgment and neither believe nor disbelieve.

EVIDENTIALISM

This way of looking at the matter has a name; it is called *evidentialism.* It is, as has been said, a rather natural way of viewing the subject—so natural, indeed that many philosophers have taken it for granted without question. Of course, it must be admitted that most ordinary people, including ordinary religious people, do not think this way at all. Most religious believers have never given much thought to arguments for or against the existence of God, and they may not feel that they have missed very much. Even those who have learned something about the arguments—say, in an introductory philosophy course—seldom make a really serious effort to find out how strong the arguments are or to guide their own beliefs by these arguments. They just go on believing, or disbelieving, without troubling themselves much about arguments.

Evidentialist philosophers, however, are not greatly concerned about the fact that most people do not think about God in the way evidentialism considers proper. The sad fact is, the evidentialists tell us, that most people are very far from being rational in the way in which they decide on important beliefs, especially religious beliefs. People believe for a variety of psychological, social, and emotional reasons that have very little to do with whether a belief is supported by evidence or whether it is likely to be true. Fortunately, however, there are a few individuals who do care about reason and truth, who do not want to be guided merely by their emotions, and it is these people who should be our example. They show what it means to be guided by evidence and arguments in determining our religious beliefs.

One of the most important developments in the philosophy of religion in recent years is the appearance of a group of philosophers who sharply reject evidentialism. These philosophers are not fideists in the sense defined in Chapter 3; they do not think that one's ultimate beliefs are immune to rational evaluation. But they maintain that it is possible for religious beliefs to be entirely rational and fully justified *even if there is no evidence supporting these beliefs*. This view is often referred to as "Reformed epistemology," because of the similarity between it and certain ideas that have been prominent in the Reformed, or Calvinistic, branch of Protestantism.[3] But the view itself is not logically tied to this branch of Christian belief; one need not be a Calvinist, or even a Christian, to be a Reformed epistemologist. The three leading exponents of Reformed epistemology are Alvin Plantinga (1932–), Nicholas Wolterstorff (1932–), and William P. Alston (1921–); we shall draw upon each of them in setting out and analyzing the position in the subsequent pages.

CRITIQUE OF EVIDENTIALISM

The first thing we need to do is to understand more precisely what is meant by *evidentialism,* so that we can see why the Reformed epistemologists object to it. Nicholas Wolterstorff presents the "evidentialist challenge" as follows:

> It was insisted, in the first place, that it would be *wrong* for a person to accept Christianity, or any other form of theism, unless it was *rational* for him to do so. And it was insisted, secondly, that it is not rational for a person to do so unless he holds his religious convictions on the basis of other beliefs of his which give to those convictions adequate evidential support. No religion is acceptable unless rational, and no religion is rational unless supported by evidence. That is the evidentialist challenge.[4]

What is so objectionable about this? Unless we are content to be irrational, the requirement that we accept only rational beliefs is hard to contest. And it certainly seems reasonable that in order for religious beliefs to be rational, they must be supported by evidence. Yet there is a problem lurking here, as we shall see.

But we need to be more precise about what it means for a belief to be *supported by evidence.* Many different views about this are possible, but many modern philosophers who are evidentialists have been committed to an epistemological perspective known as *strong foundationalism.*[5] In order to understand this perspective, we must first discuss *foundationalism* and then go on to consider what is distinctive about *strong* foundationalism.

Foundationalists distinguish between two kinds of beliefs that we all have. There are, on the one hand, beliefs that we hold because they receive *evidential support* from other beliefs that we have; these we may term *derived beliefs.* But there are also, it seems, some beliefs that are accepted *without* being supported by still other beliefs; these are our *basic beliefs,* and they form the "basis" on which our entire structure of belief and knowledge ultimately rests.

One may, of course, accept a belief in a basic way (that is, without accepting it on the basis of other beliefs that are taken as evidence for it) when it is quite unreasonable to do so. For instance, one might believe that someone is guilty of a crime simply because one dislikes that person. But there must also, it seems, be some situations in which it is *reasonable and proper* to accept certain beliefs without other beliefs as evidence; those beliefs that it is reasonable to accept without evidence are our *properly basic beliefs.*

Now, a very important question must be answered by any foundationalist: *What kinds of beliefs can be properly basic?* The answer to this question determines what the "foundations" are on which one's beliefs must be built and thus goes a long way towards deciding what the final structure of beliefs will be like.[6]

Now we are ready for the explanation of *strong* foundationalism. What makes strong foundationalism *strong* is just its idea about the sorts of beliefs that can properly be accepted as basic. The guiding idea has been that the properly basic beliefs should be *beliefs concerning which it is impossible, or nearly impossible, to go wrong.* If the foundations are as solid as it is humanly possible to make them, then the belief system erected on them can also be solid and secure. In order to achieve this, strong foundationalists usually require that properly basic beliefs should be of only two kinds: they must be either *self-evident* or *incorrigible.* *Self-evident* beliefs are seen to be true by anyone who understands them; simple truths of arithmetic, such as "1 + 2 = 3," are one example. *Incorrigible* beliefs are those that deal with one's own, immediate experience; examples include "I am feeling pain" and "I seem to be seeing something red." It may or may not be possible to go wrong over such beliefs (that has been debated), but they seem to be about as immune from doubt as any we can imagine. And if all our other beliefs can be built on these foundations, the goal of attaining real, solid, unchallengeable knowledge seems within reach.[7] To sum up, then, we may define the strong foundationalist's position as follows: *A person is rational in accepting a given belief only if that belief is self-evident or incorrigible or is derived from self-evident or incorrigible beliefs using acceptable methods of logical inference.*

From Wolterstorff's talk about the "evidentialist challenge" to religious belief it might seem that evidentialists oppose religion, but this is not necessarily the case. Quite a few evidentialists—such as Descartes (1596–1650), Locke (1632–1704), and Leibniz (1646–1716)—have thought that belief in God's existence, and other typical religious beliefs, are fully capable of being defended in a way that meets the challenge. As time has gone on, however, more and more philosophers have concluded that theism *cannot* be defended in a way that satisfies the requirements of evidentialism. And if that is true, then evidentialism and religion are indeed enemies.

But just what is wrong with evidentialism and strong foundationalism (aside from their possible conflict with theism)? Actually, the answer to this is surprisingly simple: when we apply strong foundationalism to itself it *defeats itself*—or, we may say, it *self-destructs*. (The favorite philosopher's term for this is that this view is *self-referentially incoherent*.) To see what this means, consider the statement of strong foundationalism that was given earlier: *A person is rational in accepting a given belief only if that belief is self-evident or incorrigible or is derived from self-evident or incorrigible beliefs using acceptable methods of logical inference.* Is this statement of strong foundationalism itself self-evident? Not likely!—in fact, many people have understood it and considered it carefully without thinking that it is true. Furthermore, it is not an "incorrigible" report of one's immediate experience; it is not at all like "I seem to be seeing something red." Finally, there is no reasonable way in which this statement could be *derived* from self-evident or incorrigible propositions, so as to be justified in that way. So we get the following, extremely interesting result: *If strong foundationalism is true, then no one is rational in accepting strong foundationalism.* For a strong foundationalist, this situation is downright embarrassing!

There is, however, another problem with strong foundationalism that is equally serious: *If strong foundationalism is true, then we are wrong about most of what we think we know.* This point needs some explanation. Earlier, in explaining foundationalism, we pointed out that the strong foundationalists wanted to have an *absolutely secure basis* on which the structure of our knowledge could be erected. The idea was that, by taking as foundations only beliefs that were immune to doubt, we could secure a foundation on the basis of which our other beliefs could be built up with a very high degree of confidence and certainty.

Unfortunately, this noble project has proved to be a failure again and again. Many of our ordinary beliefs—things, indeed, that we would readily say that we *know* to be true—turn out to be unsupported when tested by these standards. Consider, for instance, this question: How do you know that you have been living for longer than, say, forty-five minutes? It isn't *self-evident* that you have lived longer than that; after all, you might just have been cloned by a very speedy scientist! Nor is this something you can know by an *incorrigible* report of your own experience. You may say that you *remember* having lived for many years past—but how do we know that these are real memories of what actually happened rather than, for example, ideas that were implanted directly in your brain by a scientist?

Furthermore, there does not seem to be any way this belief can be *derived* from other beliefs that are self-evident or incorrigible. Nor is this the only sort of ordinary belief that cannot be justified to satisfy the strong foundationalist's standards. If you are going to take this view seriously, you might have to give up your beliefs that trees, mountains, and other physical objects really exist separate from your perception of them and also your beliefs that other people really have experiences and feelings of their own, as opposed to being preprogrammed robots. But this, surely, shows that there must be something badly wrong with strong foundationalism.

If strong foundationalism is rejected, does this mean that evidentialism must also be given up? Not necessarily; the two views are not logically equivalent. One might accept a version of evidentialism based on a non-classical foundationalism that allows for a broader range of beliefs to be accepted as properly basic; as we shall see in the next section, Plantinga himself adopts a foundationalism of this sort. The Reformed epistemologist, however, would question whether such a liberalized foundationalism can reasonably reject the possibility of properly basic beliefs grounded on religious experience. There can also be a *coherentist* evidentialism. Coherentism rejects the foundationalist's distinction between basic and derived beliefs and holds instead that *all* of our beliefs are justified by the way they "cohere" (fit together in a consistent, well-integrated system) with the rest of our beliefs. We cannot go into the merits of coherentism at this point. It should be noted, however, that some religious belief systems seem to be strongly coherent, so the prospects for showing religion to be irrational based on coherentism do not seem especially bright. In general, the possibility of a version of evidentialism not based on strong foundationalism is one that should be kept in mind for further study.

So far, though, all this is merely negative. Does anything of *positive value* for religion emerge if evidentialism is rejected? For consideration of this matter, we turn to Alvin Plantinga.

PLANTINGA ON PROPERLY BASIC BELIEFS

When the Reformed epistemologists criticize strong foundationalism, we must not suppose that they are rejecting foundationalism as such. They still accept the foundationalist's distinction between basic and derived beliefs, as well as the assumption that there must be *properly* basic beliefs from which all of our other beliefs have to be derived if they are to be rationally justified. What they reject is merely the strong foundationalist's overly restrictive criterion for what can qualify as properly basic beliefs.

But how then shall we decide what beliefs can be properly basic? Plantinga, following Roderick Chisholm, suggests that we should not begin by setting up in advance a general requirement, such as is done by strong foundationalism. Instead, we should begin from the structure of belief and knowledge that we already have, and we should assume provisionally that this structure of belief is pretty much in order—that, as Chisholm says, "we do know most, if not all, of those things that ordinary people think that they know."[8] And we should take our actual beliefs as examples: taking some belief we think to be reasonable and justified, we should ask ourselves whether we hold this belief because it is evidentially supported by other beliefs of ours, or whether it is one that is or could be reasonably held even if it were not supported by any other beliefs as evidence. If the latter is the case, we put this belief down as a *basic* belief and, indeed, as a *properly basic* belief. Examples of the kinds of beliefs that might turn out, through this procedure, to be properly basic might include the following: ordinary perceptual beliefs ("That is a tree over there"), memory beliefs ("I had scrambled eggs for breakfast"), beliefs about other people's thoughts and feelings ("Mary really got angry when you said that to her")—and there are other kinds as well. And when we have carried out the procedure with a number of examples of different kinds, we can begin to get an overall picture of the kinds of beliefs that can be properly basic—that is, of the *foundations* of our structure of belief.

So far, so good. But at this point, Plantinga has a radical suggestion to make: Why should the belief that *God exists* not be part of the foundation? Why should *this* not be one of our properly basic beliefs? The theist, after all, certainly thinks that this belief *is* one that she is rationally justified in holding. And if she finds (as Plantinga thinks most believers in God will find) that it is *not* a belief that she holds because it is justified inferentially from other beliefs, then the procedure just described will lead her to consider it a *basic* and, indeed, a *properly basic,* belief. And why not? What is wrong with this possibility? Is there any reason why "God exists" *cannot* be a properly basic belief? And if it is properly basic, then there is *no need* for the theist to produce proofs or arguments for God's existence in order to be justified in believing in God.

Many philosophers have found this proposal of Plantinga's to be bold and even startling. It raises a great many issues and questions, only a few of which can be taken up here. Note, first of all, that the fact that a belief is properly basic in no way guarantees the *truth* of that belief. One who *actually holds* a particular belief in a properly basic way will think that it is true, of course, but then anyone who holds *any* belief in any way whatsoever necessarily thinks that belief is true. But it is entirely possible for a properly basic belief to be false. For example, you walk into a friend's house and, because of what you are hearing, form the belief that someone is playing the saxophone in the next room. This is a basic belief, not inferred from other beliefs of yours. (You don't say to yourself, "I am hearing something that sounds like a saxophone; usually, when I hear something that sounds like a saxophone, there is a saxophone nearby; therefore, what I am hearing is probably a saxophone." Rather, you just hear the sounds and find yourself with the belief that there is a saxophone in the next room.) Furthermore, you are quite familiar with saxophones and perfectly capable of recognizing a saxophone when you hear one. This, then, is a *properly basic belief.* Nevertheless, your belief turns out to be false—your friend is testing out his new digital stereo system with a recording of solo saxophone music, and the reproduction is so good you could not tell it from the real thing.

In the same way, it *might* be true that "God exists" is a properly basic belief for some person even if God does *not* in fact exist. That a belief is properly basic for a person does not *guarantee* that the belief is true; that is one of the important differences between the strong foundationalism criticized earlier and the more moderate foundationalism embraced by Chisholm and by the Reformed epistemologists. (The other important difference is that moderate foundationalism begins by assuming the general soundness of the structure of knowledge and beliefs we already have; it is not a procedure by which to *replace* or *radically reform* that structure.) But that a belief is properly basic for some person *does* guarantee that the person is *rationally justified* in holding that belief; if "God exists" is properly basic for you, then it is rational for you to believe in God.

There is an objection to Plantinga's procedure here that has been stated forcefully by Gary Gutting (1942–):

> How can a believer just blithely claim that it's utterly obvious that he's entitled to believe without having any reasons for his belief? What of the fact that there are all sorts of honest and intelligent people who've thought a lot about religious belief and simply don't see belief in God as properly basic? . . . As philosophers, we surely have to take as clear cases only those that would be admitted as such by just about any rational person.[9]

Gutting has also said, "Isn't it just common sense to admit that, when there is widespread disagreement about a claim, with apparently competent judges on both sides, those who assert or deny the claim need to justify their positions?"[10]

Plantinga is well aware of this objection, and his response to it is illuminating:

> Criteria for proper basicality . . . should be . . . argued to and tested by a relevant set of examples. But there is no reason to assume, in advance, that everyone will agree on the examples. The Christian will of course suppose . . . that belief in God is entirely proper and rational; if he does not accept this belief on the basis of other propositions, he will conclude that it is basic for him and quite properly so. Followers of Bertrand Russell and Madelyn Murray O'Hair may disagree; but how is that relevant? Must my criteria, or those of the Christian community, conform to their examples? Surely not. The Christian community is responsible to *its* set of examples, not to theirs.[11]

Plantinga is saying, then, that a theistic philosopher is fully justified in taking "God exists" to be a properly basic belief, *even if others do not agree.* And in saying this, he is in effect giving up something that has often been thought of as an important goal of the philosophical enterprise. Philosophers have often assumed that if they hit upon the right *method* for approaching philosophical problems and applied that method carefully and correctly, then agreement on *substantive conclusions* would be bound to result. Descartes's *Discourse on Method* is a striking illustration of this assumption, but it can be found in many other philosophers going back at least as far as Plato (427–347 B.C.). To be sure, philosophers have for the most part been unsuccessful in actually *bringing about* the agreement they have sought. Plantinga is saying that it was unreasonable to expect this in the first place—that philosophers come to their task bringing with them deeply rooted *prephilosophical commitments,* and those commitments may prevent them from reaching agreement even if both sides in a dispute conduct themselves correctly in terms of the standards for philosophical reasoning and argument.[12] On the other hand, if the theist makes the mistake of allowing the atheist to set the rules for the discussion by determining what beliefs can be properly basic, then we should not be surprised if the theist comes out second best. It is clear, then, that Plantinga is thoughtful and deliberate in his rejection of a "universal rationality" that can be relied on to bring philosophers to agreement despite differences in initial beliefs. But the student of Reformed epistemology likewise needs to be aware of this and to realize that giving up this ideal of rationality is part of the price for being a Reformed epistemologist. (In considering this point, the reader may want to review the discussion of "critical rationalism" in Chapter 3, as well as the discussion of proofs as "person-relative" in Chapter 5.)

This line of thought may lead to a further objection, which may be stated as follows: Does not this mean that just anything goes? If the theist can take "God exists" as properly basic, then why cannot anyone else who holds a belief, no matter how bizarre, specify that this belief is properly basic and thus make himself immune to criticism? Thus, Linus in the *Peanuts* comic strip, who believes that the Great Pumpkin comes every Halloween to those who believe and who wait for him in a "sincere" pumpkin patch, may believe this in a properly basic way and be perfectly rational and justified in his belief. (This has become known to philosophers as the "Great Pumpkin Objection.")

Plantinga's answer to this has two parts, depending on just how the objection is taken. On the one hand, if the objector is saying that the Reformed epistemologist is bound to accept that the belief that the Great Pumpkin returns every Halloween is properly basic, then this is just wrong. Belief in the Great Pumpkin will not, of course, be among the Reformed epistemologist's "set of examples," and there is no reason whatever to suppose that the Reformed epistemologist will or should come to the conclusion that this is a properly basic belief. Plantinga admits, to be sure, that the Reformed epistemologist "is committed to supposing that there is a relevant *difference* between belief in God and belief in the Great Pumpkin if he holds that the former but not the latter is properly basic."[13] But Plantinga thinks that differences of the right sort will not be hard to find.

The objection, however, might be taken in another way, as claiming that *the Great Pumpkinite himself,* following Plantinga's procedure for determining which beliefs are properly basic, might reasonably and properly conclude that his belief in the Great Pumpkin falls into this category. Philip

Quinn (1940–) writes: "The difficulty is . . . that this is a game any number can play. Followers of Muhammed, followers of Buddha, and even followers of the Reverend Moon can join in the fun."[14]

Plantinga's reply to this is, in effect, "Sure, but what's the problem?" He says, "Different philosophers employing this method may arrive at different conclusions: true enough, but do we know of some reasonably viable philosophical method (for reaching epistemic criteria) of which this is not true? That's just life in philosophy."[15]

This answer brings us back to the point already made: philosophers, like other people, bring with them deeply held prior commitments, and these commitments may sometimes make the reaching of substantive agreement on important philosophical questions (such as the criteria for properly basic belief) impossible. No doubt this is in some way regrettable, but (say the Reformed epistemologists) it is the way things are, and there is no point in denying it.

It is possible that by this time the reader is experiencing a certain degree of frustration. Just *how is it* that the belief that God exists acquires its status as properly basic? Obviously, it is not just the fact that this *is believed* that makes it properly basic or even that it is believed *strongly,* with commitment and emotional intensity. So what is it that gives the belief this status? It seems we are in need of an answer to this question, unless we are supposed just to take the Reformed epistemologist's word for it that this belief is properly basic.

In order to answer this question fully, the Reformed epistemologist would need to use the procedure described earlier, beginning with a set of examples and using them to develop his replacement for the discredited standard of strong foundationalism. But Plantinga, in his writings on Reformed epistemology, does not actually do this; rather, he limits himself to giving examples.[16] We can, however, learn quite a bit from looking at his examples. One important point, not stressed until now, is that, generally if not always, the status of a belief as properly basic is dependent on the *conditions in which that belief is held.* In the example discussed earlier, you were rational to believe, in a basic way, that someone was playing the saxophone in the next room. But if on entering the house you had heard nothing at all, or only the sound of a child crying, you would *not* have been rational to believe there was someone playing the saxophone. The justification of your belief depends crucially on the *experiential conditions* under which you believe.

How, how might this be applied to belief in God? In answering this, it is helpful to consider some examples Plantinga gives of properly basic beliefs about God. He writes,

> There is in us a disposition to believe propositions of the sort *this flower was created by God* or *this vast and intricate universe was created by God* when we contemplate the flower or behold the starry heavens or think about the vast reaches of the universe. . . . Upon reading the Bible, one may be impressed with a deep sense that God is speaking to him. Upon having

done what I know is cheap, or wrong, or wicked, I may feel guilty in God's sight and form the belief *God disapproves of what I have done.* Upon confession and repentance I may feel forgiven, forming the belief *God forgives me for what I have done.* [17]

There are more examples, but these suffice to make the point. Clearly, what Plantinga is saying is that under certain conditions one may have an *experience* of God's majestic wisdom in creation, or of God's speaking to one through the Bible, or of God's disapproval of one's sins and his subsequent forgiveness. And when one does have such an experience, it may be entirely appropriate and rational to believe, in a basic way, the kinds of propositions cited in the examples.

There are, furthermore, a few points that should be noted about these examples. First, in the examples it is not, strictly speaking, the belief that *God exists* that is properly basic but rather certain other beliefs, beliefs about what God does or has done and says or has said. But of course, none of those other beliefs could be true if God did *not* exist, so the difference is relatively minor. Second, it is important to be clear that the beliefs in the examples are all held in a *basic* way. I do not, for example, first examine the flower, then form certain beliefs about its structure and functioning, and then go through a process of reasoning (no doubt some version of the Teleological Argument) and reach the conclusion, on the basis of all this, that something with the design and function of that flower must have been created by a divine being. I might do that on some other occasion, of course, but in Plantinga's example I simply look at the flower and *see* it as God's creature—or, what amounts to the same thing, I see that God created it. And finally, note that the experiences cited in the examples are not rare and dramatic occurrences, the sort of thing that might happen to Moses, Mohammed, the apostle Paul, or St. Francis of Assisi but not to ordinary men or women. Rather, they are the kinds of experiences that are had by many, perhaps by most, religious believers at some time or other, and by some rather frequently.[18]

The point we have come to, then, is this: the belief that God exists, and other beliefs about God, are rightly and reasonably held in a basic way by one who finds that she *experiences* God's presence and activities. (Remember Simone Weil's description of her experience at the beginning of this chapter.) This conclusion, if correct, is an important one, and requires the revision of a great deal of thinking in the philosophy of religion. It seems clear, furthermore, that the conclusion is one that calls for further discussion and investigation. For this, we turn to William P. Alston.

ALSTON ON PERCEIVING GOD

In Chapter 2 we considered Alston's argument for the similarity of religious experience to sense perception.[19] His basic thesis about the role of religious experience in religious knowledge is that "experiential awareness of God—the 'perception of God,' as I call it—can provide epistemic justification for certain kinds of beliefs about God. I call such beliefs 'M-beliefs' ('M' for manifestation), beliefs to the effect that God is doing something vis-à-vis the subject—strengthening, guiding, communicating a message, etc.—or to the effect that God has some (allegedly) perceivable property—goodness, power, lovingness, etc."[20] Evidently this is a strong claim, one that has sweeping implications. Alston does not claim, to be sure, that religious experience is our *only* way of knowing about God, any more than sense perception is our only way of knowing about the physical world. (Scientific reasoning, for example, carries us to conclusions about the world that go far beyond those that would be justified by sense perception alone.) But sense perception is the *essential basis* for our knowledge about the physical world, and in a somewhat similar way religious experience is the essential basis for our knowledge of God. In each case, certain "basic" beliefs are justified directly by the experience in question (in the case of God, the "M-beliefs"), and then various reasoning processes are used in order to justify other beliefs, those that go beyond what is "perceived."

It is evident that a great many religious believers do, in fact, have experiences that indicate to them that God is relating to them in the sorts of ways mentioned by Alston. Among philosophers, however, there has been a strong inclination to think that these experiences cannot be taken at face value. At the very least, one needs to have *independent reason* to believe that God exists and that he might be doing some of these things, before it is reasonable to believe that the experiences are what they seem to be. The experiences by themselves cannot bear the weight of justifying our beliefs.

Alston thinks this is wrong—that it shows arbitrariness and prejudice against religious experience to say that it cannot stand on its own in justifying religious beliefs. Much of his discussion is directed to defending this point and to showing that, if we accept sense perception as the basic justification for our beliefs about the physical world, then as a matter of fairness and reasonableness we ought to accept religious experience as the justification for beliefs about God. It is important, in Alston's view, that, just as for sense perception, there is a *socially established practice* of forming beliefs about God on the basis of experiential awareness of God. (Indeed, as we shall see, there are several different socially established practices of this sort.) Alston argues that such socially established practices of belief formation (*doxastic practices,* as he calls them) should be accepted as reliable until and unless we have evidence of their unreliability.

It needs to be kept in mind that in saying that M-beliefs are *directly justified* by religious experience (that, in Plantinga's terminology, they are "properly basic" beliefs), Alston is not asserting that all such beliefs are *true.* For M-beliefs as for ordinary perceptual beliefs, there can be good reasons to conclude that "things are not as they seem." In certain circumstances it may look to me as if water is running uphill, but other things I know about the world keep me from accepting that as the truth. And if I tell you that, for example,

God has ordered me to kill all Presbyterians, you will rightly disbelieve my "revelation" on the ground that God would not give me any such command. This situation is best described by saying that experience provides a prima facie justification for our beliefs,[21] which is to say that such beliefs should be accepted *unless there is compelling reason to think they are false.* And this is true both for perceptual beliefs and for M-beliefs.

Not surprisingly, other philosophers have challenged these claims. Some of them have argued that religious experience is so fundamentally different from sense experience that it can't be considered as "perceptual" experience at all. Alston, however, seems to have made out a good case for regarding some kinds of religious experiences as perceptual.[22]

But even if this is so, it may seem that we have good reason to think that sense perception is more likely to be reliable than religious experience. What we perceive with our senses shows a great deal of consistency between different observers, so long as they are not impaired in some way. Also, sense experience gives us a precise and detailed knowledge of physical things in the world and enables us to make predictions about them with considerable accuracy. None of this is true of religious experience. Many people fail to have any such experiences. Among those who do have them, different people—especially people in different cultures and religions—experience God as having contradictory characteristics, and there is no readily apparent way to check out these conflicts. In particular, there is no way to make predictions that are precise enough to serve as confirmations of religious beliefs.

Alston acknowledges the truth in these complaints; yet he maintains they do not undermine religious experience as a source of justification for M-beliefs. Rather, he argues, the differences point to ways in which our situation with respect to God is different than our situation with respect to physical objects. We could not expect to have the kind of thorough, detailed, knowledge of God we have of ordinary physical things; God is too great and mysterious, too far beyond us, for that to be possible. In the same way, it is out of the question to suppose we should be able to predict God's actions—or to run a "controlled experiment" on God. As for the fact that many people seem not to have such experiences, it is in keeping with the teachings of the major religions that "God has decreed that a human being will be aware of His presence in any clear and unmistakable fashion only when certain special and difficult conditions are satisfied."[23] These conditions, of course, pertain to the religious life, and those who make no effort to satisfy them have no reason to complain if they do not have such experiences.

Of all these objections, it seems that the most difficult ones for Alston (and also Plantinga, though he has so far shown less interest in this aspect of the problem) to deal with are those that are based on the fact that persons in different cultures and different religious traditions conceive of God—and, apparently, experience God—in quite different ways. One of the most striking differences, though by no means the only one, is the difference between theistic religions, where God is experienced as a personal being with whom one can enter into a personal relationship, and religions such as the advaita form of Hinduism (discussed briefly in Chapter 3), which conceive God as an impersonal unity and maintain that the ultimate form of religious enlightenment is to experience the fact that there simply *is no difference* between oneself and God: "That *you* are, Shvetaketu."

Suppose that what Alston has argued so far is correct, that religious experience does provide prima facie justification for M-beliefs. Then, of course, the question must be asked, *whose* experience and *whose* M-beliefs? Or, to put it differently, *which* of the different religious belief-forming practices should we take to be reliable? Should we put our trust in some theistic practice—say, that of Judaism or Christianity? Or should we rely on some Buddhist or Hindu practice where God is conceived as an ultimate, impersonal unity? It may be, of course, that both the theist's M-belief that she is in loving communion with a personal God and the advaitist's M-belief that he is indistinguishable from Brahman are prima facie justified. But these beliefs cannot both be *true,* and one's whole religious way of life will be dramatically different depending on which one is accepted. On what basis should the choice be made?

This whole matter comes up for discussion in Chapter 12 on religious pluralism. Here we must limit ourselves to mentioning a few of the ways in which the Reformed epistemologist might respond to this question. One possibility is to say that the differences between religions are not as significant as is generally thought, that they all "really" are saying the same thing. This, however, is not a very promising line to take, in view of the magnitude of the differences that exist. It seems necessary, then, to give some reason that the understanding of God in one's own tradition is more likely to be correct than its rivals' views. Perhaps this can be done by showing that the rival view is ultimately incoherent—this is sometimes said, for example, of the monistic-pantheistic scheme of advaita. Another possibility is suggested by Alston when he says, "It may be that some religious ways of life fulfill their own promises more fully than others."[24] Or, one might argue for the superiority of one's own faith-tradition on the basis of what is claimed to be divine action in history. Christians, for instance, have often argued in this way on the basis of the resurrection of Jesus. There are many possibilities, too many even to list all of them here, let alone evaluate each one. But whatever route is taken, it seems likely that we will be involved in some kind of an appeal to evidence and will not be able to rest content with "basic beliefs" resting directly on religious experience.[25] Alston takes this challenge quite seriously, and he admits that the diversity of religious belief-systems does reduce the justification for accepting the M-beliefs formed by, for example, Christians as reliable. He calls for the use of all available means to overcome this ambiguity:

> The knowledgeable and reflective Christian should be concerned . . .
> [and] should do whatever seems feasible to search for common ground on

which to adjudicate the crucial differences between the world religions, seeking a way to show in a non-circular way which of the contenders is correct. What success will attend these efforts I do not presume to predict. Perhaps it is only in God's good time that a more thorough insight into the truth behind these divergent perspectives will be revealed to us.[26]

OBSERVATIONS

At this point it may be helpful to make a few observations summarizing the significance of what has been presented and connecting Reformed epistemology with other themes in the philosophy of religion. It seems that the central and most important claim of Reformed epistemology is that religious experience plays an *independent role* in the justification of religious beliefs; it does not require a prior *argument* that might show that such experience is reliable. Furthermore, the beliefs grounded in religious experience are *basic* beliefs, just as the beliefs grounded in sense experience are basic beliefs. These claims are summed up in Plantinga's assertion that beliefs about God can be "properly basic" and Alston's claim that in our religious experience we are "perceiving God." Whether these claims are correct the reader must decide for herself. It does seem that in deciding this question, an important role is played by one's willingness (or unwillingness, as the case may be) to give up the goal of a "universal method" for reaching philosophical agreement and to accept that the different starting points and belief-commitments of philosophers may give rise to disagreements that are not decidable by means of a common philosophical rationality.

Even if the Reformed epistemologist's basic claim is accepted and religious experiences are viewed as playing a crucial role in the justification of religious beliefs, there remains the important problem created by differences of religious experiences, and the interpretations of those experiences, in different religious traditions. As we have seen, Alston now concedes that, faced with this situation, the believer may be forced to appeal to evidence and arguments that lie outside the sphere of what is directly experienced.

The abandonment of "neutral rationality" has often been associated with fideism, and Reformed epistemology is sometimes considered to be a form of fideism.[27] But this does not seem to be correct, at least when "fideism" is defined as in the present text. The Reformed epistemologist does not consider his fundamental beliefs as being exempted from rational evaluation; rather, he welcomes such evaluation. He is, however, concerned not to allow the rules for the discussion to be set in ways that prejudice the result against theism—as, for example, by strong foundationalism.

Is Reformed epistemology indifferent to evidence? Again, clearly not. Reformed epistemologists are very concerned to consider, and answer, evidence and arguments *against* the existence of God—for example, the problem of evil. Indeed, their position requires them to do so. For the justification conferred by religious experience is only prima facie justification; it could be overridden if there were compelling reasons, drawn from some other source, showing that the theistic God does *not* exist. So, they need to show that there is no such compelling reasons.

But how do Reformed epistemologists view arguments *for* the existence of God, such as the ones presented in this book? What is clear is that they hold that such arguments are not *necessary*—that one can be fully rational and justified in believing in God entirely apart from such arguments. But does this mean that there are not, in fact, good theistic arguments? Different Reformed epistemologists may hold different views about this; their basic position does not require them to answer the question one way or the other.[28] Nor need they deny that such arguments might be quite useful; Plantinga, for instance, has said that "If there were some clearly valid arguments for the existence of God . . . these arguments could obviously serve as *confirmations* of the existence of God—for at least some believers. Further, such arguments could be useful in preparing the way for faith and in leading some people closer to it."[29] We have seen, furthermore, that Alston endorses the use of such arguments (that is, of natural theology) in order to show that one's own religious belief system (in his case, Christianity) is more likely to be true than rival systems.[30] In summary, then, Reformed epistemology as such does not take any particular position with regard to the theistic arguments, except to say that such arguments are not required as a precondition for rationally accepting beliefs about God grounded in religious experience.

Perhaps more than any other topic in this book, Reformed epistemology is a recent arrival on the scene of philosophy of religion. It is too early for philosophical thought on this topic to have reached any stable resolution; what can confidently be said is that the topic will continue to be debated vigorously for many years to come.

STUDY QUESTIONS

1. What is your reaction to Simone Weil's experience and to her comments on it? After reading her account, are you inclined to agree that she was able to know with certainty that God exists?

2. What is evidentialism, and why does evidentialism tend to be opposed to religious belief?

3. What is foundationalism? What is a basic belief? What is a properly basic belief?

4. Explain what strong foundationalism is, and discuss the reasons that have led philosophers to embrace strong foundationalism.

5. Discuss the objections to strong foundationalism as given in the text. Do these objections strike you as convincing?

6. Explain the Reformed epistemologists' reasons for saying it can be reasonable to believe in God even if there are no good arguments for God's existence.

7. Is it reasonable to say that, just as in sensory experience we perceive physical objects, in religious experience we perceive God? Why, or why not?

8. How can Reformed epistemology deal with the objection that, whereas everyone has sensory experience of physical objects, many people do not have religious experiences in which they perceive God? Does the answer to this objection strike you as satisfactory? Discuss.

9. How can Reformed epistemologists deal with the problem of the conflicting ideas of God in different religions? Is their solution to this problem satisfactory? Discuss.

10. Is the belief that God exists a properly basic belief?

NOTES

1. Simone Weil, *Waiting for God*, trans. Emma Craufurd (New York: Harper, 1973), p. 24.

2. Ibid., p. 212.

3. This connection is brought out in Alvin Plantinga, "The Reformed Objection to Natural Theology," *Christian Scholar's Review* 11 (1982): 187–98; reprinted in *Rationality in the Calvinian Tradition*, ed. Hendrik Hart, Johan Van Der Hoeven, and Nicholas Wolterstorff (Lanham, Md.: University Press of America, 1983), pp. 363–83 [also reprinted in *PRSR*, Part 6].

4. From the Introduction to *Faith and Rationality: Reason and Belief in God*, ed. Alvin Plantinga and Nicholas Wolterstorff (Notre Dame, Ind.: University of Notre Dame Press, 1983), p. 6.

5. There is some variety in the terminology used at this point; Wolterstorff and Plantinga speak of "classical foundationalism" and "modern foundationalism." Sometimes, indeed, this view is simply referred to as "foundationalism" without a qualifier, but this tends to be confusing; as we shall see, the Reformed epistemologists are themselves foundationalists of a certain kind.

6. There is also, to be sure, the question about *how* one belief may support another—what sorts of arguments are used to show this, and so on. This is an important topic, but it is also quite complex and will not be discussed further here.

7. The reader may notice a similarity between strong foundationalism and *strong rationalism*, as discussed in Chapter 3; strong foundationalism is, in fact, the leading variety of strong rationalism.

8. Roderick Chisholm, *Theory of Knowledge* (Englewood Cliffs, N.J.: Prentice-Hall, 1966), p. 57.

9. Gary Gutting, "The Catholic and the Calvinist: A Dialogue on Faith and Reason," *Faith and Philosophy* 2 (1985): 241. It should be noted that, because this article is in dialogue form, one cannot automatically assume that what is said by the participants reflects the author's own view. We believe, however, that this speech of "Catholic" does reflect Gutting's view on this point. (For confirmation, see the following quotation.)

10. Gary Gutting, *Religious Belief and Religious Skepticism* (Notre Dame, Ind.: University of Notre Dame Press, 1982), p. 83. (*Note:* We have emended the text of this

quotation, with the author's agreement; the printed version actually reads "widespread agreement.")

11. Alvin Plantinga, "Reason and Belief in God," in Plantinga and Wolterstorff, eds., *Faith and Rationality*, p. 77.

12. The idea that philosophical and other scholarly work is deeply shaped by prior worldview commitments is one of the important ideas that "Reformed epistemology" takes from the Reformed tradition of Christian theology. This idea, of course, fits well with the approach of "critical rationalism" as discussed in Chapter 3.

13. Plantinga, "Reason and Belief in God," p. 78.

14. Philip Quinn, "In Search of the Foundations of Theism," *Faith and Philosophy* 2 (1985): 473.

15. Plantinga, "The Foundations of Theism: A Reply," *Faith and Philosophy* 3 (1986): 303.

16. Philip Quinn points out two problems with the way Plantinga proceeds here. The reader may see his "The Foundations of Theism Again: A Rejoinder to Plantinga," in Linda Zagzebski, ed., *Rational Faith: Catholic Responses to Reformed Epistemology* (Notre Dame, Ind.: University of Notre Dame Press, 1993), pp. 14–47. First, not all theists agree that beliefs about God can be properly basic. (They may hold, instead, that such beliefs need to be justified by the kinds of arguments set out in Chapter 5.) So it cannot be taken for granted that a theist should have such beliefs in his list of examples of properly basic beliefs. But second, even if the theist does have beliefs about God in his initial list of examples, this does not guarantee that they will still be on the list after he has gone through the process of establishing his standard for properly basic beliefs. The initial list of examples is subject to revision, and if some of the examples just do not "fit" with others and with the criteria that are developed, they may be dropped from the list. (Such beliefs would then either be derived beliefs, or they would not be rational beliefs at all.) Quinn concludes that Plantinga needs to actually go through the procedure he has outlined; it is not enough just to give a few examples.

It should be pointed out that in his more recent work Plantinga does undertake the task of establishing standards for properly basic beliefs. For more on this, the reader may consult his *Warrant and Proper Function* (New York: Oxford University Press, 1993). It is not entirely clear, however, how this recent work relates to the material on Reformed Epistemology discussed in this chapter.

17. Plantinga, "Reason and Belief in God," p. 80.

18. This point has led to yet another objection, which, because of its somewhat technical nature, is relegated to a note. In Plantinga's view it would be correct to say that the basic belief that, for example, "God has created this flower" is *grounded in* the experience of seeing the flower in that particular way, even though there is no *evidence* for the belief (because, as Plantinga is using "evidence," evidence must consist of *another belief* that is the basis of the belief in question).

This has led Philip Quinn (among others) to make the following point: whenever I *do in fact* hold such a belief as "God has created this flower" in a basic way, it is also *equally possible* for me to *infer* this belief, using as one of my premises "It seems to me that God has created this flower." And my belief in God as creator of the flower is *equally justified* whether it is basic or inferred (derived). And this, it seems, tends to undercut the importance of the question, whether such beliefs are basic or nonbasic. As Quinn says, "Although such propositions [as "God has created this flower"] would not need to be based on the evidence of other propositions, they always could be so based. So the cautious philosopher who did so base them would be every bit as justified in believing in the existence of God as the reckless mystic who did not" ("In Search of the Foundations of Theism," p. 479).

Plantinga's reply ("The Foundations of Theism: A Reply," pp. 303–306) centers on this point: in general, it simply *is not true* that experientially grounded basic beliefs could also be held in a nonbasic way without loss of justification. All of us, under certain circumstances, will believe in a basic way such propositions as "There is a tree here before me." Could one with equal justification *infer* this belief from "There seems to be a tree before me"? The answer, drawn from the history of philosophical reflection on this topic, seems to be definitely not! For, in order to do this, one would have to *justify* the inference from the "seems" statement to the "is" statement—and this amounts to solving the problem of the "proof of the external world," surely one of the hoariest, and most resistant to solution, of all philosophical problems. Yet there is no reasonable doubt (skeptics aside) that our *basic* beliefs about trees and the like are fully justified. And in the same way, basic beliefs about God may be fully justified even if *arguments* designed to show God's existence are uniformly unsuccessful.

19. See William P. Alston, "Experience of God: A Perceptual Model," paper read at Wheaton College, Wheaton, Ill., October 1989. [Also reprinted as "Religious Experience as Perception of God," in *PRSR*, Part 1.]

20. William P. Alston, "Precis of *Perceiving God*," Symposium on Alston's *Perceiving God*, *Philosophy and Phenomenological Research* 54:4 (December 1994): 863.

21. Prima facie means "at first view"; prima facie evidence is evidence that is sufficient to establish a conclusion unless it is rebutted by stronger contrary evidence.

22. See Richard M. Gale, "Why Alston's Mystical Doxastic Practice is Subjective"; George S. Pappas, "Perception and Mystical Experience"; and William P. Alston, "Reply to Commentators," all in the Symposium on Alston's *Perceiving God* cited in note 20; also, William P. Alston, *Perceiving God* (Ithaca, N.Y.: Cornell University Press, 1991), chap. 1.

23. William P. Alston, "Christian Experience and Christian Belief," in Plantinga and Wolterstorff, eds., *Faith and Rationality*, p. 129.

24. William P. Alston, "Perceiving God," *Journal of Philosophy* 83 (1986): 663.

25. For further discussion of the need for evidence at this point, see William Hasker, "On Justifying the Christian Practice," *New Scholasticism* 60 (Spring 1986): 129–44; David Basinger, "Hick's Religious Pluralism and 'Reformed Epistemology': A Middle Ground," *Faith and Philosophy* 5:5 (1988): 421–32 [reprinted in *PRSR*, Part 6]; and William Wainwright, "Religious Language, Religious Experience, and Religious Pluralism," in Thomas D. Senor, ed., *The Rationality of Belief and the Plurality of Faith: Essays in Honor of William P. Alston* (Ithaca, N.Y.: Cornell University Press, 1995), pp. 170–88.

26. Alston, *Perceiving God*, p. 278.

27. For instance, by William J. Abraham, *An Introduction to the Philosophy of Religion* (Englewood Cliffs, N.J.: Prentice-Hall, 1985), pp. 88–97.

28. Plantinga's views on this point seem to have softened. He has always maintained that none of the theistic arguments are successful when judged by the standards of strong foundationalism or of classical natural theology—but then, there are no successful arguments for *any* interesting philosophical conclusions that meet those excessively high standards. But if we are willing to lower our sights a little and accept arguments whose premises are acceptable to many sensible people if not to all, then some very interesting arguments are available. Plantinga himself has on several occasions delivered a lecture entitled "Two Dozen (Or So) Theistic Arguments"!

29. Alvin Plantinga, "The Reformed Objection Revisited," *Christian Scholar's Review* 12 (1983): 58.

30. Philip Quinn has argued ("In Search of the Foundations of Theism" and "The Foundations of Theism Again: A Rejoinder to Plantinga") that intellectually sophisticated theists in contemporary Western culture typically need such arguments in order to maintain a rational belief in God. Such persons are aware of standard objections to belief (such as the problem of evil), and Quinn thinks the prima facie justification of belief in God that comes from religious experience is not, in most cases, strong enough, by itself, to overcome these objections.

SUGGESTED READING

Alston, William P. "Christian Experience and Christian Belief." In *Faith and Rationality: Reason and Belief in God*. Edited by Alvin Plantinga and Nicholas Wolterstorff. Notre Dame, Ind.: University of Notre Dame Press, 1983.

———. *Perceiving God: The Epistemology of Religious Experience*. Ithaca, N.Y.: Cornell University Press, 1991.

———, Richard M. Gale, George S. Pappas, and Robert W. Adams. Symposium on *Perceiving God*. *Philosophy and Phenomenological Research* 54, no. 4 (December 1994): 863–99.

Gutting, Gary. "The Catholic and the Calvinist: A Dialogue on Faith and Reason." *Faith and Philosophy* 2 (1985): 236–256.

———. *Religious Belief and Religious Skepticism*. Notre Dame, Ind.: University of Notre Dame Press, 1982.

Hasker, William. "On Justifying the Christian Practice." *New Scholasticism* 60 (Spring 1986): 129–44.

McLeod, Mark S. *Rationality and Theistic Belief: An Essay on Reformed Epistemology*. Ithaca, N.Y.: Cornell University Press, 1993.

Plantinga, Alvin. "Coherentism and the Evidentialist Objection to Belief in God." In *Rationality, Religious Belief, and Moral Commitment*. Edited by Robert Audi and William J. Wainwright. Ithaca, N.Y.: Cornell University Press, 1986.

———. "The Foundations of Theism: A Reply." *Faith and Philosophy* 3 (1986): 298–313.

———. "Is Belief in God Rational?" In *Rationality and Religious Belief*. Edited by C. F. Delaney. Notre Dame, Ind.: University of Notre Dame Press, 1979.

———, "Reason and Belief in God." In *Faith and Rationality: Reason and Belief in God*. Edited by Alvin Plantinga and Nicholas Wolterstorff. Notre Dame, Ind.: University of Notre Dame, 1983.

———. "The Reformed Objection to Natural Theology." *Christian Scholar's Review* 11 (1982): 187–98.

———. "Replies." In *Alvin Plantinga*, Vol. 5. Edited by James E. Tomberlin and Peter Van Inwagen. Dordrecht: D. Riedel, 1985.

Quinn, Philip. "On Finding the Foundations of Theism." *Faith and Philosophy* 2 (1985): 469–86.

———. "The Foundations of Theism Again: A Rejoinder to Plantinga." In *Rational Faith: Catholic Responses to Reformed Epistemology*. Edited by Linda Zagzebski. Notre Dame, Ind.: University of Notre Dame Press, 1993.

Wolterstorff, Nicholas. "Can Belief in God Be Rational If It Has No Foundations?" In *Faith and Rationality: Reason and Belief in God*. Edited by Alvin Platinga and Nicholas Wolterstorff. Notre Dame, Ind.: University of Notre Dame Press, 1983.

Zagzebski, Linda, ed. *Rational Faith: Catholic Responses to Reformed Epistemology*. Notre Dame, Ind.: University of Notre Dame Press, 1993.

CHAPTER 8

RELIGIOUS LANGUAGE: HOW CAN WE SPEAK MEANINGFULLY OF GOD?

A fascinating science fiction story portrays a high lama who purchases a Mark V Automatic Sequence Computer to install in his monastery in Tibet. However, the lama requests that the computer be modified to print out letters and not numbers. The curious purpose of all this, as he expresses it, is to accelerate the completion of a list of all of the names of God that his monks are compiling. A task that would have taken another fifteen centuries will now take only a hundred days. By systematically combining sequences of letters in a special alphabet, the computer will eventually list all of the real names of God. It is not long until the computer is installed in the lamasery in the mountains of Tibet. George and Chuck, the two engineers sent to oversee its operation, are about to go stir crazy watching the monks tirelessly pasting long strips of names into books.

When Chuck is finally able to inform the high lama that the machine is on its last cycle, he receives such an enthusiastic response that he inquires further into the religious significance of the computer's activity. "Well," says the lama, "they believe that when they have listed all His names—and they reckon that there are about nine billion of them—God's purpose will be achieved. The human race will have finished what it was created to do, and there won't be any point in carrying on." Chuck later relays this incredible story to George: "When the list's completed, God steps in and simply winds things up . . . bingo!" At the thought that the end of the project will be the end of the world, George gives a nervous little laugh. Thinking the matter over, the two Americans realize if the world does not end when the project is finished, it may mean trouble for them at the hands of hundreds of angry monks whose lifework has been spoiled by a computer. They make plans to leave "Project Shangri-La," as they call it, before the computer finishes its last long series of names. On the evening of the last day, Chuck and George say good-by to the monks and ride the tough mountain ponies down the winding road from the lamasery toward the old DC-3 that is waiting for them at the end of the runway. They descend the mountain in the cold, perfectly clear Himalayan night, ablaze with the now familiar stars:

> . . . George glanced at his watch.
> "Should be there in an hour," he called back over his shoulder to Chuck. Then he added, in an afterthought: "Wonder if the computer's finished its run. It was due about now."
> Chuck didn't reply, so George swung round in his saddle. He could just see Chuck's face, a white oval turned toward the sky.
> "Look," whispered Chuck, and George lifted his eyes to heaven. (There is always a last time for everything.)
> Overhead, without any fuss, the stars were going out.[1]

HUMAN LANGUAGE AND THE INFINITE

The story reminds us of the universal preoccupation with language about God—from the primitive who thinks that naming the divine gives magical power to the intellectual who ponders how human words can appropriately apply to deity. In the twentieth century, philosophers have become particularly concerned with the nature and role of language in general and have developed a number of different theories about religious language in particular.

There are two major reasons why philosophers pay close attention to religious language. The first is that they are interested in questions of *meaning* and thus in how words about God derive their meaning. For example, the language that the Judeo-Christian tradition employs to talk about God is drawn from ordinary discourse, from the language we use daily to speak of common and familiar things. Expressions such as "God is my rock and my salvation" and "David did what was right in the eyes of the Lord" are plentiful in religious discourse. Philosophers seek an account of how it is that words used to speak of creaturely phenomena make sense when applied to God. The Judeo-Christian tradition teaches that the Creator is not the creature, that God is "high and lifted up," indeed, that God is "transcendent". And most great religions involve some kind of teaching about the transcendence of the divine. How, then, can language about the finite realm be used about God? We know what we mean when we speak, for instance, of ordinary rocks and ordinary eyes. But what can it mean to speak of God as being a "rock" or as having "eyes," since rocks and eyes are mere creaturely realities?

The second reason for the intense interest philosophers have shown in religious language is that they seek to analyze and evaluate *beliefs*. Beliefs, of course, are expressed in the form of *statements* or *propositions*. As a prelude to further philosophical scrutiny of religious beliefs, it is crucial to understand the language in which they are couched. Of course, much religious language is not used to make direct assertions of belief but is instead used for a variety of distinctively religious purposes, such as prayer, liturgy, and admonition. Yet philosophers know that other religious uses of language rest upon or assume certain prior beliefs. Worshiping God, for instance, assumes that there is such a being as God and that he is worthy of our adoration and devotion, petitioning God presupposes that God actually hears and responds to prayer, and so forth. When the precise beliefs behind these and other religious activities are made explicit, we have a set of *theological statements,* truth-claims about God and his relationship to the world. So, once we grasp the meaning of theological terms and, in turn, of the theological statements in which they appear, we can ask questions about what rational grounds one could have for accepting or rejecting those statements. While other chapters in this book concentrate on such matters as whether there is rational justification for certain theological claims, such as "God exists" or "God is perfectly good," here we examine the meaning of theological discourse itself.

THE CLASSICAL THEORY OF ANALOGY

The great medieval thinkers were well aware of the problem of using creaturely language to speak of God. They did not question whether religious language has any meaning but realized the difficult problem of accounting for its meaning. Thomas Aquinas (c. 1224–1274) developed a (now classic) theory of "analogy" or "analogical predication" as a solution to the problem. The theory has been standard fare in discussions of religious language throughout the intervening centuries and has remained attractive to many.

A predicate term in a sentence attaches some property, relation, or activity to the subject term. Thus, predicates define or characterize the subject in particular ways. Typical examples of the sorts of statements employed in both academic theology and popular religion are not difficult to find. Let us consider some examples drawn from Jewish and Christian traditions:

God created the heavens and the earth.

God brought the Israelites out of Egypt.

Yahweh spoke to the prophets.

God is just.

Aquinas held that when a word—e.g., "just"—is applied both to a created being and to God, it is not being used *univocally* (i.e., with exactly the same meaning) in the two instances. Yet neither is the word being used *equivo-*

cally (i.e., with two completely different meanings), as when "hot" is used to apply to pepper corns and race cars. There is a connection between divine justice and human justice, a similarity between a certain quality in God and a certain quality in persons. As Aquinas indicates, this allows the word to be used *analogically.*[2] It is the similarity within difference and difference within similarity that allows the analogical use of the same term in two different contexts.

James Ross (1927–) believes that the traditional analogy theory provides a helpful middle way between the univocal and the equivocal uses of terms when speaking of God and thus avoids *anthropomorphism* and *agnosticism,* respectively. *Anthropomorphism* is the view that God differs from creatures merely in degree and thus that no alteration of meaning in our terms is necessary to speak of him. *Agnosticism* is the view that God is so different from us that we cannot say anything intelligible about him at all. The promise of the analogy theory is that we can actually express truths about God in human language while never having to suppose that he has anything precisely in common with creatures.

Ross admits, however, that the theory of analogy is a very complicated matter that has already received volumes of commentary. Drawing from various passages in Aquinas, we can discern a sophisticated theory of analogy, which Ross attempts to augment and systematically present in terms of modern semantic analysis. Ross, like Aquinas, takes it to be obvious that ordinary terms already have meaning when used appropriately in religious contexts and hence offers the theory of analogy as a positive account of how meaning is transferred from ordinary contexts to religious ones. Such transfers of meaning plainly occur in a multitude of common situations in which we are already familiar with the objects and qualities involved, making analogy part of the structure of ordinary discourse that must be explained by an overall theory of language. Consider the multitude of ordinary cases in which we say things such as "Susan's anger is volcanic" or "The fox is very clever." The peculiarity of a theory of religious language is that it must describe the transfer of meaning from contexts where terms are used to speak of the familiar, observable realities of the creaturely realm to contexts where those terms speak of God and spiritual realities.

In neither ordinary contexts nor religious contexts can we simply employ any alleged analogy we choose. There are constraints built into our language on how a term can be used analogously. Aquinas and other Scholastic philosophers stated these constraints in terms of rules for analogy, with the rule called the *analogy of proper proportionality* considered to be the basis of the meaning of religious language. This rule states that God and creatures have qualities and engage in activities in proportion to their respective modes of being—infinite and finite, respectively. Thus, we can say both "God is wise" and "Socrates is wise" but make an adjustment for the shift in meaning between the two sentential contexts. And the shift is proportional to the two modes of being to which the predicate term "wise" is related.

In the two statements "God is wise" and "Socrates is wise," Socrates is said to stand in a certain relationship to some state called "being wise" in a way similar to that in which God stands to his state called "being wise." The term "being wise" is employed with respect to God and to Socrates because we recognize the similarity in the ways in which they are wise. Thus, the use of the predicate term "being wise" is not equivocal. Yet the reason that the term "being wise" is not univocal in the two statements rests on the difference between the two modes of being that are exemplified by a human and by God. Socrates is wise in the manner in which a human person is wise, in a way appropriate to his distinct creaturely mode of being, which is finite. God, too, is wise in a way appropriate to his mode of being, which is infinite.

This sort of shift in meaning occurs in many contexts. The statements "Lassie is faithful" and "John is faithful," for example, exhibit a shift in the type of faithfulness. Although the relationship of faithfulness here is similar between the two cases, it is not exactly the same relationship because the mode of being possessed by Lassie is different from that possessed by John. But there is a perceivable likeness in patterns of behavior that allows us to use the same term for both animal and human. The same rule of proper proportionality holds in many other contexts.

Frederick Ferré (1932–) maintains, as do other critics of the analogy of proper proportionality, that the theory is completely unable to provide any substantive knowledge of God. In our example, it is given that God's nature, as we shall say, is "infinite" and that one of his attributes is "wisdom." Then the formula of the analogy becomes something like the following:

$$\frac{\text{God's wisdom}}{\text{God's infinite nature}} = \frac{\text{Socrates' wisdom}}{\text{Socrates' finite nature}}$$

However, Ferré contends that the theory "cannot move a step toward explaining the 'givens' of its own formulation, nor can it explain the possibility of the independent, nonanalogical knowledge on which they depend."[3] This kind of analogy has not one but two unknowns, God's wisdom and God's infinite nature. And Ferré thinks that we just cannot have any positive knowledge of these matters.

Ross points out that Ferré's criticism distorts the theory by interpreting it on a simplistic mathematical model. The purpose of Aquinas, Ross argues, was to make the meaningfulness of religious language obvious and clear from its similarity to the way we talk in everyday life, with all of its nuances and degrees of connotation, and not to stipulate an exact mathematical relationship between uses of terms. Ross contends that Ferré's mathematical modeling of the theory confuses Aquinas's use of analogy as a *theory of meaning* with a *theory of inference* in which analogy is used to lead to some knowledge about God, a pattern of argument that Aquinas never used. According to Ross, Aquinas simply did not intend this theory of meaning to be an avenue of arriving at information about God.[4] Hence, Ross defends the doctrine of analogy as an explanation of how predicates applied to God have meaning, not as a method of spelling out the concrete character of God's attributes. Ross does believe that, equipped with this theory of meaning, we can presumably understand what assertions about God mean and thereby avoid fatal equivocation when we do construct arguments about God.

The theory of analogy merits much further discussion.[5] Questions must be faced, say, about whether the notion of "similarity" can be given any clear definition. And interesting questions arise over how the important medieval doctrine of "divine simplicity" (which claims that there is no distinction between God and his attributes such as there are between creatures and their attributes) affects the way analogy is construed. But the fact remains that religious language has historically been believed to be meaningful and that the theory of analogy has traditionally been accepted by many as an account of its meaning. It is only in the contemporary period that wholesale challenges to the meaningfulness of religious language have been waged.

VERIFICATION AND FALSIFICATION ISSUES

Traditionally, philosophers of religion had never seriously doubted that it is possible to speak meaningfully of God. Early in this century, however, a group of philosophers known as *logical positivists* strongly questioned this confidence. They developed a theory that ties the meaning of language to empirical observation. Taking science to be the best representation of careful language, logical positivists constructed a standard or criterion by which we could judge those statements that are cognitively meaningful and those that are not. Their standard came to be known as the *verifiability principle* and was applied to all statements that were not analytically (definitionally) true.[6] The principle can be stated as follows: *a statement is a genuine factual assertion if, and only if, there could be empirically observable states of affairs that would show it to be either true or false.*

A. J. Ayer (1910–1989) expressed the principle in this way:

> The criterion which we use to test the genuineness of apparent statements of fact is the criterion of verifiability. We say that a sentence is factually significant to any given person, if, and only if, he knows how to verify the proposition which it purports to express—that is, if he knows what observations would lead him, under certain conditions, to accept the proposition as being true, or reject it as being false.[7]

Ayer and other positivists thought that theological language failed to meet the empirical standard of verifiability and thus had no cognitive meaning.[8] For them, language has *cognitive* meaning only if it speaks of matters in which it is in principle possible to give empirical evidence, matters about which questions of truth and falsity make sense. Such language, then, has *factual* or *informative* status or significance and thus can be properly understood.

Positivists and their intellectual followers thought that the verifiability principle handled scientific language as well as much of our ordinary talk. Likewise, traditional attacks on theism, using the same language, are equally meaningless. For positivistic critics, then, theistic claims as well as antitheistic claims are not false but meaningless.

Interestingly, the verification principle of meaning eventually came under severe pressure. One well-known problem was that the verification principle of cognitive meaningfulness failed to meet the very empirical standards of meaning that it articulates.[9] After all, no observational experiences could possibly verify this statement of the verification principle: *a statement is a genuine factual assertion if, and only if, there could be empirically observable states of affairs which would show it to be either true or false.* (Here the verification principle of meaning encounters the problem of self-reference just as the criterion for foundational propositions becomes self-referentially incoherent as shown in the discussion of strong foundationalism presented in Chapter 7.) Another, somewhat ironic difficulty was that the verification principle of meaning did not make completely good sense of science. The history and the practice of science are replete with cases in which scientists advanced and pondered claims—claims that they took to be perfectly meaningful—for which they were unable at the time to specify exact verification conditions. The debate between the wave and the corpuscular theories of light just begins the list of such cases. In the end, positivism failed to describe correctly the conditions under which scientific statements are meaningful—and failed to do the same for numerous other kinds of statements as well (e.g., ethical statements).

Although some religious thinkers celebrated the demise of the verification principle, many in the philosophical community—positivists and others—still believed that the our statements must be linked to empirical observation. Granting that verificationist methods could supply the positive meaning for statements, they began explore the prospects for *falsification.* They developed the requirement that if anyone purports to be asserting a factual claim, he should be able to identify the conditions under which it would be would be false. In this vein, a very interesting challenge to theistic claims emerged.

Antony Flew (1923–) confronted theists with a "falsification principle." He embeds the challenge in a very powerful story patterned after an article by John Wisdom[10] (1904–1993):

> Once upon a time two explorers came upon a clearing in the jungle. In the clearing were growing many flowers and many weeds. One explorer says, "Some gardener must tend this plot." The other disagrees, "There is no gardener." So they pitch their tents and set a watch. No gardener is ever seen. "But perhaps he is an invisible gardener." So they set up a barbed-wire fence. They electrify it. They patrol with bloodhounds. (For

they remember how H. G. Wells's *The Invisible Man* could be both smelt and touched though he could not be seen.) But no shrieks ever suggest that some intruder has received a shock. No movements of the wire ever betray an invisible climber. The bloodhounds never give cry. Yet still the Believer is not convinced. "But there is a gardener, invisible, intangible, insensible to electric shocks, a gardener who has no scent and makes no sound, a gardener who comes secretly to look after the garden which he loves." At last the Skeptic despairs, "But what remains of your original assertion? Just how does what you call an invisible, intangible, eternally elusive gardener differ from an imaginary gardener or even from no gardener at all?"[11]

Flew contends that religious believers allow nothing to count against their claims, continually modifying and qualifying them in order to prevent them from being falsified.

Flew's reasoning is straightforward. When the believer states that "God loves us as a father loves his children," we would expect divine help in times of serious trouble or disease. Yet God seems distant, absent. So, the believer makes some qualification—"God's love is not like human love" or "It is an inscrutable love"—making misfortune and suffering compatible with the original theological pronouncement. In response to this maneuvering, Flew puts forth the central question: "'What would have to occur or to have occurred to constitute for you a disproof of the love of, or of the existence of, God?'"[12] The point is that if there is no state of affairs that would count against the original theological statement, then it is not really a genuine assertion at all. It says nothing, neither affirming nor denying that anything is actually the case. Flew contends that religious believers kill their own claims by a thousand qualifications.

The falsificationist critique of religious language prompted spirited discussion about whether religious claims have factual significance. And, no doubt, for many critics, the only kind of cognitive significance is factual significance. Philosophers who agreed that the falsification principle defines the issue essentially divided into two camps: those who thought that theological language is nonfalsifiable and those who thought that it could be shown falsifiable.

R. M. Hare (1919–) and Basil Mitchell (1917–) were among the many philosophers who argued that religious utterances are not falsifiable for most believers and thus were not direct statements of fact. In an effort to distinguish religious assertions from factual assertions, Hare calls the former "bliks" (a term which he coined).[13] He says that the religious believer just has a "blik" that God exists and that a certain religious way of life is correct, and nothing can change that confidence. Hare even tells a parable about a lunatic who had a "blik" that all Oxford professors were out to kill him and who could not be dissuaded from his belief by appeal to numerous inoffensive and even friendly encounters with Oxford professors. Hare indicates that all persons have "bliks" that are not held at the level of factual claims and thus cannot be overturned by contrary facts. Although

Hare's terminology tends to trivialize religious assertions, his deeper point is that they express deeply held interpretive beliefs or assumptions about the world that cannot be readily overturned by empirical observation. We might think of other important claims—such as claims about human free will or the existence of other minds—as sharing this characteristic.

Basil Mitchell also maintained that religious assertions are not straightforwardly falsifiable. Mitchell tells a story about a member of a resistance movement who meets a stranger who impresses him very much: "The Stranger tells the partisan that he himself is on the side of the resistance—indeed that he is in command of it, and urges the partisan to have faith in him no matter what happens. The partisan is utterly convinced at that meeting of the Stranger's sincerity and constancy and undertakes to trust him."[14] Although the two never meet intimately again, and the partisan sees the Stranger capturing his comrades, the young partisan remains convinced by the stranger's words. Mitchell uses this story to point out the role of trust and commitment in keeping various circumstances from conclusively falsifying a belief.[15]

By contrast, John Hick (1922–) attempted to provide specific verification and falsification conditions for establishing the factual significance of religious claims. Hick tells a parable of two travelers walking along a road, one believing that the road leads to a Celestial City and the other believing that it leads nowhere. During the journey together, both men encounter moments of refreshment and delight as well as periods of hardship and danger. One interprets the good times as previews of heavenly bliss and the bad times as obstacles to make him worthy; the other considers the journey to be aimless rambling. During the journey, the issue between the two travelers is not an experimental one; it cannot be decided by empirical observation. "And yet when they do turn the last corner it will be apparent that one of them has been right all of the time and the other wrong. It is at this point that verification and falsification become relevant. Although the issue between the two has not been experimental, it has nevertheless from the start been a real issue."[16] Hick indicates what verifying experiences might be, such as social existence in the Kingdom of God and perhaps a strong sense of the presence of God. The absence of such experiences, then, would constitute a falsification.

Hick takes the whole concern of verification and falsification to be that the factual significance of statements derives from their being connected to relevant actual or possible observational experiences. He then provides a scenario in which religious statements can be seen to be factually significant, not by virtue of experiences that are available in temporal life, but by virtue of possible experiences in the afterlife. Of course, if there is no afterlife, then there will be no verification of religious claims. Technically, Hick may have satisfied the pure logic of a verification/falsification type challenge, but one wonders what benefit it is to us presently to suppose that actual verification or falsification is located in the afterlife, which is something we cannot now experience.

While no longer at center stage in discussions of religious language, the entire verification/falsification issue presents us with a number of valuable lessons. For one, the whole concept of a *fact* needs serious review, particularly with respect to religion. Many religious believers rightly understand that there is a factual dimension to religious language that neither verificational nor falsificational analysis can properly understand. Indeed, key theological statements entail definite cosmological assertions that, while more complicated and less accessible than assertions about the physical realm, nonetheless purport to be large-scale truths about the way things are. The statement "God is always with his children," for example, when interpreted in context, entails the factual claim that "An invisible, eternal, omnipresent, omniscient spirit exists and somehow communes with and guides those who place their trust in him." After having rejected positivism, it remains to be seen how we can best account for the factual significance of such statements. A second lesson to be learned is that we must not confuse questions of *meaning* with questions of *truth,* as the positivists did. Settling the problem of how our statements have meaning cannot be made to depend on solving the quite different problem of how we can come to know their truth.

THE FUNCTIONS OF RELIGIOUS DISCOURSE

Some thinkers, holding that questions of factual significance are either peripheral or irrelevant, thought that allowing positivism to set the framework for discussing religious language was simply wrongheaded. For them, regardless of how we account for the factual significance of religious discourse, it has other important kinds of significance. Many of these philosophers turned their attention to what Frederick Ferré calls "functional analysis."[17] Following Ludwig Wittgenstein's (1889–1951) admonition to "look and see" the multifaceted aspects of language, they identified several important functions: *imperative* ("Bring me the glass"), *performative* ("I now pronounce you husband and wife"), and *interrogative* ("What time is it?"). It would be inappropriate to apply the verification principle to such statements, and yet they function perfectly well in our human linguistic commerce.

New and intriguing theories about the various functions of religious language or, better, of ordinary language used in religious contexts were pioneered. Rather than stipulate conditions of meaning that relate language to an external reality (as the positivists had tried to connect statements to observable states of affairs), functional analysts tried to understand the functioning of religious language at work. They sought to learn what kinds of tasks it performs. They came to see language as a complex social phenomenon that is adaptable to the ever-changing purposes of human beings. And religious language was seen, therefore, as serving certain unique human purposes. Although functional analysts who studied religious language differed among themselves on *the* basic function of religious language, a brief inspection of a couple noteworthy studies is enlightening.

An early leader in this approach, R. B. Braithwaite (1900–1990) declared that religious utterances function essentially as *moral* statements. One distinctive feature of religious language is that it involves stories that picture and reinforce a moral way of life—such as the tale of the Good Samaritan or the various narratives of Jesus' compassion for people. While these religious stories may appear to be direct assertions of fact, they actually serve to express the intentions of the one uttering them to live morally. For Braithwaite, it is not necessary that the stories be true or even that they be believed to be true for them to fulfill their primary purpose. He takes the connection between the stories and a moral way of life to be "a psychological and causal one," on the basis of the fact that most people find it naturally easier to act in a certain way if they associate their actions with certain stories.[18]

Braithwaite's analysis accents one important use of religious language: to express moral intentions and reinforce moral behavior. However, critics of this theory of the function of religious language say that it transforms it into the language of morality embellished by stories—a reductionist error comparable to the positivistic mistake of trying to reduce religious statements to empirical facts.[19] Donald Hudson (1940–) has called this kind of mistake a violation of the "depth grammar" of religion, arguing that religious discourse has its own unique character and function.[20] The philosopher's task, then, is to clarify how religious language works, to expose its exact role in human affairs.

Paul van Buren (1924–) developed an interpretation that places the language of Christianity "at the edges of language."[21] Following the later Wittgenstein, van Buren explains that human language is a complex phenomenon, consisting of many "language-games." The language-games metaphor points to identifiable linguistic behaviors employed by human beings in order to accomplish certain purposes: "Giving orders . . . Describing the appearance of an object . . . Speculating about an event . . . Forming and testing a hypothesis . . . Presenting the results of an experiment in tables and diagrams . . . Making up a story; and reading it . . . Play-acting . . . Singing catches . . . Guessing riddles . . . Making a joke; telling it . . . Solving a problem in practical arithmetic . . . Asking, thanking, cursing, greeting, praying."[22] Followers of Wittgenstein began to speak of the language of science, the language of romance and love, the language of ethics, the language of religion, and so forth. Each of these different linguistic activities or language-games occupies a definite region on the overall map of human language. Each language-game has rules or social understandings for how words function within its sphere. The word "solid," for example, means one thing when one is speaking of solid bodies in physics and something related to but distinct from this first meaning when one is speaking of a person's having a solid character in the area of ethics. These rules for language-games, of course, are not written in any book but are followed somewhat unconsciously by members of the linguistic communities involved. The rules, then, are there for philosophers to uncover.

In locating the language of Christianity on the linguistic map, van Buren writes of those areas of human speaking that are far from the "clear, rule-governed center" where misunderstandings seldom occur. He identifies *puns, poetry,* and *paradox* as linguistic activities that have a strong kinship with the language of Christianity. That bond is their common attempt to say more than we can normally say with our language, to stretch the use of words beyond their usual employment, almost to the point of lapsing into nonsense. Consider how a pun stretches "language ("A door is not a door when it is ajar)" or how poetic speech attempts to go beyond our normal linguistic frontiers ("Your eyes outshine the stars in heaven").

Our modern, materialistic Western culture, according to van Buren, pressures us to live linguistically within the safe, central parts of our language—science, economics, history, and common sense. But to live in the central regions of language is to forfeit a certain richness of experience, to forgo a certain way of being in the world. For van Buren, then, the vital role played by religious language is that of expressing a certain aspect of our humanity. Christians, as he indicates, refuse to be confined to the mundane center of language and seek to say more about ourselves and our world than can be said in ordinary or scientific talk. An example of Christian "edge-talk" is the utterance "God raised Jesus from the dead," which is misunderstood if taken as a statement of historical fact. It is actually a statement of faith that tries to press language to its limits in talking about Jesus and his ongoing influence; it performs an entirely different function for believers than it does for historians.[23] Talk of a God who is "personal, but not a person" and of a "spiritual body" just begins the list of examples of Christian edge-talk.

Those who engage in *functional analysis* have helped reveal a host of different employments of religious language. In a list that proceeds much like Wittgenstein's, they have shown us that language in religion is used in a variety of ways: to pray and petition, to sing praises, to comfort, to exhort, to affirm commitment, and so forth. Yet van Buren, along with all other functional analysts, runs the risk of falling into a certain form of *fideism,* the view (discussed in Chapter 3) that faith is immune to external critique.[24] Since religious language has its own unique character and function, it is not subject to the sorts of questions and linguistic procedures that occur in other linguistic territories. Perhaps we could call this position *linguistic fideism.*

It would be wholly inappropriate, according to van Buren, to ask, for example, whether the word "God" names someone or some thing—to ask whether some object bears that name or whether it refers to something real. Such questions are appropriate, say, to the physical sciences or to other factually oriented linguistic activities where the technique of naming objects is involved. But religion cannot ask whether its most fundamental term—the term "God," which constitutes and governs its whole field of discourse—can play by the rules of other fields in which naming and referring are key techniques.[25] Focusing exclusively on the *function* of religious language within a religious community neglects its informative dimension. It seems as though functional analysts have surrendered to the positivist charge that religious language is cognitively meaningless and have looked elsewhere to find some other way in which it can be meaningful, *functionally* meaningful.

Van Buren and other Wittgensteinian thinkers have rightly called our attention to the intimate connection of language to all areas of human of life; they have forced us to recognize that much of our humanity is indeed bound up with being linguistic creatures. However, only by assuming that science and ordinary talk are central linguistic practices—a capitulation to the positivists—can van Buren justify placing religion at the "edges" of language. A more adequate interpretation may well perceive that religious language has its own inherent standards of precision and sayability, just as science does, without having to relinquish matters of precision or factual communication to science.

Moreover, it appears that van Buren fails to see the complex fabric of religious language as involving metaphysical, ethical, and historical statements that are intended by religious believers to be just that—metaphysical or ethical or historical assertions. By reducing religious language to the activity of expressing a distinct perspective on the world, van Buren still leaves unresolved the more fundamental question of whether our language can be used to say anything about that Ultimate Reality that believers take to be God. Traditional thinkers, such as Aquinas, would say that van Buren's approach (like that of Braithwaite and other functional analysts) fails to take seriously what ordinary religious believers take themselves to be saying. Believers regularly take themselves to be asserting the factual truth of certain theological teachings and narratives, or at least to be engaging in liturgies and other religious behaviors that assume such factual truths.

RELIGIOUS LANGUAGE AS SYMBOLIC

Many philosophers became dissatisfied with functional analysis just as they had with verificational analysis. Verificational analysis denied cognitive meaning to religious discourse, and functional analysis sought to find uses for it that were basically noncognitive. Most contemporary philosophers now admit that religious language has legitimate cognitive meaning, but many of them believe that its meaning cannot be *literal*. That it is impossible to speak literally of God has become a fundamental assumption of contemporary theologians as well. Both philosophers and theologians fear lapsing into the *anthropomorphism* involved in talking about God as we would talk about creatures. Not satisfied with the traditional analogical theory for avoiding anthropomorphism, more recent thinkers have developed a plethora of nonliteral interpretations: some speak of theological "models," some of "stories," others of "metaphor," and still others of "parable" as the essential mode of religious discourse.[26]

The theologian Paul Tillich is well known for his position that talk of God is *symbolic.* Tillich recognizes, as do many others, that statements such as "Yahweh spoke to the prophets" and "The Lord is my Shepherd" are not commonly considered to be capable of literal interpretation. After all, God does not really "speak" by expelling air across physical vocal cords; nor is he a "shepherd" as we typically understand it. Of course, there are many cases of broadly symbolic speech in ordinary language. We speak of the "mouth of a river" or of "Christine's character being solid." In ordinary discourse, such symbolic or metaphorical talk can be cashed out literally. We can explain for instance, that the river has a "mouth" in that it has an opening out of which things flow or that Christine's character is "solid" in that it is dependable and will hold up under pressure.

All such sentences are *predications*—sentences that attach properties, relationships, and activities to a subject. Why does Tillich agree that the ordinary symbolic statements can be given literal interpretation while insisting that theological statements cannot be? According to Tillich, when God is the subject of predication, all properties, relationships, and activities ascribed to him must be symbolic because God is *transcendent, infinite, not limited by the structure of creaturely existence.* Tillich refers to God as "wholly other"[27] to emphasize that he is radically unlike anything else we know. He says that God is not *a* being at all but "the Ground of Being."[28] Accordingly, attempts to talk literally of God must be banned, for they treat God as a particular, discrete being among other beings. That is, such talk incorrectly supposes that God is a being of a certain kind, has certain properties, and performs certain actions—a supposition that violates God's ultimacy. For Tillich, God is "beyond" all of that. It is utterly impossible, on Tillich's view, to specify literally *what* it is that symbolic statements are asserting about God. Nothing can ever be asserted of God in the strict sense, since God cannot be described in terms of the predicates in our language. Thus, one can never claim with respect to some property or attribute that God possesses it and that his claim is true if, and only if, God actually possesses it. Questions of literal truth and falsity are quite beside the point.

While Tillich does not think that the religious symbol can be cashed out literally, he thinks it can be an avenue of revelation, a means of focusing on one's "ultimate concern," an occasion for encountering God. Tillich explains that both "signs" and "symbols" point beyond themselves to something else. The typical sign (e.g., the red light at the intersection of two streets) does not point to itself but to the necessity of cars stopping. Symbols also point to something beyond themselves. Tillich explains:

> The difference, which is a fundamental difference between them, is that signs do not participate in any way in the reality and power of that to

which they point. Symbols, although they are not the same as that which they symbolize, participate in its meaning and power. The difference between symbol and sign is the participation in the symbolized reality which characterizes the symbols, and the nonparticipation in the "pointed-to" reality which characterizes a sign. For example, letters of the alphabet as they are written, an "A" or an "R" do not participate in the sound to which they point; on the other hand, the flag participates in the power of the king or the nation for which it stands and which it symbolizes.[29]

Every symbol, for Tillich, opens up a level of reality for which nonsymbolic language is inadequate. For example, artistic symbols—poetry, visual art, and music—open up levels of reality that can be opened up in no other way.

In opening up the deepest level of reality, religious symbols actually open up the deepest dimension of experience in the human soul. Born out of the collective consciousness among social groups or traditions, religious symbols participate in the dimension of ultimate reality, which is the dimension of the Holy. Yet the Holy transcends every concrete symbol of the Holy. Throughout the history of religion, a rich diversity of material in time and space has become at some time or other a symbol of the Holy. According to Tillich, the key to understanding the otherwise confusing history of religion is to see religions as employing symbols that rest on the ultimate ground of being (e.g., a lotus blossom, a star, a cross). The incredible power and tenacity of religious symbols is explained by the fact that they impress upon the human mind a relationship to its own ultimate ground and meaning.

Tillich's position, then, on theological language is that it directs us to something through which the Ultimate can be experienced. For Tillich, Christians speak symbolically when they say something like: "God sent his Son into the world to save it." Tillich maintains that taking this statement literally would be absurd. But we can still come under the power of the symbol. We know, for instance, what it is to send or move something from one place to another, to cause a change. We know that talk of a son implies a father and can draw upon rich, positive images of a loving father-son relationship. We know that a basic meaning of the word "world" is "all people" and so may envision God's love being extended to all people through his son. All of this and more sensitizes us to the power of the symbol.

Tillich's view of the symbolic nature of religious language is a classic one in modern discussions. Similar positions have been taken by John Macquarrie (1919–)[30] and Sallie McFague (1933–),[31] among others. The view is both important and interesting, but one wonders if it can be consistently held. Tillich himself claims to "interpret" the meanings of religious (and particularly Christian) symbols to us. And what can this be but an attempt to give theological talk a more determinate propositional content? Others who officially endorse a symbolic view talk of "drawing implications" (both theoretical and practical) from symbols. But the notion that symbols about God have "implications" smuggles in all sorts of logical relations appropriate to literal speech. The strong tendency to move toward some form of literal talk about God, even among the pansymbolists, makes one wonder whether it is possible to avoid speaking of God in some kind of literal fashion! The rub comes in finding an adequate account of what literal speech is and of how that account would relate to our speech about God. Such an account would, of course, have to avoid the same pitfalls that various theories of religious language as nonliteral were meant to avoid, while yielding an appropriate understanding of literality that is not as artificially restrictive as those theories are.

CAN TALK OF GOD BE LITERAL?

In opposition to those thinkers who insist that talk of God must be nonliteral, William Alston (1921–) offers a sophisticated theory of how it can be literal. He begins to build his case by making a distinction between the form of our language and the reality it addresses.[32] Alston admits that human language is defective for speaking about God because its *subject-predicate structure* assumes a distinction between an *object* and its *properties*, whereas it is maintained in classical philosophy that God's essence has no distinctions. So, when a predicate term (e.g., "love") attributes a property to some subject term (e.g., "Mother Teresa"), the subject-predicate structure of the sentence assumes a distinction between Mother Teresa and her love. However, we have to use the same subject-predicate language to speak of God and God's love, although there is no parallel distinction. Alston states therefore that our conceptual grid, reflected in our language, cannot fully capture the divine reality.[33]

Alston claims, however, that the limitations of our subject-predicate language do not necessarily preclude the literal application of all predicate terms to God. The possibility still remains that our human terms are not defective for speaking of God. That is, there can be a genuine reality that is the intended target of our terms. We typically apply concepts such as love or knowledge or power or action in a literal fashion to human beings. Human beings possess creaturely characteristics—finitude, temporality, embodiment. But Alston contends that the concepts of love, knowledge, power, action, and the like do not necessarily involve creaturely conditions. Thus, he believes that there is a core of meaning for these concepts that can be literally attributed to God.

Alston focuses on a particular category of predicate terms,[34] what he calls *personalistic predicates:*

> Personalistic predicates are those that, as a group, apply to a being only if that being is a "personal agent"—an agent that carries out intentions, plans, or purposes in its actions, that acts in the light of knowledge or belief; a being whose actions express attitudes and are guided by stan-

dards and principles; a being capable of communicating with other such agents and entering into other forms of personal relations with them.[35]

Various personalistic predicates that might be applied to God include "commands," "loves," and "guides."

The key question here is not whether we can form subject-predicate sentences with a subject-term used to refer to God and make literal use of a personalistic predicate term so as to claim that it is true of the subject. Obviously, both technical theology as well as ordinary religious discourse contain numerous such sentences. "God loves us" and "Yahweh is righteous" and "Allah is merciful" merely begin the list. The real issue is whether any such truth claim can be successful. In other words, it is whether any personalistic predicate term, used literally, can be *true of* God, or *truly applied* to God, or just *literally true* of God.

Nonliteralists insist that personalistic predicates cannot literally apply to God because of God's radical "otherness." Alston recognizes that there are different respects in which God has been thought to differ from creatures, and he arranges them on a scale of increasingly radical "otherness":

A. Incorporeality.
B. Infinity. This can be divided into:
    B1. The unlimited realization of each perfection.
    B2. The exemplification of all perfections, everything it is better to be than not to be.
C. Timelessness.
D. Absolute simplicity.
E. Not *a* being. (God is rather "Being-Itself.")[36]

Different thinkers on the subject of "divine otherness" emphasize different items on the list, with those favoring the range of items near the bottom of the list representing the more extreme versions of "otherness." It would be a very rewarding project to work through each item and determine whether the type of "otherness" indicated conceptually prohibits the literal application of intrinsic, personalistic predicates to God.

Alston selects the first item on the list for inspection, the concept of God's incorporeality. His aim is to show that the concept of *incorporeality*, or of an *incorporeal being*, is not incompatible with *personalistic predicates*. If he can show that personalistic terms can be literally true of an incorporeal being, he will not thereby have proved that they are literally true of God. But he will have shown that the concept of God's incorporeality does not rule them out. There may be other divine attributes (e.g., infinity or timelessness) that inhibit us from thinking literally of God as a personal agent, but settling those issues would be part of a much larger and more comprehensive undertaking.

Alston divides *personalistic predicates* (P-predicates) into two categories:

mental predicates (M-predicates) and *action predicates* (A-predicates). *Mental predicates* have to do with cognitions, feelings, emotions, attitudes, wants, thoughts, fantasies, and other internal psychological states, events, and processes. *Action predicates,* on the other hand, have to do, broadly speaking, with what an agent does. Philosophers have different views of the meaning of mental predicates and the meaning of action predicates,

On the matter of *mental predicates,* philosophers are divided over whether they are properly defined in terms of their behavioral manifestations. According to the *Private Paradigm* view, the meaning of an M-predicate is not defined through behavioral manifestations but is known through inner experience or introspection. This is true regardless of the fact that certain inner states (e.g., feeling depressed) regularly tend to manifest themselves in certain behavioral ways (e.g,. droopy appearance and lack of vigor). Proponents of the Private Paradigm view contend that associated behaviors are not necessary to the concept of an inner state, since, in the presence of other inner states, one may not exhibit those behaviors. One could imagine, for example, that, given sufficiently high motivation not to appear droopy (e.g., wanting to do well on a job interview), one could appear more energized, even though one is feeling depressed. It seems rather unproblematic, according to Alston, to conceive of an incorporeal being having mental states on the Private Paradigm view, since this view does not require that inner states be connected to bodily behaviors.

Opposing the Private Paradigm view is the *Logical Connection* view, which asserts that there is a logical (conceptual) connection between a mental state and its overt manifestations. Alston agrees that an M-predicate is applicable to a subject S only if A-predicates are applicable to it. God, on this view, can literally know, purpose, and will only if God can literally perform overt actions. Interestingly, this thesis mirrors the fundamental place of divine agency in Judeo-Christian theology. However, many who advocate Logical Connectionism assume that a being is capable of overt action only if it is capable of bodily movements and, conversely, that a nonbodily being is not capable of performing overt actions. Concepts of such M-predicates as "making," "commanding," or "forgiving" would, then, necessarily include the concept of bodily movements of the maker, commander, or forgiver.

This discussion leads to the matter of *action predicates.* Since the concept of God is one of an incorporeal or nonbodily being, many thinkers conclude that the concept excludes the capability of overt actions. But Alston charges that it is question begging to assume that our concept of overt action requires specifications of bodily movements by corporeal beings. He sets out to show that the concept of action does not conceptually require bodily movements and thus to remove an obstacle to thinking of an incorporeal being as performing overt actions.

Alston refers to the well-known discussion in twentieth-century philosophy of a *basic action.* A *basic action* is one that is performed *not* by or in (simultaneously) performing some other action. A *nonbasic action* is one that is performed by or in (simultaneously) performing some other action. For example, signing my name on a check (a nonbasic action) is performed by moving my hand in a certain way (for present purposes, a basic action). If we were to analyze many examples like this, Alston thinks that we would conclude that our concepts of many particular human basic actions do indeed involve specifications of bodily movements. Obviously, these particular kinds of basic actions cannot apply literally to an incorporeal being. Likewise, if we were to inspect numerous examples of human non-basic actions, we would also conclude that they require bodily movements but are often not specific in regard to particular types of bodily move-ments. Making a souffle, for instance, involves causing a souffle to come into existence, but the range of bodily movements used to do this is quite open. A person can stir the ingredients with his right hand or with his left. Thus, it may well be that human beings may not bring about such consequences except by moving their bodies.

It does not follow, however, from the fact that bodily movement is involved in all of the kinds of human actions (both basic and nonbasic) with which we are acquainted that the concept of bodily movement is built into the concept of human action concepts. And, even if we were to grant that all human A-concepts do contain a bodily movement requirement, all that follows is that no *human* A-concepts are literally applicable to an incorporeal being such as God. It does not follow that *no* A-concepts what-soever are applicable. Why should we suppose that the action concepts that apply to human beings exhaust all the action concepts that there are? This opens up the question of whether we can form A-concepts that, first of all, are distinctively *action* concepts and, second, do not require any bodily movements of the agent.

To address this point, Alston narrows his discussion to *intentional* ac-tions, that is, those the agent *means* to perform. It is clear that bodily move-ment alone does not constitute an action, since many bodily movements are not intentional (e.g., automatic jerks, twitches, reflexes). So, what makes an action an *action?* Alston believes that only two theories have a chance at giving an adequate answer to this question: *psychological causation* and *agent causation.* He crafts an argument to the effect that neither of these two theories contains any inherent restrictions on incorporeal action.

The *psychological causation* theory asserts that the psychological back-ground (e.g., motives, beliefs, attitudes, intentions) gives rise to a "bodily movement" and makes it an *action* rather than a "mere" movement. Since there is no conceptual obstacle to thinking of an incorporeal being as having intentions, we are left with a question about bodily movements. In the case of an incorporeal being, something would have to substitute for the bodily movement component of a basic action. Alston suggests that it is just a fact about human beings that only bodily movements are under direct voluntary control; it is not a conceptual restraint on basic action per se. It is logically possible that there could be agents, corporeal or otherwise, such that things other than their bodies are under their direct voluntary control. Some agents might be such that they could bring a souffle into being without doing something else (i.e., it would be a basic action for them). So, it appears that any change whatsoever—and not just bodily movements—can be the core of a basic action. Precisely what changes are within the repertoire of a given incorporeal agent depends on the nature of that agent. Alston's conclusion, then, is that the *psychological causation* theory poses no conceptual road block to ascribing action predicates to an incorporeal being. In the case of God, the way is open to conceive of his "creating light" or "parting the sea of reeds" or "making a souffle" as the performance of basic actions, actions that are under Gods direct voluntary control and do not have to be brought about by his first doing something else.

The second theory, *agent causation,* is actually less problematic than the first. According to this view, a "bodily movement" is an *action* if and only if it is caused in a certain special way and not by some other event or state; it is simply caused by the *agent.* Thus, in performing a basic action, one "directly" brings about a bodily movement—not by doing something "else" to bring it about. One simply exploits one's basic capacity to perform a basic action. Given that the concept of agent causation is not restricted to corporeal substances or committed to the agent's possessing a particular kind of internal structure or mechanism, it presents no conceptual bar to attributing A-predicates to God.

Overall, then, Alston considers his case to be successful. He claims not to have proved that intrinsic predicates can be literally predicated of God but to have shown that there is no conceptual impossibility in applying mental predicates and action predicates to an incorporeal being.[37] In showing this much, he has at least established that the prospects for speaking literally about God are not dim as often thought.[38] If Alston is right, then he has gone a considerable way toward showing that theistic thinkers are not asserting and discussing propositions about God that are obviously absurd or extraneous. By the same token, he has helped show that classical critiques and denials of theistic beliefs are not beside the point.

STUDY QUESTIONS

1. Discuss various reasons for philosophical interest in religious language. Must one have a philosophical theory of religious language before using it?

2. What is the theory of analogy for explaining the meaning of religious language? What strengths is this theory supposed to have? What weakness have been pointed out?

3. Can you state the verifiability principle of meaning that was advanced by the logical positivists? Why was it supposed to be a boon for philosophy? What impact did it have on religious language? What sorts of responses ensued?

4. What could it mean to criticize the verifiability principle by saying that it confuses issues of meaning and truth?

5. Is verification or falsification a totally logical and objective process—in which case it is the same for all people? Or does it have a psychological aspect that takes into account the mental states of individual people—in which case it can differ from person to person?

6. What exactly is the difference between saying that a religious statement is meaningless and saying it is false?

7. Try to state in your own words the basic idea of functional analysis. How is it that the functional analysis of religious language generally ignores matters of truth and falsity?

8. Explore the various functions which language in general seems to fulfill within a linguistic community. Explore the functions which religious language seems to perform. Can any one function be identified as "basic"?

9. Make a case, as Paul Tillich would, for all talk of God being symbolic. Evaluate.

10. What strategy does William Alston use for showing that we can speak literally of God. Do you think his strategy is successful? Why, or why not?

11. Explore the question of whether Alston has shown how we can avoid anthropomorphism and speak univocally of God.

NOTES

1. From Arthur Clarke, "The Nine Billion Names of God," in his collection of short stories titled *The Nine Billion Names of God* (New York: Harcourt, Brace, and World, 1967).

2. Aquinas, *Summa Theologica*, Part I, Question 13, Art. 5; also see *Summa Contra Gentiles*, Book 1, chaps. 28–34.

3. Frederick Ferré, "Analogy in Theology," in *Encyclopedia of Philosophy*, vol. 1 (New York: Macmillan, 1967), pp. 94–95.

4. Accepting the rebuttal that analogy theory is distorted if it is mathematically modeled, a counter might still be made: that while the analogy theory is, admittedly, a theory of meaning, there are *two* unknowns, not one, on the God-side of the equation. Suffice it here to say that a sophisticated version of analogy theory seeks to account for the fact that the mode of God's being (which we here call "infinite"), as well as the intrinsic character of his attributes, is not really an object of full conceptual knowledge. As Ross says, the infinity of God is only approximated "when we say that God is infinitely wise, infinitely good, infinitely intelligent, etc." We can say *that* God is wise, for instance, but do not understand *how* he is wise. Such matters slip through our finite, conceptual net, so to speak. See Ross, *Philosophical Theology*, (Indianapolis: Bobbs-Merrill, 1969), p. 56.

5. An excellent treatment is James F. Ross, "Analogy as a Rule of Meaning for Religious Language," *International Philosophical Quarterly* 1, no. 30 (Sept. 1961): 468–502.

6. Most formulations of the verifiability principle included the condition that the statements in question are not analytic, that is, that their truth or falsity is not simply a function of their logical structure and not a function of their relationship to possible empirical facts.

7. A. J. Ayer, *Language, Truth and Logic* (New York: Dover, 1952), p. 35.

8. As it also turned out, neither metaphysics nor ethics fared well under the positivist criterion of meaning.

9. Actually, this point leads to an interesting debate over first-order statements and second-order rules for meaning. Defenders of the verifiability criterion held that it is just that, a criterion, and therefore that it did not have to meet its own standard of meaning. In other words, it was a second-order rule that was to be applied to first-order language. Critics held that it should have to meet its own standard of meaning and, since it is not meaningful according to its own standard, it is self-defeating.

10. John Wisdom, *Logic and Language*, vol. 1 (Oxford: Blackwell, 1951), chap. 10.

11. Antony Flew, "Theology and Falsification," in *New Essays in Philosophical Theology*, ed. Antony Flew and Alasdair MacIntyre (New York: Macmillan, 1955), p. 96.

12. Ibid, p. 99.

13. R. M. Hare, "Theology and Falsification," in Flew and MacIntyre, eds., *New Essays*, pp. 99–103.

14. Basil Mitchell, "Theology and Falsification," in Flew and MacIntyre, eds., *New Essays*, p. 103.

15. Ibid., p. 104.

16. John Hick, "Theology and Verification," *Theology Today* 17 (1960): 260–61. Hick develops his case further in his *Faith and Knowledge*, 2d ed. (New York: Macmillan, 1966), chap 8.

17. Frederick Ferré, *Language, Logic and God* (New York: Harper Torchbooks, 1961), p. 58.

18. R. B. Braithwaite, "An Empiricist's View of the Nature of Religious Belief," in *The Existence of God*, ed. John Hick (New York: Macmillan, 1964), pp. 229–52.

19. Other mistakes: first, it initially assumes an inadequate theory of moral language in which statements of objective norms ("Murder is wrong") translate into expressions of subjective intentions ("I never intend to murder anyone"). Hence, whatever course of action one intends to follow becomes *moral*—a result that blatantly conflicts with our common moral experience! Second, Braithwaite mixes religious stories of quite diverse logical types, some intended as historical statements about the life of Jesus, others as parabolic, and so forth. Thus, Braithwaite overlooks numerous subtle differences in the uses of Christian stories. And, third, he totally ignores what religious believers themselves understand as the function and meaning of their various assertions and stories.

20. W. Donald Hudson, *Ludwig Wittgenstein* (Richmond, Va: John Knox Press, 1968), p. 62.

21. Paul van Buren, *The Edges of Language* (New York: Macmillan, 1972).

22. Ludwig Wittgenstein, *Philosophical Investigations*, trans G. E. M. Anscombe (New York: Macmillan, 1953), §23 (p. 11ᵉ).

23. Van Buren, *Edges of Language*, p. 157.

24. See Chapter 3 of this book for a fuller discussion of fideism.

25. Van Buren, *Edges of Language*, p. 134; also p. 137. "The word 'God' marks the point at which the religious man has come up against the final limit of what he can say about the object of his concern" (p. 135).

26. On models, see Ian T. Ramsey, "Talking about God," *Myth and Symbol*, ed. F. W. Dillistone (London: SPCK, 1966), pp. 76–97, and James Kellenberger, *Religious Discovery, Faith, and Knowledge* (Englewood Cliffs, N.J.: Prentice-Hall, 1972), chap.

3; on story, Alasdair MacIntyre, "The Logical Status of Religious Belief," *Metaphysical Beliefs*, 2d ed. (London: SCM Press, 1970), pp. 158–201; and Ian Crombie, "The Possibility of Theological Statements," in *Faith and Logic*, ed. B. Mitchell (London: George Allen and Unwin, 1957), p. 60; on metaphor, see Paul Ricoeur, "Biblical Hermeneutics," in *Semeia* 4, ed. J. D. Crossan (Missoula, Mont.: Scholars Press, 1975); on parable, Ronald Hepburn, *Christianity and Paradox* (London: C. A. Watts & Co., Ltd., 1958), pp. 192–204.

27. Among the thinkers who take this kind of approach are Paul Tillich, Karl Barth, John Macquarrie, Emile Bruner, and Rudolph Otto.

28. This theme runs through Tillich, *Systematic Theology* (Chicago: University of Chicago Press, 1951–63) and *The Dynamics of Faith* (New York: Harper and Row, 1957).

29. Paul Tillich, "The Nature of Religious Language," *Christian Scholar* 38, no. 3 (1955): 189–97. [This piece is reprinted in *PRSR*, Part 7, 357–65.

30. John Macquarrie, *Principles of Christian Theology*, 2d ed. (New York: Scribner's, 1977).

31. Sallie McFague, *Metaphorical Theology: Models of God in Religious Language* (Philadelphia: Fortress Press, 1982).

32. Alston also has employed more classically medieval language to make the same point. Medieval thinkers spoke of the distinction between the *mode of signification* (the form of our language) and the *perfection signified* (the reality about which we speak). Here "perfection" is synonymous with "property" or "attribute." See William Alston, "Being-Itself and Talk about God," *Center Journal* 3, no. 3 (Summer 1984): 21.

33. The point here, for Alston, is that we can know *that* God loves but we cannot comprehend *how* God loves.

34. Alston states that even proponents of nonliteral talk could presumably be led to agree that *negative predicates* and *extrinsic predicates* are literally true of God. Such *negative predicates* as "immutable" or "not identical with Jimmy Carter" are literally true of God, but presumably no opponent of literal religious language means to deny this. Moreover, various *extrinsic predicates* surely seem to be true of God, such as "thought of now by me." So he restricts the point at issue to this: whether *intrinsic predicates* can truly apply to God, particularly what he calls *personalistic predicates*.

35. William Alston, "Can We Speak Literally of God?" in *Is God GOD?* ed. Axel D. Steuer and James W. McClendon Jr. (Nashville: Abingdon Press, 1981), p. 144–77. [Reprinted in *PRSR*, Part 7, pp. 367–68.]

36. William Alston, "Functionalism and Theological Language," *American Philosophical Quarterly* 22 (July 1985): 221. Also reprinted in William Alston, *Divine Nature and Human Language: Essays in Philosophical Theology* (Ithaca, N.Y.: Cornell University Press, 1989), p. 64.

37. Referring to the Thomistic project in religious language, some would see Alston as having shown the way talking univocally of both finite and infinite beings. The anthropomorphism that Aquinas feared can be avoided by defining terms in ways that do not invoke finite or corporeal elements. Such terms as "knows" (entertains a consistent set of justified true beliefs), "desires" (a strong feeling concerning goals to be achieved, in line with intentions), "creates" (brings into being), and "good" (morally responsible, virtuous in character, disposed to do the right) can be applied univocally to creatures and to God.

38. The total body of Alston's work on religious language deserves to be read in its larger context. An excellent resource is his *Divine Nature and Human Language: Essays in Philosophical Theology* (Ithaca, N.Y.: Cornell University Press, 1989).

SUGGESTED READING

Alston, William P. *Divine Nature and Human Language.* Ithaca, N.Y.: Cornell University Press, 1989.

Ayer, A. J. *Language, Truth, and Logic.* New York: Dover, 1952.

Diamond, Malcolm, and Thomas V. Lizenbury Jr., eds. *The Logic of God.* Indianapolis, Ind.: Bobbs-Merrill, 1975.

Durrant, Michael. *The Logical Status of "God."* London: Macmillan, 1973.

Ferré, Frederick. *Language, Logic and God.* New York: Harper and Row, 1969.

Gilkey, Langdon. *Naming the Whirlwind.* Indianapolis: Bobbs-Merrill, 1969.

Gilson, Etienne. *Linguistics and Philosophy.* Notre Dame, Ind.: University of Notre Dame Press, 1988.

High, Dallas, ed. *New Essays in Religion Language.* New York: Oxford University Press, 1969.

Kellenberger, James. *Religious Discovery, Faith, and Knowledge.* Englewood Cliffs, N.J.: Prentice-Hall, 1972.

Kimel, Alvin F., Jr. *Speaking the Christian God.* Grand Rapids, Mich.: Eerdmans, 1992.

Mascall, E. L. *Existence and Analogy.* New York: Longmans, Green, 1949.

———. *Words and Images.* New York: Ronald Press, 1957.

McFague, Sallie. *Metaphorical Theology.* Philadelphia: Fortress Press, 1982.

Mitchell, Basil. *Faith and Logic.* London: Allen and Unwin, 1957.

Ramsey, Ian. *Religious Language.* London: SCM Press, 1957.

———, ed. *Words about God: The Philosophy of Religion.* New York: Harper and Row, 1971.

CHAPTER 9   MIRACLES: DOES
GOD INTERVENE IN
EARTHLY AFFAIRS?

> Blinded and paralyzed on one side of his body, a retired French accoun-
> tant refused to believe that nothing would help him just because his doc-
> tors couldn't find a cure. . . . [So he] decided to journey to the famous
> "Our Lady of Lourdes" shrine and beg the Lord for a miracle. . . . Within
> hours of bathing in the spring, he regained his sight and could walk with-
> out crutches.[1]

Dramatic healings such as those linked to the spring at Lourdes form only
a small portion of the class of events alleged to be miraculous. A person
being spared in a devastating earthquake that killed everyone else directly
affected, water being turned into wine, a baby being born of a virgin—all
these events and more have been called miracles. Moreover, miracles are
typically invested with religious significance. Specifically, the concept of
miracle is normally linked with God and his relation to the world. It
should not be surprising, then, that philosophers of religion have long
been interested in this intriguing subject.

MIRACLES DEFINED

The term *miracle* is used in ordinary discussions to refer to a wide variety
of occurrences. Some individuals use it to describe any *unexpected event*—
from the unanticipated passing of a difficult exam, to the rediscovery of a
hopelessly lost heirloom, to a rapid, welcomed change in a person's behavior. Others use the term in a more restricted sense, applying it only to those
very unusual events that apparently conflict with known scientific laws—
events such as the survival of a flight attendant after a 10,000–foot fall or
the total recovery of a person dying of cancer. However, "miracle" is most
frequently defined in a distinctively religious sense. That is, for most indi-

viduals, a miracle is not only an unusual event but also the *result of some sort of divine activity.* For example, the contention in the opening story is not simply that the retired accountant regained his sight and the use of his legs but that God brought these things about. It is this sense of the term that has generated the greatest volume and intensity of philosophical discussion.

What exactly does it mean to say that God has caused a certain event? Many theists hold that many, if not most, events are acts of God in the broad, fundamental sense that God has created the universe, established the "laws" upon which causal interaction within this universe is based, and continues to sustain such interaction by divine power.[2] In this sense, the birth of a baby and a summer thunderstorm can be said to be acts of God. Most of these theists, however, also maintain that there are some events—for example, healings—that would not have occurred in the exact manner in which they did if God had not *directly* intervened—that is, if God had not at some point and in some manner directly manipulated the natural order. Miraculous occurrences, not surprisingly, are normally considered to fall within this category of *direct acts of God.* However, opinion differs on what type(s) of direct divine activity should be labeled miraculous. Since the time of David Hume (1711–1776), it has been very popular in philosophical circles to define miracles as direct acts of God that "violate" natural laws.[3] But what exactly does it mean to say that a natural law has been violated? This question stands at the threshold of a very complex and debatable issue. However, it is possible to state what most individuals seem to have in mind when they speak of miracles as violations.

Natural laws are, for present purposes, statements that describe what will (or probably will) happen or not happen under specifiable conditions. They describe the inherent tendencies or dispositions of things in the world to act and react in certain ways. Accepted scientific laws may be viewed as specifications of some of these natural laws. Our knowledge of well-established scientific laws leads us to believe, for example, that water does not turn instantly into wine and that those who have genuinely died do not (at least in a physical sense) come back to life. But let us assume that someone actually were to turn water instantly into wine or rise from the dead. Not only would we then be required to acknowledge the occurrence of an event that our knowledge of scientific laws gives us good reason to believe will not occur. More important, we would then be required to acknowledge the occurrence of an event for which it appears no natural explanation could ever be forthcoming. And thus we would be justified in assuming that a natural law has been violated.

However, many theists do not believe we should limit our application of the term "miracle" to only those events for which no plausible natural explanation is (or could be) available. Consider, for example, the following story related by R. F. Holland (1932–). A child riding his toy motor-car strays on to an unguarded railway crossing near his house when a wheel of his car gets stuck down the side of one of the rails. At that exact moment, an express train is approaching with the signals in its favor, and a curve in the track makes it impossible for the driver to stop his train in time to avoid any obstruction he might encounter on the crossing. Moreover, the child is so engrossed in freeing his wheel that he hears neither the train whistle nor his mother, who has just come out of the house and is trying to get his attention. The child appears to be doomed. But just before the train rounds the curve, its brakes are applied, and it comes to rest a few feet from the child. The mother thanks God for the miracle, although she learns in due course that there was not necessarily anything supernatural about the manner in which the brakes of the train came to be applied. The driver had fainted, for a reason that had nothing to do with the presence of the child on the line, and the brakes were applied automatically as his hand ceased to exert pressure on the control lever.[4]

The event sequence described in this situation includes no component for which a natural explanation is not available. Boys sometimes play on train tracks, drivers sometimes faint, and the brakes of trains have been constructed to become operative when a driver's hand releases the control lever. But another explanation presents itself in this case: that God directly intervened to cause the driver to faint at the precise moment. And as many theists see it, if God did directly intervene in this instance, the event could justifiably be considered a miracle, even though a totally natural explanation is also available. In short, to generalize, many theists do no want to limit the range of the term "miracle" to only those direct acts of God for which no natural explanation can presently be offered. They want to expand the definition to cover any event in relation to which God has directly manipulated the natural order, regardless of anyone's ability to construct plausible alternate causal scenarios.[5]

Moreover, even here a finer distinction is sometimes made. When we think of God's directly bringing about an event, it is quite natural to conceive of God's manipulation of the natural order as occurring *at the time* the event takes place. For instance, if we think of God bringing it about that the driver in our scenario fainted, it is quite natural to conceive of God as doing something just before the train rounds the bend. But as philosophers such as Robert Adams have pointed out, there is another way to think of God's activity in this context. We can conceive of God creating "the world in such a way that it was physically predetermined from the beginning" that nature would act in the appropriate way "at precisely the time at which God foresaw" it would be needed.[6] For example, we can conceive of God creating the world in such a way that a specific individual driving a train would faint at a specific time in order to save the life of a young boy. In this case, God does not directly intervene in the sense that he directly manipulates a natural order already in place. However, he still directly intervenes in the sense that he purposely manipulates the natural order to bring about some event that would not have occurred without this intentional divine activity.[7]

When we consider the miraculous in any of these senses, various philosophical questions arise. One set of questions is concerned with whether it is possible for God to intervene in earthly affairs and (for violation miracles) whether natural laws can be violated. Let us turn first to the question of whether a violation of a natural law is possible. Alistair McKinnon (1925–) offers us a popular negative response.[8] Natural laws, he tells us, are simply "shorthand descriptions of how things do, in fact, happen"— that is, shorthand descriptions of the "actual course of events." Accordingly, to claim that an occurrence is a violation of a natural law is to claim that the event in question is a "suspension of the actual course of events" and this, of course, is an impossibility. Events may well occur, he acknowledges, that seem at present to be incompatible with how we believe things normally happen. But a true counterinstance to what we now believe to be a natural law only shows the law to be inadequate. Since natural laws, by definition, describe "the actual course of events," we must in principle always be willing to expand our laws to accommodate any occurrence, no matter how unusual. We can, by definition, never have both the exception and the rule.[9]

However, many find this line of reasoning questionable. To maintain that a natural law accurately describes the natural order is to say only that it correctly identifies what will occur under a specific set of *natural* conditions. But to maintain that an event is a *miraculous* counterinstance to a natural law is not to maintain that some event has occurred under the exact set of *natural* conditions covered by this law and nothing more. To say that water has miraculously turned into wine, for example, is not to say that water has turned into wine under the exact set of natural conditions under which the relevant laws tell us this will not occur. It is to maintain that an additional nonnatural causal factor, namely direct divine activity, was also present in this case. Accordingly, it is argued, unless it is assumed that supernatural activity is impossible, it cannot be assumed that a miraculous counterinstance to a natural law—that a counterinstance produced in part by *divine* circumvention or modification of the natural order—is conceptually impossible.[10]

This brings us directly back to the more fundamental question concerning the possibility of miracles: Is it *possible* for God to intervene in earthly affairs? Of course, many individuals do in fact deny the existence of any type of supernatural being. And even some who affirm the existence of such a being—for example, process theists—deny that this being can unilaterally intervene in earthly affairs in the sense necessary to produce miraculous events. However, few philosophers today maintain that the existence of a supernatural being, or the ability of such a being (if it exists) to intervene, can be demonstrated to be impossible.[11]

Most philosophers are currently concerned instead with another type of question related to the miraculous: What can be known or reasonably believed? Specifically, they are interested in three related but distinct questions: Under what conditions can a person reasonably maintain that certain unusual events have actually occurred as reported? Under what conditions can a person reasonably maintain that an event could have no natural explanation? And under what conditions can a person reasonably maintain that God was directly involved in bringing about a given occurrence? Each will be considered in some detail.

MIRACLES AS HISTORICAL EVENTS

Many theists do not claim only that certain types of events could justifiably be considered miracles if they were to occur. They claim that certain events that merit the label "miraculous" have actually occurred. If these events have natural explanations available, as is the case in Holland's story about the boy and the train, the accuracy of such claims can be assessed in the same way we assess any historical report. We can, for example, try to determine whether the original source was trustworthy and whether what was originally reported has been faithfully transmitted.

Yet what of those allegedly miraculous events that are incompatible with current natural laws? What, for instance, of the Christian beliefs that Jesus came back to life after he had been dead for three days and that Jesus turned water into wine? Are there conditions under which a theist can (or at least could) justifiably claim that seemingly unexplainable events of this sort have actually occurred as reported?

Most philosophers currently grant that reports of *repeatable* counterinstances to current laws cannot justifiably be dismissed. That is, most grant that if a counterinstance to our current laws can be made to recur, given equivalent natural conditions, we are not in a position to dismiss reported occurrences of this event. However, few (if any) of the types of counterinstances to our current laws considered to be miraculous by theists—for examples, healings and resurrections—fit into this category. They are at present not repeatable under specifiable natural conditions. And there are a number of philosophers—most notably, Antony Flew (1923–)—who argue that, when considering the accuracy of reports of such events, we ought to be *much* more skeptical. It is clearly possible, Flew acknowledges, that nonrepeatable counterinstances to well-confirmed natural have occurred (or will occur). However, as Hume has rightly pointed out, the wise person proportions his or her belief to the evidence. And when we consider the evidence rationally, it is not difficult to see the problem at hand. We have well-known natural laws that justifiably lead us to believe, for instance, that dead people remain dead and that water does not turn into wine. Such laws are not the product of inaccessible scientific studies or outmoded historical hearsay. Such laws can be, and are, tested and reconfirmed daily. The dead stay dead, and untreated water persists as water.

On the other hand, the alleged counterinstances to our current natural laws are supported only by *personal testimony* from the past, and such testimonial evidence is by its very nature always weaker than the evidence for the laws it contradicts. For one thing, while many people have found the laws in question to hold, only a few, possibly biased individuals claim that the counterinstance occurred. And while the evidence supporting the laws in question is objective, the testimonial reports of those who claim to have witnessed the event are quite subjective.

Accordingly, Flew concludes, we can never have better reasons for accepting the report of a nonrepeatable counterinstance to our current laws—for example, the claim that Jesus rose from the dead—than for rejecting the report as inaccurate. If such an event were repeatable—that is, if it could be produced by anyone under specifiable natural conditions—then we would need to take it seriously. But with respect to reports of nonrepeatable counterinstances, "no matter how impressive the testimony might appear, the most favorable verdict history could ever return must be the agnostic and appropriately Scottish 'not proven'."[12]

Does not this line of reasoning, though, demonstrate an arbitrary and dogmatic naturalistic prejudice? What right, it might be argued, does Flew have to assume that the laws of science have the ultimate or final voice in relation to history? How can other, nonnatural factors be ruled out automatically? For example, many theists believe that specific "miraculous" events have occurred because they are recorded in "holy writings" such as the Bible, sources whose accuracy is thought to be guaranteed by their divine origin. Moreover, the types of miracles recorded in such revelations are often thought to furnish theists with clues as to how God still works in the world today. For example, many Christians believe the Bible to teach that God sometimes intervenes in response to prayer. Thus, when such theists are told of alleged occurrences that fit divine patterns, these reports are often initially granted a reasonable degree of reliability. In short, many theists do in fact believe nonnaturalistic evidence to be quite relevant to the question at hand. And how can Flew justifiably dismiss such evidence completely?

This criticism, however, may well be misguided. Flew repeatedly emphasizes that he is, in this context, discussing only what we can conclude on the basis of the historical (natural) evidence alone. He is not attempting to rule out the possibility that the historicity of certain events could, for some people, be settled on the basis of nonnatural criteria—for example, a revelation from God. Moreover, it is not clear that Flew's decision to consider only "natural" historical criteria can in this context be considered arbitrary. He makes this decision because he is assuming that theists generally wish to use miracles to help establish or support religious belief. And he rightly sees that an alleged miracle can have this apologetic value only if, among other things, the occurrence in question can be established objectively on "natural" grounds.[13]

Some theists today, of course, do not desire or even believe that it is possible to certify to the satisfaction of all rational individuals that particular allegedly miraculous events have actually occurred as reported. Instead, they want to hold only that they are justified in believing this for themselves. Historically, however, theists have often wanted to use miracles to support belief in God's existence, or establish that Jesus is God, or support the claim that some text is an *authentic* divine revelation. Thus, to the extent that this is still the case, it does not appear that Flew's line of reasoning can be accused of involving arbitrary, dogmatic naturalism. In this context, the question of how the actual occurrence of reported events can be authenticated in a public, objective sense remains paramount.

Even granting all this, is Flew's line of reasoning sound? No one denies that natural laws are continuously open to confirmation or disconfirmation and, thus, that we are indeed justified in using such laws to predict in general what will or will not occur under certain conditions. No one denies, for example, that we have well-established laws that justifiably lead us to believe that a withered leg does not instantly return to its normal shape, and, thus, we should not expect such an occurrence. Moreover, no one denies that reports of nonrepeatable counterinstances to well-established current laws should be viewed with a certain amount of initial skepticism. However, there are those who believe it unreasonable to assume that the evidence supporting even the most highly confirmed laws *always* furnishes a sufficient basis for dismissing reports of nonrepeatable counterinstances to them.

As some see it, to make this assumption fails to take into account the prima facie reliability of our sensory belief-forming faculties. We rely on these faculties daily, and, in general, they serve us quite well. In fact, the general reliability of such faculties must be presupposed by those who formulate our natural laws. Thus, in those cases where we had no reason to doubt the reliability of these belief-forming faculties—for instance, if we were to observe a seeming counterinstance ourselves or if it were to be directly observed by a friend whose character and objectivity were beyond question—it is not clear that it would always be justifiable to decide in favor of the natural laws in question, even if such laws were very well established and the occurrence in question could not be repeated.[14]

Moreover, Richard Swinburne (1934–) adds, we do not have merely the assumed reliability of our belief-forming faculties and the evidence of the relevant natural laws to consider; we must also consider any relevant physical traces. In the case of an alleged healing of a withered leg, such relevant traces might be X-rays (or photographs) of the leg taken just before and just after the alleged occurrence. An even more compelling physical trace would be a videotape of the incident. Of course, X-rays, photographs, and videotapes can be altered. Thus, such physical traces could not conclusively verify that the event had actually occurred as reported. And since the traces would in this case be incompatible with well-established natural laws, caution in drawing a conclusion would indeed be justified. But we have generally accepted methods for assessing (analyzing, testing) the authenticity of X-rays, photographs, and videotapes, and if it proved highly likely that they were reliable, Swinburne contends, such data would obviously stand as very strong evidence for the accuracy of the report in question.[15]

In short, to some there appears to be no strong basis for refusing automatically to acknowledge the accuracy of reports of nonrepeatable counterinstances to our current natural laws. The fact the alleged occurrence is incompatible with well-established natural laws does count strongly against the report. And it is not easy to say exactly when the assumed reliability of our faculties and/or the physical evidence can justifiably be held to counterbalance or even outweigh the long-standing scientific evidence. But a decision concerning the accuracy of such reports, it is argued, must finally be made on a case-by-case basis.[16]

MIRACLES AS UNEXPLAINABLE EVENTS

As we saw earlier, not all individuals believe that a miracle must be an event for which no plausible natural explanation is available. However, since the time of Hume, the majority of philosophers have conceived of miracles as "violations" of natural laws. That is, they have assumed for the sake of discussion that miracles are events for which no totally natural explanation could be forthcoming. And for such philosophers, a second important question quite naturally arises. Even in those cases where no one denies that a nonrepeatable counterinstance to our current laws has occurred, could we ever be in a position to claim justifiably that any such event is permanently unexplainable in this sense? If, for instance, we all agreed that someone has actually come back to life after being dead for three days, would we be in a position to claim justifiably that this acknowledged counterinstance to our current laws could never be explained naturally?

It might appear that a promising response is inherent in the very definition of miracle. As was stated earlier, miracles are probably best understood to be direct acts of God that would not have occurred in the exact manner they did if God had not directly manipulated the relevant natural cause/effect patterns. But this is simply another way of saying that such events do not have totally natural causal explanations. Accordingly, it might appear that any direct act of God is automatically an event that is permanently unexplainable naturally. That is, to be more specific, it might appear that the question of whether we can justifiably claim that an alleged miracle could have no adequate natural explanation actually collapses into the question of whether we can justifiably claim that an event is a direct act of God.

However, this line of reasoning is seen by some to be based on a confusion. It is true, they grant, that if an event is a direct act of God, this occurrence itself cannot have a totally natural causal explanation. But the primary purpose of natural science is not to determine what nature has in fact produced. The main objective of science, rather, is to determine what nature is capable of producing—what can occur under solely natural conditions. For instance, the primary purpose of natural science is not to determine whether natural factors alone actually caused any specific person's cancer to enter remission. The primary purpose of science is to determine whether natural factors alone could have produced an event of this type. Hence, when considering whether we could ever be in a position to maintain justifiably that an event is permanently unexplainable on scientific grounds, the question is not whether we could ever be in a position to maintain justifiably that a specific state of affairs itself *was* not produced by nature alone. The question, rather, is whether we could ever be in a position to maintain justifiably that an event of this type *could* not have been produced by nature alone.[17]

If we accept this reading of the issue, what ought we to conclude? Could we ever be in a position to label an event permanently unexplainable in this sense? The most common argument denying this possibility can be stated succinctly. It might now appear that some type of event could never be explained. But it is always possible that new information, generated by further scientific investigation, will force us to revise our current set of natural laws related to any given type of occurrence. Therefore, we can never decisively state that any given type of event could never be given a natural explanation.[18]

Not all philosophers agree, however. Such philosophers are not assuming that they have complete and incontrovertible knowledge of the natural order, nor do they even assume that any specific law can ever justifiably be considered immune from revision. Their claim is weaker: even granting that we might gather significant new scientific data and greatly revise our current set of laws accordingly, if some events were to occur, we could justifiably rule that events of this type could never be given a natural explanation.

But what are the criteria by which such events are to be identified? The key, according to Swinburne, lies in our ability (or inability) to devise new scientific laws to accommodate seemingly unexplainable events. We have, to some extent, good evidence about the "laws of nature," and some of these laws are so highly confirmed that any modification we would suggest to account for the odd counterinstance would be so clumsy and ad hoc that it would upset the whole structure of science. For example, let us imagine that we experience the "resurrection of . . . a man whose heart has not been beating and who was dead by other currently used criteria." Or let us assume we see "water turning into wine without the assistance of special apparatus or chemical catalysts." The relevant laws in such cases are well entrenched; they cannot be modified or given up easily. Accordingly, Swinburne concludes, if events of this type were to occur, they could justifiably be considered permanently unexplainable events.[19]

Margaret Boden (1936–) argues in an analogous manner. She grants that observable phenomena cannot normally be dismissed as lying forever outside the range of science, but she is not convinced this always has to be the case. She invites us to consider the logically possible case of a leper whose missing fingers reappear instantly under the most stringent, frauddetecting conditions—for instance, in the presence of doctors or TV cameras. Such an event, she argues, would conflict with so many accepted scientific facts that any attempt to revise our present scientific laws to accommodate events of this type would so weaken the predictive power of such laws that they would no longer be of practical value. Accordingly, she concludes, if such an event were actually to occur, the scientist, of necessity, would be forced to identify it as a permanently unexplainable phenomenon.[20]

Such reasoning has a prima facie appeal, but an obvious question arises. Swinburne and Boden freely acknowledge that the scientific enterprise is continually discovering new, often startling and unexpected, information about the causal relationships that obtain in our universe. Also, they freely acknowledge that the annals of science record numerous instances in which supposed counterinstances to long-standing scientific laws were later demonstrated—sometimes only after significant conceptual shifts—to be consistent with such laws or revisions of them. Accordingly, is it not the height of scientific provincialism for anyone to maintain solely on the basis of the data now available that certain events could justifiably be labeled permanently unexplainable?

Swinburne and Boden obviously think not, and it is important to understand why. It is not, as mentioned before, because they believe they have some privileged understanding of the "true nature of reality." It is rather that when faced with an acknowledged counterinstance to very highly confirmed laws, they see only two basic options: to either modify the laws to accommodate the occurrence or affirm the adequacy of the laws and declare the event permanently unexplainable. And they feel that in some conceivable instances, the latter would be the more reasonable choice.

But is there not another option? Let us assume that after extensive testing, we cannot explain how water has turned into wine. Why must we in this case either radically modify the relevant laws or declare the event permanently unexplainable? Why cannot we simply continue to run further tests or label the occurrence a "freak event" and await the occurrence of similar events before seriously investigating further?

According to Holland, such a noncommittal posture would place the relevant laws in a state of uncertainty and would therefore weaken the strength of the scientific method.[21] But not everyone has found such a response convincing. Acknowledged counterinstances to our current laws, it is granted, do challenge the reliability of such laws. In fact, if it were true that the occurrence of acknowledged counterinstances to well-established laws required us to either modify such laws immediately or declare the counterinstances to be permanently unexplainable, the latter might well in some cases be the most reasonable choice. But only *repeatable* counterinstances, these critics maintain, actually require us to make such a decision. With respect to nonrepeatable counterinstances, this is a false dilemma. As long as a counterinstance—no matter how unusual—is not repeatable, a third alternative is always open to us: to continue to acknowledge the functional adequacy of the current laws in question while we search for new or modified laws to accommodate the unusual occurrence in question.[22]

Even if this is correct, however, little of religious significance *necessarily* follows. As stated before, although many philosophers are interested in determining whether certain types of events can justifiably be said to be violations of natural laws, it is doubtful that most theists actually share this concern. For most theists, what is of primary importance is whether, and only whether, the events in question would have occurred at the exact time and in the exact manner they did if God had not somehow acted.

MIRACLES AS ACTS OF GOD

This brings us to our final set of questions: those concerning our ability to establish that God has directly intervened in earthly affairs. For some philosophers, the most crucial of these questions continues to be the following: Are there imaginable conditions under which all rational individuals would be forced to admit that God has directly intervened—that is, are there imaginable conditions under which no rational individual could remain a strict naturalist?

Some believe that an affirmative answer is required. Let us assume, Grace Jantzen (1948–) argues, that we have compelling evidence for believing that Jesus rose from the dead. In this case, she tells us, to attempt to revise the relevant natural law would hardly be the appropriate response—for what could be gained by making this law read, "All men are mortal except those who have an unknown quality, observed on only one occasion and hitherto accountable for only by divine intervention"? "Where there is a single exception to a perfectly well-established and well-understood law, and one that is inexplicable unless one appeals to divine intervention . . . the skeptical response would be inadequate."[23]

Robert Larmer (1954–) comes to a similar conclusion. Let us "suppose that one hears of a man who claims to perform miracles of healing through the power of God." And let us further suppose that we are "able to capture on film occasions when, immediately following the prayers of this man, fingers lost to leprosy were regrown to their original form and length in a matter of seconds, and occasions when eyes severely burned by acid were immediately restored to sight." Finally, let us assume "not only that this man appears to have the power to heal any kind of disease or injury, but also that no interposition of any [object or force] has any effect on his apparent ability to heal" and that "his power is apparently independent of distance, since people in distant countries have experienced dramatic healing after this man prayed for their cure." In such a case, Larmer argues, the most rational response would clearly be to acknowledge God's interventive activity. To hold out for a totally natural explanation would be uncritical, dogmatic and question begging.[24]

Neither Jantzen or Larmer, it must be emphasized, is arguing simply that supernatural activity can justifiably be considered a plausible causal explanation when it cannot be shown that nature left to its own devices could manage. Their claim is stronger: that if some conceivable events were to occur, it would be most reasonable for all rational individuals to assume that God has directly intervened.

Some believe, however, that those making this claim have overlooked an important factor. There are, it is acknowledged, conceivable situations that, when considered in isolation, make divine intervention a plausible causal hypothesis. But no actual event, and thus no causal hypothesis for it, can be considered in isolation from the rest of the relevant evidence. To assume, for example, that a remarkable healing is the result of direct divine intervention is to assume not only that God exists but that God's existence is compatible with other relevant experiential data. It is to assume, for example, that God's existence is compatible with the evil we experience. Accordingly, if such a "healing" were to occur, the crucial question, it is argued, would not be, as Jantzen and Larmer imply, whether divine causation is the most plausible causal explanation for this event alone. The crucial question would be whether divine causation is the most plausible explanation, given all that this implies.[25]

Now let us assume that, after comparing the plausibility of believing that God has healed the individual in question (and, hence, that God's existence is compatible with the amount and types of evil in the world) with the plausibility of believing that God's existence is not compatible with all that we commonly experience (and, hence, that God did not heal the individual in question), someone decides that the case for God's nonexistence is more compelling overall. In other words, let us assume that the prima facie evidence for God's existence that has been generated by the "healing" in question is not of sufficient weight in the mind of a given individual to make the supernatural perspective the most plausible explanation for all the relevant data. Could Jantzen or Larmer justifiably accuse such an individual of being stubborn or intellectually dishonest or irrational? Larmer believes so. Specifically, he believes that there are conceivable contexts (such as the one mentioned earlier) in which every rational person would have to acknowledge that the evidence for God's existence is so strong that it clearly outweighs any evidence against God's existence—for instance, that generated by evil.[26]

However, Larmer's contention is based on the assumption that we possess (or could in principle possess) a set of neutral, nonquestion-begging criteria for belief assessment in relation to which we can objectively determine the comparative strength of the evidence for and against God's existence. And many philosophers—in agreement with such diverse figures as Hume and Kierkegaard (1813–1885)—continue to believe that no such criteria exist, that the comparative assessment of evidence for and against God's existence will, by it very nature, ultimately always be primarily a subjective, relative matter.[27]

For many theists, though, the crucial question is not whether there are imaginable conditions under which all rational individuals would have to acknowledge divine intervention. The important issue, as they see it, is whether the *theist* can (could) justifiably claim that God is, at least in part, directly responsible for certain occurrences. That is, the important question is whether there are conditions under which the theist can reasonably claim that certain events are direct acts of God.

In response, theists might assume a purely defensive posture. They might maintain that unless it can be shown that a given occurrence is not a direct act of God, they are justified in claiming that it is. And given our discussion of this approach to religious belief in Chapter 7, they might be successful. However, many theists have positive reasons for maintaining that God does (or at least can) directly intervene in earthly affairs. Specifically, many theists claim that they have acquired—from written revelation or oral tradition or personal experience—accurate information about God's general "patterns of action" in our world. And they believe that when they observe (or at least if they were to observe) some specific event that fit such a pattern, they can (or at least could) justifiably label it a direct act of God.

To accept a *divine-pattern thesis* of this sort, it must be emphasized, is not to argue that God can act only in accordance with recognized patterns. Consider, for instance, the following situation. One day Jim notices a peculiar phenomenon in his garden: his vegetables continually grow from seed to full maturity in one hour and then quickly regress again to seed. Try as he will—for example, by discussing the occurrence with respected botanists—Jim can find no specific natural cause for this strange phenomenon. Moreover, although Jim is a proponent of the divine-pattern thesis, he is not aware of any divine action pattern with which this unusual phenomenon fits. Accordingly, Jim will quite likely refrain from claiming that this is a direct act of God. He will not thereby be claiming that the occurrence is *in fact* not a direct act of God. He will be indicating only that he has at present no sufficient reason for thinking God is directly involved.

Also, theists who accept this divine-pattern thesis are not arguing that God must always intervene in a predictable manner. Consider, for example, the following situation. John, a theist, has grown up in a home in which the Bible is accepted as literally true. He has been taught, accordingly, that if one prays to God in time of trouble, God will directly answer. In other words, John believes he has acquired "knowledge" of a specific divine behavior pattern related to petitionary prayer. One day John finds himself in a serious personal crisis. His little girl is gravely ill, and there seems little hope for her recovery. John prays to God, beseeching him to save her life. Happily, the next day the girl's health has inexplicably improved, and she later goes on to make a full recovery. However, if John claims that this is a direct act of God because the "healing" fits an accepted pattern of how God interacts with the would, he will not thereby be saying that his prayer "forced" God to act. He will be claiming only that the fact that the healing fits an accepted divine action pattern is a sufficient reason to believe God has in this case chosen to intervene directly. Moreover, in no such case are theists professing absolute certainty. They are claiming only that they are justified in believing that it is more likely than not that a given occurrence is a direct act of God.

Of course, even in light of these clarifications, an important question arises. Are the theists in question justified in assuming that the sources from which the divine action patterns are derived—revelation, tradition or personal experience—yield accurate information? In some specific cases, such an assumption may not be reasonable. Perhaps it can be shown, for example, that specific patterns affirmed by some Christians cannot actually be supported by proper biblical interpretation or by correct knowledge of Christian tradition. Or perhaps it can be demonstrated that a specific historical source trusted by some Muslims is unreliable. However, since few philosophers today maintain that God's existence can be conclusively disproved or that the concept of divine communication with humans is self-contradictory, it should not be surprising that few wish to argue that theists cannot rationally maintain belief in the accuracy of certain divine action patterns and thus cannot justifiably label events that fit such patterns direct acts of God.[28]

PRACTICAL CONSIDERATIONS

Have any miracles, though, actually occurred? This question has recently generated considerable philosophical discussion. And no purported miracle has received more attention than the resurrection of Jesus.

Those engaged in this debate—most notably Flew, Michael Martin (1932–), Stephen Davis (1940–), Gary Habermas (1950–), and James Keller (1939–)—all grant for the sake of argument that Jesus could have died, been buried, and then come back to life. But there is considerable difference of opinion on the strength of the historical evidence for this alleged occurrence and the relationship between this evidence and rational belief. Although details differ, the general "evidential" case for the resurrection of Jesus—most clearly stated by Davis and Habermas—can be summarized as follows.[29]

Almost all biblical scholars (whatever their personal perspective on the resurrection) agree (1) that Jesus of Nazareth lived, was crucified and buried, (2) that his disciples claimed soon after his death that his tomb was empty, (3) that some claimed to have experienced (met, encountered, interacted with) a live Jesus, (4) that these experiences caused his disciples to believe that Jesus had risen from the dead, and (5) that this was a key belief within early Christianity. Moreover, although New Testament accounts of the resurrection differ (and even contradict each other on specific details), the biblical record uniformly claims that Jesus died, was buried, and then rose from the dead. Furthermore, there exists no good reason to believe that the disciples were lying, since their lives were so radically changed by this belief that many were willing to die rather than denounce their faith. Nor is there good reason to believe that the disciples were hallucinating (were simply imagining things that were not actually occurring), since none of the usual causes for hallucination—food or sleep deprivation, drugs, mass hysteria—appear to have been present. Finally, there was no conclusive refutation of Jesus' resurrection by Jewish authorities (for example, they didn't produce the body), although they had the power and motivation to do so.

Accordingly, while other explanations for the historic evidence cannot be shown to be impossible, "Jesus' literal Resurrection from the dead . . . is the best explanation for the facts."[30] However, many nontheists (most notably, Martin and Flew) and some theists (most notably, Keller) have argued that such evidence is far from compelling. Again, details differ, but the essence of their critique is the following.[31]

First, while scholars agree that Jesus lived and died by crucifixion, considerable debate surrounds the question of whether either the disciples or the very early church actually believed that Jesus had risen from the dead and appeared to many. Some scholars believe that the resurrection story entered the Christian tradition well after its inception, while others believe we are simply not in an evidential position to say when this story became a key component of faith.[32]

Second, there is little, if any, independent, objective evidence for the gospel accounts of the resurrection. And the inconsistencies among the gospels on such issues as whether the stone had been rolled away from the entrance of the tomb before the women arrived, which women were present, who was in the tomb, what the women did after their discovery, and how the disciples reacted are not simply minor difficulties. They throw into serious doubt the historical reliability of the biblical texts.

Third, even if it is true that the disciples believed Jesus to have risen from the dead and were for this reason so radically altered that they were willing to die for their faith, this in no sense increases the probability that the resurrection actually occurred. History is replete with examples of religious zealots who gave their lives for what they believed to be the truth—for example, Muslim martyrs, kamikaze pilots, followers of Jim Jones or David Koresh. And most who believe in the historicity of the resurrection adamantly deny that the basic beliefs which motivated devotion in these cases are true (or even made more probable by the zeal of their adherents).

Fourth, even if the Jewish authorities were aware of the resurrection claims and could not decisively counter the resurrection story by producing the body, this does not increase the probability that an actual resurrection took place. It is just as plausible to believe that the body had been stolen and hidden by the disciples or that the Jewish authorities were not overly concerned with the followers of Jesus at this point or that they simply did not have enough evidence for an objective refutation because there were no independent, unbiased eyewitnesses to the events in question.

Fifth, the burden of proof clearly lies with those who believe Jesus to have risen from the dead. Human experience continues to confirm in the strongest possible sense an undesirable but obvious fact: dead people stay dead. Thus, the historical evidence for any claim to the contrary must be exceedingly strong. But the relevant evidence is weak at best. Hence, there simply exists no valid historical basis for maintaining that the resurrection of Jesus is an established fact (or even a reasonable probability).

Those who believe in the historicity of the resurrection are, of course, aware of these challenges and offer responses. They claim, for instance, that the gospel accounts of the resurrection, if properly interpreted, contain no significant contradictions. And the critic's contention that many sincere (but possibly misguided) individuals, in addition to the disciples, have died for what they believed to be the truth misses the point, they argue. It is the fact that the disciples were in a position to know whether Jesus came back to life that makes their perspective unique.

All involved agree, though, that this "evidential" debate clearly raises important questions about the assessment of historical data. What types of evidence are relevant when assessing the alleged occurrence of an event in the past? How strong must such evidence be to establish the actual occurrence of an event? Who is in the best position to make such determinations?

However, of equal (if not greater) philosophical significance is the current debate over the appropriate relationship between the historic evidence for the resurrection and rational belief. For some on both sides of the issue, the answer is clear. Habermas, for instance, believes the historic evidence for the resurrection of Jesus to be so strong that no sincere, knowledgeable person can rationally deny that this event actually occurred. Martin and Flew, on the other hand, believe the historic evidence to be so weak that a "rational person should disbelieve the claim that Jesus was resurrected from the dead."[33]

Davis, however, offers a middle ground, based on the currently popular distinction between simply defending one's right to hold a belief and arguing that no one can rationally disagree. As already noted, Davis believes personally that the historic evidence, considered alone, clearly supports the resurrection of Jesus. But he denies that sincere, knowledgeable individuals cannot justifiably disagree. Supernaturalists, he argues, can reasonably maintain that reality cannot be explained totally in natural terms and therefore can reasonably maintain that the historic evidence supports an actual resurrection. However, naturalists can justifiably maintain that all events are part of a natural order that is uniform, and, given this assumption, disbelief in the actual resurrection of Jesus is also rational. In short, as Davis sees it, one's perspective on whether Jesus actually rose from the dead ultimately comes down to one's basic worldview—one's basic perspective on the nature of reality. And since belief in both supernaturalism and naturalism can be held by rational people, differing rational perspectives on the historicity of the event in question must also be allowed.[34]

Yet what of the claim that Jesus was raised from the dead by God and, thus, that the resurrection was indeed a miracle? Habermas and Davis represent those who believe not only that the evidence for the resurrection is very strong but that the probability that such an event could be explained without reference to divine intervention is very low. In fact, Habermas seems to believe that when the evidence for the resurrection is conjoined "with the claims of Jesus"—Jesus' claim, for instance, that he was uniquely related to God or that the resurrection would verify this fact—the denial of direct divine activity in this case borders on irrationality.[35] Davis disagrees. While he doubts that someone can maintain that the resurrection occurred and yet deny divine intervention, he holds, remember, that naturalists can rationally deny the historicity of this event, in which case, of course, no explanation is needed.

Critics such as Martin go even further. They argue that even if one grants that the resurrection of Jesus occurred, one can rationally deny that it was brought about by God (is a miracle), since it is just as plausible that this unusual event was the result of natural laws not yet discovered or fully understood or that this event was simply uncaused naturally or supernaturally.[36]

Who is correct? Or, at least, which perspective is the most plausible? There is at present no consensus within the general philosophical community on these explanatory issues. But most philosophers agree that serious discussion of the appropriate epistemic relationship between evidence and worldviews is absolutely essential with respect to any disputed occurrence in the past.

There is, though, one other issue surrounding any miraculous claim that clearly merits attention in this context. Let us consider again our scenario concerning John and his daughter. John believes that God can and will occasionally intervene, and, thus, when his daughter becomes gravely ill, he beseeches God for assistance. When she recovers, he attributes the recovery in part to God's direct activity and thanks God for this demonstration of divine compassion.

Now let us expand our story. Tom, a friend of John, is very happy about the seemingly miraculous healing of John's daughter. He, too, has always believed that God can intervene occasionally in earthly affairs and is pleased to think that God has actually done so in the case of John's daughter. Accordingly, when Tom encounters a number of starving children during a business trip to India, he beseeches God for help. After all, he reasons, if God can heal John's daughter, surely God can also help some of these children. Yet, in spite of his fervent prayer, all the children die slow, painful deaths.

The prima facie moral tension here is obvious. Why did God intervene in one case but not in the other? When considering instances of seemingly unnecessary suffering, many believers, as discussed in Chapter 6, emphasize the extent to which God is self-limited. God cares for everyone, it is argued. But God has created a moral context in which human freedom and the natural order that undergirds it are normally allowed to function uninhibited. And in such a universe, undesired evils are unavoidable. However, why then has John's daughter been healed? If God's creative agenda keeps God from directly intervening in the case of starving children in India, how can God directly intervene in the case of John's daughter without violating the structure of our moral universe? How can we think that God intervenes on behalf of some and not for others?

The basic question here is not whether God can occasionally intervene but why such interventions do not occur in a more understandable, orderly fashion. Or, as the process theist David Griffin states the point, why would a God who can unilaterally intervene not do so more frequently "in order to prevent particularly horrendous evils?"[37]

Of course, many responses are available to theists. It can be argued that while situations may look analogous from our perspective, they may not be so from God's. It can also be argued that although situations may be analogous, God is under no moral obligation to act in ways *we think* are appropriate. God does what he wants for reasons beyond human understanding.

But for some theists the tension remains, and it is strong enough to cause them to question whether God does *in fact* intervene today. Moreover, even for those theists who have resolved this "tension" for themselves, a general point appears valid. The acknowledged frequency of undesired but unavoidable evil and the expected frequency of beneficial, direct divine intervention stand in an inverse relationship. To the extent that a theist responds to specific instances of evil by claiming that God is barred from removing them because of the nature of our moral universe, this theist has less reason to expect beneficial (miraculous) intervention in any specific situation. Moreover, to the extent that a theist resolves the tension in question by claiming that "God's ways are above our ways," the less able he is to predict when and where any such intervention might occur.

This type of tension, however, must be kept in perspective. It is true that the miraculous is a complex concept, and it is true that serious theoretical and practical questions concerning our ability to identify "miracles" do exist. But nothing argued in this chapter indicates that theists cannot in principle reasonbly believe that miracles can occur, or even that miracles have actually occurred.[38]

STUDY QUESTIONS

1. What do you think most theists have in mind when they speak of miraculous divine intervention? Specifically, is it similar to what philosophers have traditionally had in mind?

2. How do you think "miracle" is best defined? Specifically, as you see it, could an event be considered a miracle if a natural explanation were available?

3. Why does Flew believe we cannot acknowledge the occurrence of nonrepeatable counterinstances to well-established natural laws? Do you agree?

4. Are you sometimes skeptical when you hear reports of alleged miracles? Why? Under what conditions is such skepticism justified?

5. Swinburne and others believe that we can conceive of some events that could never be given natural explanations. Why? Do you agree?

6. Jantzen and Larmer believe that, if some conceivable events were to occur, it would be most reasonable to acknowledge supernatural causation. Briefly outline their line of reasoning and the types of criticism to which they must respond.

7. Those who believe God does miraculously intervene in earthly affairs face an obvious question: Given all the pain and suffering present in the world, why does God not intervene more frequently, or at least in a more systematic manner? How might a theist respond to this question?

8. Do you think that someone who believes that miracles can occur will be less likely to search for a natural solution to personal and social problems?

9. Do you believe that any miracles, as you define them, have actually occurred? Why, or why not?

10. Briefly outline the evidential case for and against the resurrection of Jesus. Which do you consider more convincing?

NOTES

1. *Prayers God Has Answered* (West Palm Beach, Fla.: Globe Communications, 1985), pp. 5–6.

2. Medieval philosophers distinguished God's "primary causation" from the "secondary causation" of creatures that the divine power upholds in existence.

3. David Hume, *Enquiries Concerning the Human Understanding and Concerning the Principles of Morals,* 2d ed., ed. L. A. Selby-Bigge (Oxford: Clarendon Press, 1972), pp. 109–31.

4. R. F. Holland, "The Miraculous," *American Philosophical Quarterly* 2 (1965): 43. It is not totally clear, however, exactly what Holland, himself, believes this story to illustrate. Christopher Hughes, for instance, believes Holland's point to be that the mother in this case "could (rationally) continue to maintain that a miracle had taken place, even if she came to believe that no divine intervention was involved" ("Miracles, Laws of Nature and Causation," *Proceedings of the Aristotelian Society* [Supplementary Volume] 66 [June 1992]: 188–89).

5. See Hughes, "Miracles, Laws of Nature and Causation," pp. 179–205, for an expanded discussion of this topic.

6. Robert Merrihew Adams, "Miracles, Laws and Natural Causation (II)," *Proceedings of the Aristotelian Society* (Supplementary Volume) 66 (June 1992): 209.

7. Not everyone is completely comfortable with this distinction. Hughes agrees that an event can be considered miraculous even if a natural explanation is avail-

able but does not want to apply the label of miraculous to providential activity during the creation of the world. He narrows the application of "miracle" in this context to "an event occurring in (an up and running) nature which is directly caused by God" (p. 202).

8. Alistair McKinnon, "'Miracle' and 'Paradox'," *American Philosophical Quarterly 4* (October 1967): 308–14.

9. The discussion of whether Hume put forth this type of a priori argument against the possibility of miracles continues. See Robert Fogelin, "What Hume Actually Said about Miracles," *Hume Studies* 16, no. 1 (1990): 81–86; Antony Flew, "Fogelin on Hume on Miracles," *Hume Studies* 16, no. 2 (1990): 141–44; Kenneth G. Ferguson, "An Intervention into the Flew/Fogelin Debate," *Hume Studies* 17, no. 2 (1991): 105–11; Joseph Elin, "Again: Hume on Miracles," *Hume Studies* 19, no. 1 (1993): 203–12.

10. See, for example, Hughes, "Miracles, Laws of Nature and Causation," or David Basinger, "Miracles as Violations," *Southern Journal of Philosophy,* 22, no. 1 (1984): 1–7.

11. See Chapter 3 for a fuller discussion of how philosophers currently view the status of arguments for and against God's existence.

12. Antony Flew, "Parapsychology Revisited: Laws, Miracles and Repeatability," *Humanist* 36 (May/June 1976): 28–30.

13. Antony Flew, "Miracles," *Encyclopedia of Philosophy,* vol. 5 (New York: Macmillan, 1967), p. 351.

14. Chapter 7 furnishes a more comprehensive discussion of this point.

15. Richard Swinburne, *The Concept of Miracle* (London: Macmillan, 1970), pp. 33–50.

16. J. L. Mackie is one of a number of nontheists who are sympathetic to Flew's line of reasoning but who want to argue only that such considerations make the occurrence of an allegedly miraculous event *"prima facie* unlikely on any particular occasion." See Mackie's *The Miracle of Theism* (Oxford: Clarendon Press, 1982), pp. 18–29.

17. This line of reasoning appears implicitly in Swinburne, *Concept of Miracle,* pp. 23–32. A more explicit discussion occurs in David Basinger and Randall Basinger, *Philosophy and Miracle. The Contemporary Debate* (Lewiston, N.Y.: Edwin Mellen Press, 1986), pp. 68–71.

18. See Michael Martin, *Atheism: A Philosophical Justification* (Philadelphia: Temple University Press, 1990), chap. 9; Flew, "Miracles," pp. 348–49.

19. Swinburne, *Concept of Miracle,* pp. 29–32.

20. Margaret Boden, "Miracles and Scientific Explanation," *Ratio* 1, no. 1 (1969): 137–41.

21. Holland, "The Miraculous," pp. 43–51.

22. Basinger and Basinger, *Philosophy and Miracle,* pp. 59–71.

23. Grace Jantzen, "Hume on Miracles, History and Politics," *Christian Scholar's Review* 8 (1979): 325.

24. Robert Larmer, "Miracles and Criteria," *Sophia* 23, no. 1 (1984): 4–10.

25. See, for example, David Basinger, "Miracles and Natural Explanation," *Sophia* 26, no. 3 (1987): 22–26.

26. Robert Larmer, "Miracles, Evidence and Theism: A Further Apologia," *Sophia* 33, no. 1 (1994): 51–57.

27. See, for instance, Alvin Plantinga, "The Probabilistic Argument from Evil," *Philosophical Studies* (Jan. 1979): 1–53.

28. An exception is Martin. See his *Atheism* or *The Case against Christianity* (Philadelphia: Temple University Press, 1991).

29. Stephen Davis, "Is It Possible to Know that Jesus Was Raised from the Dead?" Faith and Philosophy 1, no. 2 (April 1984): 147–59; "Naturalism and the Resurrection: A Reply to Habermas," *Faith and Philosophy* 2, no. 3 (1985): 303–308; "Doubting the Resurrection: A Reply to James A. Keller," *Faith and Philosophy* 7, no. 1 (1990): 99–111. See also Gary Habermas (with Antony Flew), *Did Jesus Rise from the Dead?* ed. Terry L. Miethe (San Francisco: Harper and Row, 1987), "Affirmative Statement," pp. 19–29.

30. Habermas, p. 29.

31. Martin, *The Case against Christianity*; Habermas and Flew, *Did Jesus Rise from the dead?*; James A. Keller, "Contemporary Christian Doubts about the Resurrection," *Faith and Philosophy* 5, no. 1 (1989): 40–60 and "Response to Davis," *Faith and Philosophy* 7, no. 1 (1990): 112–16.

32. See, for example, Willi Marxsen, *The Resurrection of Jesus of Nazareth*, trans. Margaret Kohl (Philadelphia: Fortress Press, 1970), pp. 36–78; Hugh Anderson, *Jesus and Christian Origins* (New York: Oxford University Press, 1964), pp. 185–240; Reginald Fuller, *The Formation of the Resurrection Narratives*, rev. ed. (Philadelphia: Fortress Press, 1980), pp. 50–154.

33. Martin, *The Case against Christianity*, pp. 96.

34. Davis, "Naturalism and the Resurrection." A somewhat analogous line of reasoning appears in J. Houston, *Reported Miracles* (Cambridge: Cambridge University Press, 1994), pp. 208–57.

35. Habermas, *Did Jesus Rise from the Dead?* pp. 39–42.

36. Martin, *The Case against Christianity*, pp. 96–100.

37. David Griffin, "Values, Evil and Liberation Theology," *Process Philosophy and Social Thought*, ed. John B. Cobb and W. Widick Schroeder (Chicago: Center for the Scientific Study of Religion, 1981), p. 193.

38. Space considerations do not allow for the discussion of a cluster of other questions related to the involvement of humans in miraculous activity. For example, it is reasonable to hold that humans can initiate divine intervention (perhaps through prayer)? More important, can it be held that God sometimes intervenes (or refrains from doing so) primarily because humans have freely chosen to request (or freely chosen not to request) that he do so?

SUGGESTED READING

Adams, Robert Merrihew. "Miracles, Laws and Natural Causation (II)." *Proceedings of the Aristotelian Society* (Supplementary Volume) 66 (June 1992): 207–24.

Basinger, David, and Randall Basinger. *Philosophy and Miracle: The Contemporary Debate*. Lewiston, N.Y.: Edwin Mellen Press, 1986.

Flew, Antony. "The Impossibility of Miracles." In *Hume's Philosophy of Religion*. Edited by Antony Flew et al. Winston Salem, N.C.: Wake Forest University Press, 1986.

Fogelin, Robert J. "What Hume Actually Said about Miracles." *Hume Studies* 16, no. 1 (April 1990): 81–86.

Houston, J. *Reported Miracles: A Critique of Hume*. Cambridge: Cambridge University Press, 1994.

Hughes, Christopher. "Miracles, Laws and Natural Causation (I)." *Proceedings of the Aristotelian Society* (Supplementary Volume) 66 (June 1992): 179–205.

Hume, David. *Enquiries Concerning the Human Understanding and Concerning the Principles of Morals.* 2d ed. Edited by L. A. Selby-Bigge. Oxford: Clarendon Press, 1972.

Larmer, Robert, ed. *Questions of Miracle.* Montreal: McGill-Queen's University Press, 1996.

Lewis, C. S. *Miracles.* Rev. ed. London: Collins, Fontana Books, 1960.

Nowell-Smith, Patrick. "Miracles—The Philosophical Approach." *Hibbert Journal* 48 (1950): 354–60.

Swinburne, Richard. *The Concept of Miracle.* London: Macmillan, 1970.

———, ed. *Miracles.* New York: Macmillan, 1989.

Walker, Ian. "Miracles and Violations." *International Journal for Philosophy of Religion* 13 (1982): 103–108.

Williams, T. C. *The Idea of the Miraculous: The Challenge of Science and Religion.* New York: St. Martin's Press, 1991.

CHAPTER 10   LIFE AFTER DEATH:
                ARE THERE
                REASONS FOR
                HOPE?

And the people from the margin,
Watched him floating, rising, sinking,
Till the birch-canoe seemed lifted
High into that sea of splendor,
Till it sank into the vapors
Like the new moon slowly, slowly
Sinking in the purple distance.
And they said, "Farewell forever!"
Said, "Farewell, O Hiawatha!"
And the forests, dark and lonely,
Moved through all their depths of darkness,
Sighed, "Farewell, O Hiawatha!" . . .
Thus departed Hiawatha,
Hiawatha the Beloved,
In the glory of the sunset,
In the purple mists of evening,
To the regions of the home-wind,
Of the Northwest-Wind, Keewaydin,
To the Islands of the Blessed,
To the kingdom of Ponemah,
To the land of the Hereafter!

                                Henry W. Longfellow,
                                The Song of Hiawatha

The theme that death does not end human life sounds through all religions. The ancient Egyptians buried their mummified nobility, along with
the food and valuables necessary for the long journey to the next life, in
elaborate tombs decorated with statues or paintings of Osiris, god of that

world. Confucians and practitioners of traditional African religions remember and appease ancestors with special ceremonies at home altars, on their graves, or at sacred sites, while Hindus and Buddhists speak of karma and reincarnation. The *Koran*, which uses the term "hereafter" (*al-'akhira*) 113 times, frequently discusses the resurrection and judgment. In worship, many Christians regularly recite the Apostles' Creed: "I believe in . . . the resurrection of the body and the life everlasting." In fact, the belief in life after death is so central to religion that one author contends that it is more fundamental than the belief in God, so that if God did not exist, God would have to be created in order to "function as the benevolent purveyor of man's immortality."[1]

Yet since we will all die, is it reasonable to believe that we will live again after our death? Polls indicate that many people believe we will. But statistics from opinion polls provide little help in determining the truth of the belief. Our task must be to clarify what is meant by life after death, determine its possibility, and assess purported evidence that it actually happens.

TERMINOLOGY

The first problem concerns the terminology we should use to discuss the subject. Though people frequently speak of *immortality*, we should use this term cautiously. Literally, it means "not-dying," and this appears to conflict with the fact that we all die. If immortality, understood literally, is to be possible, there must be some part of us, containing our personal identity, that can survive physical death and corruption. Some call such a thing a soul. When the body dies, the soul that we have (or, better, are) lives on— in another sphere of existence, with or without some sort of body.

An associated concept is *reincarnation,* according to which after death we again take up bodily existence. Typically, though not always,[2] this view invokes a belief in a soul or self that survives death and can exist independently while it transmigrates from one body to another. Those who believe in reincarnation generally hold that transmigration occurs numerous times until the person achieves final liberation.

Others use the term *resurrection* to refer to what happens sometime after death. According to one traditional interpretation, bodies are resurrected to be rejoined with a continuing soul. The Catholic tradition holds that unless the body that is reunited with the soul is the self-same body that died, the deceased and the resurrected person cannot be the same.[3]

Still others speak of the *re-creation* of individual persons sometime after their death.[4] There is no literal immortality, no persisting soul, but simply life after death. Human existence is gap-inclusive: we live and die, and our bodies disintegrate and in the future are re-created to live again. What is re-created is our entire psychophysical being, which, though it allows the re-created to be the same person as the deceased, might have many features (for example, appearance, physical composition, lack of certain diseases) different from those possessed prior to death.

It is obvious that we cannot address the topic of life after death in a philosophically neutral way. Immortality language invokes the concept of a soul or self that is both the locus of personal identity and capable of persisting through physical death. One can witness one's own funeral. Life-after-death language accords with the truism that we all die, but in doing so (if understood literally), it rules out the identification of ourselves with a persisting soul-entity. Of course, one might take a more restricted view of death as applying solely to the body and understand life after death as life after the death of the body. Then "life after death" is compatible with viewing persons as ensouled beings, but it leads to a different understanding of death (that is, death of the body versus death of the person).

In what follows we shall have to make a language choice. Since the term "life after death" seems the most neutral, we generally will speak of the problem of life after death, though in some contexts the term "immortality" will more accurately capture the thought.

CONCEPTS OF LIFE AFTER DEATH

Just as the language about life after death is diverse, so are people's concepts of life after death. Four concepts bear noting here.

1. According to one widely held view, we achieve our immortality in the living presence of ourselves in the things or persons that continue after our death. We term this view *immortality by remembrance.* African and Chinese religions espouse forms of this view, which holds that the deceased live on through the remembrance of those who knew them.[5] It also plays a subtle role in our own everyday experience. Craftspeople, writers, and artists put something of themselves—their ideas, beliefs, hopes, fears, and views of the world—into their work. They hope that their creations will have lasting significance so that their ideas or fame will long outlive them. Other persons gain immortality by painting on the canvas of history: holding political office, winning or losing battles, revolting against authority, committing outrageous crimes, or making great discoveries or inventions. Still others obtain their immortality by improving the lives of others.

The philosopher George Santayana (1863–1952) suggested that the human desire for immortality and the frustration that results from recognizing our own mortality find their outlet in human reproduction.[6] We seek to prolong our lives in the lives of our children. Consequently, many desire to have male children to continue the family "name," give their children their own or their forebears' names, or put pressure on their children to espouse their beliefs, values, and ideals or to take up the parents' own occupations.

Though immorality by remembrance surely describes a kind of immortality, it is divorced from the moral and spiritual dimensions that people often associate with immortality. In religious contexts, belief in immortality and preparation for it encourage and reinforce moral action. But immortality as remembrance advises accomplishment of the noteworthy or memorable; immoral and inhumane acts are as likely to bring remembrance as moral acts, if not more so. Lee Harvey Oswald, who shot President John F. Kennedy, is remembered by more people than is Harriet Tubman, who worked to free the slaves. Further, this view fails to touch on the factual question of our own future existence. It is not insignificant that we want others to remember us, but we also want to know what will happen to *us* after we die. Is the grave or funeral pyre the end?

2. The philosophical difficulties that allegedly haunt a belief in a literal resurrection have led some to advocate a second view of life after death. For example, Rudolph Bultmann (1884–1976) concludes that "an historical fact which involves a resurrection from the dead is utterly inconceivable!"[7] Dead persons cannot be resuscitated. Resurrection, as a mythological event, must be demythologized to ascertain its *existential significance for our present life.* Resurrection language is language about power over sin and our freedom from guilt. Resurrected persons are those who live with renewed commitment to the full realization of their authentic selves.

Similarly, D. Z. Phillips (1934–) suggests that the immortality of the soul has nothing to do with a life that extends beyond or begins after death.[8] Death is not an event that a person experiences, like drinking coffee or getting chicken pox; rather, it is the end of all that person's possibilities. Accordingly, it is necessary to reinterpret immortality in terms of our present experience and life. Eternal life is not an extension of one's life but the present reality of goodness. It is not more life but the quality of our present life. Thus, when religion speaks about the eternal life of the soul, it indicates that what is important is overcoming death not in the sense that we survive death but in the sense that we "die to ourselves" by living unselfishly for others.

The emphasis on the quality of our present life helpfully corrects the previous view of immortality as remembrance. The doctrine of life after death should have implications for our moral living. But this view wrongly takes such implications as the doctrine's meaning and thus reduces its quantitative dimensions to the qualitative. That is, this view, too, leaves the factual question untouched. As we shall see, such questions as "Is death the end of our existence?" and "Should we prepare for a future life?" are not meaningless.

3. A third view, prevalent in Vedantic Hinduism and Mahayana Buddhism, is that after death, those who have been liberated from the cycle of existences experience *union with the One* or Nondual. In Vedanta, Reality ultimately is nondual, though it can be viewed diversely either from the perspective of the reality that evolves itself as this world (*Brahman*) or of the subject or self (*atman*). The self that I am (*atman*) transcends my senses, mind, intellect, feeling, and will; it is pure consciousness. But my consciousness is not independent of all other consciousness; rather, universal consciousness manifests itself in my self. Since *atman* is *Brahman,* individual human consciousness manifests the One, though in an illusory way. We have forgotten our essential unity or identity with the One and wrongly believe we are distinct from it. Thus, we are caught in the cycle of suffering. At some future time our conception of ourselves as distinct from the Nondual will be recognized to be an illusion, and we will be liberated to (re)gain union with it.

Here the factual question about the individual's future existence is answered, but in a way that might seem to have little significance for the individual. Once union with the Nondual occurs, the individual no longer is aware of any uniqueness or distinct existence. It is like putting a drop of water into the ocean; the drop adds to the whole, but its identity is not preserved. Indeed, desire to preserve our identity is the root of our problems. The acceptance of this view of life after death depends on one's larger view of reality and the human predicament, that is, on whether one believes that all is one (whether one is a metaphysical monist) and that the source of suffering and unhappiness is our ignorance of our identity with the One.

4. A fourth view might be termed *personal life after death.* On this view, individual persons either continue to live subsequent to their body's death or begin to exist sometime after their own death. Two requirements must be met. First, that which makes for an individual's personal identity must be present in that person in the afterlife. This is necessary for the person to be the same as and not merely similar to the deceased. Second, individuals must have sufficient reason to think they are the same person that they were prior to death. That is, there must be an awareness of self-identity. If this is not present, their immortality has no more significance for *them* than would the birth of someone in Tanzania after they die. This identification can be ensured, at least in part, by an awareness of who one is and the presence of true memories about the previous life.[9]

It is this last view—the actual existence of the individual person after death—that we will examine in detail. What we want to know is whether individual, personal life after death really does or will occur. But this question presupposes a prior one, for only if it is *possible* for persons to live subsequent to their deaths can they *actually* do so. In fact, almost without exception, the denial that we have life after death is grounded not on arguments against its actuality but on the contention that it is impossible.

But what critical factors govern its possibility? One consideration involves the existence of a powerful mediating agent. If living on after death is a natural event, if the soul can survive and in some natural way acquire another body, as Hindus believe, the existence of a separate, powerful agent is unnecessary and not an issue. If living on is not a natural state, it requires the existence and action of a being who has the special power to bring it about that persons live subsequent to their deaths. That is, if it is true that we all die, not simply in body but in self, then unless an omnipotent or extremely powerful God exists, there is no ground for thinking that there can be any life after death. For purposes of argument, we assume that a God with this power exists.

The second consideration concerns the nature of human persons. If life after death is to be possible, human persons must be the sort of beings that can live subsequent to their deaths. If they are not, then arguments showing that life after death is actual are moot. Thus, before discussing the question "What good reasons can be given for believing in life after death?" we must discuss the philosophically prior question "What is the nature of human persons?" with respect to the possibility of life after death.

PERSONAL IDENTITY AND THE SOUL

One approach to the question "What is the nature of human persons?" takes the perspective that we cannot identify ourselves with our physical beings. Although our physical bodies and their components continually change, there is something about us—our *personal identity*—that does not change. Our body is something we have, a contingent part of us required for our continuing physical existence on earth, but not something we are.[10] Our posture, movement, appearance, and physical characteristics express our self but do not constitute it.

Furthermore, the person cannot be identified with individual states of consciousness, categories of thought, memories, or the particular way one experiences and understands the world. First, individual memories, conceptual categories, and states of consciousness can be altered or lost without loss of personal identity. We do not remember most of what occurred when we were five or ten, or even last year. And we think about things differently from the way we did a number of years ago.

Second, memory claims are not infallible. We might claim to remember certain things that never happened or happened differently from the way we remember them. Hence, we must distinguish between memory claims and true memory claims. Only the latter suffice as the criterion of personal identity. But what makes my memory claim a true memory claim? At least two factors do so: for one, it must accurately report what in fact occurred; for another, it must be *my* memory claim. But if only genuine memories can be used as criteria for personal identity, and if my genuine memories are memories only had by me, then it becomes impossible to hold that genuine memory claims constitute personal identity without begging the question. In sum, our mental states might be used as evidence for establishing or assigning personal identity, but they do not constitute personal identity.

Perhaps a person is an irreducible, ultimate, unanalyzable self.[11] We say not that we have a self but that we are a self. Although we recognize the personal identity of others through their distinctive physical characteristics and behavioral patterns, we know our own self either through some inner, intuitive self-awareness or through having experiences.[12] The self, the subject and center of our experiences, is the agent of thinking, remembering, feeling, and understanding.

Four kinds of evidence can be given in defense of this notion. First, one way we understand ourselves is as *conscious beings* who have self-awareness, beliefs, desires, intentions, and feelings. It is not that each of us uniquely has these but rather that each has his or her own individualized set. Further, access to this set is private. I might infer from your behavior what you are thinking or feeling, but my access to your mental life is never direct. It is always mediated or secondhand. But in my own case it is immediate or firsthand. I have a good idea about how I feel at this moment—and even if I am mistaken, I am not mistaken that I think that this is the way I feel.

The physical, however, is public. Our body and its processes are perceptible to others. Since the public and the private are contradictories, that which is about something private cannot at the same time be about something public. Consequently, introspective reports about our selves and our mental states cannot be about something public.[13]

A second line of argument begins with the observation that an essential feature of ourselves is that we are persons to whom we can ascribe *moral responsibility*. But if we are to be held morally accountable for our thoughts and actions, we must be free. But what is it to be free? The incompatibilist view of freedom maintains that given the same causal conditions, a person can choose to perform either one action or another or, alternatively described, can choose to do or refrain from doing a certain action. But if we are identified with our physical components, if our psychological language refers to nothing over and above the physiological events that occur in the brain and the central nervous system, then our choices are products of and explainable in terms of prior causal conditions, and these in terms of other causal conditions that extend beyond ourselves, even prior to our own existence.

If our choices and actions ultimately depend upon causal conditions outside ourselves, and if these in turn are placed in the larger deterministic causal chain, our actions are not free. But without freedom, the indeterminist holds, we cannot be held *morally* accountable for our deeds; neither can there be a true moral *ought,* which requires that we act one way rather than another. This suggests that for humans to be free, there must be something in us that is not part of any physical, deterministic causal chain and that, whatever this is, it is essential to our personhood, insofar as the capacity to make moral choices and to take moral accountability for our actions is an essential feature of our personhood.

A third argument is based on a strange but real phenomenon, that of *one body housing, as it were, several different personalities or persons.* Each has its own memories, its own behavioral patterns that affect the appearance of the body and can possess its own name. Some of these persons are known to the others housed in the same body and are in contact with them; others are unknown and isolated.[14] If one body can house several different persons, or if several different persons can share the same body, it appears that the body cannot be the locus of personal identity.

It is not obvious how best to describe this phenomenon. Should we say that one body houses several persons (a case of multiple personalities), or should we say that one person manifests several different personalities at different times (a case of split personality)? The fact that each person has a distinct self-concept, personality, and set of character traits and different ways of thinking and acting, and memories and that at times they can know the other as a separate person (for example, Eve Black holds that she is not married to Eve White's husband) argues that the former interpretation is correct. On the other hand, one might suggest that this is an abnormal case, that here is a single person who is so fragmented that she cannot hold the various aspects of herself together, something most of us can do. It is true that we show different sides of ourselves in different contexts, but these different perspectives do not leave us fragmented. However, in a pathological condition the person has lost what holds these perspectives together, so that a kaleidoscope results rather than a whole person. The fact that the persons have different memories or experiences does not argue for their plurality but rather results from a repression of some states, which under proper conditions reappear despite repression. Which option is correct even psychiatrists who treat such cases have difficulty deciding.[15]

A fourth argument is developed from the *alleged existence of human paranormal powers*. Minds purportedly have the power to communicate with other minds where no normal communication (in terms of a physical causal chain) is possible (telepathy), to discern physical states of affairs without being able to perceive them (clairvoyance), and to move physical objects without using physical means (psychokinesis). For example, experiments have been conducted that suggest that persons can communicate telepathically with others at a distance, even when the subject is enclosed in chambers walled with lead and iron.[16] But paranormal phenomena seem incompatible with a materialistic conception of the mind, for they presuppose that the mind is capable of receiving information about the world and other minds or producing physical effects without requiring, as brains do, intermediate physical agencies.[17]

For some, extrasensory experiences such as these are an undisputed fact.[18] Others are more dubious, grounding their worries on the possibility that the experiments either are not carefully enough constructed to exclude fraud or else are subject to serious allegations of irregularity. So, whereas some treat such experiences as established fact, others affirm that "it is fair to claim that so far, no paranormal results have been satisfactorily repeatable."[19]

For many, these four strains of evidence suggest that humans are some sort of nonphysical self (or what might be termed a *soul*) that currently exists in a body. The functions of this self include self-awareness, memory, conceiving, and emoting. Although they currently occur in conjunction with the body, it is logically possible that these functions could occur apart from it.

IMMORTALITY OF THE SOUL

The implications of this view for life after death are obvious. If the self is identified with a nonphysical entity that is currently embodied, then, since dying is a physical process, it is possible that the soul's existence does not terminate at physical death. Of course, death might significantly affect the quality of soul-life. The corruption of the body ends those functions, such as sensation, that require mutual involvement of both the physical and the nonphysical. However, what is not dependent upon the physical can survive and continue. Furthermore, since the soul is the self, there are sufficient grounds for holding that life after death is personal, that we survive physical death with our self-identity and our self-awareness essentially intact.

What kind of existence after death does the believer in the soul envision? There are three major schemas, though each has many permutations. The first view is that *the soul at death immediately unites with a body of some sort.* Some religions believe this to be another physical body; others believe that it is a spiritual body. Where the new body necessary for functioning of the soul is spiritual, verification of continued existence by other parties is impossible, for presumably the spiritual body exists in a different spatio-temporal plane. Where reincarnation takes place in a physical body on earth, verification remains problematic, for, with the exception of yogis who have achieved the higher meditative states, the reincarnate generally lacks any awareness of previous existence. Without this knowledge of previous lives, being reborn is not a meaningfully different experience from being born the first time.

In the second schema, *the soul continues to exist after death but does not function until it is united with something that provides what is requisite for it to function.*[20] Oscar Cullmann (1902–), for example, says that those in the interim state are "with Christ," "waiting," but without any mental functions. They are only sleeping.[21]

In the third schema, *the soul continues to exist and function disembodied,* either temporarily until united with a body or permanently. One can find this temporary disembodiment in the Roman Catholic doctrine of purgatory. Disembodied souls in purgatory experience mental suffering whose purpose is to exact temporal punishment for previously committed venial sins and to purify the person of guilt. The suffering includes the pain of temporary loss of and longing for the beatific vision of God.

Believers in an immortal soul suggest that during its disembodied state the soul's activities are of a paranormal sort. Perception would require the addition of new and different powers or the extension of currently little-used perceptual powers such as clairvoyance and telepathy; its agency would be described in terms of thoughts and desires alone causing certain events, as in psychokinesis. H. H. Price (1899–1984) suggested that the next world is composed of souls that have mental images, about which they have beliefs and desires. "There might be a set of visual images related to each other perspectively, with front views and side views and back views all fitting neatly together in the way that ordinary visual appearances do now."[22] Such a group of images might also contain tactile, taste, auditory, and olfactory images, so that a nexus of interrelated images would constitute an object. One might even have a visual image of the body one had in the prior life. This body image might form the center of one's image world, much as our body now does. The entire environment of the disembodied individual would be composed of such families of mental images and would serve as the immortal's world. Development of some such scenario is necessary to avoid solipsism (the view that the individual self is the whole of reality).

CRITICISM OF THE SOUL-CONCEPT

The view that identifies persons with souls is not without its difficulties. Perhaps the most substantial problem is that after death this immaterial self would have to sustain functions such as concept formation and memory recall. This implies that the physical brain is not a necessary condition for these and other sorts of cognitive processes. But this runs counter to much psychological and physiological evidence. For one thing, behavioral evidence indicates that certain mental abilities and the degree to which they function successfully are in part inherited. For example, researchers have compared the intelligence of members of natural families. The highest correlation exists between identical twins and progressively diminishes, though remaining significant, for fraternal twins, siblings, parents and children, and grandparents and grandchildren. The farther removed the genetic relation, the lower the correlation. Moreover, diseases that affect the mind (such as Down's syndrome) and susceptibility to diseases (such as some cases of Alzheimer's) are genetically based. This indicates that the physical process of heredity plays a major role in determining mental ability and function.

Second, damage to the brain directly affects awareness, consciousness, memory, and conceptual ability. For example, persons whose brain hemispheres have been severed (a split brain person), when presented with an object on the left that is sensed only by the right hemisphere of the brain, cannot tell what they saw, though they can point to it with their left hand. The right brain, which controls the left hand, knows the object, but the left brain, which is the main area for speech and communication, does not know of the object because no information passes through the severed corpus callosum.

Third, diseases that exhibit distinct mental phenomena, such as schizophrenia, cannot only be traced genetically in certain families but can be treated with drugs, such as clozapine, that help ameliorate symptoms such as hallucinations and delusions.

Fourth, certain mental abilities seem to be locatable in the brain. The operations of working memory are carried out in the prefrontal lobes of the cerebral cortex, which "is divided into multiple memory domains, each specialized for encoding a different kind of information, such as the location of objects, the features of objects (color, size and shape), and additionally, in humans, semantic and mathematical knowledge."[23] Gender differences in mental abilities likewise indicate the effect that hormones have on our minds through the brain. Whereas men tend to perform better on tests related to motor skills, women excel at verbal fluency and mathematical calculation.[24] It is true that individual thought processes cannot yet be correlated with particular energy transfers in the brain and probably never will be. Yet we can discern patterns of energy events. This makes possible brain research into mental functions.

Finally, intelligence of certain kinds, though not specifically localized, is associated with specific cerebral hemispheres. Analytic, conceptual, verbal intelligence is located in the left hemisphere of the brain, while the right hemisphere controls the artistic and intuitive mental processes.

This, along with an array of collaborative evidence, implies that a dilemma confronts defenders of the immortal soul thesis. Either they deny that after death the soul continues to be conscious and to perform cognitive activities like remembering, or else they deny the mass of psychological and physiological evidence that indicates that the brain is necessary for the existence and functioning of the mind. The latter is unacceptable in light of contemporary brain research. The former is impossible for believers in the immortality of the soul, since removal of its ability to perform mental activities effectively deprives it of any significant function.

To escape this dilemma, believers in the soul might maintain that though in our present life something physical such as a brain is necessary for consciousness and thinking, these functions can be supplied in the afterlife by something else, either some re-created physical brain or perhaps something quasi-physical.[25] For example, there might be an ethereal body appended to the soul immediately at the death of the physical body. The problem here concerns our ability to verify the existence of such a body.

THE SELF AS A PSYCHOPHYSICAL UNITY

Due to the problems of understanding the self as a soul, many contemporary philosophers have located personal identity in our mind-body (psychophysical) unity. One contemporary view, called the *Identity Theory* or *Central State Materialism*, holds that human beings are nothing more than physical organisms. This should not be taken to imply that mental or psychical states such as perceiving, conceptualizing, or remembering are not real. What it does mean is that insofar as a statement about a mental state is a report of something, that something is a brain process, a brain state, or a process within the central nervous system.[26] That is, the event that the mental language reports is ultimately the same as or identical to the event that would be reported by the neurologist. The mind is what the brain does. Thus, what those who hold these views deny is not that we can speak about minds or mental states but that states of consciousness are irreducibly psychical.

Other instances of identity between things in different categories illustrate this relationship.[27] Lightning can be reported by using either the physicist's language about an electrical discharge occurring at a particular place and time or the language of the ordinary observer who reports a bright flash of light, jaggedly etched across the stormy sky. Although the two people use noninterchangeable language systems, both genuinely report one and the same event.

The major problem facing the Identity Theory concerns the nature of this cross-category identity. Defenders of the view claim that mental and brain states are neither merely related causally nor simply constantly correlated. They opt for strict identity between the two. But according to a traditional principle (called Leibniz's principle of the identity of indiscernibles), two things are identical if and only if every property of one is also a property of the other. But the properties of mental states and brain states differ, not the least in that the former are nonspatial and private, whereas the latter are spatial and public. One might respond that Leibniz's principle does not apply to cross-category identities. In particular, one cannot expect total identity of properties where the application of the property to one category would be meaningless (as would be the case in applying spatial predicates to mental states). But then what criteria do two things with different category-sets of properties have to meet to be identical? In the case of the mind and body, we have mental events and brain events occurring at the same time. But what shows that they are not causally related rather than identical?

Recent reductionists such as Douglas Hofstadter (1945–) have taken the materialist perspective a step farther. I am not my body; I have a body. The physical body can be artificially replaced. What is significant is the brain, for were I to undergo a body transplant, I would go with the transplanted brain. I would not stay with the body from which the brain was taken. But I do not seem to be simply my brain, either. Were I to commit a crime and then be separated from my brain, which continues unabated in a vat of nutrients, the authorities would not rest content with incarcerating my brain (as me) while letting my body roam free.

What, then, are we? The self is the locus of meaning, understood on the symbolic level as a representational system, that is, "an active, self-updating collection of structures organized to 'mirror' the world as it evolves."[28] These high-level structures are composed of lower-level active patterns, and these of still lower patterns, until we reach the lowest level, which consists of nothing more than neural firings. Taken individually, these neural firings are random and meaningless, but statistical regularity reveals patterns that encode the information necessary for the organism to respond interactively to other patterns of symbols in its environment. When the patterns of firings are interpreted at the highest levels, we give them meaning, and these meaning-assigned patterns become alternative ways of explaining who we are.

Hofstadter gives the analogy of an ant colony. A colony has different levels: the colony itself, groups of different ants such as the workers, teams of ants, and the individual ants themselves. We assign meanings to the higher levels (for example, that a group of worker ants is removing the carcass of a fly) and hold that these higher levels encode information for the colony. But these higher-level patterns of behavior are ultimately the mere products of the random motions of individual, unintelligent ants.

We thus exist as programmable machines, potentially replicable by sophisticated (though yet undeveloped) computers. But computer hardware is interchangeable. One kind of hardware can be made to emulate a different kind if it is fed the proper software. Thus, ultimately, it is the patterns—the software—that matter. The precise nature of the hardware is insignificant except as it is able to cause or recognize these patterns.

But are these higher level patterns, described in language about meanings, intentions, and ends (teleological language), real? Hofstadter suggests ultimately not. These higher-level patterns only emerge from the fundamental, nonintelligent actions of the neurons, just as the ant colony emerges from the actions of individual ants. And just as there is no colony over and above individual ants, there is no person over and above neural firings. Hence, we need not appeal ultimately to meaning to account for reality. Of course, we can do so, but only because it is easier to explain things this way, because of our penchant to use language that ascribes purpose. We even speak of (unconscious) ant colonies as having the goal to reproduce. Thus, language about persons simply becomes one way of speaking about the higher-level patterns that carry coded information. Does this, then, mean that the concept of person is dispensable? Ultimately we must say yes, for "with some effort I can always remember the other point of view if necessary, and drain all these systems of meaning, too."[29] Since there cannot be any top-down causation, there seems little role for the concept of person in this model, except to cater to our need for easier explanations. Indeed, even freedom or volition is nothing more than a complicated, internal, causal configuration that enables the object to react to its environment as a representational system.

One problem with such reductionist accounts is the presence of evidence of top-down causation. Mental events seem to be genuine causes of events at adjacent but lower physiological or neurological levels. One can see this is cases where mental activity is deficient. For instance, persons suffering from agnosia receive visual stimuli but are unable to recognize what they see (for example, a face), even though they can recognize it through data conveyed through other senses.

There are other, less reductionistic models of the person, some that allow for top-down causation. For example, John Searle (1932–) argues that mental phenomena are properties that emerge from physiological microelements and, hence, are as real as any other properties. Indeed, as emergent mental properties, they are a kind of physical property, namely, a biological property, that can bring about effects though "intentional causation," where the "cause both represents and brings about the effect."[30] The mind is able to cause because it just is a higher order feature of the brain. Yet like other materialists, Searle has difficulty accounting for free human agency. "As long as we accept this conception of how nature works, then it doesn't seem that there is any scope for the freedom of the will because on this conception the mind can only affect nature in so far as it is a part of nature. But if so, then like the rest of nature, its features are determined at the basic micro-level of physics."[31]

RE-CREATION AND SPATIOTEMPORAL CONTINUITY

What are the implications of these *materialistic views of the person* for the possibility of life after death? Clearly, life after death is not guaranteed by any continuing thing like a soul. If there is to be life after death, the activity of an omnipotent and omniscient being is necessary. In what way? Since we are identical with our physiological organism, which at base is composed of coded matter, it is possible that this being could physically re-create and program us with all the physical and psychical characteristics we possessed before we died. Specifically, since consciousness is a brain process or emergent biological property of brains, our brain could be re-created and programmed to have neural components and structures identical to those we had when we died so that we would have substantially the same memories, ideas, perspectives, and personality traits as we had before we died.

The radical reductionistic view of persons makes re-creation even more feasible. If we are nothing but programs that are, to some extent, hardware independent, then an omnipotent, omniscient being could re-create us simply by re-creating our program. We would have to be programmed into hardware of some sort, but the specific hardware is insignificant, so long as it is capable of booting up and running the relevant programs.

But would the re-created person be the same as the deceased? One immediate difficulty is that the re-created is neither spatially nor temporally continuous with the deceased. Yet why should we think that spatiotemporal continuity is necessary for personal identity?

It is true that we sometimes consider spatiotemporal continuity necessary for identity. If a fire destroyed "The Reapers" by Van Gogh and then a skilled copyist precisely re-created it, I would hesitate to affirm that the re-creation is an authentic Van Gogh or to pay millions for the exact replica. But the reason spatiotemporal identity is important in "The Reapers" is that the identity of the painting *as a Van Gogh* involves more than the particular distribution of paint on canvas. It is a Van Gogh because it was painted by Van Gogh himself. If it were destroyed by fire and repainted by the skilled copyist, though the content would be identical, it would no longer be a painting he actually created. Spatiotemporal continuity is essential to the painting's identity in order to make it a Van Gogh, that is, to preserve the special causal sense captured in the identification of the painting as a Van Gogh.

But is spatiotemporal continuity necessary for the painting to have its identity as "The Reapers"? If one considers the painting insofar as it is this particular painting and not as painted by Van Gogh, then one would look to the properties of the painting to determine that it is "The Reapers" rather than Caillebotte's "The Floor Scrapers." That is, what often gives an object its identity is its unique set of characteristics.

The critic will respond that it is not merely the possession of these unique, essential characteristics but the possession of them connectedly over time and space that is necessary for something's identity. Yet there seem to be interesting exceptions to the use of the spatiotemporal continuity criterion of identity. Consider the way we treat persons in plays. We experience no logical difficulty treating them as gap-inclusive people who continue to exist after the intermissions between acts. Within the reality of the play the characters lack spatiotemporal continuity. Of course, the actors themselves have spatiotemporal continuity between scenes or acts, but one can clearly distinguish between the actor and the character in the play. The critic might respond, however, that theatergoers merely temporarily suspend their logical belief regarding identity when they enter the theater.

Whether spatiotemporal continuity is necessary for identity is not easily resolved. The a priori claim that it is necessary for identity begs the question. The a posteriori claim based on our daily experience risks the universality of the claim, for even if all of our everyday experience invoked spatiotemporal continuity, that would not establish that such is necessary to *all* cases of personal identity. Re-creation of persons could very well be the exceptional case.

Suppose that, for the sake of argument, one grants that spatiotemporal continuity is not necessary for all cases of personal identity. The question remains whether the deceased and the re-created are identical. The answer depends upon the criteria we use for constituting personal identity. If they include internal states of consciousness (including conceptual categories and memories) and personality traits or patterns, then it is possible that these can be repeated in the re-created person, and, if they are repeated, then there are grounds for suggesting that the same person lives again.

But, it is objected, it is logically possible that there could be two persons who make identical memory claims and have identical personalities. Consequently, where we have two claimants, James and John, both claiming to be re-creations of Peter, the criteria given in the previous paragraph provide no grounds for deciding which is really Peter.[32] That is, the fact that someone makes memory claims about performing an action at a previous time does not compel us to assert that that person really performed that action.

One might reply, however, that though it is true that there is no way of deducing identity from these features, two people simply cannot have the same memories (make true memory claims) about experiences had by only one person and still not be the same. Identity appears to be deducible from true memories. Hence, though we might not be able to discern whether it was James or John who was identical with the deceased Peter, both cannot be identical with him, given that only one can make true memory claims.

Of course, we could create all kinds of scenarios. For example, we might envision a case whereby one person had half of the deceased's true memories and the other person the other half. Or we could have persons dividing like amoebas into two identical beings, in which case both could be making true memory claims. This latter example suggests that any logical difficulty in James and John's both having true memories of Peter is based on certain presuppositions about humans, for example, that the same person cannot be in two different places at the same time (even if only momentarily).

Apart from the logical point, however, these speculative possibilities would create difficulties of discerning who was really that person only if there were two claimants and all these presuppositions were invoked. It does not follow that, where there is only one claimant, he or she cannot be the same as the deceased.[33] The theistic re-creationist could cogently suppose that God would re-create only one person who would make the relevant memory claims concerning the experiences of the deceased. Consequently, where there is only one claimant, it would be reasonable to hold that true memory claims, in conjunction with similarity of personality characteristics and perspectives of understanding, would provide good grounds for identifying the re-created with the deceased (provided spatiotemporal continuity is not a necessary condition for identity).[34]

The conclusion of all this is that both perspectives on the human person—that we are souled beings or that we are psychophysical unities or even mere programs—allow for the possibility of life after death. One cannot reject the doctrine on the grounds that it is contradictory or absurd. At the same time, both views face difficulties: the one grounds for thinking that souls can exist as persons, the other that spatiotemporal continuity is not necessary for all cases of personal identity.

A POSTERIORI ARGUMENTS FOR LIFE AFTER DEATH

If one grants that life after death is possible, a second question arises: Is there any reason to think that it actually occurs? Two sorts of arguments can be suggested: a priori philosophical arguments and a posteriori arguments from certain sorts of experience. We look at the a posteriori first and then turn to the a priori. Three types of a posteriori arguments seem attractive to those who think about these issues.

1. The first appeals to claims about *near-death* or *life-after-life experiences* of persons who either have almost died or have died but were resuscitated (depending on one's definition of death). As some persons lie near death in a hospital room, they hear themselves pronounced either dying or dead. They then find themselves leaving or out of their body, witnessing from a different perspective (often from above) their body, their immediate surroundings, and the health care personnel working to resuscitate their body. They now possess a new body, variously described as an amorphous cloud or a spiritual body shaped as the physical body was, which is incapable of interacting with the physical environment of their original body. After this, they experience passing through a dark place, often described as a tunnel, until they come to a different realm. Here they meet other persons, not physically embodied though often recognizable, with whom they communicate in some telepathic way. They also encounter a being of light, exuding love and compassion, who helps them recall (as if by an instantaneous videotape) and evaluate their past. Despite their strong desire to stay and enjoy this peaceful and happy experience, they either want to or are told to return to their physical bodies.[35]

There is no doubt that people have such experiences. The problem is how to understand or explain them. Some have argued that these are products of hallucination. Physiological conditions in the body can cause a person to have unusual experiences, similar in part to those described. "A change in blood pressure in the inner ear can evoke a sense of rising, hovering, floating in space." Such a change can occur when the blood flow through the body is checked, as with cardiac arrest. Likewise, the experience of visualizing one's body "as if from the outside itself becomes more common when a person is subject to serious emotional stress," as happens in near-death experiences, or is taking powerful drugs, as is sometimes the case with dying persons.[36] Yet descriptions given by these persons of the immediate circumstances surrounding their physical body have an amazing accuracy, not characterized by what one would expect in a drug-induced account. Sometimes they even describe what is going on in the room or in nearby rooms that they could not observe from their patient-bed. Paul Badham (1942–) cites a case of a patient who accurately reported the presence of two coins on the top of a high cupboard in the room. However, experiments—for example, where secret numbers have been placed in a surgical unit near the ceiling, in a position that could be viewed only from above—have failed to yield consistently positive results. People who reported having near-death experiences in such places have been unable to provide the secret numbers.

Perhaps these after-death experiences can be explained by appealing to psychological or physical factors. Christians, for example, have a penchant for interpreting the being of light as Jesus, Hindus as the death god Yama or other Hindu deities. The descriptions sometimes convey imagery distinctive to certain religions—for example, gates of pearl. This suggests that these experiences may be individual projections, colored by the persons' religious backgrounds and beliefs and occasioned by the traumatic experience through which they are going.

Yet the descriptions can vary significantly from standard religious expectations. Raymond Moody (1944–) writes, "I have not heard a single reference to a heaven or a hell anything like the customary picture to which we are exposed in this society. Indeed, many persons have stressed how unlike their experiences were to what they had been led to expect in the course of their religious training."[37]

In addition to the being of light, they also report seeing relatives. This would not be striking, except for the fact that sometimes they encounter people whom they had not met before but later recognize in a picture or people who (unknown to them) have just died. Badham gives the case of a "child met by her grandfather's mother of whom she had no previous knowledge, but whose photograph she recognized with great enthusiasm when first visiting an uncle's home some time after her recovery. Apparently she had never seen that photo before, nor did any other member of the family possess a photograph of this long departed relative."[38]

Part of the puzzle of these cases is the difficulty experienced in recounting the kind of body possessed. It is invisible, able to move through physical objects, and weightless (floating); yet it has powers of perception and can hear (though more so in terms of thought-transfer than of auditory experiences). This suggests that this world and the people in it are "embodied" in a way that makes them recognizable and locatable from a particular perspective, yet possessing only a partial, one-way relationship to our present world. That is, they are briefly aware of the physical environment, yet cannot influence it at all. However one interprets this new body, two of the elements we deemed necessary for personal immortality are present: awareness of their own identity and recollection of their past.

2. The second a posteriori argument comes from psychical research into *mediumistic communication with deceased persons*. If mediums really do communicate with deceased persons, this would provide evidence that people survive death.

Appeal to mediums who work through seances is often discounted, not only because of the possible and proven cases of fraud, but because what they recount of the deceased often can be accounted for more easily by appealing either to role-playing by various parts of the medium's conscious or unconscious personality or to telepathic communication from those present and seeking information about the deceased. It is the sitters' expectations that are met, expectations that perhaps in some way can be communicated to the alleged medium.[39]

However, some cases are more difficult to explain in this fashion. There are instances wherein deceased persons allegedly have appeared to the living and conveyed to them information that was verifiable but previously unknown. C. D. Broad (1887–1971) recounts the case of a North

Carolina farmer who appeared four years after his death to inform a surviving son about the location of his lost last will.[40] There are also the attempts by people involved in the Society for Psychical Research to communicate after their death with the living. One deceased person allegedly dictated thousands of pages through the automatic writing of mediums in Great Britain, Australia, and the United States. These writings were like a jig-saw puzzle that, individually interpreted, made little sense but when fitted together contained alleged evidence that they were produced by one person.[41]

Yet even here reasonable suspicions can be entertained. Why must the communications from these individuals be so cryptic, complex, and filled only with allusions? How these diverse messages can be correlated is itself subject to differing speculative interpretations, suggesting that the finished product is more the work of the collator than of a communicating, deceased person. Further, the communicants give no indication that their life has continued on in any meaningful way in the afterlife.[42] They give no detailed indication of their new surroundings, occupations, or interests, and what is said often contains vague generalizations easily ascribable to the medium's beliefs about the afterlife.

3. A third a posteriori argument commences from the claim that *certain persons actually have come back to life*. In Christianity, the belief that Jesus was resurrected from the dead is coupled with the theological assertion that this event both foretokens and makes possible our resurrection. The Apostle Paul's argument is this: If Christ was raised from the dead, we will be raised from the dead. Christ was raised. Therefore, we will be raised.[43]

The soundness of this argument depends on the truth of both premises. The first premise is theological. Thus, knowledge of its truth depends on accepting a number of other claims, including that God exists, that he can reveal his promises and purposes, that he is trustworthy to keep and powerful enough to implement them, and that he actually revealed this to Paul. The orthodox Christian theist presumably would have little problem with any of these presuppositions. The truth of the second premise depends on whether the claim that Jesus was resurrected is historically true. Christians often introduce claims about witnesses to the living Jesus, the empty tomb, and the rise and success of the Christian Church as evidence that it really occurred.[44]

Each of these a posteriori arguments depends upon claims persons make about experiences they have had. To evaluate the claims means that we must consider the criteria that we ordinarily invoke to evaluate the testimony or report made by other persons. The difficulty, generally, is not that people have had the experiences that they claim to have had but how to understand and interpret those experiences. This brings us back to the larger worldview that each of us brings to our experience. It is to the shaping of this worldview that this book is addressed.

A PRIORI ARGUMENTS FOR LIFE AFTER DEATH

In addition to a posteriori arguments from particular experiences, there are numerous a priori arguments that commence from ideas rather than experience. Let us note three of them.

1. The first argument was developed by Thomas Aquinas (c. 1224–1274).[45] He argued that *we are made for an ultimate end,* which is happiness. But happiness cannot be achieved in this life, for our individual fortune is fickle, our body and will weak, and our knowledge imperfect. But since God cannot have made us in vain, we must be able to achieve the end for which we were made, and this requires that we continue to live after death.

But why should one think that we cannot achieve happiness in this life? Aristotle (384–322 B.C.) suggests that happiness is not a momentary feeling of pleasure but a state in which persons manifest virtues throughout their lifetime.[46] If we engage in the activity of reason or contemplation, we can attain it. We need not lose happiness simply because of momentary adversity.

Aquinas, however, understands happiness differently. Human happiness must relate to the ultimate end for which we were made, which is God. Since our knowledge of God by faith is an act of the will, not the intellect, our present knowledge of God by natural reason can be erroneous and uncertain. Hence, knowledge or contemplation of God, in which lies our ultimate happiness, is not (except momentarily) attainable in this life. To fully experience this beatific vision, we must live subsequent to our death.[47]

Aquinas's argument rests on the very interesting (and debatable) thesis that we have been made in vain if we cannot achieve our ultimate end. But is God's creation of us compromised if we fail to achieve our ultimate end, no matter what other ends we realize? If we achieve limited fulfillment of human potential or a partially realized life of happiness, or if we come to know God in our own limited way and actualize our intellectual capacity through contemplation of what truth can be known and live a virtuous life, participating in the grace of God, there seem to be no grounds for the claim that we have lived in vain. On the other hand, if part of our end is fulfilled in contemplative communion with God, it seems reasonable to think that God would not let us fail to achieve this highest end for which we are made. Clearly, this argument comes laden with theological as well as philosophical presuppositions.

2. A second a priori proof, which uses basically the same argumentative structure as the first, commences from moral premises. In general, the *moral argument* asserts that since finite human existence is insufficient either to achieve the moral ideal or to provide an adequate basis on which to recommend the performance of good rather than evil, humans must be immortal. The former contention is advanced by Immanuel Kant (1724–1804).[48] The moral law tells us that we must strive to achieve the highest

good. But unless we can realize this highest good, we cannot be commanded to attain it. But this highest good—the perfect alignment of our individual wills with the moral law, so that we act solely out of respect for the moral law (what Kant calls holiness) and not out of inclination—is not achievable in this life. Hence, if the moral law is to have any bite, if we are to be obligated to live under it, we must be able to live past death, at least to the point at which we can become holy. Life after death is a postulate of the moral law.

But why, one might ponder, must we be able to realize completely the highest good in order to be commanded rationally to pursue it? Often goals are ideals toward which a person strives, ideals that may, at best, be only partially realizable. I have the ideal to be truthful and am commanded morally to speak the truth, though I have no illusions about attaining perfect truthfulness. In Kant's defense, however, it might be argued that there is a difference between commanding that we *strive* to attain a goal and commanding that we *attain* it. The moral law commands the latter, not the former.

3. A third argument, advanced by Plato (428–347 B.C.), applies to the dualist conception of the human person. Plato argued that the *soul is immortal because it is imperishable*, it is imperishable because it is indestructible, and it is indestructible because it is simple (not divisible into parts).[49] But why cannot the soul perish in other ways, for example, by simply being annihilated? There seems to be no reason that what is simple cannot be annihilated. On the other hand, since annihilation would require the activity of some outside agent, Plato's argument, if sound, would suggest that in itself the soul lives on and does not die with the disintegration of the physical body.

CONCLUSIONS

What conclusions can be drawn from our discussion? First, we have seen that there is considerable debate over how best to understand the human person. The conclusion the investigator draws depends not only on the particular evidence marshaled but also on how it fits into one's larger philosophical schema. We have considered arguments that life after death is possible on different perspectives on the human person, though problems persist. If one adopts the view that the soul is the real person, then it is possible that the soul persists through death, since physical death does not necessarily mean the end of the soul. If one adopts a materialistic view of the person, then the possibility of life after death depends upon the existence of a powerful, omniscient being who is capable of re-creating persons to be essentially the same as the deceased. If one denies the existence of such a being or refuses to ascribe to this being the relevant powers, or if spatiotemporal continuity is necessary for identity, then life after death for the anthropological materialist seems impossible.

What about its actuality? Here the evidence is far from clear. The *a posteriori* arguments depend upon claims that might have other plausible explanations. The *a priori* arguments rest on claims concerning, for example, the appropriate goal of human action or what the moral law requires. In both cases readers must evaluate the claims and judiciously decide which explanation best accounts for the data.

Often those who find arguments for immortality unconvincing have already adopted a nontheistic worldview, whereas those who find them convincing have adopted a particular theistic worldview in which these claims not only make sense but contribute in an important way to a present, meaningful existence in which encounter with God and the desire to realize their end in him play an essential role and in which the afterlife simply provides for a higher realization of these possibilities. This is not a defect, but a recognition that any view of the world should have a coherence of structure and meaning.

STUDY QUESTIONS

1. Do you believe in life after death? To what evidence or arguments do you appeal to support the response you give?

2. What presuppositions about the nature of human persons are made by those who talk literally about human immortality? How might these presuppositions differ from those held by someone who speaks simply about life after death? Why do you think that language matters when we speak about important topics?

3. We noted four different views of life after death. In what ways are they similar and different? Present an argument that might be given in support of each view and another that is critical of each.

4. What is involved in personal identity? What do you consider to be the most significant evidence to show that our personal identity is to be found in a nonreducible, ultimate self? Note a strength and a weakness of this evidence.

5. Give a description of the materialist conception of human persons. What problems face this view? What are the implications of this view for the possibility of life after death?

6. In what ways would the characteristics of the afterlife differ for the believer in a soul and the materialist? What problems (for example, population, human fulfillment, time consciousness) might result from humans living after their death?

7. Which of the arguments presented in this chapter for the actuality of life after death do you think is the strongest? Why do you think so? Note the critical premise of that argument, and evaluate its truth.

NOTES

1. Corliss Lamont, *The Illusion of Immortality* (New York: Philosophical Library, 1965), p. 7.

2. According to the Theravada Buddhist doctrine of *anatta*, there is no persisting self-substance to transmigrate. See David Kalupahana, *Buddhist Philosophy* (Honolulu: University of Hawaii, 1976), pp. 38–42.

3. Thomas Aquinas, *Summa Theologica*, Part III Supplement, Q. 79, A. 2. Paul Badham quotes a 1976 Catholic catechism for adults, approved in Ireland and the United States, that states that each person will one day rise again "as the same person he was, in the same flesh made living by the same spirit." Paul Badham and Linda Badham, *Immortality or Extinction?* (New Jersey: Barnes and Noble, 1982), p. 5.

4. John Hick, *Death and Eternal Life* (New York: Harper and Row, 1976), chap. 15; Bruce R. Reichenbach, *Is Man the Phoenix? A Study of Immortality* (Grand Rapids: William B. Eerdmans, 1978), chap. 5.

5. "After his death his words remain established. This is what the ancient saying means. I have heard that the best course is to establish virtue, the next best is to establish achievement, and still the next best is to establish words. When these are not abandoned with time, it may be called immortality." *Tso chuan*, in Wing-Tsit Chan, *A Source Book in Chinese Philosophy* (Princeton: Princeton University Press, 1963), p. 13. For its place in African religions, see J. S. Mbiti, *African Religions and Philosophy* (New York: Doubleday, 1970), pp. 32–33.

6. George Santayana, *Reason in Religion* (New York: Collier, 1962), pp. 174.

7. Rudolph Bultmann, *Kerygma and Myth*, ed. Hans Werner Bartsch (New York: Harper and Row, 1953), p. 39.

8. D. Z. Phillips, *Death and Immortality* (London: Macmillan, 1970), pp. 41–55.

9. A problem relating to the second of these conditions dogs those who advocate reincarnation. Alleged reincarnates are born with their unique genetic code inherited from their parents and go on to develop their own physical characteristics, personality, memories, and categories of understanding. They begin life as infants who have no recollection of former lives, and few ever remember them. One might hypothesize the continuity of a spiritual soul, but without memories, awareness of self-identity, and consciousness of continuity or consistency of experience with the past, one cannot discern whether the person is a reincarnated person or a new individual. Reincarnationists, however, point to exceptional cases where children appear to remember past existences and exhibit features (e.g., being able to speak certain languages) that seem to require previous existence.

10. Richard Swinburne, *The Evolution of the Soul* (Oxford: Oxford University Press, 1986), p. 146.

11. Richard Swinburne, *The Coherence of Theism* (Oxford: Oxford University Press, 1977), p. 119.

12. H. D. Lewis, *The Self and Immortality* (New York: Seabury, 1973), p. 45.

13. Kurt Baier, "Smart on Sensation," *Australasian Journal of Philosophy* 40 (1962); reprinted in C.V. Borst, ed., *The Mind/Brain Identity Theory* (New York: Macmillan, 1970), chap. 8.

14. Corbett H. Thigpen and Harvey M. Cleckley, *The Three Faces of Eve* (New York: McGraw-Hill, 1957), pp. 50–51. See also Flora Rheta Schreiber, *Sybil* (Chicago: Henry Regnery, 1973).

15. Thigpen and Cleckley, *Three Faces*, p. 38.

16. L. L. Vasiliev, *Experiments in Mental Suggestion* (Church Crookham: Institute for the Study of Mental Images, 1963).

17. Keith Campbell acknowledges that "parapsychology could in principle refute Central-State Materialism," though paradoxically he goes on to suggest that "if

some paranormal results were established as genuine, they might . . . be accommodated in a new, expanded, physical science." *Body and Mind* (New York: Doubleday, 1970), pp. 96–97.

18. Hick, *Death and Eternal Life*, p. 121; Badham and Badham, *Immortality*, p. 90–92.

19. Campbell, *Body and Mind*, p. 96. It is puzzling that just a page earlier Campbell apparently does grant credence to Vasiliev's work.

20. Swinburne, *The Evolution of the Soul*, chap. 10.

21. Oscar Cullmann, *The Immortality of the Soul or Resurrection of the Dead?* (London: Epworth Press, 1958), pp. 51–53. What is puzzling about Cullmann's view is that earlier he argued for a monistic view of the person who is to be resurrected in the End.

22. H. H. Price, "Survival and the Idea of 'Another World,' " *Proceedings of the Society for Psychical Research* 50, Part 182 (Jan. 1953); reprinted in Terence Penelhum, *Immortality* (Belmont, Calif.: Wadsworth, 1973), pp. 25–26. [See PRSR, Part 9, pp. 421–31.]

23. Patricia S. Goldman-Rakic, "Working Memory and the Mind," *Scientific American* (Sept. 1992): 115.

24. Doreen Kimura, "Sex Difference in the Brain," *Scientific American* (Sept. 1992): 119–25.

25. Swinburne, *The Evolution of the Soul*, chap. 15. [See PRSR, Part 9, pp. 431–42.]

26. J.J.C. Smart, "Sensations and Brain Processes," *Philosophical Review* 68 (1959); reprinted in Borst, *Mind/Brain Identity Theory*, p. 56.

27. U. T. Place, "Is Consciousness a Brain Process?" *British Journal of Psychology* 47 (1956); reprinted in Borst, *Mind/Brain Identity Theory*, p. 47.

28. Douglas R. Hofstadter and Daniel C. Dennett, *The Mind's I* (New York: Basic Books, 1981), p. 192.

29. Ibid., p. 174.

30. John Searle, *Minds, Brains and Science* (Cambridge: Harvard University Press, 1984), p. 61.

31. Ibid., p. 93.

32. B.A.O. Williams, "Personal Identity and Individuation," *Proceedings of the Aristotelian Society* 57 (1956–57): 239.

33. Hick, *Death and Eternal Life*, p. 292.

34. This stipulation is unsatisfactory if one takes these characteristics as constituting personal identity, for then whether a person's identity continues depends not on empirical factors about the person but on extraneous factors, such as whether God decided to create two beings rather than one or whether both entities of the amoeba-like split survived.

35. See Raymond A. Moody Jr., *Life after Life* (New York: Bantam, 1976).

36. Badham and Badham, *Immortality*, p. 73.

37. Moody, *Life after Life*, p. 140.

38. Badham and Badham, *Immortality*, p. 80.

39. Hick, *Death and Eternal Life*, (pp. 131–38), with others, terms this *unconscious fraud*.

40. C. D. Broad, *Lectures on Psychical Research* (London: Routledge and Kegan Paul, 1962), pp. 137–39.

41. See Badham and Badham, *Immortality*, pp. 95–98, for more details and references.

42. "The spirits do not seem to speak out of the context of a continuing life; they seem to lack a credible environment of their own, a community of which they are a part, real next-world tasks, interests and purposes. They seem instead to be still very much what they were in this world." Hick, *Death and Eternal Life*, p. 140.

43. I Corinthians 15:12–23.

44. For an extended argument to this effect, see Frank Morison, *Who Moved the Stone?* (London: Faber and Faber, 1930). We have briefly dealt with this in Chapter 9.

45. Aquinas, *Summa Theologica*, Supplement to part II, Q79, A2.

46. Aristotle, *Nicomachean Ethics* (Indianapolis: Bobbs-Merrill, 1962), Bk. I, chaps. 7–10.

47. Aquinas, *Summa Contra Gentiles*, III, ch. 35.

48. Immanuel Kant, *Critique of Practical Reason* (Indianapolis: Bobbs-Merrill, 1956), Bk. II, chap. 2.

49. Plato, *Phaedo*, 100b-107a.

SUGGESTED READING

Badham, Paul. *Christian Beliefs about Immortality*. London: Macmillan, 1976.

———— and Linda Badham. *Immortality or Extinction?* New Jersey: Barnes and Noble, 1982.

Blackmore, Susan. *Dying to Live: Near-Death Experiences*. Buffalo: Prometheus Press, 1993.

Cooper, John. *Body, Soul, and Life Everlasting*. Grand Rapids, Mich.: William B. Eerdmans, 1989.

Davis, Stephen T., ed. *Death and Afterlife*. London: Macmillan, 1989.

Edwards, Paul. *Immortality*. New York: Macmillan, 1992.

————. *Reincarnation*. Amherst, N.Y.: Prometheus, 1996.

Fischer, John Martin. "Why Immortality Is Not So Bad." *International Journal of Philosophical Studies* 2, no. 2 (Spring 1994): 257–70.

Hick, John. *Death and Eternal Life*. New York: Harper and Row, 1976.

Kvanvig, Jonathan L. *The Problem of Hell*. New York: Oxford University Press, 1993.

Lewis, H. D. *Persons and Life After Death*. London: Macmillan, 1978.

————. *The Self and Immortality*. New York: Seabury, 1973.

Lorimer, David. *Survival?* London: Routledge and Kegan Paul, 1984.

Moody, Raymond A., Jr. *Life after Life*. New York: Bantam Books, 1976.

Penelhum, Terence. *Immortality*. Belmont, Calif.: Wadsworth, 1973.

————. *Survival and Disembodied Existence*. London: Routledge and Kegan Paul, 1970.

Perry, John. *Personal Identity and Immortality*. Indianapolis: Hackett, 1979.

Phillips, D. Z. *Death and Immortality*. Macmillan, 1970.

Reichenbach, Bruce R. *Is Man the Phoenix? A Study of Immortality*. Grand Rapids: William B. Eerdmans, 1978.

————. *The Law of Karma*. London: Macmillan, 1990.

Shoemaker, Sidney, and Richard Swinburne. *Personal Identity*. Oxford: Blackwells, 1984.

Swinburne, Richard. *The Evolution of the Soul*. Oxford: Oxford University Press, 1986.

Taliaferro, "Why We Need Immortality." *Modern Theology* 6, no. (July 1990): 367–77.

Tipler, Frank. *The Physics of Immortality*. New York: Doubleday, 1994.

Walls, Jerry L. *Hell: The Logic of Damnation*. Notre Dame: University of Notre Dame Press, 1992.

CHAPTER 11   RELIGION AND
            SCIENCE:
            COMPATIBLE
            OR INCOMPATIBLE?

In 1616 the Holy Office of the Roman Catholic Church condemned the view that the earth moves around the sun as false science and contrary to biblical teaching:

> It has . . . come to the knowledge of the said Congregation that the Pythagorean doctrine—which is false and altogether opposed to the Holy Scripture—of the motion of the Earth, and the immobility of the Sun, which is also taught by Nicolaus Copernicus in *The Revolutions of the Planets* . . . is now being spread abroad and accepted by many. . . .[1]

Copernicus's work was placed on the list of censored books.

At the same time, the Church wanted Galileo (1564–1642) to abandon the Copernican position that he had been advocating in both written and public discussions. But Galileo, courageous as he was brilliant, continued to defend the Copernican position. His writings on planetary motion, sunspots, comets, and other natural phenomena clearly supported the heliocentric theory. In 1633, at the age of sixty-nine and in poor health, Galileo was summoned to appear before the Grand Inquisitor in Rome. He was found guilty of teaching falsehood, forced to recant, and placed under house arrest for the remaining eight years of his life.[2]

Historians of science know that the Church was actually willing to allow Galileo to discuss the heliocentric theory as a hypothesis, but it did not want him to claim that the theory truly depicted the behavior of the sun and planets. Wanting to protect its unique right to make pronouncements about reality, the Church offered Galileo and other progressive scientists the opportunity to say that the heliocentric theory is a mathematical fiction—just one of several possible calculational schemes that could account for observed heavenly phenomena.

When he wrote the preface to Copernicus's *Revolutions*, Andreas Osiander (1498–1552) tried to make that work more palatable to the scientific community and to church theologians. He maintained that the heliocentric hypothesis is simply a convenient device for predicting planetary motion and not a true account of the causes of planetary motion. Osiander thought that he could defuse the controversy by sharply separating the domains of science and theology: science formulates mathematical fictions, but theology describes reality. Osiander was right that the enterprises of science and theology must be differentiated. The key, however, lies in precisely how the difference is defined. Galileo did not accept Osiander's option of denying to science the task of describing reality and discovering the hidden causes of observable events. Galileo believed that the heliocentric theory genuinely described reality, and thus he remained in direct conflict with the Church's geocentric view.

The Galileo affair bristles with many complex issues: the abuses of authority by institutionalized religion, the unfair lobbying activities of Ptolemaic scientists, the theological procedure by which scientific facts were derived from Holy Scripture, the emerging tension within science between the old deductive and the new inductive methods, and Galileo's own lack of diplomacy in propagating his views. Yet the most pervasive and most significant issue revolves around the operative notions of science and religion that led to conflict between them. The Galileo affair made painfully clear the need to understand the respective natures of these two powerful and important human activities. Adopting a thoughtful position on the relationship between science and religion is a prelude to approaching a multitude of specific problems that arise at their interface.

In seeking a thoughtful position on the relationship between religion and science, we need to understand the role of philosophy. Many people do not realize that almost all areas of intellectual investigation emerged from philosophy. Early in Western culture, study of the motions of the planets, the nature of music, the forms of government, the composition of ultimate reality, and much more came under the general canopy of *philosophy*, the "love of wisdom." Gradually, as the specific objects and methods of each inquiry became more clearly defined, new disciplines were born. Ultimately, many fields of study were spawned, each capable of conducting its official investigation independent of philosophy. The constellation of different disciplines that now exists—the array of natural sciences, the various social sciences, mathematics, and so forth—has emerged through a slow process of differentiation.

Our present exploration, then, deals with three disciplines: *theology* (which is the systematic articulation of religious beliefs), *natural science* (which is the empirical study of the order of nature), and *philosophy* (which, for our purposes, is the attempt to understand the most general characteristics of reality and knowledge). The attempt to define, distinguish, and interrelate the activities of theology and natural science is a philosophical undertaking. Two broad philosophical concerns are particularly relevant to this task: *metaphysical questions* (dealing with reality) and *epistemological questions* (dealing with knowledge) are crucial to differentiating the various models. As we look at the philosophical assumptions of both theology and natural science, we will see that they may be differentiated according to how their respective *aims, objects,* and *methods* are conceived.

Ian Barbour (1923–) has identified four basic models for understanding the relationship of religion and science: *conflict, independence, dialogue,* and *integration.* Let us consider each of these models in turn. We confine our discussion of science to the broad domain of the natural sciences, since doing so is faithful to the manner in which the historical discussion of the relation between religion and science developed. This means we must leave for another time exploration of the rich and inviting questions about the relation of religion to the social sciences.

DO RELIGION AND SCIENCE CONFLICT?

The Galileo affair has long been taken as symbolic of an inherent and irresolvable conflict between religion and science. Of course, other important issues have been taken as representing the conflict as well. For example, the now familiar debate over creation and evolution has been a heated controversy for more than a hundred years, pitting a view of humanity as a complex product of nature against a view of humanity as a creation of a personal deity.[3] Other examples are abundant. Relativity theory in physics drastically reinterprets concepts of space, time, and causality and thus challenges all religious perspectives that relate God to the world.[4] Technological advances in computers and artificial intelligence seem to endanger the unique status of Homo sapiens.[5] And the discovery of the DNA molecule threatens to put "the secret of life" into the hands of scientists.[6]

In the contemporary period, two dramatically opposed schools of thought, *scientific materialism* and *biblical literalism,* agree on one key point: that religion and science are in total *conflict.* Let us sketch the basic position of each of these schools and learn why they agree on this point. *Scientific materialism* makes the epistemological assumption that the empirical method of science is the only reliable procedure for obtaining knowledge and the metaphysical assumption that physical stuff (i.e., matter and energy) is the ultimate reality in the universe. Auxiliary assumptions that complete the view of scientific materialism include the claim that only the entities studied by science are real and the claim that only science can reveal what is real. After all, science allegedly works from publicly observable, reproducible data that are taken to confirm and disconfirm its theories. Hence, science is said to be properly objective. Religious beliefs, by contrast, are not as readily connected to such data as scientific theories and thus are said to be subjective, parochial, and uncritical.

Perhaps no intellectual movement exemplifies our general characterization of scientific materialism more than *logical positivism,* a movement whose heyday ranged from about the 1920s to the 1940s. Logical positivists, such as A. J. Ayer (1910–1989), who was discussed in Chapter 8, took the strong epistemological line that the only statements that have meaning are those that are verifiable or falsifiable by empirical experience. Since religion, metaphysics, and even ethics address nonempirical or nonsensory realities, the positivists charged that these disciplines consist of pseudo-statements with no cognitive meaning. For example, religion speaks of God, an entity that cannot be observed. Metaphysics speaks of being in general, which is an abstraction that cannot be observed. And ethics speaks of values, things of which we can have no sensory experience. The logical positivists denied reality to such unobservables and thus denied cognitive meaning to statements about them. The positivists claimed that, at best, terms for unobservable entities should be viewed as expressing our own subjective, psychological states and not as referring to objective realities.

Ironically, logical positivism itself eventually collapsed as philosophers began to realize that sensory input does not even provide an indubitable starting point for science. Philosophers of science became increasingly aware that the interaction of theory and observation is much more subtle and complex than the positivists ever imagined, thus threatening their pristine version of objectivity. So, since the positivists could not account for cognitive significance in scientific statements, the intellectual community became disillusioned by their claim to have a standard of meaning for all statements in other areas, such as religion and ethics.

Outside professional philosophy, there are other representatives of scientific materialism and its attendant conviction that religion and science conflict. In popular culture, Carl Sagan (1934–1996) has been a spokesperson for scientific materialism. In his book *Cosmos*, later made into a series for educational television, he states: "The Cosmos is all that is or ever was or ever will be."[7] Sagan believes that the universe is eternal, that it is fundamentally physical, and that science is the only way to gain reliable knowledge about it. He has been openly critical of traditional ideas of God as being too mystical and subjective and as ultimately threatening to the scientific method.

At the other end of the spectrum from scientific materialism is *biblical literalism*. Biblical literalism is something of an anomaly in the history of Christian thought, which contains a variety of views on the relation of scripture and science. For example, St. Augustine (354–430) maintained that when some particular passage of the Bible appears to conflict with established scientific thought, that passage should probably be interpreted metaphorically.[8] Other medieval philosophers and theologians acknowledged that the Bible includes a rich diversity of literary forms and reveals truth at many levels. The Anglican tradition continues this approach to scripture and is open to figurative as well as literal interpretations, depending on the genre of literature and the context of scriptural text in question. Pope John Paul II (1920–), representing a stance quite different from the one the Church took toward the Galileo controversy, has said that we now have "a more accurate appreciation of the methods proper to the different orders of knowledge,"[9] clearly giving place to both religious and scientific knowledge.

By contrast, particularly during the late nineteenth and early twentieth centuries in America, a literalistic mode of interpretation became the hallmark of certain American Protestant denominations or at least of large constituencies within those denominations. Biblical literalism—often referred to as "Protestant fundamentalism" or just "fundamentalism"—can be seen as a reaction to the rise of evolutionary biology in the area of science as well as to "higher criticism"[10] in the study of scriptural texts. Fundamentalists, whose numbers seem to be strong and growing, insist that scripture is "inerrant" and should be interpreted literally. Of course, they have a certain view of what it means to interpret scripture literally. The most prominent instance of how fundamentalism employs this approach is no doubt its ongoing crusade against the scientific theory of evolution. Their so-called literal interpretation of the book of Genesis results in the belief that God created the universe in six twenty-four-hour days and instantaneously created humanity at the end of a sixth day. This belief is in direct conflict with the scientific thesis that the species Homo sapiens evolved over millions of years—and the fundamentalists are interested in no compromises.

The Scopes "monkey trial" of 1925 was a sensational clash between the forces involved in this issue.[11] In the trial, William Jennings Bryan argued that teachers should not be permitted to present biological evolution in the public schools because it is clearly contrary to Scripture. Here we have religionists making factual pronouncements of a scientific nature on the basis of their reading of the Bible. Although Brian won the decision in the trial, it was later overturned on a technicality and evolutionary theory was permitted in the schools. However, fundamentalist opposition has continued to the present day.

In the last few decades, fundamentalists have developed a new argument known as "scientific creationism." Creation scientists try to validate their creationist position by scientific means. Instead of basing belief in the instantaneous creation of the first human beings on a literal reading of the Bible alone, they claim that they have *scientific evidence* for such beliefs. "True science," they argue, correlates with a literally interpreted biblical account of creation.[12] Creation scientists typically label evolutionary theory "false science" and demand equal time for "creationist theory" in the schools. In 1981, for example, a fundamentalist group succeeded in getting an Arkansas court to rule in favor of equal time for the teaching of "creationist theory," supported by whatever scientific facts seemed to confirm it and without reference to God or the Bible. We should note that the U.S. District Court overturned the Arkansas law one year later on grounds that it favored a particular religious view and thus violated the constitutional separation of church and state. It also pronounced creation science bogus science. We should also note that quite a few people who testified against the Arkansas bill were religious leaders and theologians, many of whom argued that the fundamentalists' literalistic approach to the Bible and their co-opting of science for sectarian purposes was dangerous to our intellectual and religious freedom.

Regardless of our personal feelings on these issues, a more fundamental lesson that we may learn concerns the way in which competition and conflict between religion and science are made possible. Conflict is certainly possible when religion and science are conceived in ways that closely equate their *aims, objects,* and *methods.* When the *aims* of theology include providing an explanation for natural objects and events that would stand on the same footing as any proposed scientific explanation, then conflict is almost inevitable. Likewise, when the proper *objects* of theological investigation include the same natural or physical phenomena that science studies, the stage is set for direct competition. And, when the *method* of theology is put on a par with that of science—or at least when it is not sufficiently distinguished from the method of science—then the path is open for severe competition between the two disciplines.

One clear moral emerges from the prolonged debate over evolution and creation: when the objects, aims, and methods of religion and science are not sufficiently differentiated, the stage is set for competition and conflict. We might venture a few generalizations about the history of the issue. When disciplinary or intellectual boundaries are persistently blurred, we eventually find some theologians meddling in the affairs of science, even wanting to overturn its findings for religious rather than scientific reasons. On the other side, we find some scientists and other scientifically informed persons who try to use the results of modern science to confirm philosophical naturalism and thus to discredit religion altogether. What we might hope for is a better understanding of the nature of religion and science than either side possesses in a conflict model.

ARE RELIGION AND SCIENCE INDEPENDENT?

Instead of treating religion and science as if they are in direct conflict, some thinkers and movements have treated them as if they are totally *independent,* with each area having its own very different *aims, objects,* and *methods.* Generally, this independence model produces the attitude that each field—religion and science—should stick to its own business. The image of religion and science as sealed off from one another in air-tight compartments is appropriate here. Conflict, quite obviously, is thereby avoided.

In the medieval period, the separation of religion and science was supported by a kind of broad dualistic thinking that has both metaphysical and epistemological components. Metaphysically, the medieval mind saw reality as divided into two realms, supernature and nature. God is a supernatural reality, and the human soul and other objects of theology were associated primarily with this realm as well. The physical universe, on the other hand, comprised the mundane realm of nature. The general medieval posture, epistemologically speaking, was that the realm of supernature could be fully known only by revelation, whereas the realm of nature is known by the techniques appropriate to human rational investigation. Thus, both the *objects* and the *methods* of theology and science are greatly different. Obviously, the medieval tradition of *natural theology* (whose arguments we studied in Chapter 5) afforded some middle ground, maintaining that the existence and a few metaphysical attributes of God could be inferred from the existence and design of nature. And there was a strong conviction that the spiritual realm permeates the material realm, giving ordinary life profound significance.

In modern times, several intellectual movements, each in its own way, have advocated the strict independence of religion and science: *Protestant neo-orthodoxy, existentialism,* and *linguistic analysis.* The Protestant theologian Karl Barth (1986–1968), perhaps the most celebrated spokesperson for *neo-orthodoxy,* tried to recapture for Christianity its emphasis on the centrality of Christ and the primacy of special "revelation" for knowing God.[13] For Barth, theology deals with God's self-revelation in Christ and therefore offers a source of religious knowledge that lies beyond our human noetic powers. In fact, according to Barth, sin has so blinded human reason to the knowledge of God that it is absolutely necessary for God to bridge the gap and reveal himself to us.[14] Furthermore, the aim of religion is to effect personal encounter with God. Barth conceives of science, on the other hand, as the ongoing human search for knowledge of the natural world, employing as it does observation, experiment, rational inference, and the like. Its fundamental aim is to gain understanding about the patterns of the empirical world.

Existentialism, which influenced neo-orthodox theology, also advocated a sharp distinction between the domains of religion and science. Neo-orthodoxy sharply distinguished the transcendent realm from the finite human realm in order to support the separation of religion and science. However, the dominant distinction in the existentialist categorization of religion and science was between the realm of personal selfhood and the realm of impersonal objects. Common to all versions of existentialism is the conviction that we can understand the meaning of human existence only by being personally involved in freely making decisions. It is through commitment, being authentic, and shouldering our humanity responsibly that we work out the meaning of our own lives—not through detached speculation.

Although *atheistic existentialists,* such as Nietzsche (1844–1900) and Sartre (1905–1980) believed that we could achieve meaning without reference to God, *religious existentialists* insisted that we need to orient ourselves toward God to experience the full significance of personal life. For these existentialists, religion involves the subjective and inward orientation of one's personhood, whereas science involves the study and manipulation of objects. Once again, then, we have a strict differentiation between the *subject matter* of religion and science; the former deals with the realm of uniquely personal existence, whereas the latter deals with the realm of objects and their operations. The *methods* of knowledge are subjective and objective, respectively. And the *aim* of religion is to provide an avenue of personal meaning and significance, whereas the aim of the scientific enterprise is to explain, predict, and control the behaviors of impersonal things in our physical environment. The noted Jewish theologian Martin Buber (1878–1965) poignantly makes this distinction, stating that the relation between a person and a material object is an I-It relationship but that the religious believer's relation to God is an I-Thou relationship. It is through relationship with another person that one becomes human, and it is in relationship with God that one finds complete human fulfillment: "As a Person God gives personal life, he makes us as persons become capable of meeting with him and with one another."[15]

Linguistic analysis is another philosophical movement that envisions religion and science as totally compartmentalized human endeavors. Although positivistic philosophers restricted language to the statement of empirical facts and were fascinated by the prospect of building an ideal language on that basis, ordinary language philosophers were fascinated by the rich variety of functions that human language performs. Ordinary language philosophers are less inclined to assign reality to the respective *objects* of religion and science but are instead interested in analyzing the uses of these different stretches of language and the different human contexts in which they occur. Taking their cue particularly from the work of the later Wittgenstein, exponents of this approach said that religion and science are two distinct but equally legitimate "language games," each with its own vocabulary, categories, and logic. According to linguistic philosophers, the uses of language in religious contexts differ greatly from the uses of scientific language. For them, the aim of religious language (considered in depth in Chapter 8) is to support and recommend a certain way of life. The method by which it does this is to use language that is effective in eliciting a certain set of attitudes and encouraging allegiance to a particular moral point of view. On the other hand, the aims served by scientific language are essentially those of explanation, prediction, and technological manipulation of observable phenomena. This language must be extremely precise and highly empirical. So, for ordinary language philosophy, theology and science are treated as markedly separate linguistic activities, having intrinsically different *aims* and *methods* woven inextricably into their respective languages, with no possibility of interaction or conflict.[16]

IS DIALOGUE POSSIBLE?

One may wonder whether it is possible to move beyond the independence thesis to some conception of how religion and science can interact. Can they engage in dialogue in any fashion? Ian Barbour envisions two avenues along which these two distinct fields in can have meaningful dialogue. The first avenue relates to the discussion of what might be called *boundary questions;* the second revolves around consideration of *methodological parallels* between the two fields.

Let us proceed by talking about the *boundaries of science* along two different lines: the *presuppositions* required at the foundations of science and the questions raised at the *limits* of certain scientific theories that, by their nature, cannot be answered by further scientific investigation. Each of these approaches to the matter of boundaries offers interesting possibilities for dialogue between theology and science.

It is common among philosophers of science to say that science rests on certain *presuppositions,* beliefs that science cannot establish but that shape the whole enterprise. These presuppositions, taken together, provide a kind of sketch of the fundamental characteristics of the world in which science takes itself to operate, giving rise to more specific commitments about its *aims, objects,* and *methods.* For example, many thinkers take science to rest on the presupposition that physical nature is in a significant sense real, leading to a belief that the objects of science are empirically real entities. Another important presupposition is that nature is intelligible, that is, accessible to mind. And still another presupposition is that the world's order is contingent and not necessary, which entails that its order must be known through inductive and empirical methods. One last presupposition of science is that nature is, in an important sense, good—that it has value and worth. This presupposition supports the aim of understanding nature and entering into commerce with it.

Such presuppositions may seem rather unremarkable and almost too obvious to be interesting, but they have not always been so widely accepted. In fact, their acceptance in modern times has a long and interesting history. It is customary to speak of modern science as being indebted to classical Greek thought, to say that its confidence in the rational structure of nature provides one of the early driving forces for science. However, a deeper look into the Greek worldview raises enormous doubts about whether it could ever have evolved in the direction of modern science. Plato and Aristotle both believed that the true nature of things is found in their "form," not in their "matter." Thus, the objects of science, for them, are the essential (nonempirical) forms of things. In this vein, ancient Greek science assumed we could know the properties of a thing by logically deducing them from a definition of its essence—and without having to study it empirically! This is hardly the method that modern science follows.

The Judeo-Christian *doctrine of creation,* which was formulated centuries later and which eventually influenced pioneer thinkers, actually allowed modern science, with its careful empirical techniques and inductive reasoning, to be born. The doctrine teaches that God freely chose to bring the world into existence, which makes its operations contingent and thus amenable to inductive and empirical methods. Since God is good, his creation is also good and worthy of study. E. L. Mascall (1905–) explains that the doctrine of creation supplied a philosophy of nature that overthrew the Greek perspective and gave solid support to modern science:

A world which is created by the Christian God will be both contingent and orderly. It will embody regularities and patterns, since its Maker is rational, but the particular regularities and patterns which it will embody cannot be predicted *a priori*, since he is free; they can be discovered only by examination. The world, as Christian theism conceives, it is thus an ideal field for the application of scientific method, with its twin techniques of observation and experiment.[17]

These and other implications of the doctrine were not all seen at once but came to be understood after centuries of reflection by Christian thinkers. As further implications were drawn, Christian philosophers realized that they were committed to the rich and suggestive affirmations that matter is real and intelligible per se and that appropriate methods had to be developed for studying it. Thus, the conceptual seeds for modern science were planted by theological insights.[18] Science began to break away from the Greek conception and to flourish anew in the early modern period. This is one of the many lessons of the Galileo affair.

Another kind of *boundary issue* arises when we realize that some of the crowning theories of science take us to the *limits* of science's ability to explain. The more general and comprehensive scientific theories actually raise additional questions that science cannot answer by its own methods. These questions are essentially metaphysical, thus opening the door for dialogue between science and theology. In pushing back to the earliest history of the cosmos, astronomers and theoretical physicists, for example, ask questions about the initial conditions that existed. The physicist Stephen Hawking (1942–) once proposed that everything in the universe expanded from an initial infinitesimal point in which not even the most elemental laws of physics operated.[19] Since this is as far back as science can extend its impulse for explanation, it has reached a limit or boundary. At this level of inquiry, a profound question arises: How did the fundamental laws of physics first come into existence, if there was once a punctiliar time when they did not exist? Since science cannot answer such a question, some would say that the door is open for theology to say something about God as the creative ground of the existence and structure of the universe. By its own distinct methods, theology can help make sense of the contingency and general order that science discovers in the universe. It thereby offers a different perspective on the same range of objects.

Various thinkers envision different ways for theology to interact with the boundary questions of science. The philosopher of science Ernan McMullin (1924–), for example, distinguishes the statements and methods of theology from those of science and envisions those two enterprises as functioning on different levels of explanation. McMullin declares that, on its own level, a scientific account of the universe is in principle complete. For him, there is no need to think that the relation of theology to science is that of filling in the gaps—that is, of deriving arguments for the existence of God on the basis of incomplete explanations in science. Besides, as science advances, such gaps are eventually closed, thus preempting that role for theology. McMullin stresses, instead, that the aim of theology is to provide ultimate explanations, and its methods are oriented toward constructing them. The Christian doctrine of creation does not, he contends, explain the mechanics of how the universe began but affirms its absolute dependence on God. Interpreted in this fashion, the doctrine of creation is "consonant" with modern scientific cosmology, giving an explanation of the universe that is not incompatible with but is complementary to scientific explanation. Thus, theology—like science, history, literature, and other disciplines—contributes to a coherent worldview.[20]

David Tracy (1939–) proposes that religion can enter into genuine dialogue at the boundaries of science in a somewhat different manner. On the one hand, theology can contribute insight on the ethical issues pertaining to the uses of science (e.g., the use of atomic theory to build weapons of mass destruction). Tracy also believes that theology can shed light on the presuppositions required for the possibility of science (e.g., that the world requires a rational ground that can be understood from classic religious texts and the structures of human experience).[21] This is the impact religion can have on science: answering its boundary questions. On the other hand, science can also contribute information to theology. Tracy contends that theological doctrines are culturally conditioned and limited and that enlightened theological method takes into account new scientific advances. The way evolutionary ideas have affected modern consciousness, for example, raises the question of reformulation of the doctrine of creation.

As we indicated earlier, another avenue for dialogue between religion and science pertains to the *methodological parallels* between the two fields. Although *positivists, neo-orthodox theologians,* and *existentialist thinkers* characterized science as *objective* and religion as *subjective,* that dichotomy came under increasing pressure from studies showing that religion is more objective than originally thought and that science is subjective in important respects. Such studies opened the way for thinkers to seek parallels between the methods of religion and the methods of science, rather than concentrate on the stark differences between them. For present purposes, let us look at four factors that can be cited to make a case for the methodological parallel between science and religion: *communal paradigms, research programs, observer participation,* and *the role of models.*

In the past several decades, such philosophers as Norwood Russell Hanson (1924–1967),[22] Stephen Toulmin (1922–),[23] and Thomas Kuhn (1922–)[24] have persuasively argued that science is not as pristine and objective as previously thought. These authors represent a growing trend in philosophy of science that emphasized the fact that scientific data are in a certain sense theory-laden, that theories arise as much from the free and creative scientific imagination as they do from an analysis of evidence, and that the acceptance of theories is as much a function of the historical community of scientists as it is a calculation based strictly on the evidence. We might say that this new era in the philosophy of science stresses the theme of "personal involvement"—and it has done this in a rich variety of ways.

Probably no contemporary philosopher of science has had broader impact than Thomas Kuhn. Kuhn argued that the method of science is not totally objective in testing theories by clear-cut criteria that refer to theory-free data because both theories and data are dependent on the prevailing *paradigms* of the scientific community. Although Kuhn uses the term "paradigm" in slightly different ways throughout his work, the following statement of Kuhn's is enlightening:

> On the one hand, [the term "paradigm"] stands for the entire constellation of beliefs, values, techniques, and so on shared by the members of a given community. On the other, it denotes one sort of element in that constellation, the concrete puzzle-solutions which, employed as models or examples, can replace explicit rules as a basis for the solution of the remaining puzzles of normal science.[25]

"Normal science" simply means the collective efforts of the scientific community to solve the research problems they face according to the prevailing paradigm. The paradigm contains examples of puzzles already solved and helps decide what could count as an adequate solution of other puzzles. An established paradigm is resistant to simple falsification by a few negative instances and can often be preserved by considering these instances to be anomalies or by articulating ad hoc hypotheses.

Kuhn's idea of a *scientific revolution* is highly suggestive of parallels with religion. Normal science, which is typically conservative and controlled by tradition, enters crisis when the prevailing paradigm encounters increasing difficulty solving some important puzzles. At some point, an alternative paradigm starts seeming attractive to the community of researchers by virtue of its ability to account for existing data while handling new data in a more satisfactory way. When such conditions are present, science typically undergoes a major *paradigm shift*, which is a "scientific revolution." Likewise, when the prevailing theological paradigm—or way of looking at the world and explaining and responding to important life situations—comes under pressure and a new paradigm seems to have much promise to a significant number of the religious community, then a *theological revolution* is almost inevitably brewing. One could interpret, say, the Protestant Reformation's break from Roman Catholicism or the modern rejection and reformulation of traditional Christian doctrines by feminist theologians in this light. We could also see the emergence of Mahayana Buddhism from Theravada Buddhism, for example, as a major paradigm shift.

All of this highlights the tremendously social nature of paradigms. Although debates continue about the exact degree of subjectivity in science, Kuhn's provocative analysis inspired some thinkers to suggest that religious traditions can also be viewed as communities that share a common paradigm. The data for religious communities are religious experience, historical events, and sacred texts—all interpreted and given significance within an overarching paradigm. Challenges to religious belief, like challenges to a scientific theory under the approved paradigm, can be deflected by calling them anomalies or by proposing ad hoc hypotheses. This actually explains the tendency of religious believers to maintain their beliefs even in light of seemingly contrary evidence—and scientists, as Kuhn has shown us, often do the same thing. That is just the way paradigms operate within the communities that embrace them.

In seeking ever more adequate ways to expose methodological parallels between science and religion, some have thought that the Kuhnian-type radical paradigm shift is too extreme. Nancey Murphy (1951–) maintains that the idea of a *research program* provides a better conception of methodological parallels.[26] Imre Lakatos (1937–) advanced the idea that a community of scientists engages in ongoing projects and endeavors that preserve at their heart a core theory that is surrounded by auxiliary hypotheses. The role of the auxiliary hypotheses is to protect the core theory. Thus, they are subject to modification and even rejection and replacement in order to keep data from overturning the core theory. The idea of a research program explains the tendency of scientists to cling to their main theory in light of seemingly adverse data while at the same time accounting for their ability to make appropriate theoretical adjustments.

Murphy thinks that it is very fruitful to interpret the task of theology as a research program as well. The core of the theological research program should contain the theologian's judgment about how to sum up the essential minimum of the relevant community's faith—perhaps revolving around the trinitarian nature of God, God's holiness, and God's revelation in Jesus. The next step is to develop auxiliary hypotheses to be explained by the core and whose future modification could help protect the core. The third step, if theology is to be genuinely parallel to science, is for the theologian to seek data that help confirm the core theory and the auxiliary hypotheses. The data describe a range of religious experiences (e.g., humiliation, love, meekness, spiritual appetite, communal support).

One might describe Murphy as wanting to look for parallels between religion and science primarily by making theology more objective, whereas followers of Kuhn do it by making science more subjective. But the question arises: Why would we want to adapt a scientific method to theology (or, perhaps, adapt theology to a scientific method, depending on one's perspective)? The point of Lakatos's method is to provide an objective decision procedure for choosing between competing conceptual schemes or research programs. Those large-scale theories that generate new, confirmable data are progressive; those that fail to do so are degenerative. Obviously, theology faces a diversity of theoretical positions—Christian and non-Christian—that vie for acceptance. How do we decide among them? Murphy would answer that the respective religious research programs should project novel and important facts about human experience that can be objectively verified. Confirmation of the empirical claims that follow from these research programs would provide support for the research programs. Conversely, should the empirical claims be disconfirmed or encounter serious anomalies, the research program would seem to be degenerative rather than progressive. This would mean, at the very least, that some auxiliary hypotheses would need reevaluation so as to make the research program progressive again or, at the very most, that the program should be abandoned. Much more needs to be discussed before arriving at a final assessment of Murphy's proposal. However, we may say at this point that she envisions a positive relation between the *methods* of theology and science, a relation that reflects the fact that both can exhibit critical objectivity that makes for intersubjective testing.

Instead of arguing that religion is like science, philosopher of science Holmes Rolston (1932–) argues that science is like religion in an important respect. He explains that the role of personal involvement is coming to be recognized in science and that it is somewhat parallel to the nature of personal involvement in religion. While the methods of both religion and science call for personal involvement, Rolston admits that the distinct aim of personal involvement in religion is the reformation and reorientation of the person.[27] In modern times, the emergence of both relativity physics and quantum physics has supplied an interesting case study for those looking for parallels with religion. While the relationship between relativity and quantum theories may be debated, they both forced a reconsideration of the status of the observer in science. Traditional conceptions envision the observer in science separate from the object of observation. However, in developing an adequate quantum theory, Werner Heisenberg (1901–1976) and others asserted that the very act of observation itself influences the outcome of the observation, that the observer is somehow involved with the data. The Heisenberg Uncertainty Principle states that the more precisely we determine the location of an electron, the less precisely we can determine its velocity, and vice versa. This is because light must be used, say, to determine position, but even one quantum of light alters the velocity of the electron.[28] Relativity theory also assumes personal involvement when it asserts that the most fundamental measurements—such as mass, velocity, and length of an object—depend on the frame of reference of the observer.[29] For example, a moving object appears much shorter in the direction of motion, although it is the other objects that appear compressed when viewed from the moving object itself. All of this accents the intimate tie between—indeed, the inseparability of—the oberver and the observed, the seeker and reality.[30]

As we can see, exciting advances made in both science and the philosophy of science put pressure on the old dichotomy between science as totally objective and religion as deeply subjective by showing the personal and communal features of the scientific enterprise. However, the dichotomy also came under pressure from some writers who insisted that religion should not be typecast as utterly subjective. We can, for example, interpret religion as having its own data for public consideration, much as science does. Its data include religious experience, rituals, and scriptural texts. Furthermore, theology can approach its distinct explanatory task with a premium placed on the conceptual criteria of coherence, comprehensiveness, and fruitfulness, which are criteria also employed in the scientific evaluation of empirical theories.

Still another factor that helps reveal methodological parallels between theology and science is the use of models in each discipline. As Ian Barbour shows in *Myths, Models, and Paradigms*, religion employs metaphors and models much as science employs them to help imagine what is not directly observable.[31] A *model*, for present purposes, is an imaginative mental construct invented to account for observed phenomena. According to Barbour,

> a model is usually an imagined mechanism or process, which is postulated by analogy with familiar mechanisms or processes. . . . [I]ts chief use is to help one understand the world, not simply to make predictions. . . . Like a mathematical model, it is a symbolic representation of a physical system, but it differs in its intent to represent the underlying structure of the world. It is used to develop a theory which in some sense explains the phenomena.[32]

Clear instances of models in practiced religion as well as professional theology are not difficult to find.

The feminist theologian Sallie McFague (1933–) discusses some of the prominent models in the Christian community, models that arise from human experience and help us understand certain aspects of the divine. She analyzes three personal models: *God as Mother* (representing nurture and care), *God as Lover* (representing the divine passion toward humanity), and *God as Friend* (representing a reciprocal bond between God and the believer).[33] Again, such studies of religion help show that it has more structure and is more objective than common stereotypes allow and, furthermore, that its structure and objectivity are parallel to elements detected in the scientific quest.

ATTEMPTS AT INTEGRATION

Some thinkers hold that religion and science are capable of a more intimate and organic relationship than a *dialogue model* admits. They contend that some sort of *integration* between the two fields is not only possible but necessary if we are to achieve a unified and comprehensive understanding of reality. Barbour identifies three different versions of integration between the content of theology and the content of science: *natural theology, theology of nature,* and *systematic synthesis*.

Traditional natural theology reasons from the existence of the cosmos itself and from evidence of design in nature to the existence of God. As we saw in Chapter 5, natural theologians construct arguments based on human reason rather than on sacred revelation or religious experience. Perhaps the most widely popular piece of natural theology is the teleological argument in its various forms.[34] In contemporary times, the Anthropic Principle, based on a wealth of new scientific findings, is often employed to make the argument.[35] Thus, new theories and findings in science sometimes provide fresh grist for the mill in natural theology. While the *aims* and *methods* of natural theology differ from those of empirical science, there is a sense in which they are interested in giving their respective explanations of the same *objects*. This means that natural theology may be seen as one form of integration between the content of science and the content of theology.

A different kind of integration of religion and science is attempted by those thinkers interested in articulating a *theology of nature*. Unlike natural theology, a theology of nature does not start from science and move to God. Arthur Peacocke (1922–) states that a theology of nature starts from an accepted religious tradition, with its distinctive religious experiences and scriptural texts. A theology of nature uses the content of science to tutor, reformulate, and reinterpret traditional theological doctrines, rather than to argue for the existence of God. Within the Christian intellectual community, for example, the doctrines of creation, providence, and human nature are affected in fascinating and important ways by the most current theories propounded in the sciences. Peacocke understands that science now characterizes nature as dynamic and evolutionary, with a long history of emergent novelty brought about by the interplay of chance and law. Explaining the new scientific picture of things theologically, he says that "the natural causal creative nexus of events is itself God's creative action."[36] Many see Peacocke's approach as opening the door for a closer relationship between religion and science than seems possible in natural theology because the *objects* of science (even characterized in a general way) are interpreted as mediating God's presence and activity in the world.

A third version of integration, quite distinct from *natural theology* and the *theology of nature*, is *systematic synthesis*. This is the attempt to synthesize key religious themes with basic scientific insights under the canopy of a *comprehensive metaphysical system*, a unified worldview. The process philosophy of Alfred North Whitehead (1861–1947) is probably the most important and most influential modern example of this. We might characterize Whitehead as integrating religion and science by showing how their respective *aims* coalesce in a larger and more comprehensive aim, how each field has important insight into the nature of the *objects* that populate reality, and how the fruits of their *methods* have taught us new universal themes for understanding the universe. In short, Whitehead enlists both religion and science in the service of an overarching metaphysical vision.

Whitehead rejects the medieval view as well as the Newtonian view of nature. On the medieval view, nature embodies a fixed, unchanging, hierarchical order and operates teleologically (directed toward rational ends). All substances that make up reality, for medieval thinkers, involve a dualism of spirit and matter. Spirit is eternal and our link with the life of God, whereas matter is transitory and imperfect. The Newtonian view envisions nature as involving the continual rearrangement of unchanging components of the universe. Atomism (the belief that reality can be broken into separate particles) and determinism (the belief that reality operates by strict causal necessity) are hallmarks of the Newtonian picture of nature.

Whitehead acknowledges that the new concepts of nature picture it as evolutionary and dynamic, with new and novel forms emerging through time. Concepts of determinism are replaced by concepts of chance, randomness, and even chaos, allowing nature to be characterized by openness as well as structure. Furthermore, nature is understood as relational, ecological, and interdependent. Reality has come to be seen as constituted by events and relationships, rather than by separate substances and their operations. According to Whitehead, a holistic conception of reality invalidates virtually all forms of dualism. Dualistic views of human nature are replaced by evolutionary views that acknowledge the special capacities of our species while maintaining that it is the product of and interdependent with other creatures in the natural order. Thus, the medieval view of nature as a kingdom and the Newtonian view of nature as a machine have been replaced by the view of nature as a community.

The genius of Whitehead's philosophy is that it presents a systematic metaphysical interpretation of reality that is consistent with the evolutionary view of nature held by twentieth-century science. Central to Whitehead's metaphysics is the priority of *becoming* over *being*, of *transition* and *activity* over *permanence* and *persistence*. All entities, which Whitehead calls "actual occasions," are centers of conscious experience, each exerting influence on all other occasions, making reality interdependent, ecological. The great hierarchy of nature represents a spectrum of the organization and integration of experience: an entity such as an *electron* (which quantum physics tells us has a transitory and indeterminate existence) exhibits a relatively low level of integration; a *cell* has a considerably higher level of integration; and so on up the chain of plants and animals. A *human being* exhibits a very high level of integration in which all of the lower levels are incorporated. These key ideas led Whitehead to dub his view "the philosophy of organism."[37] In discussing process responses to evil in Chapter 6, we learned that each entity is interconnected with the whole of reality and yet retains its own individuality and power of self-determination.

Whitehead connects ideas inspired by contemporary science with theological ideas in a very sophisticated way. For Whitehead, God (in his Primordial Nature) is the ultimate ground of order in the world, offering all logical possibilities for how events can turn out. God selects certain "initial subjective aims" and imparts them to entities in the world, seeking to actualize the possibilities he envisions. However, God (in his Consequent Nature) is influenced by events in the world as he responds and adjusts to actual outcomes, always seeking to lure things toward his ideal aims for them. In his Consequent Nature, God conserves all of the valuable experiences and achievements of the creaturely world, thus leading to a process version of immortality. Between God and the world there is interdependence and reciprocity. Whitehead's God is not in monarchical control of the universe conceived as his kingdom; rather, he "persuades" and "influences" events at a very deep level.

INSIGHTS

How one conceives of the *aims, objects,* and *methods* of these two important areas of human endeavor determines whether one embraces a model of their relationship as one of *conflict, independence, dialogue,* or *integration.* Key thinkers are increasingly moving away from conceptions of the aims, objects, and methods of religion and science that lead either to outright conflict or to utter independence. There is increasing interest in the intellectual arena in some form of dialogue or integration. This shift seems correctly rooted in a fundamental intuition that the different areas of human experience should fit together somehow, in meaningful dialogue or even in an all-encompassing vision of everything. We can rest assured that scholarly interest in this endeavor is so high that there will be no shortage of creative new proposals in the foreseeable future.

STUDY QUESTIONS

1. Try to characterize the four different views presented here regarding the relationship of religion and science. Explore the basis presented for each view.

2. The relation of religion and science is very complex. On one level, it is a philosophical issue; on another level, it is a political or institutional one. Explore what this statement might mean. Use the Galileo affair and the creation-evolution debate as starting points.

3. For centuries, theological inquiry has been conducted with an awareness of the contribution of Newton to our scientific understanding of the world. Do some reading about relativity theory in physics, and then engage in your own speculation about how it might affect the way theology is done in our time. Do the same for quantum mechanics.

4. Are there significant differences between the natural and the social sciences? Begin to think about this by trying to identify the *methods, aims,* and *objects* of the social sciences and distinguishing them from those of the natural sciences.

5. This chapter discusses the relationship between theology and natural science. How do you think a discussion of the relationship between theology and social science might proceed?

6. Explore the idea that science as we know it necessitates that we make certain assumptions about the structure of reality. What do you think of the suggestion that the assumptions found within the Judeo-Christian worldview are more conducive to science than those found in other major religious worldviews? Other nonreligious worldviews?

7. Select one school of thought that tends to see religion and science as completely independent or compartmentalized. Construct an argument for the merits of the position. Then construct an argument against the position.

8. Many forms of theism assert that God created a world order that operates acording to general physical laws. Explore the suggestion that some of those natural laws are contained in the theory of biological evolution. Explore.

9. What might be the differences between a model of the relationship between religion and science that posits inherent conflict between them and a dialogue or integration model that still might allow for potential conflicts?

NOTES

1. *Opere,* XIX, 323. Quoted in Jerome Langford, *Galileo, Science and the Church* (New York: Desclee Company, 1966), pp. 97–98.

2. Ibid., chap. 6.

3. Although there were evolutionary-type works in geology and some other sciences that predated Darwin's work, it is fair to say that the heated debate as we know it started with Darwin's work. Charles Darwin, *The Descent of Man and Selection in Relation to Sex* (New York: A. L. Burtt, 1874) and *The Origin of Species by Means of Natural Selection* (Chicago: Encyclopedia Britannica, 1955).

4. Albert Einstein, *On the Method of Theoretical Physics,* delivered as the Herbert Spencer Lecture at Oxford, June 10, 1933; and *Relativity, the Special and the General Theory: A Popular Exposition,* 15th ed., trans. R. W. Lawson (London: Methuen, 1954). See also Hans Reichenbach, *The Philosophy of Space and Time,* trans. M. Reichenbach and J. Freund (New York: Dover, 1957).

5. A seminal work in this area was A. M. Turing, "Computing Machinery and Intelligence," *Mind* 59 (1960), reprinted in Alan R. Anderson, ed., *Minds and Machines* (Englewood Cliffs, N.J.: Prentice-Hall, 1964), pp. 4–30. Among recent treatments of the issues, see D. Hofstadter and D. Dennet, *The Mind's I* (New York: Basic Books, 1981).

6. A seminal work in this area is J. D. Watson and F. H. C. Crick, "A Structure for Deoxyribose Nucleic Acid," *Nature* 171 (1953): 737.

7. Carl Sagan, *Cosmos* (New York: Random House, 1980), p. 4.

8. Ernan McMullin, "How Should Cosmology Relate to Theology?" in *The Sciences and Theology in the Twentieth Century,* ed. Arthur Peacocke (Notre Dame, Ind.: University of Notre Dame Press, 1981), p. 21.

9. *Origins: NC Documentary Service* 13 (1983): 50–51.

10. For an explanation of higher criticism, see William Neil, "The Criticism and Theological Use of the Bible, 1700–1950," pp. 238–93, and Alan Richardson, "The Rise of Modern Biblical Scholarship and Recent Discussion of the Authority of the Bible," pp. 294–338, both in *The Cambridge History of the Bible: The West from the Reformation to the Present Day,* ed. S. L. Greenslade (Cambridge: Cambridge University Press, 1963).

11. See Roland Frye, *Is God a Creationist? The Religious Case against Creation-Science* (New York: Scribners, 1983), for a set of articles discussing the ensuing controversy and making a case against creationism. Also see David B. Wilson, ed., *Did the Devil Make Darwin Do It? Modern Perspectives on the Creation-Evolution Controversy* (Ames: Iowa State University Press, 1983).

12. See, for example, Henry Morris, *The Twilight of Evolution* (Grand Rapids, Mich.: Baker Book House, 1963), and Morris, ed., *Scientific Creationism* (San Diego, Calif.: Creation Life Publishers, 1974). Also see the many publications produced by the Institute for Creation Research in San Diego, California.

13. Thomas Torrance has developed further some of the major points in the neo-orthodox perspective. See his *Theological Science* (Oxford: Oxford University Press, 1969), p. 281.

14. Barth provides a manageable introduction to his thought in *Dogmatics in Outline* (London: SCM Press, 1949).

15. Martin Buber, *I and Thou*, trans. R. G. Smith (Edinburgh: T. & T. Clark, 1937), p. 136.

16. A helpful summary is given in Frederick Ferré, *Language, Logic and God* (New York: Harper and Brothers, 1961).

17. E. L. Mascall, *Christian Theology and Natural Science* (New York: Ronald Press Co., 1956), p. 132. Also see M. B. Foster, "The Christian Doctrine of Creation and the Rise of Modern Natural Science," *Mind* 43 (1934): 446–68.

18. It would be of great theoretical interest to explore the assumptions for science that nonreligious traditions offer and then see how they compare with those offered by the Judeo-Christian worldview. Although the naturalist tradition did not, as a matter of historical fact, give birth to science, we still might ponder whether, as a matter of logic, it could have done so. We might also exercise our theoretical interests by exploring conceptions of nature in non-Christian religions that could have given rise to modern science as we know it.

19. Stephen Hawking, *A Brief History of Time* (New York: Bantam Books, 1988), chap. 8.

20. See Ernan McMullin, "How Should Cosmology Relate to Theology?" in *The Sciences and Theology in the Twentieth Century*, ed. Arthur Peacocke (Notre Dame, Ind.: University of Notre Dame Press, 1981), p. 52.

21. David Tracy, *Blessed Rage for Order* (New York: Seabury, 1975) and *Plurality and Ambiguity* (San Francisco: Harper and Row, 1987).

22. Norwood Russell Hanson, *Patterns of Discovery* (Cambridge: Cambridge University Press, 1958).

23. Stephen Toulmin, *Foresight and Understanding* (Bloomington: Indiana University Press, 1961).

24. Thomas Kuhn, *The Structure of Scientific Revolutions* (Chicago: University of Chicago Press, 1970).

25. Ibid., p. 175.

26. Nancey Murphy, "Revisionist Philosophy of Science and Theological Method" (Paper delivered at the Pacific Coast Theological Society, Spring 1983); see also *Theology in the Age of Probable Reasoning* (Ithaca, N.Y.: Cornell University Press, 1990).

27. Holmes Rolston III, *Science and Religion: A Critical Survey* (New York: Random House, 1987), pp. 12. [Also see the reprinted selection in *PRSR*, Part 10, pp. 467–77.]

28. Norwood Russell Hanson, "The Philosophical Implications of Quantum Mechanics," *Encyclopedia of Philosophy*, vol. 7, ed. Paul Edwards (New York: Macmillan, 1967), p. 44. Also see Hawking, *A Brief History of Time*.

29. For a popular rendition of relativity, see Lincoln Barnett, *The Universe and Dr. Einstein* (New York: New American Library, 1952); also see Paul Davies, *Other Worlds* (London: Abacus, 1982).

30. Some adherents of Eastern religions have gone so far as to say that this discovered inseparability is nothing less than a reflection of our participation of the individual in the Absolute. Subsequent discussion of such a suggestion would have to distinguish whether the relation between the knower and the known is essentially epistemological (having to do with the nature and scope of our experimental methods) or ontological (having to do with the nature of things). See Fritjof Capra, *The Tao of Physics* (New York: Bantam Books, 1977).

31. Ian Barbour, *Myths, Models, and Paradigms: A Comparative Study in Science and Religion* (New York: Harper and Row, 1974). pp. 41–51.

32. Ibid., p. 30.

33. Sallie McFague, *Metaphorical Theology: Models of God in Religious Language* (Philadelphia: Fortress Press, 1982).

34. David Hume threads this line of argument throughout his *Dialogues Concerning Natural Religion* (Indianapolis, Ind.: Hackett, 1980). [See Part X of the *Dialogues* reprinted in *PRSR*, Part 5, pp. 235–43.]

35. L. Stafford Betty and Bruce Cordell, "The Anthropic Teleological Argument, " *International Philosophical Quarterly* 27, no. 4 (1987): 409–35. [Reprinted in *PRSR*, Part 4, pp. 198–210.]

36. Arthur Peacocke, *Intimations of Reality* (Notre Dame, Ind.: University of Notre Dame Press, 1984), p. 63. See also his *Creation and the World of Science* (Oxford: Clarendon Press, 1979).

37. The classic source of process philosophy is, of course, Alfred North Whitehead, *Process and Reality* (Cambridge: Cambridge University Press, 1929).

SUGGESTED READING

Barbour, Ian G., ed. *Ethics in an Age of Technology: The Gifford Lectures.* Vol. 2. San Francisco: Harper and Row, 1993.

———. *Religion in an Age of Science: The Gifford Lectures,* Vol. 1 (San Francisco: Harper and Row, 1990).

———, ed. *Science and Religion: New Perspectives on the Dialogue.* New York: Harper and Row, 1968.

Brooke, John Hedley. *Science and Religion.* Cambridge: Cambridge University Press, 1991.

Davies, Paul. *God and the New Physics.* New York: Simon and Schuster, 1983.

Dillenberger, John. *Protestant Thought and Natural Science.* New York: Doubleday, 1960.

Hawking, Stephen. *A Brief History of Time.* New York: Bantam, 1988.

Mascall, E. L. *Christian Theology and Natural Science.* London: Oxford University Press, 1979.

Murphy, Nancey. *Theology in the Age of Scientific Reasoning.* Ithaca, N.Y.: Cornell University Press, 1990.

Nebelsick, Harold. *Theology and Science in Mutual Modification.* New York: Oxford University Press, 1981.

O'Connor, Daniel, and Francis Oakley, eds. *Creation: The Impact of an Idea.* New York: Scribner's, 1969.

Peacocke, Arthur. *Imitations of Reality: Critical Realism in Science and Religion.* Notre Dame, Ind.: University of Notre Dame Press, 1984.

———. *Theology for a Scientific Age.* Oxford: Blackwell, 1990.

Polkinghorne, John. *One World.* Princeton: Princeton University Press, 1987.

————. *Reason and Reality: The Relationship between Science and Theology.* Philadelphia: Trinity Press International, 1991.

————. *Serious Talk: Science and Religion in Dialogue.* Valley Forge, Pa.: Trinity Press International, 1995.

————. *The Way the World Is: The Christian Perspective of a Scientist.* London: Triangle Press, 1983.

Rae, Murray, et al. *Science and Theology.* Grand Rapids, Mich.: William B. Eerdmans, 1994.

Ratzsch, Del. *Philosophy of Science: The Natural Sciences in Humans Perspective.* Downers Grove, Ill.: Intervarsity Press, 1986.

Rolston, Holmes, III. *Science and Religion: A Critical Examination.* Philadelphia: Temple University Press, 1986.

Schlesinger, George. *Religion and Scientific Method.* Dordrecht: D. Reidel, 1977.

CHAPTER 12   RELIGIOUS DIVERSITY: HOW CAN WE UNDERSTAND DIFFERENCES AMONG RELIGIONS?

A Zen Buddhist gives the following description of his religious experience and beliefs:

> Reached a white heat today. . . . Monitors whacked me time and again . . . their energetic stick wielding is no long an annoyance but a spur. . . .
>
> At next dokusan [the roshi or Zen master] again asked for Mu.[1] Quickly raised my hand as though to smack him. Didn't intend to really hit him, but the roshi, taking no chances, ducked. . . . How exhilarating these unpremeditated movements—clean and free. . . .
>
> . . . Didn't intend to tell Roshi of my insight, but as soon as I came before him he demanded: "What happened last night?" . . . [H]e began quizzing me: "Where do you see Mu? . . . How old is Mu? . . .
>
> Threw myself into Mu for another nine hours with such utter absorption that *I* completely vanished. . . . *I* didn't eat breakfast, *Mu* did. *I* didn't sweep and wash the floors after breakfast, *Mu* did. *I* didn't eat lunch, *Mu* ate. . . .
>
> Hawklike, the roshi scrutinized me as I entered his room, walked toward him, prostrated myself, and sat before him with my mind alert and exhilarated. . . .
>
> "The universe is One," he began, each word tearing into my mind like a bullet. "The moon of Truth—" All at once the roshi, the room, every single thing disappeared in a dazzling stream of illumination and I felt myself bathed in a delicious, unspeakable delight. . . . For a fleeting eternity I was alone—I alone was. . . .
>
> "I have it! I know! There is nothing, absolutely nothing. I am everything and everything is nothing!" I exclaimed more to myself than to the roshi, and got up and walked out. . . .[2]

The religious beliefs and practices expressed by this Zen Buddhist seem worlds apart from those associated with Western religions. Yet he takes these beliefs as true and this way of religious life as fulfilling. But if his beliefs differ in significant ways from others' religious beliefs, can all these beliefs be true? If so, what are the implications of this for understanding what Reality is like? If not, how do we decide which are true and which not? In short, how are we to understand and interpret diverse religious claims?

RELIGIOUS DIVERSITY

In our complex world, we cannot affirm conscientiously one particular religious perspective and merely ignore the others. Modern communications, tourism, educational exchange, immigration, and international business have produced a cultural integration that people hail as one hallmark of the second half of the twentieth century. Diversity and plurality are bywords of the new society. Yet contact among believers in diverse religions is not a new phenomenon. None of the major religions ever existed in complete isolation from other religions; their origins and development intertwine. Judaism developed its unique particularism amid numerous Semitic religions; Christianity grew out of Judaism; Islam developed later in contact with both. Hinduism was an amalgam of the thoughts and practices of Aryan invaders and of adherents of the Dravidic religion indigenous to India. Buddhism arose in reaction to Hindu ascetic culture and developed in China through interaction with both Confucianism and Taoism. And what is true of the major religions applies even more to the sects or religions that grew out of them: Bahai out of Islam; Mormonism, Christian Science, and Unitarianism from Christianity; Unificationism out of Korean Protestantism, Neo-Confucianism, and Buddhism; Sikhism out of Hinduism and Islam.

From a purely historical point of view, then, one should not think of religion in isolationist terms. Some have even argued that one could construct not only an integrated history of the individual religions but perhaps also a generic history of religious faith and practice.[3] Such an account would look very different from that found in standard religion texts, which devote distinct chapters to individual religions, their history, personages, beliefs, and practices. It would be a history that elicits how the actual beliefs, and practices of one religion influenced those of other faiths. It might contain, for example, a tale about a wealthy prince who renounces his worldly power and goes off to live in ascetic poverty, a story that originates in Hinduism or Jainism, is passed down through Buddhism, Manicheism, and Islam, and finally is Christianized to play a role in the Christian religious experience of Tolstoy. Or it might trace a religious practice like the use of prayer beads from Buddhism through Islam to Catholicism.[4]

Neither can we ignore the similarities among the practices, rituals, and beliefs of the various religions. Many religious ceremonies use candles and incense and include offerings of various sorts to the gods; Hindus and Christians eat a divine meal; Muslims, Hindus, and Sikhs remove footwear before entering places of worship. As for beliefs, Judaism, Christianity, and Islam are monotheistic; heavenly beings play roles in most religions; avatars (physical incarnations of deity) play an important role in Christianity and Hinduism; the Golden Rule is prominent in Confucianism and Christianity.

But there are notable differences as well. Theravada Buddhism is nontheistic; Vedantic Hindus believe that Ultimate Reality (termed Brahman or *nondual Absolute*) lacks any distinctions. Orthodox Christianity is trinitarian and Hinduism polytheistic, whereas Islam and Judaism are strictly monotheistic. We could go on, but a detailed study of comparative religions is beyond the scope of our book. Our point is simply that the various religions make both similar and different truth-claims, and this raises the fundamental question of this chapter: How should an advocate of one religion approach the truth-claims of another religion?

Our question is often misunderstood. We are asking not how an advocate of one religion should approach an advocate of another religion but how one should approach *what* another person advocates. On the one hand, to ask how we should approach the truth-claims found in other religions is an epistemological question about what beliefs it is rational to hold and an ontological question about what really exists. Answers to these questions require that we consider the truth-claims of the various religions. The questioner seeks to understand sympathetically other persons' religious claims, to interpret what they mean and what significance they have for believers' lives, and to evaluate critically their alleged truth. On the other hand, to ask how we should approach other persons is a moral question. Advocates of other religions should be treated, at the very least, as the ethics of our religion demand persons should be treated. Often words like tolerance, openness to understanding, caring and compassion dominate such discussions.

It is often forgotten that evaluating persons' truth-claims and relating to persons morally are separate issues. Thus, some suggest that unless we adopt the relativist claim that whatever persons think is correct is correct for them and renounce any belief that there are religious truths that can be evaluated intersubjectively and interculturally, we are being intolerant of persons from different religions. They then trot out the blemishes of religion—jihads, crusades, inquisitions, and pogroms—to demonstrate what happens when we attempt to evaluate critically other religions and their claims.

We should not ignore the wrongs that believers have done in the name of their religions; they were and are deplorable—whether committed in Amritsar, Beirut, Belfast, Jerusalem, Kashmir, or Sarajevo. But we should not make the faulty inference that statements regarding how we should treat those with whom we disagree follow directly from epistemological claims about the truths or falsehoods they hold. Nor should it imply anything about the legitimacy of disagreement. Tolerance of and openness to others does not mean that we must agree with what they believe or think.

Otherwise, the rational discussion in our book about disagreements would be morally intolerable.

EXCLUSIVISM

John Hick (1922–) has classified three approaches to the diversity of religions.[5] For the first—*exclusivism*—salvation, liberation, human fulfillment, or whatever else one considers the ultimate goal of the religion to be, is found solely in or through one particular religion. There are truths in other religions, but one religion is exclusively effective in that it alone provides the way of salvation or liberation. Adherents of other religions, although sincere in their piety and upright in their moral conduct, cannot attain salvation through their religions. To be saved, they must be told about and acknowledge the unique way. The salvific actions of this unique way are both ontologically necessary (the objective conditions for salvation must really be in place) and epistemically necessary (those seeking salvation must know about them) for salvation. Beliefs of this sort help explain religious evangelistic fervor and missionary zeal. Exclusivists argue philosophically for their view. Religions, they claim, make incompatible truth claims. But incompatible truth-claims cannot both be true. Hence, where they contradict, at least one claim must be false. Noting this fact, however, does not help one determine which claim is false; that is the function of further reflection.

Many exclusivists hold that salvation can be accomplished only by a divine act of grace. Since attempts to save ourselves are doomed to failure, it is critical that we discover the locus of the divine salvific initiative. Once we discover where God has truly revealed his unique purposes, it would be folly to go elsewhere for salvation.

For example, the Protestant theologian Karl Barth (1886–1968) contrasts religion with revelation. Religion stands opposed to faith as the defiant, arrogant, human endeavor pitted against the revelation of God. Religion is our impossible and sinful attempt to understand God from our viewpoint and overcome by our own efforts our estrangement from him. Religion is impossible because reconciliation can be accomplished only by God; it is sinful because it replaces God with something we have made and hence is idolatry.

> We cannot, therefore, interpret the attempt as a harmonious co-operating of man with the revelation of God, as though religion were a kind of outstretched hand which is filled by God in His revelation. . . . In religion man bolts and bars himself against revelation by providing a substitute, by taking away in advance the very thing which has to be given by God.[6]

Salvation comes only through the true revelation of God, in which he shows and gives himself to us. "There is only one revelation. That revelation is the revelation of the covenant, of the original and basic will of God.

. . . Apart from and without Jesus Christ we can say nothing at all about God and man and their relationship one with another."[7]

Barth does not deny that other religions contain truths, high moral ideals, and aesthetic values or that their adherents are moral or sincere. Indeed, Barth denies that Christianity is the true religion in the sense that it is the climax or fulfillment of all human religion. Christianity is not a superior religion. However, because of the uniqueness of Jesus Christ, Christianity is the *locus* of true religion. In the event of Jesus Christ, God uniquely provides and reveals the means by which we can be reconciled with God. Revelation not only destroys religion; it creates true religion. Thus, even Christians must realize the inadequacy of their own religion when viewed outside of grace and revelation.

Exclusivism is not a distinctly Christian phenomenon; most religions at heart are exclusivistic. For example, Muslims hold that, though there have been other prophets, their revelations were incomplete and mixed with untruths. Because Mohammed is the true and final prophet of God, whose "teachings are absolutely perfect, . . . the only source for anyone to know about God and His system of life is Muhammad (peace be on him)."[8] Through him the divine uniquely has spoken. Only in the Koran are the words of God unmixed with human words, only here are God's words not addressed to a particular people but to all humankind, and only the Koran contains all that is needed for right living. "It is because of these special features of the Koran that all people of the world have been directed to believe in it. They have been told to give up all other books and follow it alone."[9] Christians are heretics who believe only partial truths, and polytheists are infidels.

CRITIQUE OF EXCLUSIVISM

Many find it difficult to believe that persons in other religions are doomed because they have not heard the gospel of a given religion and sought salvation in the prescribed manner. Men and women who live morally upright or profoundly righteous lives devoted to God and to others abound in all religions. They are living evidence that their religions can deliver on their promise to transform humans. Can they be thought to have failed on the ground that they do not acknowledge a particular religious mediator, follow someone's teachings, or conceive of God or Reality in a particular manner? It is unjust for God to condemn a person who has never heard or is unable to understand what is necessary for salvation.

But not all exclusivists are committed to these tenets regarding God's condemnation of people who in this life have never had an encounter with the true religion. Some exclusivists hold that a loving and just God will provide opportunities for persons to hear and understand the message of salvation after their death. Only after this opportunity will God impose any judgment on those who continue to disbelieve the truth. Ultimately, all will have an equal opportunity for salvation,[10] and the number of people saved or liberated will depend not on the availability of the message but on people's knowledgeable acceptance.[11]

Others object to exclusivism on the grounds that if God truly desired that all persons come to know, love, and worship him, he would not narrowly bind his revelation solely to a particular time, way, person, community, or culture. Just as advertisers can tailor their message to different audiences, so an infinite God could speak in diverse ways to different cultures. But, to communicate effectively, he would have to adapt his message to the motifs and thought patterns of that culture. Hence, if there were many revelations, they would have different characteristics and contents because they were expressed in diverse cultural dresses. Thus, religion need not pit human creative reason against divine revelation but might embody diverse perceptions of the divine revelation or salvific truth. Barth presupposes that there is only one revelation; hence, he can contrast all religion with that revelation. But this presupposition might be questioned, given both an infinite God capable of communicating in different forms and different people who claim either to have received divine revelations or to be that revelation.

Finally, given that there are many exclusivist claims—not simply Christian or Muslim—to which faith ought we adhere? We cannot decide on the basis of the moral lives prescribed or lived, for the virtues and acts encouraged often do not greatly differ among the respective religions, and adherents of all faiths seem capable of living morally praiseworthy lives. One might suggest that we evaluate the truth-claims made by the respective religions; we return to this issue later in this chapter.

PLURALISM

In light of these concerns, some simply abandon exclusivist claims and acknowledge that, although different religions manifest different responses to the divine Reality, each can successfully facilitate salvation, liberation, or self-fulfillment. As Hinduism affirms, there are many coequal routes to liberation or salvation. "In whatever way men approach Me, I am gracious to them; men everywhere . . . follow My path." [12] There could be some internal checks and balances on religious claims, but these are met when the religious tradition has, through the centuries, produced profound scriptures, impressive intellectual systems, new visions of human existence, and saintly lives. This second position, adopted by Hick himself, he terms *pluralism*.

Several questions arise. First, Hick admits that some religions have fundamentally differing and incompatible views of the Real. For some, the Real is nondual, apersonal, beyond everything and nothing, transcending the illusory world in which we live and think. For others, the Real is personal, the creator God who is involved immanently in human affairs. Since these conceptions of the Real seem to be irreconcilable, it seems impossible that all these diverse religious conceptions of God could be true. How, then, does the pluralist deal with the exclusivist argument regarding incompatible truth claims?

To answer this, Hick invokes a distinction that he adopts from Immanuel Kant. He distinguishes between the Real as it is in itself (the Noumena) and the Real as it is humanly and culturally perceived and experienced (the phenomena). When religious persons try to speak about the noumenal Ultimate, all they can describe is how it appears to them. Their characterization depends upon the interpretative concepts they use to understand and structure their world and give meaning to their existence. Thus, those who hold that the Real is nondual and indescribable employ one set of interpretative concepts, metaphors, and images; those who see the Real as personal use another set. This is the reason the Real can be described in diverse ways.

Hick employs the familiar story of the blind men and the elephant:

> An elephant was brought to a group of blind men who had never encountered such an animal before. One felt a leg and reported that an elephant is a great living pillar. Another felt the trunk and reported that an elephant is a great snake. Another felt a tusk and reported that an elephant is like a sharp plough-share. And so on. . . . Of course they were all true, but each referring only to one aspect of the total reality and all expressed in very imperfect analogies.[13]

We cannot tell which perspective is correct, because there is no ultimate perspective from which we can view the blind men as they feel the elephant. In seeking the Real, we are all blind, trapped by our individual and cultural concepts.

It is not that one set of concepts or structures is true and another false. According to Hick, statements about the Ultimate are metaphors that are validated in terms of their efficacy in bringing about salvation or personal transformation; they are preserved in religious traditions because they are continually meaningful to many persons. Hick believes that those who hold that religious concepts are projections of human characteristics on the divine are partially correct. The presence of anthropomorphic projections should not be used to debunk religion, for they register our conscious attempts to relate our conceptual framework to the Ultimate and to respond to the activity of the Ultimate in our lives. But they are not wholly correct; religious concepts arise out of religious experience and thus express the ways in which we conceive of, experience, and respond to the Real. We are warned about projecting from our limits a definitive, descriptive characterization of the Real.

Second, what can pluralists say to exclusivists? For example, how can they reply to Barth, who claims that Jesus Christ is the unique revelation of God and the unique means through which salvation is attained? If God was incarnate in Jesus, so that only through him could the Father be known, it would seem that here God has revealed the one way he provides for salvation. Hick's response is to deny the orthodox view of incarnation, that Jesus really was divine.[14] He maintains that God's spirit can work in all persons, transforming them so that they fully manifest God. The incarnation is a myth describing God's activity in human lives. For Hick, a myth is a statement that, although "not literally true, nevertheless tends to evoke an appropriate dispositional attitude to" what the myth is about.[15] In the myth of the incarnation, Christians see that in Jesus they have someone who more fully realized the openness to being transformed to a Reality-centered life. But this can be true of other great religious founders and saints as well.

The center of religion, for Hick, is not theological doctrine but personal transformation.[16] Hence, he cautions that religious doctrines, such as the incarnation, should not be unduly emphasized. Neither should they be considered true or false in the way in which we consider scientific beliefs to be true or false. Religious dogmas and historical claims are attempts to answer personal questions about human existence and experience of the divine. Consequently, they are true insofar as they succeed in changing our attitudes and life-patterns. Hence, although doctrines of the various religions might seem to contradict, when properly viewed as life-expressing truths they often do not. They simply express the diverse ways people from different cultures react to the Reality they encounter. In this way Hick counters the exclusivists' premise that incompatible truth claims cannot both be true.

In other words, Hick is less concerned with theological truths (understood as propositions) than with the existential or life-changing aspects of religion, less concerned with dogma than with religious experience. Religion is significant because it transforms human existence from self-centeredness to Reality-centeredness. Exactly what one believes is not all that important; it is a mythic projection of one's own experiences, culture, and conceptual categories on the Real. For Hick, therefore, exclusivists' attempts to convert or sweep all people into one religion's kingdom fail to capture the essence of religion. What matters is that the Real so affects us that we are transformed.

CRITIQUE OF PLURALISM

Pluralism is attractive; it accords well with our attempt to accept other persons without being judgmental. Yet this appeal sometimes can involve the confusion between epistemological and ethical considerations noted earlier in this chapter. As we argued there, it is a mistake to affirm that being judgmental about truth-claims or beliefs necessitates maltreating persons who hold differing beliefs and that being tolerant implies not rationally assessing but merely accepting the diverse truth-claims. Hence, we need to consider more carefully the strengths and weaknesses of the pluralist position.

What, then, is at issue in this debate? The answer is, in part, the nature of religion. For many pluralists, the significant aspect of religion is its power to transform the individual, to move someone from concern with self to being Reality-centered. This being the case, religious beliefs and practices are important as means to personal and social transformation but are not intrinsically or ultimately significant. Thus, two people can disagree about a certain belief or practice, and it makes no ultimate difference. Hick writes, "I hold that someone who differs from me about, for example, whether Jesus had a human father is probably (though not certainly) mistaken; but in holding this I am also conscious that he/she might nevertheless be closer to the divine Reality than I. This awareness is important because it has the effect of de-emphasizing such differences of historical judgment. They can never be more than penultimately important."[17]

But is this a fully adequate view of religion? Do not religions make truth-claims about the Real? Pluralists differ among themselves on this question. For some, truth is not to be understood propositionally, as if proposition are true or false apart from the time, perspective, and individual who believes them.[18] Rather, truth must be seen humanly, in terms of what propositions and beliefs mean to individual persons, and this is both a historical and an existential matter. Truth is how reality appears to us at a particular time and place, in a particular historical perspective. Religious orientations "can be seen as less or more true in the sense of enabling those who looked at life and the universe through their patterns to perceive smaller or larger, less important or more important, areas of reality, to formulate and to ponder less or more significant issues, to act less or more truly, less or more truly to be."[19] The problem with this claim about truth is that this very general claim cannot be called true, for it is subject to the same restrictions that this view imposes on other truth-claims, namely, that truth is not propositional and is relative to a particular time and place. One could, of course, restrict this view of truth to religious truth-claims, but such a move would be arbitrary and question begging.

Other pluralists hold that religious adherents make truth-claims, but only about the Real understood phenomenally (that is, as the Real appears to them). Consequently, there can be no contradiction between religious claims. For example, the claims that something appears to me to be blue and to you not to be blue are not contradictory. They would be contradictory only if we both claimed that the object itself was the color each of us perceived it to be. Similarly, religious adherents speak about what they have encountered from their cultural-religious perspective, not from some external, objective, all-encompassing point of view. Hence, their claims cannot be said to be really contradictory.

Further, the language and concepts we use to approach the Real are not subject to the type of scientific verification that characterizes our ordinary experience. They are "linguistic pictures or maps of the universe, whose function is to enable us to find salvation/liberation. . . . They accordingly test themselves by their success or failure in fulfilling this soteriological function."[20] What Reality really is like can be verified only eschatologically, if at all.[21]

Hick does argue that we can engage in rational scrutiny of religious systems. The criterion to be used to distinguish authentic from inauthentic manifestations of the Real is "soteriological alignment." By this he means that an authentic religion fosters transformation of human existence from self-centeredness to Reality-centeredness, demonstrated by the saintly lives of the religion's followers and by its role in spiritual and politico-economic liberation.[22]

Some will find this standard too broad. Under this criterion Hick allows not only traditional religions but the great secular movements as well to count as authentic manifestations of the Real. For example, he notes that the book on post-Maoist reform in China and on Communism is still open, for these have been at least partially successful in transforming society.[23] His position might also be viewed as too narrow, for while the great religions produce saints, their success has been limited. Even the world religions have produced their share of individuals who have shown their dark side in the name of the very religion they espouse. Criteria in addition to the saintly lives of adherents must be used to distinguish authentic from inauthentic manifestations of the Real.

One also might object that the pluralist contention—that truth-claims are both historically and culturally subjective and only about the phenomena—leads inevitably to skepticism about the Real. Unless we can speak about the Ultimate, not only cannot we know anything about the real elephant (using Hick's analogy); we cannot even assert that there is an elephant. Hick responds that, although we cannot prove that the Real must exist, we must trust the basic veridicality of our religious experience and thought. And to preserve this against the claim that religious experience results merely from human projections, we must *postulate* that there is a noumenal Real.

Yet why conclude that religious experience is not a human projection, if there is no way that one can understand or say anything true about the Real in itself? Unless we can speak about Reality, what have we postulated? For any of the blind men to have postulated that what he really felt was an elephant, he must have known what an elephant was. Even Hick cannot completely resist saying something about the Real. For him it is "rich in content," the "One without a second," for there cannot be a plurality of ultimates. Further, the Real "produces . . . the phenomenal world of ours"; it is the "ground or source" of the phenomenal divine attributes, of religious experience, and of love and justice, consciousness and bliss; it has a presence and an impact on the phenomena. These suggest, at minimum, that causal predicates apply to the Real. And insofar as the Real fosters or hinders salvific transformation,[24] it must have some kind of telic consciousness and concern for human beings.

Indeed, unless pluralists can ascribe goodness, love, and justice to the Real, there is no ground for their objection, noted earlier, to exclusivism, namely, that a God with these properties would not limit his revelation and salvific work to a particular culture or religion. The criticism of exclusivism's consistency presupposes knowledge of the appropriate predicates of the Real.

In short, it is well and good for pluralists to say that there is a Reality that meets us, but what is Reality? The very willingness of some pluralists to admit atheistic Marxism and naturalistic humanism into the camp of religions alongside and on equal footing with theism[25] suggests the seriousness of the problem. Jews, Muslims, and Christians maintain there really is a God, the encounter with whom brings meaning to our lives; the naturalist holds that we can find meaningful existence apart from affirming or encountering the divine; Satanists deify evil and power. But the rational claims of these belief systems are very different. In the first, meaning comes from an encounter with a good, personal God; in the second, meaning is self-created; in the third, it is evil that gives power and meaning.

Pluralists such as Hick are faced with a dilemma. If we have no clear concept of God, if we are left with nothing to be said about God or the Real as it is in itself, our religious belief becomes indistinguishable from agnosticism. If we can speak about God, then we can employ some consistent set of predicates to describe the properties God has. Hence, we have a content about which we can make claims, and we are not in the position of being completely blind. We can, in principle, evaluate which of the blind men's claims, if any, are correct.[26]

In short, it seems that a pluralist view such as Hick's is accepted, not only at the extremely high price of skepticism, but in disregard of what believers think they are doing. In making fundamental dogmas into myths, "it rules out people's most precious beliefs in things normative. It asks Muslims, in effect, to deny that the Koran is central to God's purposes. It asks Jews to deny that God spoke definitively through Moses. It asks Christians to deny that Jesus is the Incarnation of God in history."[27] It also prevents believers from addressing certain problems facing their faith. For example, Hick's own soul-building theodicy, which we discussed in Chapter 6 as an approach to the problem of pain and suffering, he now treats as a true myth that cannot apply to the transcendent Real and hence cannot be used to justify its goodness, power, or justice.[28]

At the same time, we cannot ignore the insight of pluralism, namely, that, in some way, not only can God be encountered through other religions, but these religions can be a positive force in helping persons discover and worship the true God and lead upright lives. How, then, can we bring together concerns about truth with those about meaning and salvation?

INCLUSIVISM

If we acknowledge that there are many different religious and life-transforming experiences and that God might reveal himself or graciously act in various ways in diverse places, while at the same time we affirm that religious claims about Reality are either true or false, we might adopt what Hick terms religious *inclusivism*. On the one hand, in common with exclusivism, inclusivists hold that there is one absolute provision for salvation that only one religion truly makes known. The way of salvation is open to people only because they meet special criteria revealed in one true religion or are accounted righteous on account of a specific salvific act. On the other hand, in common with pluralists, inclusivists hold that God can be encountered and his grace manifested in various ways through diverse religions. Everyone can experience salvation, regardless of whether he or she has heard and acknowledged the basic tenets of the one true religion. Inclusivism thus extends beyond exclusivism because, though it makes exclusivistic claims for the absolute truth of one religion and what it accomplishes, it allows that adherents of other religions can be saved because of things specified by the true religion. Put in philosophical language, a particular salvific event might be ontologically necessary for salvation (salvation cannot occur without it) but not epistemologically necessary (one need not know about it to be saved or liberated).

The Catholic theologian Karl Rahner (1904–1984) argues that persons can be saved only because a particular salvific event has occurred. Christianity is an absolute religion and cannot recognize any other religion as providing *the* way of salvation. It not only tells us of God's unique Word, incarnate in Jesus who died on the cross for all persons, but provides the social context in which Jesus Christ comes to persons. However, it is also true that God is love and that he desires that all persons be saved. To accomplish this salvation, God can apply the results of Jesus' atoning death and resurrection to all human beings, even to those who have never heard of Jesus and his death or have never acknowledged his lordship. In this way God makes it possible for all persons, even those who are not within the context of historical Christianity, to be transformed and reconciled to God.

One might think of an analogous scenario. In a particular town, a large number of poor people owe debts they cannot pay from their meager resources. But unless they pay, their creditors will foreclose on all their property. A rich woman in another town, learning of their plight, deposits a large amount of money in their town bank, with the stipulation that it be used to satisfy the debts of the poor. Since the poor of the town cannot remove their debts without using these resources, the benefactor's funds are objectively necessary for relieving their plight. However, knowledge of her or of the way she provided for their financial relief is not necessary to their liberation. Even though they do not personally know their benefactor, these resources can be used to pay off their debts and transform their lives.

Rahner notes that though Christianity began historically with Jesus of Nazareth, it had a prehistory. In pre-Christian times there were many Israelites and followers of other religions whom the New Testament claims were justified or saved subjectively by their faith and objectively by the still future obedience of Christ. Some, like Melchizedek, were even priests of non-Israelite religions. The appearance of Jesus is the point at which Christianity faced the Jewish people, requiring those who heard the gospel to take a position on it. That is, when Christianity became a historical factor in first-century Palestine, it became realistic to claim that salvation depended upon some response to the proclaimed gospel. But Christianity is not a real historical factor for many other cultures, where people have never heard a proclamation of the Christian gospel. Hence, since people in these cultures remain in a position comparable to those of the pre-Christian era, we can apply what is said about the pre-Christian Jewish and non-Jewish righteous to them. Since God desires that all persons be saved, it is reasonable to think that God applies the same grace he applied to those of the pre-Christian era to those who have never heard about Jesus. The Spirit of God is at work in the lives of people who worship in other religions, even though they do not recognize God's activity in Christian terms. Rahner terms these persons *anonymous Christians* because, although they lack an explicit Christian faith, they consciously or unconsciously seek and worship God.[29]

Yet if Christianity is the true religion, whereas others contain various admixtures of falsity, should non-Christians then practice their own religion? Rahner holds that religious faith is not solely an internal matter; a social form is necessary for salvation. This form is always culturally embodied in the religion (including the practices and beliefs) that a person embraces. Since different religions embody different degrees of truth, they have different degrees of lawfulness, that is, ability to facilitate a right relationship with God. But just as the theological impurity of pre-Christian Judaism did not prevent its adherents from encountering God in and through their religion, so the theological impurity of contemporary religions does not prevent their adherents from finding God. Indeed, these religions can be the mediators of supernatural grace. It is not an all-or-nothing matter; supernatural grace can be manifested in various degrees in all religions. It is only that the New Testament delineates the definitive difference between right and wrong and the unique, salvific revelation of God in Jesus Christ, and it is only through a relationship with God in Jesus Christ that the fullness of God can be known and experienced.

This analysis might apply just as well to inclusivist advocates in other religions. Just as the Christian might speak of Christianity as the only true religion and of persons whose lives manifest the grace of God as anonymous Christians, so the Muslim might speak of the absolute truth of Islam and of Christians or Jews as anonymous Muslims. The Jew might see others as anonymous Jews, while the Buddhist might see others as anonymous Buddhists. Each could hold that though one particular religion is the absolute or true religion, there are significant truths in other religions as well; other religions perceive dimly, partly, and perspectivally the truths that are found in clearer form in the one true religion. Since not all religious doctrines or practices in all religions are true, cross-religious criticism is in order. This, then, can provide an authentic basis for interreligious dialogue, for the differences are appreciated and worthy of rational discussion and debate.

CRITIQUE OF INCLUSIVISM

If persons can achieve salvation without knowing anything at all about a particular religious tradition, why then should one try to convert them? Why not simply encourage them to continue to live according to what they know and believe so that they can lead transformed lives in that light? Rahner holds that bringing members of other religions to the knowledge of what their faith is truly about and of the basis for that faith is a stage of the development of those persons' Christianity. "The reflex self-realization of a previously anonymous Christianity is demanded (1) by the incarnational and social structure of grace and of Christianity, and (2) because the individual who grasps Christianity in a clearer, purer and more effective way, has, other things being equal, a still greater chance of salvation than someone who is merely an anonymous Christian."[30] Other inclusivists might reply that it does matter that persons know the true basis of their salvation because, since liberation comes through knowledge, truth matters. Hence, we have an obligation to enlighten others about the objective basis of their transformation. In any case, the exclusivist content of inclusivism provides a basis for justifying proselytizing.

Others have questioned the confidence that Rahner has in the lawfulness of other religions. The Christian theologian Clark Pinnock (1937–), for example, sees that religion at times is "dark, deceptive, and cruel. It harbors ugliness, pride, error, hypocrisy," and other characteristics that do not lead to salvation. He notes the dark side found in Aztec sacrifices, Haitian voodoo, and the Hindu deities Kali and Shiva, as well as the caste system of India that "sanctions pious neglect of the poor."[31] Yet, though religions as social phenomena might be idolatrous, God is at work in lives of individuals outside the Christian faith. He suggests two criteria for discovering where God is present in persons: their fear of God and their pursuit of righteousness in their behavior.

More seriously, given that many religions hold themselves to be the absolute religion, how can one decide which makes the correct claim? Some feel it is simply a matter of determining the locus of unique divine revelation. Rahner and Barth are certain that God has come in Jesus Christ; Muslims hold that Mohammed gave us Allah's mature revelation. But this simply pushes the problem back. How do we adjudicate claims to divine revelation? Some have suggested that we can do this by evaluating the life of the claim maker. But are we able to know enough about the individual religious founders to make comparisons that could establish the spiritual or moral superiority of one over another? Is the moral life of Jesus superior to that of the Buddha? Others have appealed to the character of the tradition that grew out of the work of the founder; yet this is risky, for the history of each religion is strewn with events that both credit and discredit the teachings of the religion.

A different way of assessing religions appeals to criteria by which we can evaluate the religious systems themselves. To this approach let us now turn.

CRITERIA FOR ASSESSING RELIGIONS

One conclusion we might draw from the discussion to this point is that we must take seriously the contention that religions make specific truth-claims about reality. Some say there is a god, others not. Some assert there are many gods, others that there is one God. Some declare that God becomes incarnate, others not. Some claim that Jesus is the God incarnate, others that it is Krishna. Some claim that Christ is actually present in the bread and wine of Holy Communion, others that the elements are symbolic only. Some accept Ali, Mohammed's son-in-law, as the first Imam and rightful successor of the Prophet; others do not. Some believe we should pray facing Mecca; others face the Wailing Wall. We could go on presenting contrasts. The point, however, is that there is good reason to think that religious believers are making truth-claims about Reality or (in some traditions) God's acts in history and that these must be given their due place.

If they are making truth claims about reality, it follows that specific beliefs are subject to rational evaluation. We can use the canons of logic, human experience, and perhaps trained intuition to establish probabilistically that some beliefs are true and others false. In fact, much of what has already transpired in this book is directed toward evaluating religious claims. Other claims cannot be tested (e.g., Christ is present in the bread and wine of Holy Communion) except in terms of whether they make sense and the degree to which they are consistent with or implied by other relevant religious claims. In any case, there are legitimate grounds for rationally evaluating many individual religious beliefs.

But probably we want to go beyond this. We want not only to claim that individual beliefs are true or false but to be able to make comparative evaluations of religions themselves. In deciding whether to be a Muslim, Hindu, Sikh, Jew, Christian, or whatever, we want to know whether a particular religious system is true or more true than any other. This is more difficult, for religious systems contain many propositions, some of which are true and others false. Thus, one has to weigh not only individual statements but whole systems of statements, according to some criteria.

What criteria might be used to evaluate religious systems? Keith Yandell (1938–) suggests the following:

1. The propositions essential to that religion must be consistent with each other.

2. Knowing that the religious system is true must be compatible with its being true. If the truth of the system demands that we cannot know it is true—for example, if, like Madhyamika Buddhism, it claims that all views are false—that is reason to suspect its truth.

3. The truth of a religious system must be compatible with what must exist for it to be true. For example, the claim that Ultimate Reality has no distinctions is incompatible with the claim that religious statements that affirm this are true and not false.

4. If the only reason for offering the religious system is that it promises to provide a solution to a problem, and it fails to do so, there is no reason to accept the system. For example, if a religious system were introduced to resolve the problem of pain and suffering, but it clearly did not accomplish this, there would be no reason to advocate that religious system.

5. Essential truths of the system should not contradict well-established data, for example, in the sciences or psychology.

6. Ad hoc hypotheses designed to counter evidence contrary to the religious system count against that religious system.

7. A system should be able to account for and explain broad reaches of human experience.[32]

To Yandell's criteria one might add

8. It should satisfy some basic moral and aesthetic intuitions and provoke and inspire persons to live more morally responsive and responsible lives.

Reflection on this list suggests that further thought is necessary about evaluative criteria. Are these good criteria? Are there others? Can these criteria be applied to systems as diverse as religions?

This brings up one final issue: What is it that we evaluate when we evaluate a religious system? Although we have spoken of religions as systems that make propositional truth-claims, at the same time it is wrong to view religious systems as consisting of impersonal, objective statements of religious beliefs that are accepted by all advocates of that religion. Religious systems are complex bodies of belief that have grown and developed historically. What a Christian or Hindu believes today differs (for some, remarkably) from what first-century Christians or eighth-century Hindus held. This is not to say that these persons today are not Christians or Hindus, but they are Christians or Hindus not only because they embrace certain beliefs but because they participate in a historical tradition that is Christian or Hindu. The tradition is not pristine; we cannot get back to the original founders and believe exactly what they believed and practice as they did. The tradition is cumulative and dynamic, social and personal. Hence, there is an important subjective dimension to any description of that religion.

Religions are embodied historically in cultures, making it difficult to isolate distinctively religious beliefs from cultural ones (for example, is monogamy a Christian religious or a Western cultural prescription? Is Hinduism isolable from the caste system?). Religions are embodied in individual believers, and there are no two believers who hold exactly the same beliefs. Thus, in assessing religions we must not speak about the totality of the assertions made by an advocate of a religion but about what might essentially describe that religion. Yet even here difficulties emerge, for what must a person believe to be a Christian, Muslim, or Hindu? The diversity within each of these traditions bears witness to the difficulty of discerning a particular credal essence.

The claim that each religion is a strand in the religious history of the world is an intriguing notion. Yet even if there are generic religious concepts such as faith and God, not every claim about these concepts is true. Suppose there is a universal religion in which humans have participated throughout history in the same way as one can affirm that there is a universal science in which persons have participated. In science, not every avowed scientific belief is true, nor every practice sanctioned; alchemy, for instance, was wrongheaded. Yet each scientist grapples with reality, seeking to understand how it operates and to discern what causal explanations best suffice. Similarly, in many religions humans grapple religiously with the God who comes to them, attempting to understand that Reality and to apply it meaningfully to their own existence. Some of their beliefs are false, some of their practices wrongheaded. If there is a Reality, a God who operates in the world, encountering humans, it becomes as much an intellectual task to understand that Reality as an existential task to appropriate it in our own lives.

STUDY QUESTIONS

1. Make a list of some of the differences between various religions you know about. Are these differences significant or not? Defend your view, noting in particular the criteria you used to decide significance.

2. What is religious exclusivism? What arguments might be given in defense of this view? What critique might be given of this view? How might the exclusivist respond to each of the objections?

3. How does the story of the blind men and the elephant help one understand religious pluralism? How might this analogy be turned into a criticism of plural-

ism? Would the story and its point change significantly if the men were not blind but partially sighted? Explain.

4. Why does Hick think personal transformation is more important than religious beliefs? What do you see as the proper relation between personal transformation and religious beliefs? Do beliefs matter? Defend your view.

5. Develop two criticisms of Hick's religious pluralism. How would Hick respond to each of these criticisms?

6. How is religious inclusivism similar to and different from both exclusivism and pluralism? How does Rahner defend his view?

7. Develop two criticisms that might be given of inclusivism. How would the inclusivist reply to each?

8. Compare and contrast pluralism with inclusivism on the question whether religions make truth claims about reality. What dilemma does Hick face on this issue? How might he respond to that dilemma?

9. Use the criteria suggested by Yandell to evaluate your own or another religious tradition.

NOTES

1. *Mu* is part of an ancient Zen *koan* or saying. Literally it means "not, not having, or having nothing."

2. Philip Kapleau, ed., *The Three Pillars of Zen* (Garden City, N.Y.: Anchor Press, 1980), pp. 237–39.

3. This is a central theme in Wilfred Cantwell Smith, *Towards a World Theology* (Philadelphia: Westminster, 1981).

4. Both are described in more detail in ibid., pp. 6–13.

5. John Hick, ed., *Problems of Religious Pluralism* (New York: St. Martin's Press, 1985), chaps. 3, 4.

6. Karl Barth, *Church Dogmatics* I, 2 (Edinburgh: T. & T. Clark, 1956), p. 303.

7. Ibid., IV, 1, p. 45.

8. A. A. Maududi, *Towards Understanding Islam* (Pakistan: np, nd), p. 60.

9. Ibid., p. 81.

10. Jerry L. Walls, *Hell: The Logic of Damnation* (Notre Dame, Ind.: University of Notre Dame Press, 1992), chap. 4. Not all exclusivists are comfortable with post-mortem evangelization. See Ronald H. Nash, *Is Jesus the Only Savior?* (Grand Rapids, Mich.: Zondervan, 1994), pp. 150–58. More is said about this issue in Chapter 14.

11. It might be noted that this view begins to narrow the gap between exclusivism and inclusivism, about which we speak later.

12. *Bhagavad-Gita*, trans. Eliot Deutsch (New York: Holt, Rinehart and Winston, 1968), IV, 11.

13. John Hick, *God and the Universe of Faiths* (London: Macmillan, 1977), p. 140. [See *PRSR*, Part 11, pp. 518–19.]

14. Hick, *Problems*, p. 35; also John Hick, ed., *The Myth of God Incarnate* (London: SCM, 1977). [See *PRSR*, Part 11, p. 517.]

15. John Hick, *An Interpretation of Religion* (New Haven: Yale University Press, 1989), p. 348.

16. Hick, *An Interpretation*, chap. 3.

17. Hick, *Problems*, p. 89.

18. Smith, *Towards a World Theology*, p. 190.

19. Ibid., p. 94.

20. Hick, *Problems*, p. 80.

21. Whether Hick can consistently hold this is problematic, since there is reason to think that the same epistemological difficulties that plague our present awareness would still apply. This is exacerbated for Hick when one considers the variety of views of the afterlife, some of which, such as metaphysical Absolutism, where the individual unites with the Nondual, would not allow for any individual verification. Eschatological verification would seem to be a remnant of Hick's earlier days as a Christian theist.

22. Hick, *An Interpretation*, pp. 248, 300–301.

23. Ibid., p. 308.

24. Ibid., pp. 243, 247, 249, 350.

25. Smith, *Towards a World Theology*, chap. 7.

26. Peter Byrne, "John Hick's Philosophy of World Religions," *Scottish Journal of Theology* 35, no. 4 (1982): 297.

27. Clark Pinnock, *A Wideness in God's Mercy* (Grand Rapids, Mich.: Zondervan, 1992), p. 70.

28. Hick, *An Interpretation*, pp. 359–60.

29. Some have objected to this terminology, claiming that it is either patronizing or that it "tends to obscure the difference that Jesus makes when he is known through faith in the Gospel." Pinnock, *A Wideness*, p. 105.

30. Karl Rahner, "Christian and the Non-Christian Religions," in John Hick and Brian Hebblethwaite, eds., *Christianity and Other Religions* (Glasgow: Collins, 1980), pp. 76–77. [See *PRSR*, Part 11, p. 512.]

31. Pinnock, *A Wideness*, pp. 90–91.

32. Keith E. Yandell, "Religious Experience and Rational Appraisal," *Religious Studies* 8 (June 1974): 185–86.

SUGGESTED READING

Barnes, Michael. *Religions in Conversation*. London: SPCK, 1989.

Byrne, Peter. "John Hick's Philosophy of World Religions." *Scottish Journal of Theology* 35, no. 4 (1982): 289–301.

D'Costa, Gavin. *Theology and Religious Pluralism: The Challenge of Other Religions*. Oxford: Blackwell, 1986.

———, ed. *Christian Uniqueness Reconsidered: The Myth of a Pluralistic Theology of Religions*. Maryknoll, N.Y.: Orbis, 1990.

Griffiths, Paul. *An Apology for Apologetics: A Study in the Logic of Interreligious Dialogue*. Maryknoll, NY: Orbis, 1991.

Hick, John. *God and the Universe of Faiths*. London: Macmillan, 1977.

———. *An Interpretation of Religion*. New Haven: Yale, 1989.

———, ed. *Problems of Religious Pluralism*. New York: St. Martin's Press, 1985.

Hick, John, and Brian Hebblethwaite, eds. *Christianity and Other Religions*. Glasgow: Collins, 1980.

Knitter, Paul. *No Other Name? A Critical Survey of Christian Attitudes Toward World Religions*. Maryknoll, N.Y.: Orbis, 1985.

Nash, Ronald. *Is Jesus the Only Savior?* Grand Rapids, Mich.: Zondervan, 1994.

Pinnock, Clark H. *A Wideness in God's Mercy*. Grand Rapids, Mich.: Zondervan, 1992.

Rice, Alan. *Christians and Religious Pluralism*. Maryknoll, N.Y.: Orbis, 1982.

Sanders, John. *No Other Name! A Biblical, Historical, and Theological Investigation into the Destiny of the Unevangelized*. Grand Rapids, Mich.: William B. Eerdmans, 1992.

Smith, Wilfred Cantwell. *Towards a World Theology*. Philadelphia: Westminster, 1981.

Vroom, Hendrik. *Religion and the Truth: Philosophical Reflections and Perspectives*. Grand Rapids, Mich.: William B. Eerdmans, 1989.

Yandell, Keith E. "Religious Experience and Rational Appraisal," *Religious Studies* 8 (June 1974): 173–87.

CHAPTER 13　RELIGIOUS ETHICS:
THE RELATION OF
GOD TO MORALITY

> While my own view is that the balance of considerations sup-
> ports permitting the practice of [voluntary active euthanasia]
> . . . there is reason to expect that legalization of voluntary ac-
> tive euthanasia might soon be followed by strong pressure to
> legalize some nonvoluntary euthanasia of incompetent pa-
> tients unable to express their own wishes.
>
> DAN BROCK,
> *Hastings Center Report*
> (March-April 1992)

What are we talking about when we discuss ethics? As we shall see, this
is a very complex question. But a basic distinction may help us get started.
Let us assume that we want to engage in an ethical discussion about the
right of terminally ill patients in severe or unbearable pain to end their
lives. Some of the issues we might consider would be primarily *descriptive*.
That is, they would relate to what *actually* is the case. How many individuals experiencing what they believe to be severe or unbearable pain attempt
to end their lives? Does public opinion currently support some forms of
active euthanasia? Would some who are terminally ill feel obligated to end
their lives if this were allowed? What abuses are possible? Other issues,
however, would be primarily *normative* (prescriptive); that is, they would
center around what we *should* believe or how we *ought to* behave. Should
any individual who is thinking clearly have the legal right to end her life
when it no longer seems worth living? Should only terminally ill individuals have this right? Should anyone have the right to make such a decision
for a mentally incompetent individual? Ought we ever allow physicians to
assist people in ending their lives?

Philosophers certainly do not deny that *descriptive ethics* is important.

They realize that we cannot, for example, create proper public policies if we do not know what people actually believe and how they live or do not consider the possible consequences of any change in policy. Most philosophers, though, feel that such considerations lie primarily in the domain of the anthropologist, sociologist, or political scientist. On the other hand, philosophers continue to be very interested in *normative ethics.* That is, they continue to be interested in the question of what people ought or ought not believe or how they ought or ought not act. Specifically, philosophers continue to be very interested in questions of the following type: What is the origin of the normative ethical principles we affirm? Under what conditions can such principles be rationally affirmed? Which set of normative ethical principles (hereafter simply referred to as *ethical principles)* is the correct one?

THE SOURCE OF RELIGIOUS ETHICAL TRUTH

There is no standard order in which ethical issues such as those mentioned are discussed. But in the area of religious ethics a rather natural progression arises. All of us affirm ethical principles related to almost every aspect of our lives. That is, we believe we have some understanding of how we, our family and friends, and even those with whom we will never have any direct contact *ought* to behave. But what is the origin of the ethical principles we believe to be true? At one level, an answer is readily available. We initially acquired the vast majority of our ethical principles the same way we initially acquired what we believe to be true about U.S. presidents or proper nutrition or types of automobiles: *from some respected authority.* For instance, most of us initially believed it was wrong to disobey our parents or engage in certain forms of sexual behavior because of what our parents, teachers, and religious leaders told us. What, however, is the *ultimate* origin of the ethical principles we hold to be true? Are they solely the product of human thought? Were they "created" by God? Do such principles originate in some source independent of both? Or are there multiple sources?

All of these options have their proponents. Even among theists, a wide variety of opinion exists. However, the vast majority of theists continue to claim that the basic ethical principles they affirm in some sense have their origin in God, as opposed to human thought or some source totally independent of both.

What exactly does it mean to say that ethical principles originate in God? One interpretation is the seemingly paradoxical contention that, although the basic ethical principles we affirm are not totally independent of God, they are *not* a divine creation. An analogy with the laws of logic may help. Consider the law of noncontradiction—the contention that something cannot be both what it is and what it is not at the same time. Few theists have thought this law to be totally independent of God, or something that God discovered. But it is also true that few theists hold that this law was created by God, or that it somehow came into existence as the result of divine decree. It is, rather, normally thought to be an eternal truth that has always existed in the mind of God. For example, according to this line of reasoning, the fact that humans cannot be both alive and not alive in the same sense at the same time is not true because God decreed that it should be so. Rather, the nature of reality (what is it to be alive or not to be alive) simply makes such a state of affairs an impossibility. What God did was decide whether humans would actually come into existence and, thus, whether the logical truth in question would actually apply to the world as it is.

Some have suggested that basic ethical principles might reasonably be viewed the same way. Let us consider, for instance, the widely accepted moral belief that it is wrong to inflict pain unnecessarily. We should not, we are told, view this ethical principle as independent of God in the sense that it is a principle with which God came in contact and then determined should guide all divine and human behavior. And, of course, if God had not created beings capable of experiencing pleasure and pain, this specific "truth" would have no relevance for our world. But this ethical principle did not come into existence as the result of some divine decree, nor can God do away with it at will. Rather, the fact that inflicting unnecessary pain is wrong is simply *inherent* in the very concept of any being who can experience such pain. Hence, much like the laws of logic, this principle is best viewed as having always existed in God's mind.[1]

Moreover, proponents of this "autonomy thesis," as it is often called, deny that viewing the origin of our ethical principles in this manner is a threat to theism. Louis Pojman (1935–), for instance, argues that

> if there is an inherent logic to goodness that precludes God's inventing right and wrong, why should that bother religious people? It is widely recognized that God's omnipotence isn't threatened by the fact that the laws of logic exist independently of him. Why should the fact that there is a logic to ethics threaten the notion of God's sovereignty or omnipotence?[2]

Many theists, however, have not liked the idea of anything in *any* sense being independent of God or limiting divine activity. Thus, they have wanted to argue that the basic ethical principles they believe to be true have their origin *solely* in God in a stronger sense. One popular way in which this has been envisioned—by individuals often labeled divine command theorists—is to maintain that ethical principles find their inception in God's commands.[3]

To claim that this is so, it is important to point out, is not to hold that the commands themselves are seen as the *origin* of these ethical principles. God is not envisioned as mindlessly "uttering" statements that somehow magically become the basis for ethical standards the moment they leave "God's lips." God's commands are seen as an expression of God's will.[4]

Just as a parent's command for a child to go to bed is best interpreted as an expression of what the parent wants the child to do, so, too, are God's commands best seen as an expression of how God wants us to live.

However, even given this clarification, a well-known challenge remains. If the ethical principles by which we are to live originate in the commands that express God's will, then it appears that we would be justified in doing anything God commanded. It appears, for instance, that even if God commanded us to kill innocent people routinely, or arbitrarily and capriciously commanded us to treat small children kindly one day but torture them the next, our obedience would be justified (indeed, required), simply because God has said this should be done. And surely, argues the critic, this is unacceptable. Surely a rational theist would not affirm a theory about the origin of correct ethical principles that had *this* implication.[5]

One popular response has been developed by the ethicist Robert Adams (1937–).[6] He wants to tie the origin of ethical truth to the will of God but denies that the "believer is committed to doing the will of God just because it is the will of God." That is, Adams denies that the theist would always be required to do what God commanded solely because God commanded it. He grants, for instance, that it would not be wrong for the theist to refrain from practicing cruelty, even *if* God commanded cruelty. This is so, we are told, because God's commands can be viewed as worthy of obedience "only if certain conditions are assumed—namely, only if it is assumed that God has the character which [we] believe Him to have, of loving His human creatures."[7] Otherwise, it would not be wrong to disobey him. Stated in more positive terms, Adams's response is that if we assume that God is a personal agent who loves his human creatures—an assumption Adams believes we can justifiably make—then we need not fear that commands that originate in the will of God will obligate us to act in a capricious, unloving manner.[8]

Others have elaborated more fully on the important connection between God's commands and character. It is certainly true, they acknowledge, that God has the ability to command us to kill innocent people. God obviously can formulate the relevant concepts and communicate the divine intentions to us. However, the divine moral will expressed by God's commands does not exist in a vacuum, nor is it dependent on some autonomous moral standard that has existed eternally in God's mind. God's will, rather, is an aspect of God's nature—that is, it is an expression of the type of being God really is. And once we understand the type of being God really is, it is argued, the criticism in question loses its force.

First, God is the all-knowing creator of everything. Thus, God knows exactly how all aspects of the divine creation function best. God knows, for example, exactly what will satisfy us individually and what will help us to live together harmoniously. Second, God does not just happen to be caring and loving most or even all of the time. God could not be unloving because God's essential nature is never-changing. God necessarily wills our individual and corporate fulfillment. Accordingly, it is concluded,

God's commands could not be arbitrary and capricious in the way the critic envisions. God, for instance, could not command us to kill innocent children "just for the fun of it," since this would be inconsistent with God's nature.[9]

But could God not have been a different type of being, one who believed that lying, cheating, or killing innocent children was an intrinsically meritorious action? A powerful, supernatural being who held such beliefs could conceivably exist, theists respond. However, the God we worship is not such a being. In fact, the vast majority claim, he could not have been such a being. Thus, the criticism in question simply fails to apply, and, accordingly, it remains perfectly reasonable to maintain that God's nature is the ultimate origin of the ethical principles we believe to be true.[10]

THE AUTHORITATIVE BASIS OF RELIGIOUS ETHICAL TRUTH

Even given that God's nature is the origin of ethical principles, a significant question remains: What gives the ethical principles that originate in God their authority? Why ought the theist obey what God communicates? Or, as Alasdair MacIntyre (1929–) has phrased this question, "What conditions must be satisfied for it to be rational for someone to treat God's [ethical] beliefs as authoritative?"[11]

In reality, some theists may follow God's commands primarily out of fear, others out of love or the belief that doing so will generate the best consequences, and still others primarily because their culture has ingrained this desire or duty in them. However, as MacIntyre and others rightly point out, theists could not justifiably view the ethical principles that originate in God as the ultimate ethical standard if they did not think that God was *perfectly good*.

What basis, though, do theists have for maintaining that God is good? The religious critic Kai Nielsen (1925–) contends that there are only two possible avenues of response.[12] One option, we are told, is for theists to claim that God's goodness is a factual or evidential matter. That is, they might claim that God is good because God has, for example, given them a purpose for living or healed a loved one or offered guidance in times of need.

However, this will not do, Nielsen is quick to point out. We can claim that an individual possesses a certain characteristic only if we already have some understanding of the characteristic in question. For instance (to cite an example not found in Nielsen's writings), we can claim that a new acquaintance is friendly *only if* we already understand what it means for someone to be friendly. In a similar fashion (to return to Nielsen's argument), we can claim that God is good by appealing to the actions God has performed *only if* we already have in mind a standard of goodness by which God's actions can be judged. But if this is true, Nielsen concludes, then it can obviously no longer be claimed that the ethical principles that originate in God provide the ultimate ethical standard. Rather, our own ethical intuitions must be acknowledged to be the ultimate standard.

The other option, Nielsen informs us, is to claim that the statement "God is good" is true by definition or, more correctly, to claim that "goodness" is a necessary defining characteristic of "God." God's attitudes (and actions) are then good simply because God possesses (or performs) them. But this response generates another question: Upon what basis do theists label the being they worship "God"? Or, to state Nielsen's question in a somewhat different fashion: How do theists know that the being from whom they have received those ethical principles that they accept as authoritative is actually God?

Theists, Nielsen points out, cannot justifiably claim that such a being is God simply because this being says it is good. The question then simply becomes: Upon what basis can the claims of such a being be believed? Nor, he argues, can theists claim that the actions of the being they worship are good and, thus, that the being can justifiably be considered God, just because they believe this being is the omniscient, omnipotent creator of the universe. It may be true that it would be unwise not to follow the commands of such a being, but it is not impossible for an omnipotent, omniscient creator to be wicked. The only valid response, we are told, is for theists to admit that the being they worship is called "God" because they possess an independent ethical standard of goodness with which the actions and attitudes of this being are consistent.

An analogy may help clarify this important point. Let us assume that someone declares the statement "All puppies are young" to be a definitional truth. This alone does not allow her to maintain justifiably that a dog that has just entered the room is a puppy. To make this claim justifiably, she must first determine whether the dog is young. And to do this she must already have in mind the characteristics that young dogs possess—for instance, oversize feet and an excitable personality. Likewise, Nielsen is arguing, theists can claim that the being whose commands they follow is God, and thus an acceptable ethical authority, only if they can determine (possibly in addition to other things) that this being is good. But this can be accomplished only if they already have in mind a concept of goodness by which this being can be judged. Thus, again, theists must admit that their own ethical intuitions are the ultimate ethical standard.

Is Nielsen correct? First, it must be emphasized that Nielsen's argument applies only to those theists who maintain that ethical truth originates totally in God—for example, in God's nature. His comments are not relevant to those theists (noted earlier) who maintain that, although ethical truth is in some sense dependent on God, it is also in some sense independent of him.

What, though, of those theists who hold that ethical truth *does* originate totally in God? Is Nielsen's argument compelling in this case? It may well be true that many theists maintain that God is good because the attitudes and actions of the being in question are consistent with their own ethical sensibilities. That is, it may well be true that many theists generally judge God to be good by ethical standards they possessed before this judgment is made. But to grant Nielsen this much is innocuous. The crucial part of his thesis is his contention that the ethical criteria used by the theist to evaluate God's goodness constitute an ethical standard that is separate from, and more fundamental than, the basic ethical beliefs of the divine code-giver being judged.

However, it is not clear that the theist need grant Nielsen this point. The ethical criteria by which theists judge the goodness of God are "separate" and "more fundamental" in the sense required by Nielsen only if they are formulated by each theist apart from divine influence. But Judeo-Christian theology, for example, has traditionally maintained that humans and the environment in which they function are both divine creations. More specifically, it has traditionally been held that the basic ethical principles that we as humans find ourselves affirming are actually divine in origin. As we shall see, theists differ in their beliefs about the exact sense in which this is so. Yet if such principles are in any sense divine in origin, then it is not clear that theists need grant, in the last analysis, that they judge God by an ethical standard that is separate from, and more ultimate than, God's. They can claim, rather, that they judge God by a standard that God has brought it about that they possess. In short, it appears that by affirming the "divine" origin of their own ethical sensibilities, theists can grant that they judge the goodness of God by their own ethical standards and yet justifiably deny that their own personally formulated ethical code is the final seat of ethical authority.[13]

Nielsen, of course, does not accept this religious understanding of the origin of humanity's basic ethical intuitions. But this is not relevant. Nielsen is not assessing the truth or falsity of the theist's beliefs concerning God's existence, attitudes, or actions. His contention, rather, is that theists cannot consistently maintain that their ethical decisions are based on a ethical standard ultimately independent of human thought, even if they make certain religious assumptions. However, this contention, it seems, can be countered successfully.

THE ACQUISITION OF RELIGIOUSLY BASED ETHICAL TRUTH

Let us assume, then, for the sake of argument, that theists can justifiably maintain not only that ethical truth originates in God but also that such truth is authoritative for this reason. This still leaves us with the question of how theists acquire this ethical insight.

Three distinct, although not mutually exclusive, methods of acquisition are mentioned most frequently. First, theists often claim that God has communicated ethical truths through some form of *written revelation*—for example, the Bible or the Koran. Opinions differ widely on the extent to which God is thought to have been directly involved in the production of this revelation. Some believe God is directly responsible for every word, others believe God is responsible for the basic concepts, and still others believe that God is responsible only for helping to collate the most accurate human ethical insights. But many, if not most, theists hold that written revelation is a very important source of information about the ethical principles by which God wants us to live.

It is here, though, that conservative Jewish and Christian theists—those who believe the Torah or the Bible to be a clear, direct communication from God—run into a well-known dilemma. The problem is that, at face value, some of the actions attributed to God appear to be ethically questionable. For example, in Numbers 31 it is God who declares that all members of an enemy tribe are to be killed by the Israelites and then decides how to divide up the 32,000 virgin girls who were not destroyed. And in I Chronicles 21, it appears that God brings it about that 70,000 individuals die solely to punish King David, not because of any wrongdoing on their part.

Some conservative theists respond by separating the ethical principles by which God operates from those applicable to human behavior. God, it is argued, has created a consistent, thoughtful ethical standard for humans, a standard that, if followed, will bring about what God desires and the greatest fulfillment for all. But God is not bound by such a standard. God can do whatever he wants for whatever reasons he possesses, and such actions are ethically justifiable simply because he has performed them.[14]

Of course, this contention generates obvious questions. If God operates by a different ethical standard, how can God remain the object of our ethical admiration? We might well obey a being who has created rules for us because we recognize that these rules maximize human fulfillment or because we fear the rule-giver. But could we truly worship or revere a being who not only could but did violate the most basic ethical concepts by which we have been told (and created to feel) we should live?

Many theists think the answer is no. They deny that two distinct standards exist. Of course, they grant, God has created some ethical tenets that apply only to humans. For example, rules related to the well-being of our physical bodies are not relevant to God because God has no such body. However, the basic ethical principles God has communicated to us are the same ethical principles that also "guide" God's activity. Accordingly, they conclude, any seeming violation of these principles must ultimately be a problem of human perspective. If we could see the whole picture from God's perspective—if we were aware of all the contextual factors—we would see that everything God has actually said and done is consistent with God's nature, which is loving in the basic manner in which we understand the term.[15]

Second (to return to our primary question of how theists acquire their ethical beliefs), some theists, in the *natural law tradition* of Thomas Aquinas (c. 1224–1274), continue to believe that human reason is capable of discovering divine ethical truth. According to this perspective, God is the ultimate source of all ethical knowledge. That is, God establishes the ultimate distinction between good and evil. However, as the result of being created in God's image, we humans possess the rational capacities to comprehend those aspects of this ethical standard that have been revealed in nature. That is, from our observation of the natural order, we can deduce how human beings are to act and be treated.

We have, for example, a natural tendency to preserve ourselves, to produce offspring, and to live in a social setting with others. From these principles we can deduce that God sanctions self-defense. And from the fact that we have a natural tendency to protect young children and the fact that we all desire to avoid pain, we can deduce that God does not sanction the killing of innocent children.

Thomistic natural law theorists are quick to point out that such ethical reflection is not a more trustworthy avenue for discerning ethical truth than written revelation. In fact, many have acknowledged that written revelation must be given precedence in the event of a conflict. But, although written revelation is *sufficient* for giving us God's basic ethical perspective, it is not *always necessary*. Human reflection on the nature of things, it is held, can discover much about God's basic ethical standards and their application to our daily lives.[16]

Third, as we have already implicitly stated, some theists also claim that *divine ethical truth is, at least in part, innate.* Each of us, they maintain, has been created in the "image of God," including God's "ethical image." And this means that our basic ethical intuitions—for example, the belief that we should not kill innocent children—automatically mirror God's basic ethical perspectives. As Gottfried Leibniz (1646–1716) and others rightly noted, such innate intuitions may require some external illumination before we become consciously aware of them.[17] We may, for instance, need to understand what a child is, and what killing means, before we become consciously aware of the fact that killing children is wrong. Moreover, not all available ethical insight comes to us in this fashion. Written revelation and reason are also necessary. But some of the basic ethical principles we believe to be true, these theists argue, were not "learned." We, as divine creations, were simply "born" with them.

There is, however, a seemingly serious problem that proponents of all three of these modes of acquiring divine ethical truth must face. Why is there so much ethical diversity among theists? That is, why do seemingly sincere, knowledgeable theists differ significantly on so many issues related to human thought and action? If theists have access to basic ethical truth, as they claim, why is there not greater ethical consensus among them?

Some of this diversity can, of course, be reasonably attributed to the diversity in religious perspectives themselves. It is true that proponents of almost all religions claim to have access to ethical truth through reason, inborn awareness, and/or written revelation. However, given that religious perspectives differ not only with respect to the content of their "written revelations" but also with respect to the role that innate awareness and rational reflection can play in the discovery of truth, it should not be surprising that there exists a great deal of ethical diversity in the general religious community.

What can be said, though, about the significant amount of ethical diversity that remains *within* various religions—for instance, within the Judeo-Christian perspective? Such diversity can be explained in part by distinguishing between basic ethical principles and their practical application. Consider, for instance, the question of whether we should allow physicians to help terminally ill patients end their lives. There will be little debate within most religious perspectives at the level of principle. Conscientious theists, it will be held, ought to respond in a just, caring manner. But what does this mean in practice? Does it mean that theists ought to work to ensure the legal right of those in unbearable pain to be helped to end such suffering? Or should theists fight any attempt to legalize a "right to die" that might ultimately cause those in the final stages of dying to feel morally obligated to end their lives? Since either can reasonably be construed as a just, caring response, it should not be surprising that sincere theists within almost all religions disagree (sometimes strongly) on the appropriate response in this case. In short, since the general ethical principles of most religions allow for varied application, the fact that we encounter some diverse ethical behavior, even within a given religious perspective, is to be expected.

Ethical diversity within a given religion is also at times clearly a function of differing "factual" assumptions. Abortion is a good example. Most in the Judeo-Christian tradition affirm the same relevant ethical principles: for instance, that taking an innocent life is wrong. What they differ on is whether the fetus is sufficiently human to fall within the protective bounds of this principle.

Even granting, though, that some diversity can be explained in these ways, the basic tension remains in that some theists within any given religious tradition differ on the *basic* "innate" or "rational" principles themselves. For example, while some Christians believe it is never right to use life-threatening force, others believe this is justified in times of war or to defend an innocent person. And while some proponents of given religions believe that men and women should function as equals in all contexts, other adherents to the same religions maintain that men must still exercise authority over women, especially in the home and the church. Can diversity of this fundamental sort justifiably be viewed as compatible with the contention that the proponents of a given religion have access to authoritative ethical truth?

In response, many theists emphasize the important distinction between affirming *different* basic ethical principles and ranking the *same* basic ethical principles differently. Take, for example, the case of Christians who were hiding Jews in their homes during World War II. When the Nazis came to ask if Jews were within, some thought it right to lie, while others did not. But the issue here was not primarily one of principle. All the Christians involved thought it was their God-sanctioned duty both to protect innocent lives *and* not to lie. They differed on the question of which principle was properly to be given precedence in this case.[18]

Other theists hold that the human ability to identify divine ethical principles accurately has been severely damaged by "the fall"—that is, by a break in the relationship between humans and God that was precipitated by an act of rebellion by humans. Thus, they claim that although many of us at times are able to discern with relative accuracy the ethical principles affirmed by God, some of us will inevitably be unable to do so, or at least be unable to do so consistently.[19]

Finally, those theists who maintain that some ethical truth is "inborn" often emphasize the significance of cultural conditioning. It is one thing, they argue, to say that each human has some basic understanding of the divine ethical law, but quite another thing to say that such an understanding will always be consciously felt as predominant. Individuals are greatly influenced by their culture. If, for instance, they are raised in a culture where stealing or cheating or lying is condoned, they will have a strong disposition to believe that it is right to engage in such activities. They may have some vague feeling that such actions are wrong, but it need not be held that this "divine perspective" will always be most influential.[20]

Of course, even if all this is granted, pervasive ethical diversity among and within religious perspectives still leaves us with the following question: Which religious ethical standard most closely resembles God's standard? This surely is an important question, for much strife historically has been the result of individuals or groups acting on what they perceived to be the correct set of divinely sanctioned ethical principles. In fact, it is so important that it may well be true that the reality of pervasive diversity stands as a good reason for theists to periodically reassess their ethical beliefs (and the behavior such beliefs generate). That is, such diversity may well stand as a real challenge to ethical dogmatism, especially in action.

We must be careful to keep all this in perspective. There is diversity in the methods used by theists to acquire ethical truth *and* in the "truths" allegedly acquired. However, just as the reality of diversity in political opinion does not necessarily require us to become political relativists or skeptics, the reality of ethical diversity does not necessarily require us to become ethical relativists or skeptics. Ethical diversity ought to be recognized and considered by theists as they put their ethical beliefs into action, but it does not follow from the fact that theists acknowledge the reality of ethical diversity that they cannot justifiably claim that there exists any ethical truth, that such truth is divine in origin, or even that they have access to it.

THE SIGNIFICANCE OF RELIGIOUSLY BASED ETHICAL TRUTH

What does all this mean for those individuals who are not religious? If theists are correct in holding that ethical truth originates in God and that they have access to such truth, what are the implications for those who do not believe in God (or at least deny that ethical truth is in any sense dependent on God)?

Does it mean, for instance, that those who do not believe that ethical truth is in any sense dependent on God cannot meaningfully communicate about matters of moral significance with those who do? Most theists do not hold this to be the case and do not claim that one must believe in God (or believe that ethical truth is dependent on God) to be aware of any of God's basic ethical beliefs. Most maintain, rather, that God has created all individuals with an "inborn" understanding of, or the rational ability to discover, certain basic ethical principles and that the mutual possession of these principles allows for meaningful ethical dialogue between the two groups, even if nontheists do not recognize the "divine" origin of their basic ethical beliefs.[21]

However, a significant question remains: Can a nonreligious person, or anyone else who does not believe ethical truth to be dependent on God, justifiably affirm ethical absolutes? That is, can someone who does not ground ethical truth in God justifiably claim that some actions are wrong (or right) for all persons at all times and places? In reality, of course, most nonreligious individuals do affirm ethical absolutes. The vast majority believe, for instance, that innocent children ought, in principle, never to be tortured. But can such absolutes be justifiably affirmed? Most theists ground absolutes in an objective, external standard: God's nature. But if there is no God, are not all ethical beliefs ultimately human in origin? That is, if there is no God, how can it be said justifiably that one human or group of humans has the right to dictate how all others *ought* to live? Does it not follow rather, in the words of Jean-Paul Sartre (1905–1980), that "everything is permissible if God does not exist?"[22]

In response, Nielsen argues that the "nonexistence of God does not preclude the possibility of there being an objective standard on which to base moral judgments." There are, he tells us, "good reasons, of a perfectly mundane sort, why we should have the institution of morality as we now have it. . . . Morality has an objective rationale in complete independence of religion."[23]

Yet what is this "objective rationale" that is "independent of religion"? Such objectivity, Nielsen maintains, can be founded on ethical beliefs such as "happiness is good" and "all persons should be treated fairly," since such beliefs are not only ethical principles that most persons intuitively know to be true but are principles that, if put into practice, are normally most advantageous for all involved.

Suppose, however, that it is pragmatically advantageous for individuals to treat others unfairly—for example, to cheat on their taxes—and that they therefore do so. Or suppose that individuals claim to have radically different ethical intuitions—for example, that lying and stealing are right. On what basis can such persons be judged ethically wrong? Nielsen is aware of such difficulties. He admits that he cannot prove that happiness is good, arguing that he "can only appeal to our sense of psychological realism to persuade us to admit intellectually what in practice we acknowledge." And he admits that he cannot prove that fairness is always the most advantageous principle to employ, but he argues that "to be moral involves respecting [human] rights."[24] Or, as he phrases this point in another context, unless such a principle is affirmed, there can be "[no] understanding of the concept of morality, [no] understanding of what it is to take the moral point of view."[25]

Is Nielsen correct? Has he offered us a sound nontheistic basis for objective morality? As we consider this question, it is important first to realize that Nielsen is clearly not defining "objective morality" as it is usually defined by theists. For most theists, absolute (objective) ethical principles are nonexperientially grounded (a priori) statements that are true for all persons at all times in all places. For Nielsen, "absolute" ethical principles are experientially grounded (a posteriori) statements that ought, on the basis of rational considerations, to be affirmed *at present* by everyone. Thus, while most theists see "Thou shalt not kill" as a timeless truth affirmed by, but not founded on, human reasoning, Nielsen sees this ethical principle as a truth that all individuals ought to affirm, at present, on the basis of rational thought.

However, does this not make Nielsen's "objective" ethical perspective quite relative to the obvious variations in human thought and the amount of relevant data being considered? In response, Nielsen is willing to admit that if ethical principles are solely the product of human thought, then they are to a certain degree relative in this sense. However, to maintain that ethical truth is relative can also be taken to mean that there is no objective basis for preferring one ethical perspective to another—that what is *right* in every case is solely a function of what each individual personally thinks is right. It can be taken to mean, for example, that there is no stronger *objective* basis for favoring capital punishment than for opposing it. And Nielsen obviously does want to deny that his ethic is relative in this sense. He believes, as we have seen, that, given the human desire for happiness and given that there are good, pragmatic reasons for believing that certain forms of behavior will generally help us reach this goal, nontheists do have an objective basis in some contexts for saying that most people should behave in certain ways most of the time.

Some continue to claim, though, that to base ethical beliefs on common elements in human thought or experience is to confuse factual and ethical issues—to deduce unjustifiably that people *ought* to affirm certain ethical norms solely from the observable fact that such norms *are* affirmed. In response, Nielsen grants that we cannot simply "deduce that people ought to do something from discovering that they do it or seek it any more than we can conclude from the proposition that a being exists whom people call God that we ought to do whatever that being commands." However, he adds, "we do justify moral claims by an appeal to factual claims, and there is a close connection between what human beings desire on reflection and what they deem to be good."[26]

It appears that Nielsen is at least partially correct at this point. The majority of philosophers agree that neither the religious nor the nonreligious individual can directly deduce an *ought* from an is. But it does seem that religious as well as nonreligious individuals justify their ethical claims at least in part by appealing to factual contentions—for example, by appealing to certain claims about the nature of God, natural human desires, or shared ethical intuitions.[27]

Moreover, even if we reject Nielsen's basis for an objective nonreligious morality, it is not clear that a nonreligious person is committed to radical ethical relativism. It may be that nonreligiously based ethical norms must be somewhat relative to the context to which they apply or must at least be more relative than religiously based norms. However, to establish the total relativity of nonreligiously based ethics—to establish that ethical truth for the nonreligious person is nothing more than personal preference—it must be demonstrated that there exists no rational basis for humanity (all rational individuals) in general to affirm any given ethical norm, and it does not appear that this has yet been done. In fact even some theists think it is misguided to attempt to do so. Louis Pojman, for instance, agrees with Nielsen that "secular morality based on a notion of the good life is inspiring in itself, for it promotes human flourishing and can be shown to be in all of our interests, whether or not God exists."[28]

Even granting this fact, if ethical truth is solely a human invention—if there exists no ultimate standard of value apart from our human perspective—can life have any real meaning? Or, to state the question differently, is it at least true, as some theists have claimed, that belief in God is necessary if life is to have any significant purpose?

To answer this question, we must more clearly understand what theists have in mind when they claim that ethical relativism leads to "meaninglessness." Most argue at the very least that nontheists can posit no ultimate purpose for the universe as a whole. Hans Küng (1928–), for example, maintains that "by denying God, man decides against an ultimate reason, support, and end of reality."[29] This contention, however, has limited significance. Although it may be true that some nontheists need to be reminded that a godless universe is ultimately nonpurposeful, thoughtful nontheists readily acknowledge this fact.

Some theists, however, have wanted to go further. They have wanted to argue that, once nontheists realize that there exists no ultimate purpose for the universe as a whole, they will no longer experience any personal meaning. Rather, in the words of Küng, they will be exposed "quite personally to the danger of an ultimate abandonment, menace and decay, resulting in doubt, fear, even despair."[30]

Not surprisingly, however, most nontheists do not find this line of reasoning compelling. First, while they grant that some nontheists may experience a loss of personal meaning when they come to recognize that there exists no ultimate cosmic meaning in a godless universe, they deny that this is the case for most.

More important, however, nontheists argue that this type of "head-counting" approach to the question of personal meaning begs the question by its very nature. They do not deny that many theists have found in their own experience a significant tie between cosmic and personal meaning. They do not deny, for example, that many theists truly hold, with St. Augustine (354–430), that the human "heart" is restless until it finds its rest in God. In fact, many nontheists do not even deny that the theist is justified in maintaining that some such connection exists.

The key issue, they point out, however, is not what the theist can rationally affirm; the issue is what the nontheist can rationally affirm. And here, it is argued, the burden of proof clearly lies with the theist. What the theist must establish is not that she is justified in claiming that she would possess no personal meaning if there were no God or even that some nontheists also feel this way. What the theist must establish is that nontheists who deny cosmic meaning but still claim to possess personal meaning are not justified in maintaining this position. And this, most nontheists contend, the theist has not done. In fact, given that there appears to be no widespread scientific (psychological or physiological) or logical support for the claim that one cannot justifiably claim to have personal meaning if one denies cosmic meaning, most nontheists do not see how the theist could even attempt to establish such a connection in a nonquestion-begging manner.

It appears the nontheist is correct, at least given the manner in which he has structured the debate. A nonreligious worldview may require some reworking of the traditional concept of personal meaning. Some nontheists may, in fact, not experience personal meaning. But it does not follow necessarily from this that nontheists cannot justifiably affirm an enduring sense of personal meaning. A separate argument is needed for this end, an argument that does not already assume the truth of what is to be proved.

CURRENT ISSUES

One approach to which philosophers have recently been giving considerable attention is called *virtue ethics,* and this attention has carried over into the religious realm.[31] To understand any aspect of this discussion, we must first bring to the forefront the well-known distinction between *what* individuals do and *why* they do it. Consider, for example, the following situations.

Case A: One day while walking to the Post Office, Grandmother Smith trips and falls. Tim is cycling past on his way to a ball game and sees what occurs. Because he is late, he momentarily considers riding on. But this thought is quickly replaced by his concern for Grandmother Smith's welfare. Thus, he stops, helps her up, and makes sure she is not hurt before continuing on his way.

Case B: One day while walking to the Post Office, Grandmother Smith trips and falls. Bill, who is cycling by on his way to a ball game for which he is late, observes the event. But he has no intention of stopping. He is late for his game, but, even more important, he dislikes Grandmother Smith. Thus, he is actually pleased that she has fallen. However, just as he is ready to leave the scene, he notices at a distance a person who looks very much like the pastor of his church, and he fears that this person has seen Grandmother Smith fall and will see him riding away without helping. Thus, Bill stops, helps her up, and makes sure she is not hurt before riding on.

The observable behavior in each case is identical. Grandmother Smith has fallen, and a young man has stopped to help. Hence, any ethical theory that states that ethical judgment should be based solely on observable behavior would have to consider the actions of Tim and Bill as ethically equivalent. But for many of us in the Western ethical tradition, this would not be acceptable. We are happy with the "ethical output" in each case—we are glad Grandmother Smith has been helped. But our ethical assessment of Bill and Tim would not solely, or even primarily, be based on their observable behavior. It would be based primarily, or at least significantly, on our assessment of their "ethical input"—their motivation or intentions. And in this regard Bill and Tim do differ significantly. Tim wanted to help; Bill did not.

It is possible, however, to discuss this difference in ethical input in terms of either *duty* or *virtue* (virtuous character). In terms of duty, we might say that Tim's behavior is praiseworthy because he desired to act in accordance with the recognized ethical duty to help those in need, whereas Bill deserves no commendation because his actions were not motivated by this or any other relevant ethical duty. In terms of virtue, we might say that Tim alone deserves praise because his behavior was an expression of a virtuous character trait—for example, benevolence.

Of course, these two ways of describing ethical input are not mutually exclusive. In fact, it seems to many that both are necessary to a full understanding of ethical behavior. However, there has recently been a great deal of interest in whether we should view duty or virtue as the more basic or primary ethical concept. Those who want to emphasize duty argue that it is because we have a duty to do something that our intention to do it is virtuous. Or, to state this point more formally, they argue that it is because we have a basic disposition to want to act in accordance with recognized duties that we can be said to have a praiseworthy character. In terms of our current illustration, this would be to say that Tim's desire to help

Grandmother Smith is virtuous because he acted in accordance with the recognized duty to help those in need.

Those who want to emphasize virtue argue instead that we have the ethical duty to act, or refrain from acting, in certain ways because such duties are expressions of virtuous character traits. In terms of our illustration, this would be to say that Tim can be praised for fulfilling his ethical duty to attempt to help Grandmother Smith because this duty is the expression of his benevolent character. Still other philosophers see neither virtue nor duty as primary but rather see them as two partially overlapping and mutually interdependent perspectives on ethics.

The relevance of this question for religious ethics is obvious. The discussion of traditional ethical issues in this chapter has generally been couched in terms of ethical principles, which can quite plausibly be understood to be statements describing ethical duties. That is, it might appear from the tone of this chapter that to be ethical from a religious perspective is to act in accordance with the revealed rules (duties) that have their grounding in God. But the recent interest in virtue ethics has led some to conceive of religious ethics differently. Specifically, they no longer conceive of ethical activity primarily in terms of doing what God wants, or even of wanting to do what God wants, but rather in terms of being the type of person God wants us to be.[32]

To help make this distinction clearer, let us consider the common religious belief that we should love one another. In the traditional framework of a duty ethic, the theist's primary task is to apply this principle to each aspect of daily life. Such a process, of course, is in part contextual. For instance, how one responds in love to a three-year-old throwing a tantrum or to an unhelpful store clerk is allowed to differ from situation to situation. But, in each case, the theist's task is to determine consciously what would be the most loving response.

Under a virtue ethic, however, the situation is fundamentally different. The essence of ethical activity is not seen as conscious adherence to a set of duties. Specifically, the key to ethical living is not thought to be something that can be abstracted from the religious tradition and rationally applied to culture. The essence of ethical living is to *be* religious—for example, to be Christian or to be Islamic. We must become part of a tradition—a faith community—in which the character of this community—its intentions, desires, and values—become our own. We will then quite naturally find ourselves living as we should. Stated differently, once we *become* religious, we will act in a proper religious manner. The development of our religious character is prior to the realization of our religious duty.

This perspective also leads, not surprisingly, to a de-emphasis on the traditional philosophical responses to ethical issues. For example, many theists have traditionally thought it important to respond to the problem of evil: Why does there exist so much seemingly unnecessary pain and suffering in a world allegedly created by an omnipotent, omniscient, perfectly good being? But, in the words of one influential Christian "virtue ethicist," for a Christian to even attempt to answer this question "is a mistake." Evil is not a "metaphysical problem needing a solution" but rather a "practical challenge needing a response." And the appropriate response is a "community of care which [makes] it possible to absorb the destructive terror of evil that constantly threatens to destroy all human relations."[33]

There are, of course, many theists who think both duty and virtue are important ethical concepts. But the emphasis on virtue ethics appears to be something that will have an impact on the nature of religious ethics for the foreseeable future.

Another approach to ethics to which philosophers are also giving increasing attention has come to be called *feminist ethics*. Given the widely divergent interpretations of what constitutes feminism itself, it should not be surprisingly that there is no unambiguous understanding of what constitutes this approach to ethics. But there are some points on which almost all who claim to be doing ethics of this type agree.

All feminist approaches to ethics maintain that the traditional ethical theories—whether utilitarian or rights based—are inadequate. Most important, it is argued that traditional Western ethical theories are biased in the sense of uniformly "representing the experiences of men, not women."[34] Specifically, Alison Jaggar (1942–) tells us, these theories have "either devalued or ignored issues or spheres of life that are associated with women . . . women's virtues have been seen as less significant than those associated with men; women's work has gone unrecognized or its creativity has been unappreciated; the abuse of women and children, especially girls, has been ignored."[35]

Moreover, while feminists differ on the extent to which any ethical system needs general moral rules from which we can deduce appropriate behavior in specific contexts, there is general agreement that traditional ethical systems rely too heavily on abstract generalized principles applied to hypothetical situations, often at the expense of the immediate needs of actual individuals.

Finally, feminists hold that the recognition of, and respect for, women's moral experience is indispensable in that such experience enables us to identify "previously unrecognized ethical issues . . . introduce fresh perspectives on issues already acknowledged as having an ethical dimension . . . and [counter] traditional stereotypes of women as less than full moral agents, as childlike or close to nature."[36]

It should not be surprising, accordingly, that feminist ethics is overtly "political"—that is, concerned with the actual rules and regulations that govern our human interaction. This should not be construed to mean that proponents of feminist ethics do not concern themselves with theoretical issues. They explicitly acknowledge the need to "develop theoretical understandings of the nature of morality that treat women's moral experience respectfully but not uncritically."[37] But they are also firmly committed to challenging "actions and practices that perpetuate women's subordination, [prescribing] morally justifiable ways of resisting such actions and practices, and [envisioning] morally desirable alternatives that will promote women's emancipation."[38] In other words, feminists desire not only to theoretically "unmask and challenge the oppression, discrimination and exclusion that women have faced" but also to influence relevant public policy.[39]

As is true of feminist ethics in general, religious or theological feminist ethics is quite divergent in nature and scope. But again several common factors are apparent.

First, and foremost, religious feminists believe it is necessary to identify in the traditional theological ethical systems those "powers and forces, the structures and practices that oppress women."[40] Many, if not most, religions, it is argued, continue to deny equal ethical status to both men and women. Within a few branches of conservative Christianity, for instance, women are still viewed as the ones ultimately responsible for evil. But even within those religions where this is not the case, men are still often considered more "rational" than women and thus more responsible for creating and/or interpreting the ethical standards by which we are to live, standards that are often quite different for women than for men. Men are told not to take advantage of others as they strive to accomplish their goals; women are often explicitly or implicitly told to give of themselves so that others (especially men) can accomplish their goals. Men are asked to control their sexual behavior; women are still often encouraged to remain totally pure in thought and deed. Men are encouraged to make the ultimate decisions; women are encouraged to offer helpful advice. Moreover, religious feminists emphasize, it is not enough simply to identify this sort of male bias in religious ethics. Such bias must be openly challenged.[41]

In addition to this "deconstructive" project, there is also the desire on the part of most religious feminists to "reconstruct" a religious ethical perspective compatible with basic feminist tenets. Specifically, there is an attempt to construct an ethic that not only frees women from patriarchal oppression but encourages women's self-affirmation as equal participants in the religious and ethical arenas. Such attempted reconstruction takes various forms. Some religious feminists base their efforts on the assumption that since "all men and all male thought and action are different from and opposed to all women and all female thought and action," what men have said and done in the area of religious ethical theory (as in all other areas) must be repudiated. Accordingly, they have as their goal to create a wholly new religious ethic, one based on the concepts and language that arise from women's experiences.[42]

Other feminists, however, reject the contention that the traditional theological ethical systems are necessarily hostile to the interests of women. Some Christian feminists have argued, for instance, that aspects of the manner in which the early Christian church envisioned the relationships among those with unequal power are quite compatible with contemporary feminist thought.[43] Thus, as those in this camp see it, what must be done is to identify and challenge those aspects of the traditional systems that discriminate on the basis of gender, while retaining those aspects that are inclusive of women's experience.[44]

There are, not surprisingly, some theists who feel that theological feminists place too much emphasis on gender equality—that is, they wrongly identify gender equality as the primary factor in assessing the value of a religious ethical traditions. But few theists today deny that male bias continues to exist to some extent and, thus, that the feminist concerns noted must be taken seriously.

STUDY QUESTIONS

1. What do you think most theists really mean when they say that ethical truth has its origin in God? Given this interpretation, are theists still open to the charge that God's commands could be arbitrary and capricious?

2. Do you believe that ethical truth originates solely in God? If not, what is its origin?

3. Why does Kai Nielsen believe that the religious person's ethical standard is ultimately based on his own ethical intuitions, not God's commands? How do theists respond?

4. Why does ethical pluralism—the wide variety of ethical perspectives—pose a challenge for religious ethics? Which of the responses to such pluralism discussed in this chapter do you find most convincing?

5. Is there any truth to the claim that, apart from belief in God, life can have no ultimate meaning?

6. Why do some claim that ethics must be totally relative if there is no God? Briefly outline and assess Kai Nielsen's response to this claim.

7. Those theists who consider the Torah or the Bible to be a trustworthy source of information about God must grapple with the seemingly questionable behavior sometimes attributed to God in these texts. Which of the responses discussed did you find most convincing? Why?

8. What is "virtue ethics"? Do you think either "virtue" or "duty" is the more basic ethical concept? Why?

9. Do you think that religious individuals behave more ethically than nonreligious individuals? If not, is the opposite true?

10. Do you agree with religious feminists that the traditional ethical systems have been (continue to be) male biased? Why or why not?

NOTES

1. See, for example, A. C. Ewing, "The Autonomy of Ethics," in Janine Marie Idziak, ed., *Divine Command Morality* (Lewiston, N.Y.: Edwin Mellen Press, 1979), pp. 228–30.

2. Louis P. Pojman, *Ethics: Discovering Right and Wrong* (Belmont, Calif.: Wadsworth, 1990), p. 188.

3. See, for example, Emil Brunner, *The Divine Imperative* (W. L. Jenkins, 1947); Carl F. H. Henry *Christian Personal Ethics* (Grand Rapids: William B. Eerdmans, 1957).

4. William of Ockham, *On the Four Books of the Sentences,* book 11, quest. 19, in Idziak, ed., *Divine Command Morality,* pp. 55–59.

5. See, for example, Patrick Nowell-Smith, "Religion and Morality," *Encyclopedia of Philosophy,* vol. 7 (New York: Macmillan, 1967), p. 156; A. C. Ewing, *Prospect for Metaphysics* (London: George Allen and Unwin, 1951), p. 39.

6. See, for example, Robert Adams, "A Modified Divine Command Theory of Ethical Wrongness," in Louis Pojman, ed., *Philosophy of Religion* (Belmont, Calif.: Wadsworth, 1987), p. 527.

7. Ibid., pp. 533–34.

8. It is sometimes argued that Adams's "modified" divine command theory is actually just a "modified" version of the "autonomy thesis," since it appears that some independent ethical principles are accorded preference over God's commands. In one sense, this appears true. Adams does maintain hypothetically that if God were to utter certain commands, we could appeal to a higher, independent ethical standard in refusing to obey such commands. But Adams denies that it is possible for God to utter such commands, and concludes, therefore, that God's actual commands can justifiably be viewed as the actual basis of our ethical principles.

9. Bruce Reichenbach, "The Divine Command Theory and Objective Good," in R. Porreco, ed., *Georgetown Symposium on Ethics* (New York: University Press of America), pp. 219–31. It should be noted that Adams is not necessarily in agreement with all aspects of this line of reasoning.

10. Adams, "Modified Theory," pp. 525–37.

11. Alasdair MacIntyre, "Which God Ought We Obey and Why?" *Faith and Philosophy* 3 (1986): 359.

12. Kai Nielsen, *Ethics Without God* (London: Pemberton, 1973), chap. 3.

13. E. I. Carnell, *Christian Commitment* (New York: Macmillan, 1957), p. 134.

14. See, for example, Gordon Clark, *Religion, Reason and Revelation* (Philadelphia: Presbyterian and Reformed Publishing Company, 1961), pp. 221–41.

15. Adams, "Modified Theory," pp. 525–37.

16. See, for example, R.E.O. White, *Christian Ethics* (Atlanta: John Knox Press, 1981), pp. 124–35; Garth L. Hallet, *Christian Moral Reasoning* (Notre Dame, Ind.: University of Notre Dame Press, 1983), pp. 83–84, 114–15; E. Albert, T. Denise, and S. Peterfreund, *Great Traditions in Ethics,* 5th ed. (Belmont, Calif.: Wadsworth, 1984), pp. 106–25.

17. Gottfried Leibniz, *New Essays on the Human Understanding* (1765), book 1, chap. sec. 5.

18. See Norman Geisler, *The Christian Ethic of Love* (Grand Rapids, Mich.: Zondervan, 1973), pp. 76–127.

19. See Mark Talbot, "On Christian Philosophy," *Reformed Journal* 34 (September, 1984): 19–20.

20. John Hick, "The Philosophy of World Religions," *Scottish Journal of Theology* 37 (1984): 231–36.

21. Adams, "Modified Theory," pp. 535–37.

22. Jean-Paul Sartre, "The Humanism of Existentialism," in Burton Porter, ed., *Philosophy: A Literary and Conceptual Approach* (New York: Harcourt Brace Jovanovich, 1974), pp. 70–71.

23. Nielsen, *Ethics*, pp. 48, 64.

24. Ibid., pp. 86, 62.

25. Kai Nielsen, "On Religion and the Grounds of Moral Belief," *Religious Human- ism* II (Winter 1977): 33–34.

26. Nielsen, *Ethics*, p. 56.

27. Reichenbach, "Divine Command Theory," p. 230.

28. Pojman, *Ethics*, p. 191.

29. Hans Küng, *On Being a Christian* (Garden City, N.Y.: Doubleday, 1976), p. 75.

30. Some theists make a weaker claim. To Louis Pojman, for instance, "it seems plausible to assert that in some ways the world of the theist is better and more satisfying than one in which God does not exist." Ibid. p. 194.

31. See, for example, Alasdair MacIntyre, *After Virtue* (Notre Dame, Ind.: Notre Dame University Press, 1981); Stanley Hauerwas, *The Peaceable Kingdom* (Notre Dame, Ind.: University of Notre Dame Press, 1983).

32. Stanley Hauerwas, *The Peaceable Kingdom and A Community of Character* (Notre Dame, Ind.: University of Notre Dame Press, 1981).

33. Stanley Hauerwas, "God, Medicine and the Problems of Evil," *Reformed Journal* (April 1988): 19.

34. John D. Arras and Bonnie Steinbock, "Moral Reasoning in the Medical Con- text," in *Ethical Issues in Modern Medicine*, 4th ed., Arras and Steinbock (Palo Alto, Calif.: Mayfield Publishing Company, 1995), p. 28.

35. Alison M. Jaggar, "Feminist Ethics: Projects, Problems, Prospects," in *Feminist Ethics*, ed. Claudia Card (Lawrence: University of Kansas Press, 1991), p. 85.

36. Ibid., pp. 86, 91.

37. Ibid., p. 99.

38. Ibid., p. 98.

39. Arras and Steinbock, "Moral Reasoning," pp. 28–29.

40. Sally B. Purvis, *The Power of the Cross: Foundations for a Christian Feminist Ethic of Community* (Nashville, Tenn.: Abingdon Press, 1993), p. 14.

41. See, for instance, ibid.; Linda Woodhead, "Feminism and Christian Ethics," in *Women's Voices: Essays in Contemporary Feminist Theology*, ed. Teresa Elwas (London: Marshall Pickering, 1992); Marilyn J. Legge, *The Grace of Difference: A Canadian Femi- nist Theological Ethic* (Atlanta: Scholars Press, 1992); McClintock Fulkerson, *Changing the Subject: Women's Discourses and Feminist Theology* (Minneapolis: Fortress Press, 1994); Denise Lardner Carmody, *Virtuous Woman: Reflections on Christian Feminist Ethics* (Maryknoll, N.Y.: Orbis Books, 1992).

42. Woodhead, "Feminism," p. 58.

43. Purvis, *Power of the Cross*, pp. 13–14.

44. Woodhead, "Feminism," p. 58.

SUGGESTED READING

Carmody, Denise Lardner. *Virtuous Woman: Reflections on Christian Feminist Ethics* Maryknoll, N.Y.: Orbis Books, 1992.

Donagan, Allan. *The Theory of Morality*. Chicago: University of Chicago Press, 1977.

Frankena, William. *Ethics*. 2nd ed. Englewood Cliffs, N.J.: Prentice-Hall, 1973.

Fulkerson, Mary McClintock. *Changing the Subject: Women's Discourses and Feminist Theology.* Minneapolis: Fortress Press, 1994.

Gill, Robin. *A Textbook of Christian Ethics.* Edinburgh: T. & T. Clark, 1985.

MacIntyre, Alasdair. *After Virtue.* Notre Dame, Ind.: University of Notre Dame Press, 1981.

McClendon, James W., Jr. *Ethics: Systematic Theology.* Vol. 1. Nashville, Tenn.: Abingdon, 1986.

Mitchell, Basil. *Morality: Religious and Secular.* Oxford: Oxford University Press, 1980.

Nielsen, Kai. *Ethics Without God.* London: Pemberton, 1973.

Outka, Gene, and John P. Reeder, Jr., eds. *Religion and Morality.* Garden City, N.Y.: Anchor Books, 1973.

Pojman, Louis, ed. *Ethical Theory: Classic and Contemporary Readings.* Belmont, Calif.: Wadsworth, 1989.

Quinn, Philip. *Divine Commands and Moral Requirements.* Oxford: Oxford University Press, 1978.

CHAPTER 14

PHILOSOPHY AND THEOLOGICAL DOCTRINE: CAN PHILOSOPHY ILLUMINE RELIGIOUS BELIEF?

> I do not seek in order that I may believe, but I believe in order that I may understand.
>
> ST. ANSELM OF CANTERBURY (1033–1109)

As we have seen, philosophers continue to be interested in discussing basic religious concepts such as God's existence and attributes, religious experience, evil, and miracles. Moreover, there is an increasing interest in analyzing the relationship between religion and other disciplines: science, ethics, linguistics, and psychology. Historically, however, philosophers have also thought it important to help clarify and defend specific religious doctrines—for example, the Trinity or Incarnation. Such use of philosophy in the service of theology has become less common in modern times, but recently some philosophers of religion have once again turned their attention to specific theological doctrines. Typically, these philosophers are not trying to prove or establish these doctrines philosophically. Rather, in the spirit of Anselm, they assume a particular doctrine as a given topic of religious concern and set about to analyze its meaning and assess whether it can be affirmed by a rational person.

In this chapter, representative samples of this type of philosophical activity are presented. Specifically, we consider Thomas Morris's examination of the Incarnation of God in Jesus Christ, Philip Quinn's reevaluation of the classical understanding of Christ's atonement for sin, attempts by Eleonore Stump as well as by Michael Murray and Kurt Meyers to identify the purpose for petitionary prayer, Jonathan Kvanvig's and William Craig's consideration of the relationship between God's love and eternal damnation, and George Mavrodes' analysis of divine revelation.

Each of these philosophers is a Christian, and most discuss the doctrine in question primarily from within a Christian context. However, the discussions of prayer, eternal damnation, and divine revelation are also quite relevant to other religious traditions. It is also important to note that our primary goal is not to engage in a critical dialogue. For instance, our primary goal is not to determine the extent to which we believe the work considered illuminates what we see as the crucial philosophical questions related to the doctrines in question. Nor is it our primary goal even to offer a *comprehensive* critique of what has been produced. We do briefly assess the work of each philosopher, and at the end of the chapter we consider some recent comments about the value and appropriateness of this sort of philosophical activity. But our *primary* goal is simply to expose the reader to a rather new, exciting emphasis in contemporary analytic philosophy of religion.

THE INCARNATION

I believe in God the Father Almighty, Maker of heaven and earth; and in Jesus Christ his only Son our Lord.

Apostles' Creed

Historically, one of the most fundamental tenets of the Christian faith has been the Incarnation: the belief that God became human in the person of Jesus Christ. Specifically, it has been held that Jesus Christ was both *fully human* and *fully divine*. However, even some Christians have begun to question not only whether the Incarnation actually occurred but whether it is possible. Could one person be fully human and fully divine at the same time? Is it still possible for a rational, well-informed, intelligent person to accept this doctrine?

Recently, Thomas Morris (1952–) has attempted to respond to this question.[1] He makes it quite clear that his goal is not to prove that Jesus Christ was in fact fully human and fully divine or even to argue that all Christians ought to believe this is so. His main objective is to demonstrate that none of the criticisms of this belief has to date been successful and, thus, that belief in the traditional doctrine of the Incarnation remains rational.

As Morris points out, the most common current criticism of the Incarnation is that it is an incoherent concept. To say that a property of a thing or person is essential is to say that the thing or person in question could not be what it is without this property. For example, having three sides is an essential property of any triangle; nothing without this characteristic can be rightly called a triangle. And being unmarried is essential to being a bachelor. Married men sometimes claim to be bachelors, but none can actually be a bachelor.

But the essential properties of being human, some critics are now arguing, are incompatible with the essential properties of being divine. Humans are, for instance, essentially limited in power, restricted in knowledge, fleshly, and liable to sin, while God is essentially all-powerful, all-knowing, without a fleshly body, and unable to sin. Thus, one person could never be fully human and fully divine at the same time. This is no more possible than it is for a figure to be both fully a square and fully a circle at the same time.

The key to countering this criticism, Morris tells us, is to understand the distinction between a thing being *fully* what it is and *merely* what it is. For example, diamonds and turtles are both fully physical objects. That is, both possess all the essential properties of being a physical object: mass, spatiotemporal location, and so on. However, a turtle is not merely a physical object in the sense of being only a physical object. It has the properties of being animate and organic as well. In like fashion, we are told, an individual can be *fully* human without being *merely* human. Individuals are fully human if they have all the properties essential to being human—for example, the capacity to exercise power and the ability to formulate true beliefs and freedom of choice. Thus, Jesus, as well as we, can be considered fully human. And we are *merely* human in that we "possess all these properties plus some additional limitation properties as well, properties such as being less than omnipotent, less than omniscient, and so on." Jesus, however, was not *merely* human. He possessed all the properties essential to being human "but had higher properties as well, properties constitutive of deity." He was, for instance, all-powerful, all-knowing, and incapable of sin. Thus, Jesus was also fully God.[2]

However, if Jesus was fully divine, does not this commit us to saying that he was all-knowing, all-powerful, and omnipresent as he lay crying in his crib? Are we not committed to saying, for instance, that "the bouncing baby boy of Mary and Joseph [directed] the workings of the cosmos from his crib?" And does this not "sound just too bizarre for even a moment's consideration?"

The answer, Morris maintains, lies in reaffirming a distinction that Christians have held since the earliest times: that Jesus Christ, the God-Man, possessed "something like two distinct ranges of consciousness." The distinctively divine consciousness was all-knowing; it was aware of all that exists in the eternal mind of God. The distinctively earthly consciousness, on the other hand, "grew and developed as the boy Jesus grew and developed." This "range of consciousness, and self-consciousness, was thoroughly human, Jewish and first-century Palestinian in scope."

Moreover, Morris adds, the divine consciousness contained, but was not contained by, the earthly range of consciousness. That is, Jesus Christ's divine mind had full access to his earthly experiences. The divine mind knew, for example, exactly what would occur in the future. But the earthly consciousness did not have access to the divine mind—for example, did not know what would occur in the future. Thus, Jesus really was able to suffer temptation, doubt, and fear and to experience real intellectual and spiritual growth.

In short, although Jesus Christ was not two persons in one body, he was "one person with two natures, and two ranges of consciousness" and "in this doctrine," Morris maintains, there is "no apparent incoherence whatsoever."[3]

There exists, however, one other "major sort of objection" to which Morris believes he must respond. Both critics and "many prominent professors of Christian theology" have recently been emphasizing the fact that the doctrine of the Incarnation was originally developed within a prescientific perspective quite different from the one "modern scientifically minded people have today." Thus, they have concluded that ancient religious claims, which may well have made sense in their original context, can rightly be said to "have lost much, if not all, of their plausibility in the modern age."

In response, Morris first chides Christians for being so quick to relinquish or 'reinterpret' important doctrines on no better grounds than that those beliefs can appear to some secular critics to be somehow "out of step with the march of science." However, he is willing to grant that occasionally an interesting challenge of this sort does arise: for instance, the "geocentric challenge." It seems clear that the doctrine of the Incarnation was formulated during a time when "it was believed by great numbers of people, including the best educated, that we human beings live in a relatively circumscribed universe, the entirety of which has been created for the benefit of human life . . . [and] around which all else literally as well as figuratively revolves." In such a setting, of course, it would seem reasonable to assume that God would be so interested in earthly affairs that he would even appear among us. But, of course, we now know that we and our world are only a small, insignificant peripheral cog in a vast, complicated machine. Thus, the assumption that God would believe it important to become human and dwell among us loses much of its plausibility.

Morris, though, sees no reason to believe that God's attention and care cannot extend fully to every part of the universe and therefore views sheer size as an irrelevant consideration. Moreover, "it is simply wrong to think there to be a necessary link between spatial centrality and value." Accordingly, he concludes, "it is a bit surprising to find that a challenge to Christian belief which seems to have such widespread emotional appeal for critics has so little substance when examined closely."[4]

But if it is, then, possible for a rational person to believe in the Incarnation, how is it possible? On what grounds can a person be rational in maintaining that Jesus was literally God in human form? There is, Morris holds, no deductive or single inductive argument that can establish this fact. But, he asks, could there not be an innate human capacity that, when functioning properly, allows us to recognize God in various contexts? If so, then perhaps traditional Christians have just *seen* Jesus to be God Incarnate. That is, perhaps when Christians see the portrait of Jesus in the Gospels or experience what they take to be Jesus's presence in prayer or his transforming power in their lives, they simply find themselves believing that they are having experiences of God Incarnate. And from Morris's perspective, there is no reason to believe this is not actually the case. In fact, he feels it is perfectly reasonable to think this is so.

Of course, he acknowledges that for belief in the Incarnation to remain reasonable, one must be able to formulate sufficient responses to challenges. But he believes he has shown that the significant challenges to date fail. Thus, he concludes that there is no obstacle to accepting the rationality of the widespread Christian assumption that Jesus is God Incarnate.[5]

Not surprisingly, for those who believe that limited knowledge or power is an *essential* property of any fully human person, Morris's arguments carry little weight.[6] And because it is difficult to see how one would even begin to try to argue that there is a single *correct* conception of humanity, it is difficult to see how those who affirm a conception of full humanity different from Morris's could be proven wrong. However, Morris never claims to be arguing that all persons, even all Christians, must acknowledge that belief in the Incarnation is rational for them personally. He is arguing, rather, that it cannot be said that no rational person can affirm this doctrine, and thus he need establish only that his understanding of what it means for someone to be fully human is not, itself, incoherent. Not all are convinced he has done so. However, most grant that Morris's contribution to the philosophical discussion of the Incarnation is significant.

THE ATONEMENT

Having become the sin of all men, he washed away the sin of the human race.

St. Ambrose (339–397)

Christians have traditionally held that we are born separated from God because of the sin of the first humans—Adam and Eve—and can be reconciled to God only as a result of the suffering and death of Jesus Christ. But exactly what role did Christ's death play in reconciling humans to God? And why was it necessary? These are the types of questions that Philip Quinn (1940–) has considered. Specifically, he has been interested in analyzing Thomas Aquinas's position on these issues.[7]

Aquinas (c. 1224–1274) believed that the sin with which we are born has three effects on us. First, it stains our souls. We have a natural desire to turn away from God and to attempt to satisfy ourselves in ways that are contrary to both reason and divine law. In short, we are born not wanting to think and act as we should. Second, we are born in bondage to Satan (the devil). That is, not only do we have our own natural tendency to think and act improperly, but Satan is also able to influence us strongly. And, finally, our sin (both what we are born with and what we ourselves produce) deserves punishment because it is a transgression against the divine order of justice. In fact, since to be in sin is to have turned away from

God, and turning away from God is the ultimate insult to God's holiness, eternal punishment is the only appropriate "sentence." Or, stated even more simply, eternal punishment is the debt we owe God because of our sin.

God could, Aquinas believed, justly have freed humans from the debt of sin without any restitution being required. Specifically, since God alone is the one who has been wronged by our sins, God could have pardoned us without exacting a penalty. In other words, God could simply have canceled the debt, much as a grocer might simply cancel a debt rightly owed for food purchased on credit by a customer. However, since we do in fact owe a debt to God because of our sin, God is not unjust in requiring that the debt be paid. This does demonstrate that God is *severe,* but it is within God's moral rights to require restitution, just as it is within a grocer's rights to demand payment from a customer. Unfortunately, none of us can pay the debt for our own sins. We cannot collectively pay the debt for original (inherited) sin because no set of human acts can make up for the harm done to the whole of the human race by Adam's sin. Furthermore, we cannot individually pay the price for our own sins. We are finite, and, since God is infinite, any offense against God is infinite in magnitude. Thus, since God demanded that the debt for sin be paid and we as humans could not pay it, God's only option was to pay it himself, which was done through Christ's suffering and death. In fact, not only was Christ's death sufficient to pay the debt for all humanity; it was superabundant. That is, the dignity of Christ as an infinite being and the quality and amount of his love and the magnitude of the suffering he endured made his death a much more satisfactory payment than God's justice required.

Such an account of the atonement, Quinn is quick to point out, raises some obvious questions. For example, if Christ's suffering and death are not only sufficient but superabundant restitution for the sins of the whole human race, why does anyone need to suffer for his own sins? Why will anyone be in hell? Why do individuals suffer in this life?

Aquinas's answer, with which Quinn has no quarrel, is that although Christ's death was a sufficient payment, it must be appropriated by us. That is, to use a modern analogy, Christ's death functions much as does the power supply in a home. The power supply is normally more than enough to light all the lamps in a house. But the lamps will in fact be lit only if they are connected to the power source. In like manner, Christ's death was more than enough to pay our debt to God, but it will in fact function in this manner only if we make use of it, and the way humans come to appropriate or claim Christ's payment is through the sacraments— baptism, penance, and so on.[8]

But there are other questions to which Quinn believes Aquinas does not have adequate answers. First, Quinn is dissatisfied with the role that Satan plays in Aquinas's account. According to Aquinas, remember, we are in bondage to Satan. To be more specific, Aquinas believed that God justly allows Satan to punish us for our sins; yet he also believed that Satan unjustly holds us in bondage because the debt for sin is owed to God, not Satan. But it is not clear to Quinn that Aquinas can have it both ways. If we conceive of Satan serving as a sort of deputized punisher for God, then it cannot be said that Satan is inflicting the punishment unjustly. On the other hand, if Satan's punishment is actually unjustly inflicted, then it appears that God cannot justly allow it. The most reasonable way of avoiding this type of dilemma, Quinn concludes, is to give up the belief that Christ's atonement in some sense ransomed sinners from Satan and to think of the atonement solely in terms of the payment of a debt to God.[9]

Quinn is also concerned with the seemingly harsh consequences of Aquinas's view. For instance, since only those who have appropriated Christ's death through baptism can have the debt for original sin paid, and the punishment for unpaid original sin is exclusion from God's presence, it follows for Aquinas not only that all babies who die unbaptized are eternally excluded from heaven but also that all those who have never heard about God suffer the same fate. Quinn suggests that we consider modifying the conditions under which Christ's atonement can be appropriated. Specifically, he is sympathetic to the view that Christ's payment automatically applies to those who, through no fault of their own, lack either the ability or the opportunity to demonstrate faith in Christ.[10]

Quinn is most troubled, though, by Aquinas's belief that *Christ's* death can be viewed as an acceptable payment for *our* debt. In Aquinas's day, Quinn points out, monetary compensation was common for crimes, sometimes even for crimes as serious as murder. Given such a model of compensation, the idea of someone paying the debt for someone else's crime makes good sense. But we no longer view things this way, we are reminded. We might, for example, allow that a mother can pay her son's fine. But if her son has been sentenced to spend time in jail, she cannot pay his debt for him. Even if she volunteers to spend the required time in jail for him, *his* debt will not have been paid. Of course, it is possible that he will not be asked to serve his sentence because of ill health or a pardon. But even then, his debt will not have been paid. We are simply allowing the debt to remain unpaid. In other words, as Quinn sees it, our moral intuitions clearly tell us that the idea of one person actually absolving another person of his moral duty to pay for his crimes by volunteering to take his place no longer makes much sense.

Quinn is quick to acknowledge that our moral intuitions are fallible and, thus, could be mistaken. "But if they remain stable under reflection," we are told, "we should trust them." And he believes that after reflection we will continue to be convinced that a just punishment for a serious crime cannot be totally transferred to an innocent person. Thus, he doubts that it is rational to accept the idea of Christ's totally paying our justly incurred debt for us.[11]

But how then should we conceive of the atonement? Quinn offers us a "fable" to point the way to what he sees as a plausible modification of Aquinas's position.

> Suppose a great magnate makes his two sons stewards of the two finest farms on his estate. The elder son irresponsibly neglects and thus ruins his farm, but the younger son conscientiously makes his own farm flourish. As a result of his negligence, the elder son has come to deserve punishment at the hands of his father; it would be severe but just for the father to disinherit him if he does not restore the ruined farm to prosperity. Unfortunately, the elder son is not a good enough farmer to accomplish this task, even though he could have prevented the ruin of the farm if he had tried.
>
> Then the younger son wonderfully intervenes. Moved by love for his brother as well as by devotion to their father and the welfare of his estate, the younger son undertakes to restore the farm his brother has ruined. This new undertaking requires tremendous sacrifice from him: he now has to maintain one farm and rehabilitate another. But the sacrifices so works upon the father's heart that he is persuaded to be merciful rather than severe toward his elder son. He forgives his elder son for the damage he has done to the estate and does not disinherit him, even though the elder son has not himself repaired the damage.[12]

In this case, Quinn argues, there is still a sense in which it can be said that the younger son has paid his brother's debt. But it seems more accurate to say that the father was moved by his younger son's sacrifice to forgive the debt. And this, Quinn believes, is a plausible way to conceive of Christ's atonement. We do owe God a debt that God can justly demand us to pay but that we cannot pay alone. However, Christ's voluntary suffering and death for us has so moved God that God has decided not to be so severe with us. In other words, Christ's suffering and death does not pay our debt in whole; rather, it generates divine mercy. It leads God to forgive that part of the debt we cannot pay. Hence, Christ's suffering and death remain a necessary condition for reconciliation with God, as orthodoxy demands, but we need no longer view it as payment in full for our debt, which reason will not allow.[13]

Some Christians will be troubled by the "authority" Quinn gives to moral intuitions and rational argumentation. They will see in his comments a devaluation of the role of Scripture and tradition in the search for religious truth. Specifically, they will be troubled by his use of reason in interpreting Revelation. And other questions arise. For instance, if God was persuaded by the voluntary suffering of Jesus Christ on our behalf to be lenient with us, what are we to say about the voluntary suffering we do for one another? Does this, too, move God to leniency? But even those who disagree with his conclusions or methodology can appreciate the manner in which he highlights the important philosophical question of what constitutes just recompense.

PETITIONARY PRAYER

The effectual fervent prayer of a righteous man availeth much.

HOLY BIBLE (KJV)

Christians (and the proponents of many other religions) frequently petition God in the sense that they ask God to bring about events that they believe might not occur without direct divine assistance. God is often asked, for instance, to soothe a troubled mind, or to help reconcile the broken marriage of friends, or sometimes even to do such things as calm hurricanes or heal diseased bodies.

But why exactly do Christians approach God in this manner? At first glance, it might appear that the answer is obvious. We often petition our human parents because we need help and believe they can offer assistance. Christians believe God is their "heavenly parent," so it seems perfectly reasonable to assume that they will petition God for assistance in times of need.

However, the situation is actually much more complex. Let us suppose that a college student, Fred, is in need of money for his school bills and calls home to ask his parents for help. And let us further suppose that he is able to convince his parents to send the money. In this case, we can rightly maintain that Fred's petition was effective in the sense that it brought about something that otherwise probably would not have occurred. But what if Fred knows that the school has informed his parents about his bill, and what if they have repeatedly told him that they will meet his financial needs when they think it is best to do so? It then appears that a call by Fred is not capable of changing anything. It is *already* the case that his parents will do what they think is best. In fact, a call to his parents under these conditions could quite plausibly be read as displaying Fred's lack of confidence in his parent's integrity.

However, is this not exactly the situation in which Christians find themselves with respect to God? If God is all-knowing, then God does not need to be informed by prayer of *any* problematic situation. And if God is all-good, then God is surely willing to bring about anything that is really needed. Thus, it might appear that petitioning God is pointless or even displays a lack of faith. If what is requested is something that God—as an all-powerful, perfectly good being—believes should be brought about, will it not be brought about, regardless of whether someone has requested that it be done? On the other hand, if what is being requested is something God believes ought not be brought about, then will God not refrain from bringing it about, regardless of whether a request is made? For example, if God believes that it is best for Mary to be healed, then will God not heal her regardless of whether someone asks him to do so, whereas if God believes Mary should not be healed, will he not refrain from healing her in spite of any request that he intervene? In short, it might appear that while petitioning humans can often change things, petitioning God cannot. Petitioning God, it seems, makes sense only if the petitioner does not have confidence in God—does not believe that God will automatically always do what is best.

Eleonore Stump (1947–) is one of a number of philosophers of religion who have been thinking seriously about this dilemma.[14] God, she maintains, desires a loving, interactive relationship with us. But in any relationship between two individuals unequal in power and knowledge, it is possible for the more powerful to dominate or overwhelm the other in the sense of imposing his or her will on the less powerful. For example, it is very possible for a teacher who sees a child at academic risk to impose her will on the child (for instance, by calling the child's home or making the child stay after class) to the extent that she infringes on the child's autonomy. Moreover, it is also possible for the less powerful person to become spoiled in the sense that she becomes dependent on the more powerful or simply takes what is given for granted. A student, for example, who is always automatically offered all available help by a teacher may come to assume that she deserves nothing less and thus not appreciate the effort the teacher is expending.[15]

The same is true, Stump believes, with respect to the relationship between God and us. Since God is so much more powerful and knowledgeable than are we, it would be quite easy for God to impose his will on us to the point that we become simply slavish followers who lose "all sense of [our] own tastes and desires and will" or to furnish us with that which we need to the point where we become spoiled—where we come to depend upon, or even expect, God to do everything for us.[16]

However, petitionary prayer, she maintains, can be a safeguard against these dangers. Just as a teacher might at times refrain from helping a student until requested so as not to dominate the student, it seems reasonable to assume that God at times refrains from giving us all he can and desires to give us until petitioned in order to preserve our autonomy as independent creatures. And just as parents sometimes refrain from giving their children all that they would like to give them so as not to spoil them, it seems reasonable to assume that God at times refrains from automatically giving us all that he can and desires to give us so that we do not become indulgent or fail to appreciate the source of that which we receive.

This line of reasoning, by Stump's own admission, is less persuasive with respect to those petitions in which God is asked to help others in the sense that God is asked to intervene uninvited in the lives of others for their benefit. For in this case, she acknowledges, God can avoid the charge of oppressive meddling only if the person God has been asked to help comes to the place where he "has willing shared his thoughts and feelings and the like with God." But as a explanation for why God might refrain from intervening in a person's own life until assistance is requested, Stump's proposal has been considered by many quite plausible.[17]

Michael J. Murray (1963–) and Kurt Meyers (1971–) have recently suggested another reason that beneficial divine activity might sometimes be withheld until requested: namely, to help the petitioner learn more about, and thus become more like, God.[18] Human parents, they point out, sometimes use the opportunity to respond to their children's petitions to "teach their children what is right and important and what is not." By refraining from granting certain requests—for example, the request of a sixteen-year-old for a new red Corvette—"the parents indicate to the child that there are certain things that, for various reasons, are not in their interests, contrary to the child's belief." On the other hand, by granting certain requests—for example, a child's request for help in making a gift for a sick neighbor—parents have "the opportunity to foster important virtues in the child."[19]

The same basic principle, they maintain, may hold for the Christian and his or her heavenly parent: "The believer is enjoined not merely to pray for perceived needs but to do so with the sort of humility that permits her to say, 'Thy will be done.' If the request is granted, she not only has a need fulfilled; she has continued the process of learning what sorts of things are in accordance with God's will. Likewise, if the believer prays and her request is not granted, she learns that her desires are not in accordance with God's will."[20]

And by learning in this fashion about God's moral will, Murray and Meyers conclude, "the believer may in turn learn to become more righteous, and thus better conformed to the image of God."[21] They realize, of course, that we can learn about God's moral nature from what occurs after our petitions only to the extent that we can know with some degree of certainty that we are receiving (or not receiving) what we have requested as a result of a decision made by God and that this decision was made *primarily* because our request was consistent (or inconsistent) with his values—with how God would have us live. But, as they see it, there are contexts in which a petitioner "would surely be epistemically permitted, if not obligated, to believe that . . . God brought about (or failed to bring about) something that was petitioned for because He wanted things to come about in that way." And, in these cases, something about God's values could be learned.[22]

But questions remain. With respect to a prayer in which a petitioner fails to receive that which is requested, it is, of course, *possible* that this is so because the request was not consistent with God's values. But does not an *equally plausible* alternative always exists: that although what we requested was perfectly compatible with God's moral nature, God decided for some other reason—for instance, for the overall good of the petitioner or someone else—not to grant the request (at least at this time)?

On the other hand, a petitioner can learn something new about God's values *as a result of an answer* to her prayer only if she is not certain when the petition is offered whether a request of this type is in keeping with God's moral nature. But some believe that a necessary condition for maintaining that any occurrence has been brought about by God is that this event be compatible with God's moral nature. And if this is so, can answered prayer actually teach a petitioner anything new about God's values?

Moreover, while it seems reasonable to assume that God might at times withhold discretionary provisions—the "little extras"—to keep the petitioner from becoming spoiled or dominated, is it reasonable to assume that God would withhold basic provisions—for instance, not protect a person's life—solely or primarily for the purpose of "relationship maintenance"?[23]

Murray and Meyers have offered us an interesting, innovative response to the important question of why God would wait to act until requested to do so, a response that most agree deserves continued consideration.

GOD'S LOVE AND ETERNAL DAMNATION

He who believes in the Son has eternal life; but he who does not obey the Son shall not see life, but the wrath of God abides on him.

JOHN 3:36 (NASB)

Historically, orthodox Christians have claimed that while many will spend eternity heaven, others will eternally experience a conscious state of damnation (hell). However, if God is all-loving, he surely wants no one in hell, and if God is all-powerful, he can surely bring it about that no one will spend eternity in hell. Thus, how can the traditional concept of God be reconciled with eternal damnation?

Jonathan Kvanvig (1954–) is one of a number of philosophers who have recently considered this "problem of hell."[24] Some today still hold what Kvanvig identifies as the traditional Christian position: that God can justly consign certain individuals to hell as an eternal punishment for sin committed on earth. Kvanvig agrees that, since God is intimately and immediately related to the universe, violating moral obligations is an offense against God and hence merits his punishment. But he doubts that God could invoke any moral principle to justify his infliction of infinite punishment for sins committed on earth. Moreover, he doubts that God could justly impose the same infinite sentence for acts of significantly different moral seriousness—for example, the same sentence for individuals who sin with quite different intentions or whose actions produce quite different degrees of harm. Consequently, Kvanvig concludes that a view of hell in which some people are inescapably consigned to exist forever in hell as retribution for acts committed against God must be rejected.

Others have denied the finality of hell by providing people an escape based on their repentance while in hell. Kvanvig likewise thinks this fails, for even if people are eventually paroled from hell, this does not justify sending them to hell as punishment for sin in the first place. If hell is an unjust response for earthly sin, then it remains unjust, even if some ultimately escape punishment by "apologizing" for their earthly behavior.

Still others affirm versions of universalism: that a good, merciful, and powerful God will eventually "save" all persons. John Hick (1922–), for instance, suggests that following their earthly existence, those not rightly related to God will exist in self-reflective contexts that will allow them to become properly related to God.[25] Kvanvig rejects this alternative because he sees any attempt on God's part to guarantee universal salvation as coercive. It both restricts human freedom in that it requires all to acknowledge God as Lord and wrongly assumes that individuals will choose God once the impediments to knowledge are removed.

Finally, there are those who believe divine annihilation of the damned to be most just. Richard Swinburne, for example, agrees that God would not punish someone beyond what he or she deserves, and everlasting physical punishment would exceed such deserts, making God vindictive rather than just. But at the same time, Swinburne argues, there is no "point of keeping a totally corrupt being alive. He has lost the center of his being. There would be no point in giving him the 'vision' of God, for he could not enjoy it." And for such a person, Swinburne suggests, annihilation is appropriate, since God has no obligation to keep anyone in existence.[26] Kvanvig rejects this view because he sees divine annihilation as a kind of capital punishment, which for him is the ultimate punishment. And not all acts against God deserve this punishment.

Kvanvig's own justification for hell is based on his understanding of God's nature. God is essentially good, and as such he is committed to preserving both our existence and our rational freedom of choice (our ability to decide freely among options open to us). However, since we are dependent on God to sustain our existence, we ultimately have only two options: to freely accept dependence on God (which is to choose continued existence) or to reject dependence on God (which is to choose nonexistence). God sustains all persons (allows them to exist) for as long as necessary for them to come to the point where they can make a rational, settled choice between God and nonexistence. Those who choose God will remain in existence with God in the heavenly community. However, even though God is committed to preserving our existence, God is even more strongly committed to our rational freedom. Thus, those who ultimately make a rational choice to be independent of God (and thus choose not to exist) will be allowed by God to annihilate themselves in this fashion. Finally, some "may never get to the end of the road toward annihilation." Some may "eternally exist in hell," a state of existence that "is as bad as anything can be (compatible with God's perfect goodness)," and thus never come "to see the alternatives clearly or never chang[e] their opposition to the heavenly community, and yet never achiev[e] rationality for those beliefs or desires."[27]

To say that this is so, Kvanvig is quick to point out, is not to argue that anyone will or will not actually exist in the state of hell eternally. Nor is it to state that anyone in hell will in fact make the settled rational choice for annihilation or that anyone will in fact not do so. This is an empirical matter. To argue as he has, rather, is simply to explain how the concept of hell can be conceived of in a manner consistent with God's power and goodness.

In response, few question the value of love or that freely given love is preferable to coerced love. Some have questioned, though, whether freedom ought in this context always to be considered a higher value than existence. For instance, asks Frances Howard-Snyder (1963–), if we suppose that the highest state for human beings—to love God freely—cannot be guaranteed, "what, then, is the second highest state for us: freely arrived at rebellion against God, or coerced love of God? Why should we think that the former is preferable? Does freedom have infinite value, enough to outweigh the infinite evil of eternal separation from God?" And it is her belief that Kvanvig has not given us an adequate answer.[28]

Others will surely question the role of punishment in Kvanvig's perspective. Kvanvig maintains that his view does involve punishment in that, by choosing to reject God, individuals are deprived of a good. But it is questionable whether self-deprivation can be considered a punishment. Moreover, some may find in Kvanvig's rejection of hell as just punishment for sin what they consider an overemphasis on divine love at the expense of divine justice.

At the very least, though, Kvanvig has shown us that theists who believe both that hell is a punishment for those who have committed offenses against God and that God is loving and just have their work cut out for them. And he has surely offered us an interesting, thoughtful alternative conceptualization of hell and its relationship to God.

Many orthodox Christians, however, still reject the possibility that some individuals will be given the opportunity to accept God after death. That is, many continue to believe we must restrict the choice that will determine our eternal destiny to our earthly existence. Moreover, they believe that each person will exist eternally and inescapably in one of these two realms.

It seems an indisputable fact that many individuals have never had the opportunity to either accept or reject God's plan of salvation. Thus, an obvious question arises for such Christians: What is the eternal destiny of that sizable portion of humanity that has never heard the gospel?

One increasingly popular response is to maintain that in addition to God's self-revelation in Christ—God's Special Revelation—God has also revealed himself in nature—God's general revelation. Specifically, it is held God has so construed humans and the world that his existence as creator and sustainer is evident to everyone capable of accepting or rejecting him and that those who have never had meaningful access to the gospel will be judged on the basis of how they respond to that natural light that is available to them.

However, many who believe this to be so also believe that while God's natural revelation is sufficient to make all responsible for their eternal destiny, God's Special Revelation—the gospel—is more effective. That is, they believe that those who hear the gospel are much more likely to respond positively.[29] But if this is true, asks the philosopher William Craig (1949–), then why did a loving God not "supply special revelation to persons who, while rejecting the general revelation they do have, would have responded to the gospel of Christ if they had been sufficiently well-informed concerning it?"[30]

An intriguing response has recently been offered by Craig himself.[31] Craig believes that God knows before he makes any decision exactly what will occur given all of his options (that God possesses middle knowledge).[32] Thus, he begins by acknowledging an obvious question: If God knew before creation exactly what would occur given every creative option, why did he not create a world in which he knew all would be saved?

In response, Craig maintains that, if God could have created a world in which many individuals freely choose to accept him and none reject him, he certainly would have done so. But a theist can reasonably assume, Craig tells us, that in every world God could have actualized that contains many individuals who freely choose to accept God, there would also exist some individuals who freely choose to reject him. Moreover, it is reasonable to believe that all of those individuals who have not responded positively to God in the world God has chosen to create—and are thus bound for hell—are individuals who God knows, via middle knowledge, "would not freely receive Christ under any circumstances"—for example, "no matter how much the Spirit of God [had] worked on their hearts, no matter how favorable their upbringing [had been], no matter how many times and ways they [had] heard the gospel."[33]

Accordingly, Craig concludes, the Christian who acknowledges that some who have never heard the gospel will spend eternity in hell need not resort to "afterlife opportunities" to defend God's goodness. For, given the plausible creative scenario just outlined, the theist can reasonably assume that all "who would want to be saved will be saved" during their earthly existence.[34]

An increasing number of orthodox Christians, however, question whether God does or even can possess middle knowledge—that is, whether God does or even can know ahead of time exactly what will happen given all of his creative options.[35] And, given Craig's position, the question of why a God who could not create a world in which none would go to hell would have created any world containing free creatures remains.

There is clearly an increasing desire within the orthodox Christian community to defend God's goodness by offering plausible explanations for seemingly questionable divine behavior. And Craig appears to have made a meaningful contribution to the ongoing attempt to clarify the relationship between God's love and the eternal fate of "those who have never heard."

REVELATION

It is expedient to have . . . what God has revealed, in addition to the philosophical researches pursued by human reasoning.

THOMAS AQUINAS

Many theists have a healthy respect for human reason. They normally see our ability to do such things as observe, hypothesize, test, deduce, and create as a gift from God that enables us to discover a great deal of useful information about our world. They are quite willing to grant, for example, that human reason has enabled us to conquer many dreaded diseases and produce inventions that have made life easier. And many are even willing to grant, as we have seen, that human reason can discover some moral and religious truths.

However, as we have also seen, many hold that some religious knowledge is not acquired by the use of reason but is revealed in some other way. It is often held, for example, that some information about how we can come to know God or how we ought to live is known only because it has been *revealed* to us by God, apart from rational considerations. But what exactly are we to make of this concept of revelation? Is direct divine revelation of this sort possible? And if so, what forms might it reasonably be said to take? These are the types of questions with which George Mavrodes (1926–) has recently grappled.[36]

If we define revealed theology as that religious truth that lies beyond the range of reason, then, as Mavrodes sees it, three distinct models of revelation emerge. First, there is the *Causation Model,* within which "revelation" is used to label what has traditionally been called *innate knowledge* (truth not acquired from our ordinary encounters with the ordinary world). The claim that some religious knowledge is innate, we are told, can be understood in two ways. One can claim that the theist has the type of innate knowledge described in Plato's Socratic discussion (in the *Meno*) of a slave boy and geometry. Socrates begins to converse with a slave boy who has had no exposure to geometry. But in response to persistent questions by Socrates about the areas of various squares, the boy begins to display a rather sophisticated knowledge of this subject matter, a phenomenon that Plato explains by arguing that the boy was "born" with this knowledge in the form of a dormant memory that was simply brought to consciousness by Socrates' questions.

In a similar fashion, Mavrodes explains, theists such as Descartes have held that certain types of religious information—for example, the concept or idea of God—are in our intellect when it comes into existence.

But there is, he informs us, another way in which theists have held that religious information can be innate. John Calvin (1509–1564), for example, apparently did not believe that God directly implanted in us the idea of the divine. What he seemed to believe, rather, is that God implanted in the human intellect the natural disposition to believe that there is a God, a disposition activated by a variety of natural sensations—for example, by "seeing the blazing beauty of the sky on a clear night."

Is it possible that we acquire religious content in either of these innate fashions? Of course, Mavrodes grants, if one believes there is no God, then one will rightly hold that no such revelation can occur. But if there is a God, he contends, then there appears to be no good reason to deny that one way in which we acquire certain beliefs about God is that God has "implanted" these beliefs in us or created us with the natural tendency to form such beliefs under the appropriate conditions.[37]

Mavrodes then turns his attention to what he labels the *Manifestation Model* of revelation. The key to understanding this model, we are told, is the distinction between *claiming* that something is the case and *manifesting* or exhibiting this fact. Bill might, for example, *claim* that he can speak English by passing Mary a note that says this is so. But Bill would *manifest* or exhibit this ability by actually speaking English in Mary's presence. Applied to divine revelation, this allows us to distinguish between God's claiming (revealing) that he exists—for example, by bringing it about that this is written in the Bible—and God's manifesting (revealing) his existence by allowing us to have "something like an *experience* of God, a sort of perception, or quasi-perception of the divine presence."[38]

Mavrodes's first task in this context is to specify further the types of manifestation that this model might include. In almost all such cases God is clearly the revealer, but many things can plausibly be said to be revealed, sometimes by the very same act. Just as "the eavesdropper, when he steps from behind the drapery, may with equal propriety be said to reveal *himself*, to reveal his presence, and to reveal *that he is there*," there is no reason to think that God could not by some act—for instance, by making himself present to us in a time of need—reveal *himself* and *his presence* and that he is *there or that he is good*.

But even if we believe that God exists and can reveal himself and information about himself in this fashion, how are we to know that we have really experienced a manifestation of God? "What is it about an experience that warrants that belief?" Mavrodes explores two possibilities. Perhaps we have a means of recognizing God's presence that is analogous to the way we recognize a friend's presence without being able "to describe that way in any satisfactory and illuminating manner." Or perhaps we have no *way* of recognizing God's presence in the sense that we recognize it by doing something else—for example, consciously or subconsciously utilizing some line of reasoning. Perhaps it is simply a basic cognitive act. That is, perhaps we simply have the spiritual capacity for recognizing God, just as we have the physical capacity for recognizing trees. And if we are "God's creatures, it also seems plausible . . . to suppose," Mavrodes concludes, "that this capacity, if [we] indeed [have] it, is part of His endowment to [us]."[39]

Finally, Mavrodes turns to the most prominent model of revelation: the *Communication Model*, within which God is viewed as revealing himself by *speaking* with us in much the same sense we speak with one another. And here Mavrodes's strategy is basically to respond to criticisms or potential misunderstandings.

Some have argued that communicating with humans is beneath the dignity of God. But to this Mavrodes replies simply that "if God in fact speaks to men and women, then . . . so much the worse for any conception of the divine nature with which such speaking is incompatible." In fact, he doubts that this type of revelation need even be restricted to important theological and religious truth: It is "a real possibility . . . that God is just not as spiritually minded as are some theologians."

Others have argued that divine revelation might somehow damage human autonomy. After all, if we are spoon-fed important information by the author of truth, what need is there for us to utilize our own powers of thought? But again Mavrodes is not impressed. First, it seems obvious to him that many reject what God reveals. And even in those cases in which divine communication is accepted as such, "there seems to be no appreciable damage to human autonomy and initiative." Perhaps, he acknowledges, if God were to reveal every important fact to us, our natural human activities might be inhibited. But most theists hold that God reveals only some things. And just as we need not suppose that the autonomy of chemists is damaged by the fact that they rely on the accuracy of the labels on the bottles of chemicals they utilize, we need not suppose that the autonomy of theists is damaged by the fact that they rely on *some* important divine information about fundamental aspects of reality.[40]

Finally, Mavrodes takes up the question of whether God *can* in fact communicate to us personally through other persons or things—for example, through stories in the Bible or events in our lives or the lives of others. Specifically, can God communicate more to us personally than we might receive simply by taking the relevant stories or events at face value? The answer, he believes, is yes. In fact, he thinks this may be the work of the Holy Spirit.

But what reason other than the testimony of others do we have for believing that such mediated communication actually occurs? We do in fact have little to go on, Mavrodes grants, as long as we ourselves never hear (or recognize) the voice of God. But if we do hear that voice, "then we can make our own stab" at determining how God's voice has come to us.[41]

There are, of course, important philosophical issues that Mavrodes has chosen not to consider in detail. What is the proper relationship between reason and revelation? How does one identify a divine revelation as such? Moreover, there is one important issue that is not discussed at all. Almost all religions believe that God has revealed himself to us in the ways Mavrodes indicates. However, the revelations of the major religions do not simply differ in many ways; they are at points clearly incompatible. Even within the same religious perspective, significant revelatory differences appear. For example, some conservative Christians clearly find God revealing in Scripture that it is always wrong to use life-threatening force or that one must be baptized to be "saved," while others find just the opposite. In fact, wars have been fought over such issues. Why is this so? What does this say, specifically, about the plausibility of believing that any one of us has actually received a divine revelation or that we have interpreted it correctly?

Few will deny, however, that there is much of value in what Mavrodes has done. The first step in any philosophical analysis is to clarify the meaning of the concepts in question, and no other philosopher has recently attempted to clarify in such detail the various meanings of "divine revelation."

DOCTRINE AND INTERPRETATION

As we indicated at the beginning of this chapter, the philosophers currently under consideration are not trying to *prove or establish* the theological doctrines they discuss but rather to *analyze* their meaning and determine whether a rational person can affirm them. And this is surely an important goal. That is, it is important for all theists to understand what the doctrines they hold actually mean and to identify the conditions under which they can justifiably continue to hold them. It is important as well for those who are not theists to be able to understand the logic and import of these doctrines.

It is equally important, however, to remember that there is a related and even more fundamental task facing theists (including all philosophers who are theists). What has been clarified and defended in almost every case in this chapter is the orthodox (classical, traditional) interpretation of the doctrines in question. However, all of these doctrines are currently subject to a wide variety of interpretations. Views on the Incarnation, for example, range all the way from the traditional claim that Jesus Christ was fully human and fully God to the contention that Jesus was a man who received divine insight to the highest degree humanly possible. Views on scriptural revelation range from the claim that God directly dictated every word to the contention that the text at best contains the most illuminating human thoughts about God to date. Views on the efficacy of petitionary prayer range from the claim that this activity is primarily for the psychological benefit of the petitioner to the contention that our petitions are primarily intended to "change God's mind." And views on the Atonement range from the traditional claim that Christ died to "pay the price for sin" to the claim that Christ's death was a moral example of what divine love can lead one person to do for another.

Accordingly, while it is perfectly acceptable for a theist to clarify and defend a given interpretation of one of these doctrines, it is also important to emphasize that theists (including philosophers who are theists) cannot concern themselves solely or even primarily with this endeavor. As the philosophers discussed in this chapter would be the first to admit, theists need also to engage in the often complex task of determining exactly which interpretation (or set of interpretations) is actually most worthy of clarification and defense.[42]

STUDY QUESTIONS

1. Try to state in your own words the distinction Thomas Morris draws between an individual being *fully* human and *merely* human. Do you think this distinction resolves the problem it is intended to address?

2. Do you believe that Jesus Christ was fully human and fully divine? If not, could any person have both of these properties simultaneously?

3. Philip Quinn's moral intuitions tell him that one person cannot, by volunteering to take someone's place, absolve that other person of her obligation to pay for a crime. Do you agree? Why?

4. What is your response to Quinn's own model of Atonement?

5. Both Jonathan Kvanvig and William Craig attempt to explain how a good God could allow some who do not hear the gospel before they die to spend eternity in hell. Do you personally find either explanation to be reasonable?

6. Can you think of other ways in which a theist might respond to the seeming tension between God's love and the eternal damnation of (even some of) those "who have never heard the gospel"?

7. Many theists maintain both that God is in total control of earthly affairs and that prayer changes things. Can both beliefs justifiably be affirmed at the same time?

8. What do you think of Eleonore Stump's "solution" to the problem of petitionary prayer? Do you consider it stronger than the solution offered by Murray and Meyers?

9. Compare and contrast George Mavrodes's three models of Revelation. Which one seems to you most significant?

10. Do you believe there are many different written revelations that come from God? Why is the same written revelation often subject to so many different interpretations? Should this fact bother a theist?

NOTES

1. Thomas V. Morris, "Rationality and the Christian Revelation," in *Anselmian Explorations* (Notre Dame, Ind.: University of Notre Dame Press, 1987), pp. 213–41; also Morris, *The Logic of God Incarnate* (Ithaca, N.Y.: Cornell University Press, 1986).

2. Morris, *Anselmian Explorations* pp. 219–22.

3. Morris, *Anselmian Explorations* p. 224.

4. Morris, *Anselmian Explorations* p. 229.

5. Morris, *Anselmian Explorations* pp. 239–41.

6. Two representative critiques of Morris on this point can be found in Bruce Reichenbach, *Christian Scholar's Review* 16 (September 1986): 77–79, and Eleonore Stump, *Faith and Philosophy* 6 (April 1989): 218–23.

7. Philip L. Quinn, "Aquinas on Atonement," in *Trinity, Incarnation and Atonement*, ed. Ronald Feenstra and Cornelius Plantinga Jr. (Notre Dame, Ind.: University of Notre Dame Press, 1990).

8. Ibid., pp. 164–65.

9. Ibid., pp. 167–69.

10. Ibid., pp. 169–71.

11. Ibid., pp. 171–74.

12. Ibid., pp. 174–75.

13. Ibid., pp. 175–76.

14. Eleonore Stump, "Petitionary Prayer," *American Philosophical Quarterly* 16 (April 1979): 81–91.

15. This illustration is not explicitly found in Stump's discussion but is consistent with it.

16. Stump, p. 180. In an analogous manner, Vincent Brummer notes that if God did not in some cases provide for us only upon request, our relationship with God would become depersonalized in the sense that we would have no need to share our desires with him. See *What Are We Doing When We Pray?* (London: SCM Press, 1984), p. 47.

17. This synopsis of Stump's position is a variation on what first appeared in David Basinger, *The Case for Freewill Theism* (Downers Grove, Ill.: InterVarsity Press, 1996), chap. 5.

18. Michael J. Murray and Kurt Meyers, "Ask And It Will Be Given To You," *Religious Studies* 30 (1994): 311–30.

19. Ibid., 319.

20. Ibid.

21. Ibid.

22. Ibid., pp. 321–22. This synopsis of Murray and Meyers's position is a modified version of what first appeared in David Basinger, "A Response to Murray and Meyers," *Religious Studies* 31 (1995): 475–84.

23. See Basinger, "A Response to Murray and Meyers."

24. Jonathan Kvanvig, *The Problem of Hell* (New York: Oxford University Press, 1993).

25. John Hick, *Death and Eternal Life* (San Francisco: Harper and Row, 1976), p. 41.

26. Richard Swinburne, *Responsibility and Atonement* (Oxford: Clarendon Press, 1989), p. 182.

27. Kvanvig, *Problem of Hell*, pp. 152, 155.

28. Frances Howard-Snyder, "Jonathan Kvanvig: The Problem of Hell," *Faith and Philosophy* 12, no. 3 (1995): 449.

29. Neal Punt, *What's So Good About the Good News* (Chicago: Northland Press, 1938), pp. 93–101.

30. William Lane Craig, " 'No Other Name': A Middle Knowledge Perspective on the Exclusivity of Salvation through Christ," *Faith and Philosophy* 6 (April 1989): 185.

31. William Lane Craig, *The Only Wise God* (Grand Rapids: Baker Book House, 1987), chap. 12; see also Craig, " 'No Other Name' ", pp. 172–88.

32. See Chap. 4 in this book for a fuller discussion of this form of omniscience.

33. Craig, *The Only Wise God*, p. 147.

34. Craig, "No Other Name," p. 185.

35. See, for instance, William Hasker, *God, Time and Knowledge* (Ithaca, N.Y.: Cornell University Press, 1989), chap. 2.

36. George I. Mavrodes, *Revelation in Religious Belief* (Philadelphia: Temple University Press, 1988).

37. Ibid., pp. 73–74.

38. Ibid., p. 75.

39. Ibid., pp. 105, 106, 109.

40. Ibid., pp. 116, 125–26.

41. Ibid., pp. 130–52, 153.

42. See, for example, James Keller, "Reflections on a Methodology for Christian Philosophers," *Faith and Philosophy* 5, no. 2 (1988): 144–58.

SUGGESTED READING

Alston, William. "Christian Experience and Christian Belief." In *Faith and Rationality: Reason and Belief in God*. Edited by Alvin Plantinga and Nicholas Wolterstorff. Notre Dame, Ind.: University of Notre Dame Press, 1983.

Brummer, Vincent. *What Are We Doing When We Pray?* London: SCM Press, 1984.

Feenstra, Ronald J., and Cornelius Plantinga Jr., eds. *Trinity, Incarnation, and Atonement*. Notre Dame, Ind.: University of Notre Dame Press, 1988.

Hick, John. "The Logic of God Incarnate." *Religious Studies* 25 (December 1989): 409–23.

Jantzen, Grace. "Incarnation and Epistemology." *Theology* 83 (May 1983).

Kvanvig, Jonathan L. *The Problem of Hell*. New York: Oxford University Press, 1993.

Morris, Thomas. *The Logic of God Incarnate*. Ithaca, N.Y.: Cornell University Press, 1986.

Quinn, Philip. "Christian Atonement and Kantian Justification." *Faith and Philosophy* 3 (1986): 440–62.

Swinburne, Richard. *Responsibility and Atonement*. Oxford: Clarendon Press, 1989.

———. Revelation. Oxford: Clarendon Press, 1991.

Talbot, Thomas. "The Doctrine of Everlasting Punishment." *Faith and Philosophy* 7 (1990): 19–42.

Van Inwagen, Peter. *God, Knowledge and Mystery: Essays in Philosophical Theology*. Ithaca, N.Y.: Cornell University Press, 1995.

Walls, Jerry. *Hell: The Logic of Damnation*. Notre Dame, Ind.: University of Notre Dame Press, 1992.

Wolterstorff, Nicholas. *Divine Discourse*. Cambridge: Cambridge University Press, 1995.

CHAPTER 15 THE CONTINUING
QUEST: GOD
AND THE
HUMAN VENTURE

The Oxford philosopher J. L. Mackie (1917–1981) writes:

> It is my view that the question whether there is or is not a god can and
> should be discussed rationally and reasonably, and that such discussion
> can be rewarding, in that it can yield definite results. This is a genuine,
> meaningful question, and an important one—too important for us to take
> sides about it casually or arbitrarily. Neither the affirmative nor the nega-
> tive answer is obviously right, but the issue is not so obscure that relevant
> considerations of argument and evidence cannot be brought to bear upon
> it.[1]

These words begin Mackie's book, *The Miracle of Theism.* As the title suggests, Mackie takes it to be astonishing—or, to speak in hyperbole, "miraculous"—that theism has endured for centuries as a credible idea in the
minds of intelligent people. For him, when the arguments and evidence
are fairly evaluated, it is more reasonable to believe that theism is false
than that it is true.

Mackie echoes the judgment of numerous influential philosophers,
both past and present: Lucretius (c. 99–55 B.C.), David Hume (1711–1776),
Friedrich Nietzsche (1844–1900), W. K. Clifford (1845–1879), Bertrand Russell (1872–1970), Antony Flew (1923–), Michael Martin (1932–), William
Rowe (1931–), and many more. On the other side, there have been equally
distinguished philosophers who think that, when all of the relevant considerations are weighed, it is indeed rational to believe that theism is true.
The names of Augustine (354–430), Anselm (1033–1109), Aquinas (c.1224–
1274), René Descartes (1596–1650), Richard Swinburne (1934–), William
Alston (1921–), and Alvin Plantinga (1932–) merely begin the list of highly
esteemed theistic philosophers.

As we have seen throughout this book, a host of important issues is relevant to a full-scale discussion of theism: the significance of religious experience, the viability of arguments for and against God's existence, the question of whether rational argument is relevant or necessary to the acceptance of theism, the problem of how religious statements are meaningful, the difficulty of making sense of the concept of miracle, the extent to which the plurality of other religious belief systems affects the appraisal of theism, and many more. Other areas of philosophy that have a bearing on issues in religion are also relevant. Such considerations provide a basis for informed discussion about the overall acceptability or unacceptability of theism.

THE INTELLECTUAL PROCESS

All of the issues related to theism that we have discussed—religious experience, miracles, evil, and the like—are of enduring interest. Every generation and every thoughtful person must raise and ponder them afresh. Fortunately, we are not without help in our intellectual investigation of religion, since great thinkers of past and present have left for us a legacy on which to build. They have helped to clarify the main problems, identify the options, show where burdens of proof lie, and find the most reasonable positions. We need the wisdom of past and present in addition to the best thinking we can bring to the task.

In other words, we have been engaging in a great dialogue, a dialogue that inquiring minds have carried on for centuries. It will continue as long as people raise philosophical questions regarding religious belief. This is an exciting intellectual process of argument and counterargument, of carefully considering alternatives, and of trying to gain insight into the issues surrounding religious belief. This text itself stands, as do other classic and contemporary works in the philosophy of religion, as a refutation to all those who say that human reason cannot meaningfully consider matters of religion. All important issues in human life must be subject to responsible, reflective reason. This holds for beliefs associated with a particular theistic religion and beliefs drawn from theistic religions generally and beliefs maintained by nontheistic religions. If religious beliefs are not subject to the earnest, objective approach of reason, then prospects for the human venture are bleak indeed.

But if rational analysis is appropriate, are there limits to the philosophical investigation of religious belief? The answer here depends on precisely how one takes the question. If the question is about *psychological* limits, the answer may well be *yes*. Obviously, each individual or personality type will have some idiosyncratic limitations. There may be points at which a given individual's cultural background, family upbringing, religious convictions, capacity for abstract thought, and the like will produce real limitations. There may even come a point at which a particular person simply says that she can press the investigation no further.

Yet if the question is whether there are *theoretical* limits (or perhaps *logical* limits) to the rational investigation of religious belief, then the answer must be *no*. In principle, there is no fixed terminus or predetermined point at which investigation must stop. We may grant that certain individuals reach their own idiosyncratic limits, and these vary widely among people. However, we must also recognize a fundamental a lesson of intellectual history: when someone declares a limit to thought in some area of human endeavor, someone else eventually goes beyond it. No person or group can prescribe for others the limits to their rational search, not even in matters of religion.

Some will object that the vast mystery of God or Brahman or Nirvana or some other Ultimate Reality is inaccessible to finite human minds. Even if God is beyond our thoughts in certain respects, rational investigation is simply an inquiry into *concepts* of God and *beliefs* about God. It is the enterprise of trying to make our thoughts about God and related subjects clear and coherent, informed, and reasonable. God may well be infinite, but concepts and beliefs about God are not infinite and are entirely open to rational investigation.

To maintain, though, that there are no theoretical limits to the examination of religious belief is not to say that the process is in any way infallible or complete. The nature of the human rational quest seems to be that of bringing our best thinking to bear upon the problems we face, realizing full well that our results are tentative and incomplete, revising and moving ahead cautiously. Yet this process is all we have. Even if some revelation is true or if a certain religious vision is authentic, its credentials still must be rationally evaluated, and it must stand or fall in light of the arguments and evidence. The recognition of our own fallibility, as well as the strong proclivity of some religious dogmatists to claims of infallibility, suggests to us that the hope is brightest for progress when we strive hard for objectivity, fairness, and tolerance.

PHILOSOPHICAL ACTIVITY AND RELIGIOUS FAITH

Although many will admit that religion is subject to rational appraisal, some would insist that the results of philosophical inquiry are irrelevant or antithetical to authentic religious faith. Some will claim, for instance, that the sacredness of the subject makes critical, penetrating inquiry disrespectful or blasphemous or that it encourages unwholesome doubt. But while the subject matter may be deemed sacred, every major religion recognizes and encourages responsible thought. The major world religions have long histories of debate and discussion of their key doctrines and themes. Besides, nothing encourages intractable doubts as much as forbidding free and open inquiry. Or consider the opening words of Pascal's Memorial (dated November 23, 1654), which make a strict distinction between "the God of Abraham, God of Isaac, God of Jacob," on the one hand, and the God of the "philosophers and scholars," on the other. For Pascal (1623–1662) and for many other people, even if the existence of God could be validly inferred from acceptable premises, it would be of merely academic interest. Deeply religious people often claim that they already live in a dynamic relationship with God and that rational argument and other intellectual exercises are therefore patently beside the point. The proper response to their claim runs along two lines.

First, it is quite right to distinguish carefully between philosophical activity, on the one hand, and vital religious faith, on the other. *Philosophical* interest in God is simply different from *religious* interest in God, a different mode of human activity. In general, we can say that engaging in rigorous analysis and argument is neither a necessary nor a sufficient condition for a robust religious faith. Philosophical understanding is not a *necessary condition* for faith because some persons may not have the mental ability to engage in the sophisticated intellectual study of religion—and thus cannot produce any persuasive argument for, say, the existence of God—and yet may clearly possess religious faith.

Second, some persons may be quite skilled in philosophical matters and able to advance impressive arguments in favor of God's existence and not have religious faith at all. They might be intellectually persuaded, for example, that Christianity is true and yet not commit themselves to or find themselves in relation to the God worshiped in that religion. Likewise, a person might be intellectually persuaded that Hinduism is true and yet not be personally devoted to Shiva or Vishnu. The same holds for all who merely assent to the truth of other religions. Thus, the philosophical examination of religion is not a *sufficient condition* for religious faith, either.

While the rigorous philosophical examination of religion is neither necessary nor sufficient for religious faith, we must not suppose that faith is entirely divorced or separated from the rational process. It seems, rather, that religious faith (conceived as trust in a divine being and the like) is predicated on at least some amount of rational thought—and perhaps on more thought than some might initially suspect. The particular form of rational thought involved is belief that a statement or proposition is true. Many such beliefs that are taken to be true constitute a religious believer's set of intellectual commitments, conscious or unconscious.

As we have seen, having faith in God involves having certain beliefs about God and how God relates to the world. Granted, many ordinary religious believers may not be fully conscious of their own beliefs or may not critically attend to those beliefs when acting as one of the faithful. However, those beliefs are present and operative nonetheless, and much the same general rules and constraints for reasonable believing apply to them as to other human beliefs. This point is often punctuated when some religious believers realize that their own intellectual integrity depends on having their beliefs conform to some basic standards of rationality. They intentionally decide to probe and make good sense of their beliefs, to have their beliefs comport well with both *logic* and *fact*. Their religious faith is not, as Mark Twain once remarked, "believin' what you know ain't so."

Whether or not religious believers are aware of the beliefs that under-gird their faith, these beliefs can nonetheless be abstracted and system-atized for philosophical study and reflection. Philosophy of religion applies standard methods of analysis and argument, as well as the insights from metaphysics, epistemology, and other fields of philosophy, to these ab-stracted beliefs. Of course, this means that such concerns as consistency, coherence, and correspondence to the facts really do pertain to religious believing. It means that matters of plausibility and truth are relevant. But then, it is possible for religious believers, wittingly or unwittingly, to vio-late these intellectual standards.

This is true not only of religious believers but also of nonbelievers who fail to recognize the intellectual or belief component of faith. Nonbe-lievers can mistakenly characterize faith as purely emotional response or as socially conditioned behavior and thus fail to perceive the underlying beliefs that are appropriately subject to intellectual investigation. These persons may reject religious belief without engaging in a responsible ratio-nal process. Thus, anyone—believer or nonbeliever—considering the via-bility of a religious perspective must maintain a conscientious respect for the general intellectual standards that philosophy employs. It is these kinds of rational considerations that figure prominently into the decision as to whether a religious faith is sensible and warranted or confused and misguided.

WHERE DO WE GO FROM HERE?

We have just scratched the surface of the philosophy of religion in the preceding chapters. Each issue could be pursued in much more depth and detail. As one moves beyond the standard core of issues presented here, other fascinating topics arise and provide material for further consider-ation of *classical theism*. For example, the problem relating to divine action in the world would be interesting to pursue in light of the theistic concept of God and our ordinary concepts of agency. Another fascinating topic to pursue at greater length would be that of the "hiddenness of God."

There are still other kinds of topics for philosophers of religion to treat, topics that pertain more specifically to the doctrines and beliefs unique to specific historic religions. Many key theological conceptions within Christianity—such as creation, heaven, hell, and forgiveness—need further philosophical attention in the vein and spirit of our Chapter 14.[2] Although it is rarely done among current philosophers of religion, it would also be enlightening to apply philosophical analysis to important religious activities. Within Christianity, say, liturgy and the Eucharist appear to be fertile ground for philosophical attention.[3]

Another area for philosophers of religion to explore is the relationship between philosophy and theology. Although philosophy and theology had an intimate relationship in the medieval period, dialogue between philosophers and theologians since modern times has become problematic. This is in part because of differences in how the assumptions and methods of their two disciplines are conceived.[4] Theologians claim revelation as the final authority and arbiter in religious matters, whereas philosophers recognize only reason. One interesting controversy revolves around the use of modern logical techniques and conceptual analysis by philosophers and the insistence by theologians that such methods cannot do justice to human experience and history. Although the insulation of the two fields of theology and philosophy continues in many quarters, there are encouraging signs that some thinkers are attempting to break down old barriers.[5]

While many theologians—particularly those associated with historical theology and biblical exegesis—have largely avoided contact with academic philosophy, other theologians have consciously shaped their perspectives around certain philosophical concepts. These "new theologies" cover a wide range: *process theology, liberation theology, feminist theology, environmentalist theology, postmodern theology,* and other new theologies supply the substance for much philosophical thought and reflection.[6]

The philosophical scrutiny of other major religious conceptions offers another direction for further study and reflection. For example, some specific nontheistic religion—its particular beliefs and living practices—could be a fruitful object of philosophical scrutiny. In this text, for example, Hindu pantheism (or panentheism) was mentioned from time to time for the primary purposes of comparison and contrast with Western theism. But it would be wholly appropriate for a text analogous to this one to be written on the religious beliefs emerging primarily from Hinduism. A more complete treatment of Hindu beliefs would, for example, discuss the precise shape of the problem of evil as it arises for Hinduism. Also, the implications of the Hindu belief system for human morality could be traced out. Fundamental Hindu theological conceptions—such as *karma* and *samsara*—could be analyzed and their logical structure clarified.[7] In fact, it would be possible to provide a careful, philosophical treatment of the beliefs of any other world religion following the approach used in this book. Of course, one complicating factor, which is of great philosophical interest itself, is the fact that each major religion has its own philosophical tradition, a tradition that may not endorse the approach we have used.[8]

Ideally, the serious study of religion will lead one eventually to other disciplines: anthropology, sociology, and psychology. The additional perspectives that these other disciplines offer on the complex reality of religion allow the philosophical scrutiny of religion to be relevant and informed. In fact, the whole question of the bearing of these other disciplines on religion or on the philosophy of religion is itself a philosophical question.

All of this shows that the philosophy of religion is a dynamic and expanding field, filled with stimulating and important issues. It appears that recent efforts to establish grounds for theological-philosophical dialogue will be in the forefront for some years to come. Serious thinkers will find that the perennial problems continue to offer an inexhaustible supply of possibilities for research and reflection. They will also devise new strategies and approaches, providing countless permutations on old issues. And virgin territory always remains to be pioneered, opening up new and important problems for consideration. All of this taken together, then, becomes part of the growing edge of the philosophy of religion.

Those interested in the important problems related to theistic belief can do additional background study in philosophy of religion and follow the new developments in the field. This process is intellectually stimulating because we cannot always predict the outcome of classic issues, nor can we perfectly anticipate the direction of future debate. However, to understand the value of the rational appraisal of religious belief is to take a large step toward being able to navigate religious issues and to fulfill one's intellectual responsibilities. We will show ourselves willing, as Aquinas put it, "to inquire, in a rational way, into the things human reason can disclose concerning God."[9]

STUDY QUESTIONS

1. Discuss the kinds of attitudes appropriate to the fair and objective discussion of religious beliefs.

2. After engaging in the analysis and appraisal of religious belief throughout this book, how would you assess the reasonableness or the truth of classical theistic belief?

3. In light of all you have read so far, try to make the best case you can for theistic belief.

4. In light of all you have read so far, try to make the best case you can against theistic belief.

5. What topics in the philosophy of religion covered in this book would you be interested in pursuing more thoroughly?

6. What issues in fields related to the philosophy of religion would you be interested in pursuing?

7. In what ways, if any, has studying the issues presented in this text changed your approach to religion?

NOTES

1. J. L. Mackie, *The Miracle of Theism* (Oxford: Clarendon Press, 1982), p. 1. Also see pp. 11–12 for a further explanation of the title of the book.

2. Fred Freddoso, *The Existence and Nature of God* (Notre Dame, Ind.: University of Notre Dame Press, 1983).

3. Nicholas Wolterstorff, "The Remembrance of Things (Not) Past: Philosophical Reflections on Christian Liturgy," in *Christian Philosophy*, ed. Thomas Flint (Notre Dame, Ind.: University of Notre Dame Press, 1990), pp. 118–61. The volume in which this essay appears is devoted entirely to exploring the philosophical ramifications of a variety of Christian ideas (e.g., the effects of sin) and practices (e.g., creedal affirmation).

4. Note the differences between theology and philosophy assumed in such pieces as Gordon Kaufmann, "Evidentialism: A Theologians's Response," *Faith and Philosophy: Journal of the Society of Christian Philosophers* 6, no. 4 (1989): 353–77; Maurice F. Wiles, "Review of *The Logic of God Incarnate*," *Journal of Theological Studies* 38 (April 1987): 272; Thomas V. Morris, "Philosophers and Theologians at Odds," *Asbury Theological Journal* 44, no. 2 (1989): 31–41; William Abraham, "Oh God, Poor God," *The American Scholar* (Autumn 1989): 557–63.

5. One piece of evidence that there is some interchange is a conference, "Philosophical Theology and Biblical Exegesis," held at the University of Notre Dame, March 15–17, 1990. Theologians and biblical scholars are also starting to invite philosophers to speak at their professional conferences (e.g., American Academy of Religion, Society of Biblical Literature). Another piece of evidence of the contact between philosophy and theology is the Cornell Studies in Philosophy of Religion series of scholarly monographs and the Library of Religious Philosophy series from the University of Notre Dame Press. The Society of Christian Philosophers continues to sponsor conferences and seminars on topics related to theology. *Faith and Philosophy: Journal of the Society of Christian Philosophers* continues to seek dialogue with major theologians (e.g., see the October 1989 issue, which is devoted entirely to the topic of the Bible and philosophy).

6. For a good survey of modern theological movements, see R. Kliver, *The Shattered Spectrum* (Atlanta: John Knox Press, 1981). Some classic sources of feminist theological thought include Carol P. Christ and Judith Plaskow, eds., *Womanspirit Rising: A Feminist Reader in Religion* (New York: Harper and Row, 1979); Mary Daly, *Beyond God the Father: Toward a Philosophy of Women's Liberation* (Boston: Beacon Press, 1973); and Rosemary Ruether, *New Woman—New Earth: Sexist Ideologies and Human Liberation* (New York: Crossroad, 1975). For the impact of postmodernism, see Jean Luc Harion, *God without Being*, trans. T. Carlson (Chicago: University of Chicago Press, 1991).

7. For an example of how the philosophical examination of concepts in a nontheistic religion might be carried out, see Bruce Reichenbach, *The Law of Karma: A Philosophical Study* (London: Macmillan, 1990).

8. A notable example is Nagarjun's Madhyamfia Buddhism. Another example is Dogen's Zen Buddhism.

9. St. Thomas Aquinas, *Summa Contra Gentiles*, trans. Anton C. Pegis (Notre Dame, Ind.: University of Notre Dame Press, 1975), 1, 9, n. 4.

SUGGESTED READING

Alston, William P. *Divine Nature and Human Language: Essays in Philosophical Theology*. Ithaca, N.Y.: Cornell University Press, 1989.

Audi, Robert, and William Wainwright, eds. *Rationality, Religious Belief, and Moral Commitment: New Essays in the Philosophy of Religion*. Ithaca, N.Y.: Cornell University Press, 1986.

Freddoso, Fred. *The Existence and Nature of God.* Notre Dame, Ind.: University of Notre Dame Press, 1983.

Mackie, J. L. *The Miracle of Theism.* Oxford: Clarendon Press, 1982.

Martin, Michael. *Atheism: A Philosophical Justification.* Philadelphia: Temple University Press, 1990.

Plantinga, Alvin, and Nicholas Wolterstorff, eds. *Faith and Rationality: Reason and Belief in God.* Notre Dame, Ind.: University of Notre Dame Press, 1983.

Ross, James. *Philosophical Theology.* Indianapolis, Ind.: Bobbs-Merrill, 1969.

Stump, Eleonore, and Thomas Flint, eds. *Hermes and Athena: Biblical Exegesis and Philosophical Theology* (Notre Dame, Ind.: University of Notre Dame Press, 1993).

NAME INDEX

Name Index

Hofstadter, Douglas, 223–24
Holland, R. F., 191, 194, 197, 201
Howard-Snyder, Frances, 315
Hudson, Donald, 176
Hughes, Christopher, 208nn. 4, 7
Hume, David, 101, 122, 191, 194, 197, 201, 324
Husserl, Edmund, 59n. 15

Irenaeus, 136–37
Isaiah (Old Testament), 18, 19

Jagger, Alison, 296
James, William, 23, 37
Jantzen, Grace, 200, 201
Jesus (Christ), 21, 159, 228, 230, 262–63, 271
Job (Old Testament), 131
John Paul II (Pope), 240
Jones, Rev. Jim, 43, 51
Joshua (Old Testament), 51–52

Kane, G. Stanely, 137
Kant, Immanuel, 68, 98, 106, 231–32, 265
Katz, Stephen, 36–39
Keller, James, 203–4
Kierkegaard, Sören, 47, 49–52, 55–57, 201
Kretzmann, Norman, 83n. 36
Kuhn, Thomas, 247–49
Kung, Hans, 117, 292
Kvanvig, Jonathan, 302, 313–15

Lakatos, Imre, 249
Larmer, Robert, 200–201
Leibniz, Gottfried, 131–33, 142n. 9, 150, 253, 287
Lewis, C. S., 106–8
Lewis, H. D., 218
Locke, John, 46–47, 150
Lucretius, 324
Luther, Martin, 51

MacIntyre, Alasdair, 283
Mackie, J. L., 209n. 16, 118, 120–21, 324
Macquarrie, John, 179–80
McCloskey, H. J., 134
McFague, Sallie, 180, 251
McKinnon, Alastair, 283
McMullin, Ernan, 246–47
Madden, Edward, 117, 122, 123, 140
Malcolm, Norman, 89–90
Martin, C. B., 32
Martin, Michael, 32, 108–9, 122, 123, 203–6, 324
Martineau, James, 8
Mascall, E. L., 245
Mavrodes, George, 54, 82n. 19, 302, 317–20
Meyers, Kurt, 302, 311–13
Mill, John Stuart, 133
Mitchell, Basil, 173–74
Molina, Luis de, 83n. 29
Moody, Raymond, 229

Moon, the Reverend, 155
Morris, Thomas, 96, 302–6
Moses (Old Testament), 20–21, 156
Muhammed, 155, 156
Murphy, Nancey, 249–50
Murray, Michael, 302, 311–13

Nicholas of Cusa, 21–22
Nielsen, Kai, 283–85, 290–92
Nietzsche, Friedrich, 243, 324

O'Hair, Madalyn Murray, 8, 153
Osiander, Andreas, 237–38
Otto, Rudolph, 22–23, 30

Paley, William, 101
Pascal, Blaise, 44–45, 59n. 7, 326–27
Paul, the Apostle (New Testament), 44, 230
Peacocke, Arthur, 252
Penelhum, Terence, 124
Peter, the Apostle (New Testament), 21
Peterson, Michael, 143n. 26, 145n. 55
Phillips, D. Z., 215
Pike, Nelson, 83n. 30
Pinnock, Clark, 83n. 33, 272
Plantinga, Alvin, 82n. 11, 112n. 12, 119–121, 122–23, 126, 127–29, 142n. 8, 148, 151–56, 158, 161, 324
Plato, 154, 232, 317
Pojman, Louis, 281, 300n. 30
Popper, Karl, 60n. 23
Price, H. H., 221
Proudfoot, Wayne, 27–29, 30

Quinn, Philip, 154–55, 163n. 18, 165n. 30, 281, 306–9

Rahner, Karl, 270–72
Reichenbach, Bruce, 83n. 22, 145n. 55
Rolston, Holmes, 250
Ross, James, 169–171
Rowe, William, 12, 100, 124–25, 324
Russell, Bertrand, 14, 59n. 15, 99, 153, 324

Sagan, Carl, 240
Salmon, Wesley, 122–23, 127, 143n. 16
Santayana, George, 214
Sartre, Jean-Paul, 243, 290
Schleiermacher, Friedrich, 22, 29
Searle, John, 225
Shankara, 70
Smart, Ninian, 8
Smith, Quentin, 95–96
Spinoza, Baruch de, 66, 74
St. Francis (of Assissi), 156
Stace, Walter T., 35–36, 39, 41n. 36
Stump, Eleonore, 83n. 36, 302, 311, 322n. 15, 324
Swinburne, Richard, 20, 31, 87, 99, 105, 196, 198–99, 314

GENERAL INDEX

Advaita, 70, 159
Allah, 7
American Humanist Association, 8
Analysis, rational and reflective, 2, 11, 15, 325–28. *See also* Philosophical analysis
Anthropic principle, 104–5, 113n. 44
Apologetics, 16n. 6, 45, 60n. 24
Arguments for God's existence. *See* Theistic arguments
Assessment of religions, 273–75
Association of American Atheists, 8
Atheism, 95, 108–10, 117, 122, 124, 324. *See also* Atheist
Atheist (antitheist), 3, 8, 93, 227
Atonement, doctrine of, 306–9

Bahai, 51
Beliefs
  basic (properly basic), 149–57, 159–60, 163n. 18. *See also* Reformed epistemology
  belief-forming practice, 157–60
  derived (nonbasic), 149
  incorrigible, 149–51
  justification of, 29–33, 163n. 18
  religious beliefs justified, 157–61
  self-evident, 149–51
Bible, 155–56, 195, 202, 285, 286, 318, 319
  God portrayed in, 109
  Hebrew Bible, 66
  literalistic use of, 202, 240–42, 285–86
  as revelation from God, 318–19
  use in theodicy, 128
Biblical exegesis, 329
Big Bang Theory, 67, 94–96, 104
Blik, 173
Brahman, 34, 63, 70, 159, 215–16, 261

Buddhism and Buddhists, 20, 21, 24, 37, 159, 213, 215, 260–61
  Mahayana, 215, 248
  Theravada, 234n. 2, 248, 261
  Zen, 37–38, 259, 276n. 1

Causal principle, 92–93, 97, 101–2, 112–13n. 30
Causation
  divine, 190–94, 200–3
  natural, 190–94, 197–200
Christian
  anonymous, 271–72
  thinker, 46, 65
Christianity, 203, 63, 159, 161, 203, 297
Classical theism. *See* Theism: classical
Cognitive component to faith. *See* Faith: as involving beliefs (cognitive)
Coherentism, 151
Commitment (of faith). *See* Faith: as commitment
Compatibilism, 75
Confucianism, 213
Contingency, as an aspect of things, 97–100
Control, divine, 52, 75–76
Cosmological argument. *See* Theistic arguments: cosmological
Creation
  fundamentalist understanding of, 241–42
  Judeo-Christian doctrine, 69–71, 245–46
  out of God (ex Deo), 54–55, 108, 211–14
  out of pre-existing material, 69
Creator, God as. *See* God: attributes
Credulity, Principle of, 31–32, 34
Critical rationalism, 33, 53–57, 154, 163n. 12
Cumulative case argument. *See* Theistic arguments: cumulative case argument

General Index

Defense against the problem of evil. *See* problem of evil: defense
Determinism, 76
Divine hiddenness, 13–14, 328

Eschatological verification, 277 n. 21
Eternal Damnation, 313–16
Ethics
  of duty, 294–95
  feminist, 296–97
  natural law tradition, 107
  relation to God, 74, 132–33
  of virtue, 293–95
Evidentialism, 60 n. 24, 147–51
Evil
  apparently gratuitous, 124–25
  conditions for justifying, 133
  df. of moral evil, 117
  df. of natural evil, 117–18
  gratuitous, 123–27
Evolution, scientific theory of, 102, 239, 241
Exclusivism, religious, 262–64, 276 n. 11
Existence
  arguments for God's existence. *See* Theistic arguments
  as a property, 89–90
Existentialism, 51
Experience
  of God, 18–32
  near-death, 228–29

Faith
  as involving beliefs (cognitive), 4, 9–10, 24, 58 n. 2, 204, 326–28
  in relation to reason, 43–60
  as trust, 58 n. 2
  as commitment, 50–51, 57, 58 n. 2, 154–55
Fallacy of composition, 98
Falsification principle, 172–73
Feeling in religious experience, 22–23
Feminist theology, 251
Fideism, 49–53, 56, 148, 160
Foundationalism, 149–56
  classical, 133 n. 5
  modern, 162 n. 5
  moderate, 153
Free Will, 74–78
  compatibilist, 75–76
  relation to divine control, 52
  incompatibilist, 75–78, 218

Galileo affair, 237–38, 239
God
  arguments against the existence of. *See* Problem of evil
  arguments for the existence of. *See* Theistic arguments
  attributes of (God's nature), 11, 62–84
    agent (agency of), 157–59, 278
    creator, 69–71, 80, 280, 304–5
    eternal, 67, 78–80, 81 n. 2

    everlasting, 78–80
    free, 69–70
    impassible, 66, 81 n. 2
    just, 73, 116
    loving, 73
    necessary (existence), 66–68
      necessary being. *See* Necessary being
      necessary existence, 90–91
    omnipotent (all-powerful), 71–72, 74–75, 117, 303–4, 310–12
    omniscient (all-knowing), 71–73, 76–78, 303–4, 310–12
    perfection, 64–66. *See also* Theistic arguments: ontological
    perfectly good, 71–74, 117, 282–85, 303–4, 307–10, 313–16
    personal, 69, 159
    self-existent, 66–68
    sustainer, 69–70, 80, 97
    timeless, 78–80, 81 n. 2
    worthy of worship, 64–66, 74
  concept of in process thought, 137–39, 252–54
  experience of. *See* Experience: of God
  image of. *See* God's image
  relation of philosophical and religious ideas of, 109–110
God's body, world as, 71
God's image, 287
God's nature of, 62–84. *See also* God: attributes of
Great Pumpkin objection, 154

Heaven, 229, 308, 313–14
Hell, 229, 313–16
Hinduism, 21, 34, 63, 159, 213, 215–16, 228, 264
  Vedantic, 63, 70, 215, 260–61
Human predicament, 9, 20, 216

Identity theory (mind-body), 222–23
Immortality, 54, 213–14, 232
  a posteriori arguments for, 227–30
  a priori arguments for, 231–33
  definitions of, 214–17
  of immaterial soul, 220–21
Incarnation, doctrine of, 303–6
Inclusivism, religious, 270–72, 276 n. 11
Incompatibilisim, 75–78
Ineffability in mystic experience, 21, 23, 35–38
Infinite regress in cosmological argument, 98–99
Islam, 260–61

Jews, 82 n. 13, 66
Judaism, 66, 159
Justification
  epistemic, 157–61
  prima facie, 158–59, 161